THE UNITED METHODIST
MUSIC AND
WORSHIP PLANNER

2017–2018

David L. Bone
and
Mary J. Scifres

Abingdon Press
Nashville

THE UNITED METHODIST MUSIC AND WORSHIP PLANNER 2017–2018

Copyright © 2017 by Abingdon Press

All rights reserved.

Worksheets in this book may be reproduced by local congregations, provided the following credit line and copyright notice appear on all copies: "From *The United Methodist Music and Worship Planner.* Copyright © 2017 by Abingdon Press. Used by permission." No other part of this work may be reproduced or transmitted in any form or by any means, electronic or mechanical, including photocopying and recording, or by any information storage or retrieval system, except as may be expressly permitted by the 1976 Copyright Act or in writing from the publisher. Requests for permission should be addressed to Abingdon Press, 2222 Rosa L. Parks Boulevard, Nashville, TN 37228 or e-mailed to permissions@abingdonpress.com.

This book is printed on acid-free, recycled paper.

ISBN 978-1-5018-3489-9

All scripture quotations unless noted otherwise are taken from the New Revised Standard Version of the Bible, copyright 1989, Division of Christian Education of the National Council of the Churches of Christ in the United States of America. Used by permission. All rights reserved

17 18 19 20 21 22 23 24 25 26—10 9 8 7 6 5 4 3 2

MANUFACTURED IN UNITED STATES

USING THIS PLANNER

How We Organize the Resource Lists

This *United Methodist Music and Worship Planner (UM Planner)* is designed to give you as many ideas as possible about a given worship service. Use it alongside a worship plan notebook that you create and copies of *The United Methodist Hymnal, The United Methodist Book of Worship, The Faith We Sing,* and *Worship & Song*. Features of the *UM Planner* include:

- The lectionary verses found on left-hand pages of the *UM Planner* come from the New Revised Standard Version of the Bible (NRSV). Where available, we have added psalter numbers from the *UM Hymnal*. The *UM Planner* is also available with lectionary texts from the Common English Bible, the CEB (9781501834264).
- Each week **Primary Hymns and Songs for the Day** are suggested first. These suggestions include various helps for singing the hymns. These hymns and songs have the closest relationship to the scriptures and are widely known. The lengthier lists of **Additional Hymn Suggestions** and **Additional Contemporary Suggestions** will add variety to your musical selections.
- The musical suggestions are chosen to suggest a wide variety of styles, using *The United Methodist Hymnal, The Faith We Sing,* and *Worship & Song* to their fullest.
- Each item is referenced to scripture or occasion.
- **Opening (O)** and **Closing (C)** hymns are suggested for each worship service.
- At least one **Communion (Comm.)** hymn is recommended for the first Sunday of each month and liturgical season. When appropriate, Communion hymns related to the scriptures are noted on other days as well.
- **Additional Contemporary Suggestions** include not only praise choruses but also global and ethnic music, folk music, and meditative music from traditions such as Taizé. Information about resources referenced in this section can be found on page 7.
- **Vocal Solos** and **Anthems** provide ideas for vocal music "performance" offerings, and may also inspire ideas for additional congregational selections.
- The recommended **Vocal Solos** are taken from a group of eleven collections that range from contemporary settings of hymn texts and praise choruses to spirituals to well-known classics (see p. 7). Augment these suggestions from your own library.
- The **Anthem** suggestions include new works as well as generally known works that are already in many church choral libraries. Your study of the scripture and hymn texts will lead you to anthems in your church library that are appropriate.
- **One word of advice**: Be sure to consult all the music suggestions regardless of the type of service you are planning. In the changing world of worship, no one style defines a song or a worship service. Many items appropriate for contemporary and emergent styles are listed under the **Additional Hymn Suggestions** and many resources for traditional and blended services can be found in the **Additional Contemporary Suggestions** list. **Vocal Solos, Anthems,** and **Other Suggestions** may be appropriate for congregational use as well. Don't let the "category" here deter you from using any item that will enhance your worship service. Planners should consult all lists when choosing congregational music.
- Suggestions for "**Visuals**" are offered for each service. See the article "Visuals in Worship" (p. 4) for discussion of these suggestions. Visual ideas are found in the **Other Suggestions** lists. They have been compiled by Ashley M. Calhoun and supplemented by our authors. Ashley is known for his inventive use of "found" items in creating visual worship settings. Worship committees, visual artists, dancers, and altar guilds can use these ideas to create their own unique worship centers, altar pieces, banners, and dance images. Screen visual artists can use these themes to select appropriate background and theme screens for worship.
- **Other Suggestions** also include words for worship, primarily from *The United Methodist Book of Worship and Worship & Song* (Worship Resources edition); suggestions for choral introits and sung benedictions; and ideas for musical responses related to the spoken liturgy.
- A two-year, at-a-glance **2017–2018 Calendar** follows the **Worship Planning Sheets** (see p. 144). It includes a note on the lectionary years covered in this edition of *The UM Music and Worship Planner.*

Planning Worship with These Resources

When planning any worship service, it is always best to start with the scripture and let it guide your thoughts and plans. If your church is not using the *Revised Common Lectionary,* but you do know what the scripture text will be for a service, look up that text in the **Scriptures Index** on page 136.

As you read and study the scripture passages, read all of the suggested hymn texts. The hymns may remind you of anthems, solos, or keyboard selections. It is wise to mark your hymnal with the dates individual hymns are sung to avoid singing some too frequently. The **Hymn Resources** (see p. 7) can enhance congregational singing, but should be used sparingly.

Use a three-ring binder to organize your plans. For each service of worship, include a copy of one of the **Worship Planning Sheets** found on pages 140–142 (or design your own!) along with blank paper for listing further ideas. Do not simply "fill in the blanks" for each service, but use the Planning Sheet to guide your work.

Use the suggestions in the *UM Planner* along with your own page of ideas to begin making decisions about worship. Will the choir sing a "Call to Worship"? Can a hymn verse serve as a prayer response? Can a particular anthem or vocal solo give direction to the sermon? What prayers will be used?

Once your decisions are made, complete the **Worship Planning Sheet**. Make a separate list of tasks related to that service. Planning worship is an awesome responsibility, but one that can be accomplished with an organized effort along with spiritual guidance.

VISUALS IN WORSHIP
Ashley M. Calhoun

The suggestions for visuals in this planner are meant to help worship leaders use objects and images to increase the impact of the gospel on a people who are increasingly visually oriented. These suggestions can be incorporated into many visual elements: hanging and processional banners, worship settings (whether on the altar or in the chancel or narthex), worship folder covers, and bulletin boards. The ideas can also be used to suggest ways to use classical and contemporary works of art, sculpture, needlework, and photography in worship services.

With more churches incorporating screens and video walls into their worship spaces, there is tremendous potential for the use of still or moving imagery. Also, interpretive movement and drama can be very strong in visual impact.

The visual suggestions in this *Planner* have several characteristics:

- The suggestions are not meant to give detailed plans, but to spark your imagination and creativity.
- Some are drawn literally from the lessons; others are thematic.
- The suggestions are organized by reference to the lectionary passages:

O	Old Testament or Easter season, Acts reading
P	Psalm reading or Canticle
E	Epistle or New Testament reading
G	Gospel reading

- Chapter and verse numbers are sometimes given to indicate actual phrases in the scripture passage that can serve as visual elements.
- Themes such as "forgiveness," "love," or "rejoicing" are offered to encourage creative use of video and photographic images of people engaged in demonstrating those themes.

So much about worship is visual and intended to strengthen the proclamation of the gospel. The worship space is filled with visual elements that send a message. The church year is a treasure trove of color, texture, symbolism, and visual imagery. Special Sundays and special days in the cultural and denominational calendars also offer opportunities for visual expression. Evaluate the visual aspects of your worship services and find ways to enhance the worship experience with thoughtful, intentional use of visual elements and images.

PLANNING CORPORATE WORSHIP WITH A TEAM

Mary J. Scifres

Planning worship provides an important opportunity for church staff members to work together as a team. Such planning also provides an opportunity for worship committees to find an important aspect of their ministry.

Unfortunately, our fast-paced society and the production focus in current culture pushes far too many pastors into a solo effort in worship planning. We call this all-too common model "The Lonesome Approach."

The Lonesome Approach—A Non-team Model for Worship Planning

- Preaching pastor picks the scripture readings, prayers, hymns, and sermon title.
- Church secretary or pastor types and prints bulletins.
- Musician(s) pick up note in mailbox with hymn numbers for coming Sunday. If time permits, choir rehearses hymns during evening rehearsal along with anthem(s) and choral responses for Sunday.
- Preaching pastor writes sermon.
- Lay liturgist arrives early to review worship plans.
- Worship commences.

Is this how worship most often comes together in your church? If so, you may want to consider other models for planning worship. Although some find this "lonesome approach" convenient, worship planning with this approach is neither integrated into nor representative of the worshiping community. Within the book you hold in your hands, we hope that pastors, musicians, and worship leaders find encouragement and assistance for planning worship in cooperation with one another.

Perhaps the "Lonesome Approach" will one day be the exception rather than the rule.

The Team-based Approach

We suggest that pastors, musicians, and worship leaders consider a **Team-based Approach** to planning. First, gather a team: review the talents of your church for artists, visionaries, leaders, organizers, and workers. Choose team members, balancing gifts and talents, as well as time and commitment levels. Members of the worship planning team can expect to meet at least biannually. Some worship teams find weekly, monthly, or seasonal planning meetings helpful, but even two meetings a year can improve communication and coordination efforts immensely. Consider hiring worship consultants, such as Mary Scifres or Marcia McFee, to run planning retreats—a helpful gift to many worship planning teams and pastors. Organizations such as The Fellowship of United Methodists in Music and Worship Arts (UMFellowship.org) often provide convocations and training events to assist worship leaders and teams in developing skills for planning worship as well.

Many models exist for the actual planning; one model is offered here. In order to use this model, the team needs several copies of this *UM Planner* (particularly for use of scripture readings and hymn lists), a Bible, hymnals, and *The United Methodist Book of Worship*. Musicians may find it helpful to have copies of the music collections suggested in this planner as well as a single-copy file of the anthem collection and praise song collection of your church. Distribute copies of the **Worship Planning Sheets** from pages 140–142 to each team member for each Sunday being discussed.

Using a Team-based Model for Worship Planning

1) Prior to meeting, pastor(s) prepares scripture and sermon themes; musicians prepare repertoire lists as well as special performance plans.

2) Team meets for a designated time period. (A retreat setting is particularly helpful, followed by monthly or weekly meetings.)

3) Open meeting with prayer and discussion of worship. Worship leaders may bring a diversity of views about the meaning and focus of worship, enhancing the process by expressing philosophies and values honestly.

4) Read or review scriptures, with emphasis on the pastor's primary focus.

5) The pastor(s) introduces and outlines sermon topics or emphases.

6) Discuss and outline seasonal needs.

7) Team discusses visual focus options, perhaps helping visual artists and screen artists to choose specific visual themes for a season or a day.

8) Team discusses hymns, perhaps helping musicians and pastor to choose hymns. Keep in mind thematic and scriptural emphases, musical abilities, sermon topics, congregational hymn preferences, and plans to introduce new music.

9) Introduce and discuss special ideas or plans for specific worship services (e.g., Palm Sunday cantata, Christmas Eve candlelight service, children's Sunday).

10) Choose spoken words (prayers, responsive readings, blessings). The entire team or part of the team may do this, depending on number of participants.

11) Choose vocal, choral, and keyboard music (team or part of team).
12) Review services for integration, unity, and diversity.
13) Address specific service logistics.
14) Close with worship, music, and prayer.

In any one of these steps, all members of the planning team may have valuable input. A pastor may have an idea for a choral anthem to enhance a sermon idea; a musician may have an insight into a sermon topic as it relates to the congregation. At any of these steps, all members of the team will find helpful suggestions in this *UM Planner*. Each week's entry provides the text of each scripture reading, season, and liturgical color, suggestions of visual images for artists, hymn and music suggestions, liturgical suggestions, and other ideas that may spark interest in an innovative type of worship service occasionally.

When worship leaders, pastors, musicians, visual artists, and other worship leaders coordinate their work, they can educate one another about preparation timing and skills. Pastors need to know the time requirements for planning music. Choir directors can alert the pastor to the time needed to choose, obtain, and rehearse an anthem prior to a worship performance. Organists and pianists can communicate the time needed to choose, obtain, and rehearse instrumental music prior to use in worship. Likewise, organists, pianists, and choir directors need to advise the pastor of the time needed to prepare congregational music for use in worship. (Pastors often discover that both play-ing and singing improve greatly on hymns rehearsed a few weeks in advance!) Finally, the musicians can share with the pastor their visions for music ministry in worship.

Pastors, likewise, need to inform musicians of how they might interact not only in worship planning but also in worship leadership. Some pastors establish cues to alert musicians when light background music is needed during worship. A pastor can educate musicians about their roles as worship leaders. Additionally, the pastor can communicate with the musicians what her or his visions are for music ministry in worship.

These initial communications are essential when worship planners begin to work together and also as personnel changes impact the worship planning team. Constant communication and interaction in the creative and logistical planning processes of worship flow through the worship leaders into the congregation, with the unity of the worship leadership team strengthening the entire worshiping community.

Worship planning can be a point of unity and team-building for worship staff. The team that works together models corporate worship for the congregation. If we expect people to walk in the church doors on Sunday mornings from their many walks of life to have a corporate experience, we need to avoid individual approaches for planning worship and begin team planning. In so doing, we will find that the Holy Spirit has found a new freedom in which to work within the body of Christ.

RESOURCE KEY

UM   Young, Carlton R., ed. *The United Methodist Hymnal.* Nashville: The United Methodist Publishing House, 1989. ISBN: 9780687431328.

2000 or S2000   Hickman, Hoyt L., ed. *The Faith We Sing.* Nashville: Abingdon Press, 2000. Cokesbury Ord. #090547 (Pew Edition). NOTE: All hymn numbers 2000 and higher are from this hymnal.

3000 or WS3000   Smith, Gary Alan, ed. *Worship & Song.* Nashville: Abingdon Press, 2011. Accompaniment, singer, guitar, and planning editions available. ISBN: 9781426709937 (Pew edition). NOTE: All hymn numbers 3000 and higher are from this hymnal.

4000 or AH4000   *The Africana Hymnal.* Nashville: Abingdon Press, 2015. ISBN #9781426776441. NOTE: All hymn numbers 4000 and higher are from this hymnal.

WSL   Smith, Gary Alan, ed. *Worship & Song Leader's Edition.* Nashville: Abingdon Press, 2011. ISBN: 9781426709944 (Leader's edition). *These resources, WSL1–WSL222, refer to the written words for worship (prayers, litanies, benedictions) available in worship resource editions of* Worship & Song.

BOW   Langford, Andy, ed. *The United Methodist Book of Worship.* Nashville: Abingdon Press, 1992. Leader and accompaniment editions available. ISBN: 9780687035724.

HYMN RESOURCES

S-1   Smith, Gary Alan, ed. *The United Methodist Hymnal: Music Supplement.* Nashville: Abingdon Press, 1991. Cokesbury Ord. #431476.

S-2   Bennett, Robert C., ed. *The United Methodist Hymnal: Music Supplement II.* Nashville: Abingdon Press, 1993. Cokesbury Ord. #430135.

H-3   Hopson, Hal H. *The Creative Church Musician Series.* Carol Stream, IL: Hope Publishing Co.
Hbl Vol. 1. *The Creative Use of Handbells in Worship. 1997.* Cokesbury Ord. #921992.
Chr Vol. 2. *The Creative Use of Choirs in Worship. 1999.* Cokesbury Ord. #732807.
Desc *The Creative Use of Descants in Worship. 1999.* Cokesbury Ord. #732864.
Org *The Creative Use of the Organ in Worship. 1997.* Cokesbury Ord. #323904.

VOCAL SUGGESTION RESOURCES

V-1   Kimbrough, Steven, ed. *Sweet Singer: Hymns of Charles Wesley.* Chapel Hill, NC: Hinshaw Music, 1987. Catalogue #CV-1 Cokesbury Ord. #811712

V-2   Handel, George Frederick. *Messiah.* Various editions available.

V-3   Hayes, Mark. *The Mark Hayes Vocal Solo Collection*
V-3 (1) *Ten Spirituals for Solo Voice.* Alfred Music Publishing, 2007. ISBN: 9780882848808.
V-3 (2) *Seven Praise and Worship Songs for Solo Voice.* Van Nuys, CA: Alfred Music Publishing, 2010. ISBN: 9780739037249.
V-3 (3) *Ten Hymns and Gospel Songs for Solo Voice.* ISBN: 9780739006979.

V-4   Scott, K. Lee. *Sing a Song of Joy.* Minneapolis, MN: Augsburg Fortress, 1989. ISBN: 9780800647889 (Medium High Voice) ISBN: 9780800647889 (Medium Low Voice) ISBN: 9780800652821.

V-5   Various Editors. *With All My Heart: Contemporary Vocal Solos.* Minneapolis, MN: Augsburg Fortress, 2004.
V-5 (1) Volume 1: Autumn and Winter. ISBN: 978 0800676841
V-5 (2) Volume 2: Spring and Summer. ISBN: 978 0800676858
V-5 (3) Volume 3: Baptisms, Weddings, Funerals. ISBN: 978 0800679460

V-6   Walters, Richard, Arr. *Hymn Classics: Concert Arrangements of Traditional Hymns for Voice and Piano.* Milwaukee, WI: Hal Leonard Publishing, 1993. ISBN: 9780793560080. High Voice: Cokesbury Ord. #811290. Low Voice: Cokesbury Ord. #811233.

V-7   Johnson, Hall, Arr. *Thirty (30) Spirituals.* New York: G. Schirmer, Inc., 1949. ISBN: 9780793548033.

V-8   Wilson, John F., Don Doig, and Jack Schrader, eds. *Everything for the Church Soloist.* Carol Stream, IL: Hope Publishing Company, 1980. Cokesbury Ord. #810103.

V-9   Scott, K. Lee. *Rejoice Now My Spirit: Vocal Solos for the Church Year.* Minneapolis, MN: Augsburg Fortress, 1992. ISBN: 9780800651084.

V-10   Hayes, Mark, et al. *From the Manger to the Cross—Seasonal Solos for Medium Voice.* Dayton, OH: The Lorenz Corporation, 2006. Cokesbury Ord. #526369.

V-11   Pote, Allen. *A Song of Joy.* Carol Stream, IL: Hope Publishing, 2003. Cokesbury Ord. #505068.

CONTEMPORARY RESOURCES

SP   Various. *Songs for Praise and Worship Singalong Edition.* Waco, TX: Word Music, 1992. ISBN: 9783010203494.

M1-M55   Barker, Ken, ed. *More Songs for Praise and Worship Choir/ Worship Team Edition.* Waco, TX: Word Music, 2000. Cokesbury Ord. #509802 (*Keyboard Edition*: Cokesbury Ord. #509776. *Piano/Guitar/Vocal Edition*: Cokesbury Ord. #509764).

M56-M115   Barker, Ken, ed. *More Songs for Praise and Worship 2 Choir/ Worship Team Edition.* Waco, TX: Word Music, 2002. Cokesbury Ord. #512053 (*Keyboard Edition*: Cokesbury Ord. #512075. *Piano/Guitar/Vocal Edition*: Cokesbury Ord. #080689314186).

M116-M168   Barker, Ken, ed. *More Songs for Praise and Worship 3 Choir/ Worship Team Edition.* Waco, TX: Word Music, 2005. Cokesbury Ord. #523357 (*Keyboard Edition*: Cokesbury Ord. # 523418. *Piano/Guitar/Vocal Edition*: Cokesbury Ord. #523369).

M169-M219   Barker, Ken, ed. *More Songs for Praise and Worship 4 Choir/ Worship Team Edition.* Waco, TX: Word Music, 2006. Cokesbury Ord. # 529198 (*Keyboard Edition*: Cokesbury Ord. # 529244. *Piano/Guitar/Vocal Edition*: ISBN: 9785557996822).

M220-M279   McClure, Mark and Sarah G. Huffman, eds. *More Songs for Praise and Worship 5.* Waco, TX: Word Music, 2011. (*Piano/Guitar/Vocal Edition.* ISBN: 9781458418807. *Choir/Worship Team Edition.* ISBN: 9781458418814; *Keyboard/SATB Edition.* Catalog #080689500879).

See also Vocal Solo suggestions from V-3 and V-5 volumes.

Exodus 3:1-15

[1] Moses was keeping the flock of his father-in-law Jethro, the priest of Midian; he led his flock beyond the wilderness, and came to Horeb, the mountain of God. [2] There the angel of the LORD appeared to him in a flame of fire out of a bush; he looked, and the bush was blazing, yet it was not consumed. [3] Then Moses said, "I must turn aside and look at this great sight, and see why the bush is not burned up." [4] When the LORD saw that he had turned aside to see, God called to him out of the bush, "Moses, Moses!" And he said, "Here I am." [5] Then he said, "Come no closer! Remove the sandals from your feet, for the place on which you are standing is holy ground." [6] He said further, "I am the God of your father, the God of Abraham, the God of Isaac, and the God of Jacob." And Moses hid his face, for he was afraid to look at God.

[7] Then the LORD said, "I have observed the misery of my people who are in Egypt; I have heard their cry on account of their taskmasters. Indeed, I know their sufferings, [8] and I have come down to deliver them from the Egyptians, and to bring them up out of that land to a good and broad land, a land flowing with milk and honey, to the country of the Canaanites, the Hittites, the Amorites, the Perizzites, the Hivites, and the Jebusites. [9] The cry of the Israelites has now come to me; I have also seen how the Egyptians oppress them. [10] So come, I will send you to Pharaoh to bring my people, the Israelites, out of Egypt." [11] But Moses said to God, "Who am I that I should go to Pharaoh, and bring the Israelites out of Egypt?" [12] He said, "I will be with you; and this shall be the sign for you that it is I who sent you: when you have brought the people out of Egypt, you shall worship God on this mountain."

[13] But Moses said to God, "If I come to the Israelites and say to them, 'The God of your ancestors has sent me to you,' and they ask me, 'What is his name?' what shall I say to them?" [14] God said to Moses, "I AM WHO I AM." He said further, "Thus you shall say to the Israelites, 'I AM has sent me to you.'" [15] God also said to Moses, "Thus you shall say to the Israelites, 'The LORD, the God of your ancestors, the God of Abraham, the God of Isaac, and the God of Jacob, has sent me to you':

This is my name forever,
and this my title for all generations."

Psalm 105:1-6, 23-26, 45c (UM828)

[1] O give thanks to the LORD, call on his name,
  make known his deeds among the peoples.
[2] Sing to him, sing praises to him;
  tell of all his wonderful works.
[3] Glory in his holy name;
  let the hearts of those who seek the LORD rejoice.
[4] Seek the LORD and his strength;
  seek his presence continually.
[5] Remember the wonderful works he has done,
  his miracles, and the judgments he has uttered,
[6] O offspring of his servant Abraham,
  children of Jacob, his chosen ones.
. . . .

[23] Then Israel came to Egypt;
  Jacob lived as an alien in the land of Ham.
[24] And the LORD made his people very fruitful,
  and made them stronger than their foes,
[25] whose hearts he then turned to hate his people,
  to deal craftily with his servants.
[26] He sent his servant Moses,
  and Aaron whom he had chosen.
. . . .
[45c] Praise the LORD!

Romans 12:9-21

[9] Let love be genuine; hate what is evil, hold fast to what is good; [10] love one another with mutual affection; outdo one another in showing honor. [11] Do not lag in zeal, be ardent in spirit, serve the Lord. [12] Rejoice in hope, be patient in suffering, persevere in prayer. [13] Contribute to the needs of the saints; extend hospitality to strangers.

[14] Bless those who persecute you; bless and do not curse them. [15] Rejoice with those who rejoice, weep with those who weep. [16] Live in harmony with one another; do not be haughty, but associate with the lowly; do not claim to be wiser than you are. [17] Do not repay anyone evil for evil, but take thought for what is noble in the sight of all. [18] If it is possible, so far as it depends on you, live peaceably with all. [19] Beloved, never avenge yourselves, but leave room for the wrath of God; for it is written, "Vengeance is mine, I will repay, says the Lord." [20] No, "if your enemies are hungry, feed them; if they are thirsty, give them something to drink; for by doing this you will heap burning coals on their heads." [21] Do not be overcome by evil, but overcome evil with good.

Matthew 16:21-28

[21] From that time on, Jesus began to show his disciples that he must go to Jerusalem and undergo great suffering at the hands of the elders and chief priests and scribes, and be killed, and on the third day be raised. [22] And Peter took him aside and began to rebuke him, saying, "God forbid it, Lord! This must never happen to you." [23] But he turned and said to Peter, "Get behind me, Satan! You are a stumbling block to me; for you are setting your mind not on divine things but on human things."

[24] Then Jesus told his disciples, "If any want to become my followers, let them deny themselves and take up their cross and follow me. [25] For those who want to save their life will lose it, and those who lose their life for my sake will find it. [26] For what will it profit them if they gain the whole world but forfeit their life? Or what will they give in return for their life?

[27] "For the Son of Man is to come with his angels in the glory of his Father, and then he will repay everyone for what has been done. [28] Truly I tell you, there are some standing here who will not taste death before they see the Son of Man coming in his kingdom."

Primary Hymns and Songs for the Day

116   "The God of Abraham Praise" (Exod) (O)
       H-3   Hbl-62, 95; Chr-59; Org-77
       S-1   #211. Harm.
448   "Go Down, Moses" (Exod)
       H-3   Chr-215; Org-46
3029 "In the Desert, on God's Mountain" (Exod)
2129 "I Have Decided to Follow Jesus" (Matt)
2242 "Walk with Me" (Exod, Matt)
415   "Take Up Thy Cross" (Matt) (C)
       H-3   Chr-178, 180; Org-44
       S-1   #141-3 Various treatments

Additional Hymn Suggestions

64   "Holy, Holy, Holy! Lord God Almighty" (Exod)
111   "How Can We Name a Love" (Exod)
113   "Source and Sovereign, Rock and Cloud" (Exod)
116   "The God of Abraham Praise" (Exod)
315   "Come, Ye Faithful, Raise the Strain" (Exod)
436   "The Voice of God Is Calling" (Exod)
506   "Wellspring of Wisdom" (Exod)
577   "God of Grace and God of Glory" (Exod)
2060 "God the Sculptor of the Mountains" (Exod)
2180 "Why Stand So Far Away, My God" (Exod)
2230 "Lord, We Come to Ask Your Blessing" (Exod) (O)
2246 "Deep in the Shadows of the Past" (Exod)
3009 "Praise God for This Holy Ground" (Exod)
3012 "When Words Alone Cannot Express" (Exod, Pss)
87   "What Gift Can We Bring" (Exod, Pss)
100   "God, Whose Love Is Reigning o'er Us" (Exod, Pss)
124   "Seek the Lord" (Pss)
336   "Of All the Spirit's Gifts to Me" (Rom)
383   "This Is a Day of New Beginnings" (Rom)
390   "Forgive Our Sins as We Forgive" (Rom)
411   "Dear Lord, Lead Me Day by Day" (Rom)
431   "Let There Be Peace on Earth" (Rom)
434   *Cuando El Pobre* ("When the Poor Ones") (Rom)
670   "Go Forth for God" (Rom) (C)
2169 "God, How Can We Forgive" (Rom)
2202 "Come Away with Me" (Rom)
2205 "The Fragrance of Christ" (Rom)
2213 "Healer of Our Every Ill" (Rom)
2254 "In Remembrance of Me" (Rom, Comm.)
3093 "Fill My Cup, Lord" (Rom, Comm.)
       UM641 (refrain only)
3169 "You Feed Us, Gentle Savior" (Rom, Comm.)
3117 "Rule of Life" (Rom)
465   "Holy Spirit, Truth Divine" (Rom, Matt)
534   "Be Still, My Soul" (Rom, Matt)
581   "Lord, Whose Love Through Humble Service" (Rom, Matt)
297   "Beneath the Cross of Jesus" (Matt)
338   "Where He Leads Me" (Matt)
399   "Take My Life, and Let It Be" (Matt)
419   "I Am Thine, O Lord" (Matt)
424   "Must Jesus Bear the Cross Alone" (Matt)
442   "Weary of All Trumpeting" (Matt)
453   "More Love to Thee, O Christ" (Matt)
528   "Nearer, My God, to Thee" (Matt)
553   "And Are We Yet Alive" (Matt)
608   "This Is the Spirit's Entry Now" (Matt, Baptism)
2102 "Swiftly Pass the Clouds of Glory" (Matt)
2137 "Would I Have Answered When You Called" (Matt)
2149 "Living for Jesus" (Matt)

Additional Contemporary Suggestions

S2087   "We Will Glorify" (Exod)
S2272   "Holy Ground" (Exod)
M36   "Awesome in This Place" (Exod)
M55   "Jehovah Reigns" (Exod)
UM84   "Thank You, Lord" (Pss)
WS3003 "How Great Is Our God" (Pss)
S2195   "In the Lord I'll Be Ever Thankful" (Pss)
S2219   "Goodness Is Stronger than Evil" (Rom)
S2171   "Make Me a Channel of Your Peace" (Rom)
S2224   "Make Us One" (Rom)
S2222   "The Servant Song" (Rom)
S2223   "They'll Know We Are Christians" (Rom)
S2226   "Bind Us Together" (Rom)
S2179   "Live in Charity" ("*Ubi Caritas*") (Rom)
WS3117 "Rule of Life"
WS3148 "There's a Spirit of Love in This Place" (Rom)
WS3153 "O God in Whom We Live" (Rom)
WS3154 "Draw the Circle Wide" (Rom)
WS3167 "Feed Us, Lord" (Rom, Comm)
WS3160 "We Will Follow" ("*Somlandela*") (Matt)
M53   "Let It Be Said of Us" (Matt)
M122   "Every Move I Make" (Matt)
M150   "Everyday" (Matt)
M76   "The Wonderful Cross" (Matt)

Vocal Solos

"In Remembrance" (Rom, Comm.)
   V-5(2)   p. 7
"May the Mind of Christ" (Rom)
   V-8   p. 114
"Nothing . . . Everything" (Matt)
   V-8   p. 162
"Here I Am" (Matt)
   V-11   p. 19

Anthems

"Love Shall Overcome" (Rom)
Carlos Colón-Quintana; MorningStar 50-8715
SATB, with Piano, opt. Clarinet or C Instrument

"Take Up Your Cross" (Matt)
Arr. Jonathan Shippey; Hinshaw HMC2073
2-part mixed, piano, opt. hammered dulcimer

Other Suggestions

Visual Suggestions
  O   sandals, burning bush, mountain, milk/honey, 3:14
  P   musical notes, singing
  E   images of love overcoming hate, service to others,
  G   wooden cross on its side, self-denial, sandals (follow
        me), (stumbling) block
Introit: WS3047, stanza 1. "God Almighty, We Are Waiting"
  (Exod)
Opening Prayer: BOW462 (Exod, Rom)
Act of Congregational Centering: BOW470 (Rom)
Prayers of Confession: BOW481 or BOW493 (Rom)
Canticle: UM646. "Canticle of Love" (Rom)
Prayer: WSL57. "Days pass and the years vanish" (Exod)
Prayer: UM392 or BOW510 (Exod, Matt)
Prayer: UM401 or BOW522 (Rom)
Offertory Prayer: WSL103. "Blessed God" (Rom)
Blessing: BOW566. Sarum Blessing (Exod, Rom)
Blessing: WSL165. "Go out into the world" (Rom)
Sung Benediction: WS3159. "Let Our Earth Be Peaceful" (Rom)

Exodus 12:1-14

[1]The LORD said to Moses and Aaron in the land of Egypt: [2]This month shall mark for you the beginning of months; it shall be the first month of the year for you. [3]Tell the whole congregation of Israel that on the tenth of this month they are to take a lamb for each family, a lamb for each household. [4]If a household is too small for a whole lamb, it shall join its closest neighbor in obtaining one; the lamb shall be divided in proportion to the number of people who eat of it. [5]Your lamb shall be without blemish, a year-old male; you may take it from the sheep or from the goats. [6]You shall keep it until the fourteenth day of this month; then the whole assembled congregation of Israel shall slaughter it at twilight. [7]They shall take some of the blood and put it on the two doorposts and the lintel of the houses in which they eat it. [8]They shall eat the lamb that same night; they shall eat it roasted over the fire with unleavened bread and bitter herbs. [9]Do not eat any of it raw or boiled in water, but roasted over the fire, with its head, legs, and inner organs. [10]You shall let none of it remain until the morning; anything that remains until the morning you shall burn. [11]This is how you shall eat it: your loins girded, your sandals on your feet, and your staff in your hand; and you shall eat it hurriedly. It is the passover of the LORD. [12]For I will pass through the land of Egypt that night, and I will strike down every firstborn in the land of Egypt, both human beings and animals; on all the gods of Egypt I will execute judgments: I am the LORD. [13]The blood shall be a sign for you on the houses where you live: when I see the blood, I will pass over you, and no plague shall destroy you when I strike the land of Egypt.

[14]This day shall be a day of remembrance for you. You shall celebrate it as a festival to the LORD; throughout your generations you shall observe it as a perpetual ordinance.

Psalm 149

[1]Praise the LORD!
Sing to the LORD a new song,
    his praise in the assembly of the faithful.
[2]Let Israel be glad in its Maker;
    let the children of Zion rejoice in their King.
[3]Let them praise his name with dancing,
    making melody to him with tambourine and lyre.
[4]For the LORD takes pleasure in his people;
    he adorns the humble with victory.
[5]Let the faithful exult in glory;
    let them sing for joy on their couches.
[6]Let the high praises of God be in their throats
    and two-edged swords in their hands,
[7]to execute vengeance on the nations
    and punishment on the peoples,
[8]to bind their kings with fetters
    and their nobles with chains of iron,
[9]to execute on them the judgment decreed.
    This is glory for all his faithful ones.
Praise the LORD!

Romans 13:8-14

[8]Owe no one anything, except to love one another; for the one who loves another has fulfilled the law. [9]The commandments, "You shall not commit adultery; You shall not murder; You shall not steal; You shall not covet"; and any other commandment, are summed up in this word, "Love your neighbor as yourself." [10]Love does no wrong to a neighbor; therefore, love is the fulfilling of the law.

[11]Besides this, you know what time it is, how it is now the moment for you to wake from sleep. For salvation is nearer to us now than when we became believers; [12]the night is far gone, the day is near. Let us then lay aside the works of darkness and put on the armor of light; [13]let us live honorably as in the day, not in reveling and drunkenness, not in debauchery and licentiousness, not in quarreling and jealousy. [14]Instead, put on the Lord Jesus Christ, and make no provision for the flesh, to gratify its desires.

Matthew 18:15-20

[15]"If another member of the church sins against you, go and point out the fault when the two of you are alone. If the member listens to you, you have regained that one. [16]But if you are not listened to, take one or two others along with you, so that every word may be confirmed by the evidence of two or three witnesses. [17]If the member refuses to listen to them, tell it to the church; and if the offender refuses to listen even to the church, let such a one be to you as a Gentile and a tax collector. [18]Truly I tell you, whatever you bind on earth will be bound in heaven, and whatever you loose on earth will be loosed in heaven. [19]Again, truly I tell you, if two of you agree on earth about anything you ask, it will be done for you by my Father in heaven. [20]For where two or three are gathered in my name, I am there among them."

Primary Hymns and Songs for the Day

2172	"We Are Called" (Rom) (O)	
149	*"Cantemos al Señor"* ("Let's Sing unto the Lord") (Exod, Pss)	
	S-2	#154. Performance note
720	"Wake, Awake, for Night Is Flying" (Rom)	
	H-3	Chr-174, 203; Org-172
632	"Draw Us in the Spirit's Tether" (Rom, Matt, Comm.)	
	H-3	Chr-62
	S-1	#337. Performance Note
557	"Blest Be the Tie That Binds" (Matt) (C)	
	H-3	Hbl-49; Chr-14; Desc-27; Org-25

Additional Hymn Suggestions

448	"Go Down, Moses" (Exod)
3047	"God Almighty, We Are Waiting" (Exod)
2060	"God the Sculptor of the Mountains" (Exod)
2234	"Lead On, O Cloud of Presence" (Exod)
2246	"Deep in the Shadows of the Past" (Exod)
2045	"Sing a New Song to the Lord" (Pss)
62	"All Creatures of Our God and King" (Pss) (O)
77	"How Great Thou Art" (Pss)
3010	"Sing of the Lord's Goodness" (Pss)
3012	"When Words Alone Cannot Express" (Pss)
206	"I Want to Walk as a Child of the Light" (Rom)
513	"Soldiers of Christ, Arise" (Rom)
551	"Awake, O Sleeper" (Rom)
2213	"Healer of Our Every Ill" (Rom)
2254	"In Remembrance of Me" (Rom, Comm.)
2260	"Let Us Be Bread" (Rom, Comm.)
384	"Love Divine, All Loves Excelling" (Rom, Matt)
402	"Lord, I Want to Be a Christian" (Rom, Matt)
408	"The Gift of Love" (Rom, Matt)
549	"Where Charity and Love Prevail" (Rom, Matt)
560	"Help Us Accept Each Other" (Rom, Matt)
617	"I Come with Joy" (Rom, Matt, Comm.)
390	"Forgive Our Sins as We Forgive" (Matt)
2178	"Here Am I" (Matt)

Additional Contemporary Suggestions

UM123	"El-Shaddai" (Exod)
	S-2 #54 Verses for Vocal Solo
WS3038	"Mighty to Save" (Exod)
S2270	"I Will Enter His Gates" (Exod, Pss)
S2031	"We Bring the Sacrifice of Praise" (Exod, Pss)
S2028	"Clap Your Hands" (Pss)
SP23	"Sing unto the Lord a New Song" (Pss)
M46	"I Will Celebrate" (Pss)
	SP147
M59	"Let Everything That Has Breath" (Pss)
M241	"As It Is in Heaven" (Pss, Lord's Prayer)
M63	"I Could Sing of Your Love Forever" (Pss, Rom)
M242	"Salvation Is Here" (Rom)
UM432	*"Jesu, Jesu"* (Rom)
	S-1 #63 Vocal part
S2224	"Make Us One" (Rom)
S2192	"Freedom Is Coming" (Rom)
WS3002	"Blessed Be Your Name" (Rom)
WS3163	"Walking in the Light of God" (Rom)
S2171	"Make Me a Channel of Your Peace" (Rom, Matt)
S2179	"Live in Charity" ("*Ubi Caritas*") (Rom, Matt)
S2223	"They'll Know We Are Christians" (Rom, Matt)
2226	"Bind Us Together" (Rom, Matt) (C)
SP240	"As We Gather" (Matt)
M154	"Dwell" (Matt)

Vocal Solos

"Sing a Song of Joy" (Pss)
    V-4   p. 2
"All Creatures of Our God and King" (Pss)
    V-6   p. 55
"Make Me a Channel of Your Peace" (Pss)
    V-3(2)   p. 25
    V-3(3)   p. 28
"There's a Quiet Understanding" (Matt)
    V-8   p. 2

Anthems

"Sing Praise to the Lord" (Pss)
Sandra T. Ford; Hinshaw HMC2439
SAB with piano, opt. flute

"At the Table of the Lord" (Comm.)
Jay Althouse: Hope C5849
Two-part Mixed with piano (SATB C5180; SAB 5336)

Other Suggestions

Visuals:
	O	Sin/salvation (black/gold), darkness/light, lamp, candles, Passover meal, lamb, blood, wine/bread
	P	Dancing figures, tambourine, lyre
	E	Paschal Lamb, portrait of Christ
	E/G	Reconciliation, bridges, alarm clock
	G	Worship, reconciliation, joined hands, four hands folded in prayer

Introit: WS3147, stanza 3. "Built on a Rock" (Matt)
Greeting: BOW378 (Pss)
Act of Congregational Centering: BOW470 (Matt)
Prayer of Confession: BOW484 or BOW488 (Matt)
Call to Prayer: BOW202. "Where Two or Three Are Gathered" (Matt)
Prayer: UM412. Prayer of John Chrysostom (Matt)
Prayer: BOW507. For Creation (Pss)
Prayer: BOW535. At the Beginning of a New School Year (Season)
Prayer: BOW443. Labor Day Prayer (Labor Day)
Litany: BOW496. The Ten Commandments (Rom)
Litany of Preparation: WSL73. "We come broken" (Exod, Matt)
Baptism Response: UM609. "You Have Put on Christ" (Rom)
Response: S2179. "Live in Charity" ("*Ubi Caritas*") (Rom)
For additional ideas, see The Abingdon Worship Annual 2017.

Exodus 14:19-31

¹⁹The angel of God who was going before the Israelite army moved and went behind them; and the pillar of cloud moved from in front of them and took its place behind them. ²⁰It came between the army of Egypt and the army of Israel. And so the cloud was there with the darkness, and it lit up the night; one did not come near the other all night.

²¹Then Moses stretched out his hand over the sea. The Lᴏʀᴅ drove the sea back by a strong east wind all night, and turned the sea into dry land; and the waters were divided. ²²The Israelites went into the sea on dry ground, the waters forming a wall for them on their right and on their left. ²³The Egyptians pursued, and went into the sea after them, all of Pharaoh's horses, chariots, and chariot drivers. ²⁴At the morning watch the Lᴏʀᴅ in the pillar of fire and cloud looked down upon the Egyptian army, and threw the Egyptian army into panic. ²⁵He clogged their chariot wheels so that they turned with difficulty. The Egyptians said, "Let us flee from the Israelites, for the Lᴏʀᴅ is fighting for them against Egypt."

²⁶Then the Lᴏʀᴅ said to Moses, "Stretch out your hand over the sea, so that the water may come back upon the Egyptians, upon their chariots and chariot drivers." ²⁷So Moses stretched out his hand over the sea, and at dawn the sea returned to its normal depth. As the Egyptians fled before it, the Lᴏʀᴅ tossed the Egyptians into the sea. ²⁸The waters returned and covered the chariots and the chariot drivers, the entire army of Pharaoh that had followed them into the sea; not one of them remained. ²⁹But the Israelites walked on dry ground through the sea, the waters forming a wall for them on their right and on their left.

³⁰Thus the Lᴏʀᴅ saved Israel that day from the Egyptians; and Israel saw the Egyptians dead on the seashore. ³¹Israel saw the great work that the Lᴏʀᴅ did against the Egyptians. So the people feared the Lᴏʀᴅ and believed in the Lᴏʀᴅ and in his servant Moses.

Exodus 15:1b-11, 20-21 (UM135)

¹ᵇ "I will sing to the Lᴏʀᴅ, for he has triumphed gloriously;
   horse and rider he has thrown into the sea.
²The Lᴏʀᴅ is my strength and my might,
   and he has become my salvation;
this is my God, and I will praise him,
   my father's God, and I will exalt him.
³The Lᴏʀᴅ is a warrior;
   the Lᴏʀᴅ is his name.

⁴"Pharaoh's chariots and his army he cast into the sea;
   his picked officers were sunk in the Red Sea.
⁵The floods covered them;
   they went down into the depths like a stone.
⁶Your right hand, O Lᴏʀᴅ, glorious in power—
   your right hand, O Lᴏʀᴅ, shattered the enemy.
⁷In the greatness of your majesty you overthrew your adversaries;
   you sent out your fury, it consumed them like stubble.
⁸At the blast of your nostrils the waters piled up,
   the floods stood up in a heap;
   the deeps congealed in the heart of the sea.
⁹The enemy said, 'I will pursue, I will overtake,
   I will divide the spoil, my desire shall have its fill of them.
   I will draw my sword, my hand shall destroy them.'
¹⁰You blew with your wind, the sea covered them;
   they sank like lead in the mighty waters.

¹¹"Who is like you, O Lᴏʀᴅ, among the gods?
   Who is like you, majestic in holiness,
   awesome in splendor, doing wonders?"

²⁰Then the prophet Miriam, Aaron's sister, took a tambourine in her hand; and all the women went out after her with tambourines and with dancing. ²¹And Miriam sang to them:
"Sing to the Lᴏʀᴅ, for he has triumphed gloriously;
   horse and rider he has thrown into the sea."

Romans 14:1-12

¹Welcome those who are weak in faith, but not for the purpose of quarreling over opinions. ²Some believe in eating anything, while the weak eat only vegetables. ³Those who eat must not despise those who abstain, and those who abstain must not pass judgment on those who eat; for God has welcomed them. ⁴Who are you to pass judgment on servants of another? It is before their own lord that they stand or fall. And they will be upheld, for the Lord is able to make them stand.

⁵Some judge one day to be better than another, while others judge all days to be alike. Let all be fully convinced in their own minds. ⁶Those who observe the day, observe it in honor of the Lord. Also those who eat, eat in honor of the Lord, since they give thanks to God; while those who abstain, abstain in honor of the Lord and give thanks to God.

⁷We do not live to ourselves, and we do not die to ourselves. ⁸If we live, we live to the Lord, and if we die, we die to the Lord; so then, whether we live or whether we die, we are the Lord's. ⁹For to this end Christ died and lived again, so that he might be Lord of both the dead and the living.

¹⁰Why do you pass judgment on your brother or sister? Or you, why do you despise your brother or sister? For we will all stand before the judgment seat of God. ¹¹For it is written,
"As I live, says the Lord, every knee shall bow to me,
   and every tongue shall give praise to God."
¹²So then, each of us will be accountable to God.

Matthew 18:21-35

²¹Then Peter came and said to him, "Lord, if another member of the church sins against me, how often should I forgive? As many as seven times?" ²²Jesus said to him, "Not seven times, but, I tell you, seventy-seven times.

²³"For this reason the kingdom of heaven may be compared to a king who wished to settle accounts with his slaves. ²⁴When he began the reckoning, one who owed him ten thousand talents was brought to him; ²⁵and, as he could not pay, his lord ordered him to be sold, together with his wife and children and all his possessions, and payment to be made. ²⁶So the slave fell on his knees before him, saying, 'Have patience with me, and I will pay you everything.' ²⁷And out of pity for him, the lord of that slave released him and forgave him the debt. ²⁸But that same slave, as he went out, came upon one of his fellow slaves who owed him a hundred denarii; and seizing him by the throat, he said, 'Pay what you owe.' ²⁹Then his fellow slave fell down and pleaded with him, 'Have patience with me, and I will pay you.' ³⁰But he refused; then he went and threw him into prison until he would pay the debt. ³¹When his fellow slaves saw what had happened, they were greatly distressed, and they went and reported to their lord all that had taken place. ³²Then his lord summoned him and said to him, 'You wicked slave! I forgave you all that debt because you pleaded with me. ³³Should you not have had mercy on your fellow slave, as I had mercy on you?' ³⁴And in anger his lord handed him over to be tortured until he would pay his entire debt. ³⁵So my heavenly Father will also do to every one of you, if you do not forgive your brother or sister from your heart."

Primary Hymns and Songs for the Day

2234	"Lead On, O Cloud of Presence" (Exod) (O)	
	H-3	Hbl-74; Chr-123; Desc-64; Org-71
	S-1	#9-197. Various treatments
134	"O Mary, Don't You Weep" (Exod)	
149	*Cantemos al Señor* ("Let's Sing unto the Lord") (Exod, Canticle)	
	H-3	Chr-128; Org-129
	S-2	#154. Performance note
356	*Pues Si Vivimos* ("When We Are Living") (Rom)	
	S-1	#320. Orff Instr. Arr.
	H-3	Chr-218; Org-155
2169	"God, How Can We Forgive" (Rom, Matt)	
	H-3	Hbl-62, 95; Chr-59; Org-77
	S-1	#211. Harm.
390	"Forgive Our Sins as We Forgive" (Matt)	
	H-3	Chr-68; Desc-28; Org-27
	S-1	#85. Choral Harm.
389	"Freely, Freely" (Matt) (C)	
	S-1	#135. Vocal Desc. idea

Additional Hymn Suggestions

105	"God of Many Names" (Exod)
315	"Come, Ye Faithful, Raise the Strain" (Exod) (O)
448	"Go Down, Moses" (Exod)
508	"Faith, While Trees Are Still in Blossom" (Exod)
2060	"God the Sculptor of the Mountains" (Exod)
2107	"Wade in the Water" (Exod, Baptism)
2120	"Spirit, Spirit of Gentleness" (Exod)
2238	"In the Midst of New Dimensions" (Exod)
2246	"Deep in the Shadows of the Past" (Exod)
166	"All Praise to Thee, for Thou O King Divine" (Rom)
168	"At the Name of Jesus" (Rom)
169	"In Thee Is Gladness" (Rom)
463	"Lord, Speak to Me" (Rom) (C)
121	"There's a Wideness in God's Mercy" (Rom, Matt)
170	"O How I Love Jesus" (Rom, Matt)
187	"Rise, Shine, You People" (Matt)
271	"The Lord's Prayer" (Matt)
368	"My Hope Is Built" (Matt)
402	"Lord, I Want to Be a Christian" (Matt)
560	"Help Us Accept Each Other" (Matt)
2269	"Come, Share the Lord" (Matt, Comm.)

Additional Contemporary Suggestions

S2023	"How Majestic Is Your Name" (Exod)
S2144	"Someone Asked the Question" (Exod)
SP58	"The Lord Reigns" (Exod)
WS3038	"Mighty to Save" (Exod)
WS3042	"Shout to the North" (Exod, Pss)
M1	"Ancient of Days" (Exod, Rom)
UM176	"Majesty" (Exod, Rom)
S2032	"My Life Is in You, Lord" (Exod, Rom)
SP18	"I Exalt You" (Exod, Rom)
M140	"We Will Dance" (Exod, Rom)
M230	"The Highest and the Greatest" (Exod, Rom)
S2070	"He Is Exalted" (Pss, Rom)
S2071	"Jesus, Name above All Names" (Rom)
S2164	"Sanctuary" (Rom)
UM177	"He Is Lord" (Rom)
WS3176	"Come, Now Is the Time to Worship" (Rom)
M111	"The Heavens Shall Declare" (Rom)
S2162	"Grace Alone" (Matt)
S2171	"Make Me a Channel of Your Peace" (Matt)

Vocal Solos

"Wade in the Water" (Exod)
  V-5(2)   p. 46
"Oh, Freedom" (Exod)
  V-7   p. 10
"In Jesus' Name" (Rom)
  V-8   p. 188
"Make Me a Channel of Your Peace" (Matt)
  V-3(2)   p. 25

Anthems

"Miriam's Song" (Exod)
Michael R. Barker; Choristers Guild CGA740
Unison with piano

"He Never Failed Me Yet" (Exod)
Ray, Arr. Christopher; Hal Leonard 44708014
SATB with piano

Other Suggestions

Visuals:
	O	Symbols of hope: cloud, pillar of fire, rainbow, star
	P	Musical notes, sea, tambourine, dancing, Exod 15:21b
	E	Reconciliation, unity, clasped hands, Christ, scales of justice
	G	Reconciliation, forgiveness, embrace, no. 77, 70x7, scales of justice

Call to Worship: UM149, stanza 1. *Cantemos al Señor* ("Let's Sing unto the Lord") (Exod)
Prayer of Confession: BOW481 (Matt)
Canticle: UM135. "Canticle of Moses and Miriam" (Exod)
Canticle: UM167. "Canticle of Christ's Obedience" (Rom)
Affirmation of Faith: WSL82 (Rom)
Prayer: UM268 (Exod) or UM366 (Matt)
Prayer: BOW514. For the Mind of Christ (Rom, Matt)
Response: BOW189 or BOW191. "May This Mind Be in Us" (Rom, Matt)
Prayer: BOW517 or BOW547 (Exod)
Prayer: BOW522. For Purity (Rom)
Response: S2207. "Lord, Listen to Your Children" (Rom)
Scripture Response: UM402, stanza 2. "Lord I Want to Be a Christian" (Matt)
Prayer of Thanksgiving: BOW556 (Exod)
Blessing: UM666. "Shalom to You" (Exod, Matt)

Exodus 16:2-15

²The whole congregation of the Israelites complained against Moses and Aaron in the wilderness. ³The Israelites said to them, "If only we had died by the hand of the LORD in the land of Egypt, when we sat by the fleshpots and ate our fill of bread; for you have brought us out into this wilderness to kill this whole assembly with hunger."

⁴Then the LORD said to Moses, "I am going to rain bread from heaven for you, and each day the people shall go out and gather enough for that day. In that way I will test them, whether they will follow my instruction or not. ⁵On the sixth day, when they prepare what they bring in, it will be twice as much as they gather on other days." ⁶So Moses and Aaron said to all the Israelites, "In the evening you shall know that it was the LORD who brought you out of the land of Egypt, ⁷and in the morning you shall see the glory of the LORD, because he has heard your complaining against the LORD. For what are we, that you complain against us?" ⁸And Moses said, "When the LORD gives you meat to eat in the evening and your fill of bread in the morning, because the LORD has heard the complaining that you utter against him—what are we? Your complaining is not against us but" against the LORD.

⁹Then Moses said to Aaron, "Say to the whole congregation of the Israelites, 'Draw near to the LORD, for he has heard your complaining.'" ¹⁰And as Aaron spoke to the whole congregation of the Israelites, they looked toward the wilderness, and the glory of the LORD appeared in the cloud. ¹¹The LORD spoke to Moses and said, ¹²"I have heard the complaining of the Israelites; say to them, 'At twilight you shall eat meat, and in the morning you shall have your fill of bread; then you shall know that I am the LORD your God.'"

¹³In the evening quails came up and covered the camp; and in the morning there was a layer of dew around the camp. ¹⁴When the layer of dew lifted, there on the surface of the wilderness was a fine flaky substance, as fine as frost on the ground. ¹⁵When the Israelites saw it, they said to one another, "What is it?" For they did not know what it was. Moses said to them, "It is the bread that the LORD has given you to eat."

Psalm 105:1-6, 37-45 (UM828)

¹O give thanks to the LORD, call on his name,
   make known his deeds among the peoples.
²Sing to him, sing praises to him;
   tell of all his wonderful works.
³Glory in his holy name;
   let the hearts of those who seek the LORD rejoice.
⁴Seek the LORD and his strength;
   seek his presence continually.
⁵Remember the wonderful works he has done,
   his miracles, and the judgments he has uttered,
⁶O offspring of his servant Abraham,
   children of Jacob, his chosen ones.
· ·
³⁷Then he brought Israel out with silver and gold,
   and there was no one among their tribes who stumbled.
³⁸Egypt was glad when they departed,
   for dread of them had fallen upon it.
³⁹He spread a cloud for a covering,
   and fire to give light by night.
⁴⁰They asked, and he brought quails,
   and gave them food from heaven in abundance.
⁴¹He opened the rock, and water gushed out;
   it flowed through the desert like a river.
⁴²For he remembered his holy promise,
   and Abraham, his servant.

⁴³So he brought his people out with joy,
   his chosen ones with singing.
⁴⁴He gave them the lands of the nations,
   and they took possession of the wealth of the peoples,
⁴⁵that they might keep his statutes and observe his laws.
   Praise the LORD!

Philippians 1:21-30

²¹For to me, living is Christ and dying is gain. ²²If I am to live in the flesh, that means fruitful labor for me; and I do not know which I prefer. ²³I am hard pressed between the two: my desire is to depart and be with Christ, for that is far better; ²⁴but to remain in the flesh is more necessary for you. ²⁵Since I am convinced of this, I know that I will remain and continue with all of you for your progress and joy in faith, ²⁶so that I may share abundantly in your boasting in Christ Jesus when I come to you again.

²⁷Only, live your life in a manner worthy of the gospel of Christ, so that, whether I come and see you or am absent and hear about you, I will know that you are standing firm in one spirit, striving side by side with one mind for the faith of the gospel, ²⁸and are in no way intimidated by your opponents. For them this is evidence of their destruction, but of your salvation. And this is God's doing. ²⁹For he has graciously granted you the privilege not only of believing in Christ, but of suffering for him as well— ³⁰since you are having the same struggle that you saw I had and now hear that I still have.

Matthew 20:1-16

¹"For the kingdom of heaven is like a landowner who went out early in the morning to hire laborers for his vineyard. ²After agreeing with the laborers for the usual daily wage, he sent them into his vineyard. ³When he went out about nine o'clock, he saw others standing idle in the marketplace; ⁴and he said to them, 'You also go into the vineyard, and I will pay you whatever is right.' So they went. ⁵When he went out again about noon and about three o'clock, he did the same. ⁶And about five o'clock he went out and found others standing around; and he said to them, 'Why are you standing here idle all day?' ⁷They said to him, 'Because no one has hired us.' He said to them, 'You also go into the vineyard.' ⁸When evening came, the owner of the vineyard said to his manager, 'Call the laborers and give them their pay, beginning with the last and then going to the first.' ⁹When those hired about five o'clock came, each of them received the usual daily wage. ¹⁰Now when the first came, they thought they would receive more; but each of them also received the usual daily wage. ¹¹And when they received it, they grumbled against the landowner, ¹²saying, 'These last worked only one hour, and you have made them equal to us who have borne the burden of the day and the scorching heat.' ¹³But he replied to one of them, 'Friend, I am doing you no wrong; did you not agree with me for the usual daily wage? ¹⁴Take what belongs to you and go; I choose to give to this last the same as I give to you. ¹⁵Am I not allowed to do what I choose with what belongs to me? Or are you envious because I am generous?' ¹⁶So the last will be first, and the first will be last."

Primary Hymns and Songs for the Day

127	"Guide Me, O Thou Great Jehovah" (Exod, Pss) (O)	
	H-3	Hbl-25, 51, 58; Chr-89; Desc-26; Org-23
	S-1	#76-77. Desc. and Harm.
519	"Lift Every Voice and Sing" (Exod, Pss)	
	H-3	Chr-128
2036	"Give Thanks" (Pss, Matt)	
356	*"Pues Si Vivimos"* ("When We Are Living") (Phil)	
	S-1	#320. Orff Instr. Arr.
	H-3	Chr-218; Org-155
433	"All Who Love and Serve Your City" (Matt, Pss)	
	H-3	Chr-26, 65; Org-19
	S-1	#62. Desc.
553	"And Are We Yet Alive" (Phil) (C)	
	H-3	Hbl-49; Chr-14; Desc-27; Org-25

Additional Hymn Suggestions

586	"Let My People Seek Their Freedom" (Exod)
631	"O Food to Pilgrims Given" (Exod, Comm.)
648	"God the Spirit, Guide and Guardian" (Exod) (C)
671	"Lord, Dismiss Us with Thy Blessing" (Exod) (C)
3030	"Eternal God Transcending Time" (Exod)
3031	"God Leads Us Along" (Exod)
2126	"All Who Hunger" (Exod, Matt)
2234	"Lead On, O Cloud of Presence" (Exod)
2238	"In the Midst of New Dimensions" (Exod)
2264	"Come to the Table" (Exod, Comm.)
3098	"Dust and Ashes" (Exod)
3169	"You Feed Us, Gentle Savior" (Exod, Comm.)
130	"God Will Take Care of You" (Exod, Pss)
132	"All My Hope Is Firmly Grounded" (Exod, Pss)
731	"Glorious Things of Thee Are Spoken" (Exod, Matt)
2279	"The Trees of the Field" (Pss)
102	"Now Thank We All Our God" (Pss)
124	"Seek the Lord" (Pss)
131	"We Gather Together" (Pss)
133	"Leaning on the Everlasting Arms" (Pss)
565	"Father, We Thank You" (Pss)
3012	"When Words Alone Cannot Express" (Pss)
169	"In Thee Is Gladness" (Phil)
2149	"Living for Jesus" (Phil)
2153	"I'm Gonna Live So God Can Use Me" (Phil)
2179	"Live in Charity" (*"Ubi Caritas"*) (Phil)
3110	"By Grace We Have Been Saved" (Phil)
3115	"Covenant Prayer" (Phil)
121	"There's a Wideness in God's Mercy" (Matt)
339	"Come, Sinners, to the Gospel Feast" (Matt)
340	"Come, Ye Sinners, Poor and Needy" (Matt)
426	"Behold a Broken World" (Matt)
435	"O God of Every Nation" (Matt)
517	"By Gracious Powers" (Matt)
581	"Lord, Whose Love Through Humble Service" (Matt)
2177	"Wounded World That Cries for Healing" (Matt)
2268	"As We Gather at Your Table" (Matt, Comm.)
3123	"Here Is Peace" (Matt)

Additional Contemporary Suggestions

WS3099	"Hungry" ("Falling on My Knees") (Exod)
WS3094	"Come to Me" (Exod)
WS3096	"Gentle Shepherd" (Exod)
WS3167	"Feed Us, Lord" (Exod, Comm.)
M4	"Let It Rise" (Exod)
M159	"All Who Are Thirsty" (Exod)
M160	"Enough" (Exod)
M257	"Came to My Rescue" (Exod, Pss)

S2132	"You Who Are Thirsty" (Exod, Comm.)
S2144	"Someone Asked the Question" (Pss)
WS3003	"How Great Is Our God" (Pss)
S2032	"My Life Is in You, Lord" (Phil)
S2164	"Sanctuary" (Phil)
S2224	"Make Us One" (Phil)
M247	"The Stand" (Phil)
S2131	"Humble Thyself in the Sight of the Lord" (Matt)
S2176	"Make Me a Servant" (Matt)

Vocal Solos

"Leanin' on Dat Lamb" (Exod)		
	V-7	p. 42
"God Will Make a Way" (Exod, Pss)		
	SP40	
"If My People Will Pray" (Exod, Pss)		
	V-8	p. 66
"Patiently Have I Waited for the Lord" (Exod, Matt)		
	V-4	p. 24

Anthems

"There Is a Balm in Gilead" (Exodus)
Robert Lau; Hinshaw HMC1891
SAB with Organ or piano

"Ubi Caritas" (Phil)
Peter Mathews; MorningStar 50-3077
SATB with organ

Other Suggestions

Visuals:

O	Bread, quails, hungry being fed
P	Singing, praising, cloud, fire, bread, quails, rock/water
E	People at work, service to God with people (bowl/pitcher/towel)
G	Grapes, leaves, tools for work, clocks set at 6:00 a.m., 9:00 a.m., noon, 3:00 p.m., 6:00 p.m.

Call to Worship: UM127. "Guide Me, O Thou Great Jehovah." A selected stanza may be used each Sunday from today until Oct. 30, when the Hebrew scripture tells of Israel's crossing the Jordan.

Greeting: BOW456 (Exod)

Opening Prayer: BOW465 (Exod, Matt)

Call to Prayer: S2132. "You Who Are Thirsty" (Exod)

Prayer of Confession: BOW485 (Exod)

Prayer: WSL55 (Exod)

Prayer: UM409. For Grace to Labor (Matt)

Prayer: BOW514. For the Mind of Christ (Phil)

Song of Preparation: UM563, stanza 1. "Father, We Thank You" (Pss)

Scripture Response: UM731, stanza 3. "Glorious Things of Thee Are Spoken" (Exod)

Prayer of Thanksgiving: BOW552 or BOW557 (Exod)

Response: S2195. "In the Lord I'll Be Ever Thankful" (Pss)

Exodus 17:1-7

[1]From the wilderness of Sin the whole congregation of the Israelites journeyed by stages, as the LORD commanded. They camped at Rephidim, but there was no water for the people to drink. [2]The people quarreled with Moses, and said, "Give us water to drink." Moses said to them, "Why do you quarrel with me? Why do you test the LORD?" [3]But the people thirsted there for water; and the people complained against Moses and said, "Why did you bring us out of Egypt, to kill us and our children and livestock with thirst?" [4]So Moses cried out to the LORD, "What shall I do with this people? They are almost ready to stone me." [5]The LORD said to Moses, "Go on ahead of the people, and take some of the elders of Israel with you; take in your hand the staff with which you struck the Nile, and go. [6]I will be standing there in front of you on the rock at Horeb. Strike the rock, and water will come out of it, so that the people may drink." Moses did so, in the sight of the elders of Israel. [7]He called the place Massah and Meribah, because the Israelites quarreled and tested the LORD, saying, "Is the LORD among us or not?"

Psalm 78:1-4, 12-16 (UM799)

[1]Give ear, O my people, to my teaching;
    incline your ears to the words of my mouth.
[2]I will open my mouth in a parable;
    I will utter dark sayings from of old,
[3]things that we have heard and known,
    that our ancestors have told us.
[4]We will not hide them from their children;
    we will tell to the coming generation
the glorious deeds of the LORD, and his might,
    and the wonders that he has done.

[12]In the sight of their ancestors he worked marvels
    in the land of Egypt, in the fields of Zoan.
[13]He divided the sea and let them pass through it,
    and made the waters stand like a heap.
[14]In the daytime he led them with a cloud,
    and all night long with a fiery light.
[15]He split rocks open in the wilderness,
    and gave them drink abundantly as from the deep.
[16]He made streams come out of the rock,
    and caused waters to flow down like rivers.

Philippians 2:1-13

[1]If then there is any encouragement in Christ, any consolation from love, any sharing in the Spirit, any compassion and sympathy, [2]make my joy complete: be of the same mind, having the same love, being in full accord and of one mind. [3]Do nothing from selfish ambition or conceit, but in humility regard others as better than yourselves. [4]Let each of you look not to your own interests, but to the interests of others. [5]Let the same mind be in you that was in Christ Jesus,
[6]who, though he was in the form of God,
    did not regard equality with God
    as something to be exploited,
[7]but emptied himself,
    taking the form of a slave,
    being born in human likeness.
And being found in human form,
    [8]he humbled himself
    and became obedient to the point of death—
    even death on a cross.
[9]Therefore God also highly exalted him
    and gave him the name
    that is above every name,
[10]so that at the name of Jesus
    every knee should bend,
    in heaven and on earth and under the earth,
[11]and every tongue should confess
    that Jesus Christ is Lord,
    to the glory of God the Father.

[12]Therefore, my beloved, just as you have always obeyed me, not only in my presence, but much more now in my absence, work out your own salvation with fear and trembling; [13]for it is God who is at work in you, enabling you both to will and to work for his good pleasure.

Matthew 21:23-32

[23]When he entered the temple, the chief priests and the elders of the people came to him as he was teaching, and said, "By what authority are you doing these things, and who gave you this authority?" [24]Jesus said to them, "I will also ask you one question; if you tell me the answer, then I will also tell you by what authority I do these things. [25]Did the baptism of John come from heaven, or was it of human origin?" And they argued with one another, "If we say, 'From heaven,' he will say to us, 'Why then did you not believe him?' [26]But if we say, 'Of human origin,' we are afraid of the crowd; for all regard John as a prophet." [27]So they answered Jesus, "We do not know." And he said to them, "Neither will I tell you by what authority I am doing these things.

[28]"What do you think? A man had two sons; he went to the first and said, 'Son, go and work in the vineyard today.' [29]He answered, 'I will not'; but later he changed his mind and went. [30]The father went to the second and said the same; and he answered, 'I go, sir'; but he did not go. [31]Which of the two did the will of his father?" They said, "The first." Jesus said to them, "Truly I tell you, the tax collectors and the prostitutes are going into the kingdom of God ahead of you. [32]For John came to you in the way of righteousness and you did not believe him, but the tax collectors and the prostitutes believed him; and even after you saw it, you did not change your minds and believe him.

Primary Hymns and Songs for the Day

166   "All Praise to Thee, for Thou, O King Divine" (Phil)
       (O)
        H-3   Hbl-58; Chr-65; Org-152
        S-1   #314-318. Various treatments
117   "O God, Our Help in Ages Past" (Exod, Pss)
        H-3   Hbl-87; Chr-60, 143; Desc-93; Org-132
        S-1   #293-296. Various treatments
2100 "Thou Didst Leave Thy Throne" (Phil)
        H-3   Chr-200
620   "One Bread, One Body" (World Comm.)
        H-3   Chr-156
467   "Trust and Obey" (Phil, Matt) (C)
        H-3   Chr-202
        S-1   #336. Harm.

Additional Hymn Suggestions

127   "Guide Me, O Thou Great Jehovah" (Exod) (O)
130   "God Will Take Care of You" (Exod, Pss)
132   "All My Hope Is Firmly Grounded" (Exod)
448   "Go Down Moses" (Exod)
506   "Wellspring of Wisdom" (Exod)
3030 "Eternal God Transcending Time" (Exod)
3031 "God Leads Us Along" (Exod)
3098 "Dust and Ashes" (Exod)
519   "Lift Every Voice and Sing" (Exod, Pss)
586   "Let My People Seek Their Freedom" (Exod)
648   "God the Spirit, Guide and Guardian" (Exod) (C)
2126 "All Who Hunger" (Exod)
2234 "Lead On, O Cloud of Presence" (Exod)
2238 "In the Midst of New Dimensions" (Exod) (O)
2264 "Come to the Table" (Exod, Comm.)
340   "Come, Ye Sinners, Poor and Needy" (Exod, Matt)
731   "Glorious Things of Thee Are Spoken" (Exod, Matt)
168   "At the Name of Jesus" (Phil)
193   "Jesus! The Name High Over All" (Phil)
292   "What Wondrous Love Is This" (Phil)
536   "Precious Name" (Phil) (C)
554   "All Praise to Our Redeeming Lord" (Phil)
561   "Jesus, United by Thy Grace" (Phil)
562   "Jesus, Lord, We Look to Thee" (Phil)
692   "Creator of the Stars of Night" (Phil)
2082 "Woke Up This Morning" (Phil)
2186 "Song of Hope" ("*Canto de Esperanza*") (Phil) (C)
3030 "Eternal God Transcending Time" (Phil)
3039 "Jesus, the Saving Name" (Phil)
3075 "Glory in the Cross" (Phil)
3089 "O Living God" (Phil)
3115 "Covenant Prayer" (Phil)
155   "All Hail the Power of Jesus' Name" (Phil, Matt)
261   "Lord of the Dance" (Matt)
343   "Come Back Quickly to the Lord" (Matt)
438   "Forth in Thy Name, O Lord" (Matt) (C)
2170 "God Made from One Blood" (World Comm.)
2221 "In Unity We Lift Our Song" (World Comm.)
3120 "Amazing Abundance" (World Comm.)

Additional Contemporary Suggestions

WS3093 "Fill My Cup, Lord" (Exod, Comm.)
        UM641 (refrain only)
WS3094 "Come to Me" (Exod)
WS3096 "Gentle Shepherd" (Exod)
WS3099 "Hungry" ("Falling on My Knees") (Exod)
WS3167 "Feed Us, Lord" (Exod, Comm.)
M159 "All Who Are Thirsty" (Exod)
M160 "Enough" (Exod)
M257 "Came to My Rescue" (Exod, Pss)
S2132 "You Who Are Thirsty" (Exod, Comm.)

WS3042 "Shout to the North" (Phil)
WS3176 "Come, Now Is the Time to Worship" (Phil)
UM176 "Majesty" (Phil)
UM177 "He Is Lord" (Phil)
S2023 "How Majestic Is Your Name" (Phil)
S2070 "He Is Exalted" (Phil)
S2071 "Jesus, Name above All Names" (Phil)
S2131 "Humble Thyself in the Sight of the Lord" (Phil)
S2224 "Make Us One" (Phil)
SP234 "At the Name of Jesus" (Phil)
M3   "Jesus, Your Name" (Phil)
M38   "In the Secret" ("I Want to Know You") (Phil)
M140 "We Will Dance" (Phil)
M178 "Majestic" (Phil)
M263 "From the Inside Out" (Phil)
M53   "Let It Be Said of Us" (Phil, Matt)
M91   "Take My Life" (Phil, Matt)
S2161 "To Know You More" (Phil, Matt)
S2167 "More Like You" (Phil, Matt)
UM405 "Seek Ye First" (Matt)
S2224 "Make Us One" (World Comm.)

Vocal Solos

"God Will Make a Way" (with "He Leadeth Me") (Exod)
    V-3(2)   p. 9
"May the Mind of Christ" (Phil)
    V-8   p. 114

Anthems

"Who Is This?" (Matt)
John Ferguson; Morningstar 50-6509
SATB divisi with viola

"Holy Banquet, Feast of Love" (World Comm.)
Normand Gouin; MorningStar 80-837
SATB or SAB with keyboard, opt. C- or Bb- Inst.

Other Suggestions

Visuals:
O/P/G   Rock, flowing water, sand, staff, images of baptism
    E   Reminders of Crucifixion, Resurrection, Birth of
        Christ
    G   Vineyard, grapes, vine, leaves, "Reconsider Your Call"
World Communion   Flags, costumes, artifacts of nations, unity,
    breads of the world, globe
Greeting and Opening Prayer: BOW456 and BOW465 (Exod)
Call to Worship: WSL61 (Matt)
Prayer of Confession: BOW485 (Exod)
Canticle: UM167. "Canticle of Christ's Obedience" (Phil) (See
    S-1, p. 381.)
Scripture Response: UM731, stanza 2. "Glorious Things of Thee
    Are Spoken" (Exod)
Prayer: BOW514. For the Mind of Christ (Phil)
Response: BOW189/191. "May This Mind Be in Us" (Phil)
Prayer: BOW529. A Prayer of Saint Patrick (Phil)
Prayer: BOW527. For the World and Its Peoples (Exod)
Prayer: WSL19. "God of the wilderness" (Exod)
Prayer: WSL55. "Almighty God, you sustained" (Exod)
Prayer: WSL204. "God of compassion (Matt)
Prayer: BOW539, BOW540, or BOW541 (Matt)
Prayer of Thanksgiving: BOW552 or BOW557 (Exod)
World Communion resources include: BOW 432, BOW488,
    BOW 492, BOW495, BOW505, BOW562, UM556, UM564,
    WSL67/68

Exodus 20:1-4, 7-9, 12-20

¹Then God spoke all these words:

²I am the Lord your God, who brought you out of the land of Egypt, out of the house of slavery; ³you shall have no other gods before me.

⁴You shall not make for yourself an idol, whether in the form of anything that is in heaven above, or that is on the earth beneath, or that is in the water under the earth. . . .

⁷You shall not make wrongful use of the name of the Lord your God, for the Lord will not acquit anyone who misuses his name.

⁸Remember the sabbath day, and keep it holy. ⁹Six days you shall labor and do all your work. . . .

¹²Honor your father and your mother, so that your days may be long in the land that the Lord your God is giving you.

¹³You shall not murder.

¹⁴You shall not commit adultery.

¹⁵You shall not steal.

¹⁶You shall not bear false witness against your neighbor.

¹⁷You shall not covet your neighbor's house; you shall not covet your neighbor's wife, or male or female slave, or ox, or donkey, or anything that belongs to your neighbor.

¹⁸When all the people witnessed the thunder and lightning, the sound of the trumpet, and the mountain smoking, they were afraid and trembled and stood at a distance, ¹⁹and said to Moses, "You speak to us, and we will listen; but do not let God speak to us, or we will die." ²⁰Moses said to the people, "Do not be afraid; for God has come only to test you and to put the fear of him upon you so that you do not sin."

Psalm 19 (UM750)

¹The heavens are telling the glory of God;
    and the firmament proclaims his handiwork.
²Day to day pours forth speech,
    and night to night declares knowledge.
³There is no speech, nor are there words;
    their voice is not heard;
⁴yet their voice goes out through all the earth,
    and their words to the end of the world.
In the heavens he has set a tent for the sun,
⁵which comes out like a bridegroom from his wedding canopy,
    and like a strong man runs its course with joy.
⁶Its rising is from the end of the heavens,
    and its circuit to the end of them;
    and nothing is hid from its heat.
⁷The law of the Lord is perfect,/reviving the soul;
the decrees of the Lord are sure,/making wise the simple;
⁸the precepts of the Lord are right,/rejoicing the heart;
the commandment of the Lord is clear,
    enlightening the eyes;
⁹the fear of the Lord is pure,/enduring forever;
the ordinances of the Lord are true
    and righteous altogether.
¹⁰More to be desired are they than gold,
    even much fine gold;
sweeter also than honey,
    and drippings of the honeycomb.
¹¹Moreover by them is your servant warned;
    in keeping them there is great reward.
¹²But who can detect their errors?
    Clear me from hidden faults.
¹³Keep back your servant also from the insolent;
    do not let them have dominion over me.

Then I shall be blameless,
    and innocent of great transgression.
¹⁴Let the words of my mouth and the meditation of my heart
    be acceptable to you,
    O Lord, my rock and my redeemer.

Philippians 3:4b-14

^{4b}If anyone else has reason to be confident in the flesh, I have more: ⁵circumcised on the eighth day, a member of the people of Israel, of the tribe of Benjamin, a Hebrew born of Hebrews; as to the law, a Pharisee; ⁶as to zeal, a persecutor of the church; as to righteousness under the law, blameless.

⁷Yet whatever gains I had, these I have come to regard as loss because of Christ. ⁸More than that, I regard everything as loss because of the surpassing value of knowing Christ Jesus my Lord. For his sake I have suffered the loss of all things, and I regard them as rubbish, in order that I may gain Christ ⁹and be found in him, not having a righteousness of my own that comes from the law, but one that comes through faith in Christ, the righteousness from God based on faith. ¹⁰I want to know Christ and the power of his resurrection and the sharing of his sufferings by becoming like him in his death, ¹¹if somehow I may attain the resurrection from the dead.

¹²Not that I have already obtained this or have already reached the goal; but I press on to make it my own, because Christ Jesus has made me his own. ¹³Beloved, I do not consider that I have made it my own; but this one thing I do: forgetting what lies behind and straining forward to what lies ahead, ¹⁴I press on toward the goal for the prize of the heavenly call of God in Christ Jesus.

Matthew 21:33-46

³³"Listen to another parable. There was a landowner who planted a vineyard, put a fence around it, dug a wine press in it, and built a watchtower. Then he leased it to tenants and went to another country. ³⁴When the harvest time had come, he sent his slaves to the tenants to collect his produce. ³⁵But the tenants seized his slaves and beat one, killed another, and stoned another. ³⁶Again he sent other slaves, more than the first; and they treated them in the same way. ³⁷Finally he sent his son to them, saying, 'They will respect my son.' ³⁸But when the tenants saw the son, they said to themselves, 'This is the heir; come, let us kill him and get his inheritance.' ³⁹So they seized him, threw him out of the vineyard, and killed him. ⁴⁰Now when the owner of the vineyard comes, what will he do to those tenants?" ⁴¹They said to him, "He will put those wretches to a miserable death, and lease the vineyard to other tenants who will give him the produce at the harvest time."

⁴²Jesus said to them, "Have you never read in the scriptures:
'The stone that the builders rejected
    has become the cornerstone;
this was the Lord's doing,
    and it is amazing in our eyes'?

⁴³Therefore I tell you, the kingdom of God will be taken away from you and given to a people that produces the fruits of the kingdom. ⁴⁴The one who falls on this stone will be broken to pieces; and it will crush anyone on whom it falls."

⁴⁵When the chief priests and the Pharisees heard his parables, they realized that he was speaking about them. ⁴⁶They wanted to arrest him, but they feared the crowds, because they regarded him as a prophet.

Primary Hymns and Songs for the Day

559	"Christ Is Made the Sure Foundation" (Matt) (O)	
	H-3	Chr-49; Desc-103; Org-180
	S-1	#346. Desc.
77	"How Great Thou Art" (Pss)	
	H-3	Chr-103; Org-105
	S-1	#163. Harm.
368	"My Hope Is Built" (Phil, Matt)	
	H-3	Chr-191
	S-2	#171-172. Trumpet and Vocal Desc.
546	"The Church's One Foundation" (Phil, Matt) (C)	
	H-3	Hbl-94; Chr-180; Desc-16; Org-9
	S-1	#25-26. Desc. and Harm.

Additional Hymn Suggestions

390	"Forgive Our Sins as We Forgive" (Exod)
404	"Every Time I Feel the Spirit" (Exod)
2120	"Spirit, Spirit of Gentleness" (Exod)
2230	"Lord, We Come to Ask Your Blessing" (Exod)
3029	"In the Desert, on God's Mountain" (Exod)
398	"Jesus Calls Us" (Exod, Phil)
425	"O Crucified Redeemer" (Exod, Pss, Matt)
529	"How Firm a Foundation" (Exod, Matt)
149	*Cantemos al Señor* ("Let's Sing unto the Lord") (Pss)
685	"Now, on Land and Sea Descending" (Pss, Evening)
2012	"Let Us with a Joyful Mind" (Pss)
175	"Jesus, the Very Thought of Thee" (Phil)
701	"When We All Get to Heaven" (Phil)
709	"Come, Let Us Join Our Friends Above" (Phil)
298	"When I Survey the Wondrous Cross" (Phil)
363	"And Can It Be that I Should Gain" (Phil)
413	"A Charge to Keep I Have" (Phil)
2213	"Healer of Our Every Ill" (Phil)
433	"All Who Love and Serve Your City" (Matt)
2220	"We Are God's People" (Matt)
3147	"Built on a Rock" (Matt)

Additional Contemporary Suggestions

S2018	"Honor and Praise" (Exod)
M229	"Forevermore" (Exod)
S2002	"I Will Call Upon the Lord" (Pss)
S2040	"Awesome God" (Pss)
WS3034	"God of Wonders" (Pss)
WS3041	"Praise Him" (Pss)
M58	"All Heaven Declares" (Pss)
M111	"The Heavens Shall Declare" (Pss)
M126	"Famous One" (Pss)
M235	"Sing, Sing, Sing" (Pss)
M93	"Rock of Ages" (Pss, Matt)
S2066	"Praise the Name of Jesus" (Pss, Matt)
S2208	"Guide My Feet" (Phil)
S2163	"He Who Began a Good Work in You" (Phil)
S2161	"To Know You More" (Phil)
UM394	"Something Beautiful" (Phil)
M30	"Knowing You" ("All I Once Held Dear") (Phil)
M38	"In the Secret" ("I Want to Know You") (Phil)
M76	"The Wonderful Cross" (Phil)
S2264	"Come to the Table" (Phil, Comm.)
S2162	"Grace Alone" (Phil, Matt)
S2043	"Alleluia" (Matt)
WS3105	"In Christ Alone" (Matt)
WS3186	"Days of Elijah" (Matt)

Vocal Solos

"Ev'ry Time I Feel De Spirit" (Exod)
    V-7   p. 78
"The Heavens Declare His Glory" (Pss)
    V-8   p. 248a

Anthems

"The Church's One Foundation" (Phil, Matt)
Arr. Michael Burkhardt; MorningStar 60-9032
SATB with organ, brass quintet, opt. handbells

"Christ Is Made the Sure Foundation" (Matt)
Purcell/Arr. Rutter; Hinshaw HMC1796
SATB with organ; opt. congregation

Other Suggestions

Visuals:

O	Clay tablets, Ten Commandments, lightning, trumpet, mountain
P	Tent, wedding canopy, planets/stars/space, gold, rock, honey/comb
E	"Yet," rubbish, portrait of Christ, resurrection, crown of laurel leaves, trophy
G	Vineyard, wine press, building cornerstone, fruit

Call to Worship: UM211, stanza 3. "O Come, O Come, Emmanuel" (Exod)
Greeting: BOW450 (Pss) or BOW456 (Matt)
Act of Congregational Centering: BOW470 (Phil)
Litany: BOW496. The Ten Commandments (Exod)
Prayer: BOW524. For Strength (Phil)
Offering Prayer: WSL156. "Almighty God, you gave." (Exod)

Exodus 32:1-14

[1]When the people saw that Moses delayed to come down from the mountain, the people gathered around Aaron, and said to him, "Come, make gods for us, who shall go before us; as for this Moses, the man who brought us up out of the land of Egypt, we do not know what has become of him." [2]Aaron said to them, "Take off the gold rings that are on the ears of your wives, your sons, and your daughters, and bring them to me." [3]So all the people took off the gold rings from their ears, and brought them to Aaron. [4]He took the gold from them, formed it in a mold, and cast an image of a calf; and they said, "These are your gods, O Israel, who brought you up out of the land of Egypt!" [5]When Aaron saw this, he built an altar before it; and Aaron made proclamation and said, "Tomorrow shall be a festival to the LORD." [6]They rose early the next day, and offered burnt offerings and brought sacrifices of well-being; and the people sat down to eat and drink, and rose up to revel.

[7]The LORD said to Moses, "Go down at once! Your people, whom you brought up out of the land of Egypt, have acted perversely; [8]they have been quick to turn aside from the way that I commanded them; they have cast for themselves an image of a calf, and have worshiped it and sacrificed to it, and said, 'These are your gods, O Israel, who brought you up out of the land of Egypt!'" [9]The LORD said to Moses, "I have seen this people, how stiff-necked they are. [10]Now let me alone, so that my wrath may burn hot against them and I may consume them; and of you I will make a great nation."

[11]But Moses implored the LORD his God, and said, "O LORD, why does your wrath burn hot against your people, whom you brought out of the land of Egypt with great power and with a mighty hand? [12]Why should the Egyptians say, 'It was with evil intent that he brought them out to kill them in the mountains, and to consume them from the face of the earth'? Turn from your fierce wrath; change your mind and do not bring disaster on your people. [13]Remember Abraham, Isaac, and Israel, your servants, how you swore to them by your own self, saying to them, 'I will multiply your descendants like the stars of heaven, and all this land that I have promised I will give to your descendants, and they shall inherit it forever.'" [14]And the LORD changed his mind about the disaster that he planned to bring on his people.

Psalm 106:1-6, 19-23 (UM829)

[1]Praise the LORD!
O give thanks to the LORD, for he is good;
for his steadfast love endures forever.
[2]Who can utter the mighty doings of the LORD,
or declare all his praise?
[3]Happy are those who observe justice,
who do righteousness at all times.
[4]Remember me, O LORD, when you show favor to your people;
help me when you deliver them;
[5]that I may see the prosperity of your chosen ones,
that I may rejoice in the gladness of your nation,
that I may glory in your heritage.
[6]Both we and our ancestors have sinned;
we have committed iniquity, have done wickedly.

. . . .

[19]They made a calf at Horeb
and worshiped a cast image.
[20]They exchanged the glory of God
for the image of an ox that eats grass.

[21]They forgot God, their Savior,
who had done great things in Egypt,
[22]wondrous works in the land of Ham,
and awesome deeds by the Red Sea.
[23]Therefore he said he would destroy them—
had not Moses, his chosen one,
stood in the breach before him,
to turn away his wrath from destroying them.

Philippians 4:1-9

[1]Therefore, my brothers and sisters, whom I love and long for, my joy and crown, stand firm in the Lord in this way, my beloved.

[2]I urge Euodia and I urge Syntyche to be of the same mind in the Lord. [3]Yes, and I ask you also, my loyal companion, help these women, for they have struggled beside me in the work of the gospel, together with Clement and the rest of my co-workers, whose names are in the book of life.

[4]Rejoice in the Lord always; again I will say, Rejoice. [5]Let your gentleness be known to everyone. The Lord is near. [6]Do not worry about anything, but in everything by prayer and supplication with thanksgiving let your requests be made known to God. [7]And the peace of God, which surpasses all understanding, will guard your hearts and your minds in Christ Jesus.

[8]Finally, beloved, whatever is true, whatever is honorable, whatever is just, whatever is pure, whatever is pleasing, whatever is commendable, if there is any excellence and if there is anything worthy of praise, think about these things. [9]Keep on doing the things that you have learned and received and heard and seen in me, and the God of peace will be with you.

Matthew 22:1-14

[1]Once more Jesus spoke to them in parables, saying: [2]"The kingdom of heaven may be compared to a king who gave a wedding banquet for his son. [3]He sent his slaves to call those who had been invited to the wedding banquet, but they would not come. [4]Again he sent other slaves, saying, 'Tell those who have been invited: Look, I have prepared my dinner, my oxen and my fat calves have been slaughtered, and everything is ready; come to the wedding banquet.' [5]But they made light of it and went away, one to his farm, another to his business, [6]while the rest seized his slaves, mistreated them, and killed them. [7]The king was enraged. He sent his troops, destroyed those murderers, and burned their city. [8]Then he said to his slaves, 'The wedding is ready, but those invited were not worthy. [9]Go therefore into the main streets, and invite everyone you find to the wedding banquet.' [10]Those slaves went out into the streets and gathered all whom they found, both good and bad; so the wedding hall was filled with guests.

[11]"But when the king came in to see the guests, he noticed a man there who was not wearing a wedding robe, [12]and he said to him, 'Friend, how did you get in here without a wedding robe?' And he was speechless. [13]Then the king said to the attendants, 'Bind him hand and foot, and throw him into the outer darkness, where there will be weeping and gnashing of teeth.' [14]For many are called, but few are chosen."

Primary Hymns and Songs for the Day

160   "Rejoice, Ye Pure in Heart" (Phil) (O)
      H-3   Hbl-17, 90; Chr-166; Desc-73; Org-85
      S-1   #228. Desc.
      H-3   Chr-166; Desc-102
3023   "Forever" (Pss)
339   "Come, Sinners, to the Gospel Feast" (Matt)
      H-3   Chr-68; Desc-52; Org-55
      S-1   #164-166. Various treatments
427   "Where Cross the Crowded Ways of Life" (Matt) (C)
      H-3   Chr-178, 180; Org-44
      S-1   #141-3 Various treatments

Additional Hymn Suggestions

115   "How Like a Gentle Spirit" (Exod)
151   "God Created Heaven and Earth" (Exod)
352   "It's Me, It's Me, O Lord" (Exod)
426   "Behold a Broken World" (Exod)
428   "For the Healing of the Nations" (Exod)
450   "Creator of the Earth and Skies" (Exod)
2120   "Spirit, Spirit of Gentleness" (Exod)
2136   "Out of the Depths" (Exod)
3029   "In the Desert, on God's Mountain" (Exod)
3077   "Blessed Is He Who Comes in God's Name" (Exod)
2177   "Wounded World that Cries for Healing" (Exod, Pss)
2182   "When God Restored Our Common Life" (Exod, Pss)
2183   "Unsettled World" (Exod, Pss)
102   "Now Thank We All Our God" (Exod, Pss)
131   "We Gather Together" (Exod, Pss) (O)
121   "There's a Wideness in God's Mercy" (Exod, Matt)
398   "Jesus Calls Us" (Exod, Matt)
443   "O God Who Shaped Creation" (Exod, Matt)
161   "Rejoice, Ye Pure in Heart" (Phil) (O)
395   "Take Time to Be Holy" (Phil)
526   "What a Friend We Have in Jesus" (Phil)
562   "Jesus, Lord, We Look to Thee" (Phil)
70   "Go Forth for God" (Phil) (C)
715   "Rejoice, the Lord Is King" (Phil) (C)
2128   "Come and Find the Quiet Center" (Phil)
2202   "Come Away with Me" (Phil)
2205   "The Fragrance of Christ" (Phil)
2212   "My Life Flows On" (Phil)
2218   "You Are Mine" (Phil)
3048   "View the Present through the Promise" (Phil)
3125   "Peace for the Children" (Phil)
2197   "Lord of All Hopefulness" (Phil, Matt)
340   "Come, Ye Sinners, Poor and Needy" (Matt) (O)
396   "O Jesus, I Have Promised" (Matt)
348   "Softly and Tenderly Jesus Is Calling" (Matt)
381   "Savior, Like a Shepherd Lead Us" (Matt)
467   "Trust and Obey" (Matt)
612   "Deck Thyself, My Soul, with Gladness" (Matt, Comm.)
2175   "Together We Serve" (Matt)
2236   "Gather Us In" (Matt)
2263   "Broken for Me" (Matt, Comm.)
2265   "Time Now to Gather" (Matt, Comm.)
2268   "As We Gather at Your Table" (Matt, Comm.)

Additional Contemporary Suggestions

S2134   "Forgive Us, Lord" ("*Perdón, Señor*") (Exod)
S2056   "God Is So Good" (Pss)
S2036   "Give Thanks" (Pss)
S2195   "In the Lord I'll Be Ever Thankful" (Pss)
WS3026   "God Is Good All the Time" (Pss)

WS3027   "Hallelujah" ("Your Love Is Amazing") (Pss)
WS3014   "You Are Good" (Pss)
M189   "Your Love, Oh Lord" (Pss)
S2270   "I Will Enter His Gates" (Phil)
S2145   "I've Got Peace Like a River" (Phil)
S2156   "Give Peace" ("*Da Pacem Cordium*") (Phil)
S2193   "Lord, Listen to Your Children Praying" (Phil)
S2273   "Jesus, We Are Here" ("*Yesu Tawa Pano*") (Phil)
WS3049   "Wait for the Lord" (Phil)
WS3148   "There's a Spirit of Love in This Place" (Phil)
M260   "I Will Rise" (Phil)
M87   "Let the Peace of God Reign" (Phil)
M157   "Surrender" (Matt)
M195   "The King of All of Me" (Matt)
S2264   "Come to the Table" (Matt, Comm.)
WS3168   "Come to the Table of Grace" (Matt, Comm.)

Vocal Solos

"Stan'in' In De Need of Prayer" (Exod)
    V-7   p. 40
"A Song of Trust" (Phil)
    V-4   p. 20
"Chosen of the Lord" (Matt)
    V-8   p. 34

Anthems

"The Peace Which Passeth Understanding" (Phil)
James F. Hopkins; ECS Publishing 4672
SATB with organ

"Rejoice in the Lord Always" (Phil)
George Rathbone; Novello 15652
SATB with organ

Other Suggestions

Visuals:
    O/P   Gold, jewelry, golden calf, hands folded/lifted in prayer
    E   Praying hands, "Rejoice in the Lord always," "Again I say, Rejoice"
    G   Wedding garments, other wedding items (invitations, rings, flowers)
Introit: S2271, BOW199. "Come! Come! Everybody Worship" (Pss, Phil)
Greeting: BOW454 (Exod, Matt)
Call to Worship: WSL61 (Matt)
Opening Prayer: BOW464 (Exod)
Prayer of Confession: BOW479 or BOW482 (Exod)
Call to Prayer: S2157. "Come and Fill Our Hearts" (Phil)
Prayer: UM329 or UM459 (Phil)
Prayer: UM392. Prayer for a New Heart (Exod, Phil)
Prayer: BOW512. For Guidance (Phil)
Prayer: WSL19 or WSL182 or BOW516 (Exod)
Prayer: BOW519. For Others (Phil, Matt)
Prayer: BOW530. A Prayer of Saint Thomas Aquinas (Phil)
Prayer: BOW544. For Leaders (Exod)
Prayer and Response: S2201. "Prayers of the People" (Phil)
Prayer of Thanksgiving: BOW552 (Exod, Phil)
Response: S2195. "In the Lord I'll Be Ever Thankful" (Pss)
Blessing: Phil 4:8-9
Response: UM668. "Let Us Now Depart in Your Peace" (Phil)

Exodus 33:12-23

[12]Moses said to the Lord, "See, you have said to me, 'Bring up this people'; but you have not let me know whom you will send with me. Yet you have said, 'I know you by name, and you have also found favor in my sight.' [13]Now if I have found favor in your sight, show me your ways, so that I may know you and find favor in your sight. Consider too that this nation is your people." [14]He said, "My presence will go with you, and I will give you rest." [15]And he said to him, "If your presence will not go, do not carry us up from here. [16]For how shall it be known that I have found favor in your sight, I and your people, unless you go with us? In this way, we shall be distinct, I and your people, from every people on the face of the earth."

[17]The Lord said to Moses, "I will do the very thing that you have asked; for you have found favor in my sight, and I know you by name." [18]Moses said, "Show me your glory, I pray." [19]And he said, "I will make all my goodness pass before you, and will proclaim before you the name, 'The Lord'; and I will be gracious to whom I will be gracious, and will show mercy on whom I will show mercy. [20]But," he said, "you cannot see my face; for no one shall see me and live." [21]And the Lord continued, "See, there is a place by me where you shall stand on the rock; [22]and while my glory passes by I will put you in a cleft of the rock, and I will cover you with my hand until I have passed by; [23]then I will take away my hand, and you shall see my back; but my face shall not be seen."

Psalm 99 (UM819)

[1]The Lord is king; let the peoples tremble!
   He sits enthroned upon the cherubim; let the earth quake!
[2]The Lord is great in Zion;
   he is exalted over all the peoples.
[3]Let them praise your great and awesome name.
   Holy is he!
[4]Mighty King, lover of justice,
   you have established equity;
you have executed justice
   and righteousness in Jacob.
[5]Extol the Lord our God;
   worship at his footstool.
   Holy is he!
[6]Moses and Aaron were among his priests,
   Samuel also was among those who called on his name.
   They cried to the Lord, and he answered them.
[7]He spoke to them in the pillar of cloud;
   they kept his decrees,
   and the statutes that he gave them.
[8]O Lord our God, you answered them;
   you were a forgiving God to them,
   but an avenger of their wrongdoings.
[9]Extol the Lord our God,
   and worship at his holy mountain;
   for the Lord our God is holy.

1 Thessalonians 1:1-10

[1]Paul, Silvanus, and Timothy, To the church of the Thessalonians in God the Father and the Lord Jesus Christ:
   Grace to you and peace.

[2]We always give thanks to God for all of you and mention you in our prayers, constantly [3]remembering before our God and Father your work of faith and labor of love and steadfastness of hope in our Lord Jesus Christ. [4]For we know, brothers and sisters beloved by God, that he has chosen you, [5]because our message of the gospel came to you not in word only, but also in power and in the Holy Spirit and with full conviction; just as you know what kind of persons we proved to be among you for your sake. [6]And you became imitators of us and of the Lord, for in spite of persecution you received the word with joy inspired by the Holy Spirit, [7]so that you became an example to all the believers in Macedonia and in Achaia. [8]For the word of the Lord has sounded forth from you not only in Macedonia and Achaia, but in every place your faith in God has become known, so that we have no need to speak about it. [9]For the people of those regions report about us what kind of welcome we had among you, and how you turned to God from idols, to serve a living and true God, [10]and to wait for his Son from heaven, whom he raised from the dead—Jesus, who rescues us from the wrath that is coming.

Matthew 22:15-22

[15]Then the Pharisees went and plotted to entrap him in what he said. [16]So they sent their disciples to him, along with the Herodians, saying, "Teacher, we know that you are sincere, and teach the way of God in accordance with truth, and show deference to no one; for you do not regard people with partiality. [17]Tell us, then, what you think. Is it lawful to pay taxes to the emperor, or not?" [18]But Jesus, aware of their malice, said, "Why are you putting me to the test, you hypocrites? [19]Show me the coin used for the tax." And they brought him a denarius. [20]Then he said to them, "Whose head is this, and whose title?" [21]They answered, "The emperor's." Then he said to them, "Give therefore to the emperor the things that are the emperor's, and to God the things that are God's." [22]When they heard this, they were amazed; and they left him and went away.

Primary Hymns and Songs for the Day

73	"O Worship the King" (Pss) (O)	
	H-3	Hbl-85; Chr-154; Desc-71; Org-82
	S-1	#223-226. Various treatments
103	"Immortal, Invisible, God Only Wise" (Exod)	
	H-3	Hbl-15, 71; Chr-65; Desc-93; Org-135
	S-1	#300. Harm.
427	"Where Cross the Crowded Ways of Life" (Matt)	
	H-3	Chr-178, 180; Org-44
	S-1	#141-3 Various treatments
444	"O Young and Fearless Prophet" (Matt)	
	S-2	#27. Desc.
399	"Take My Life, and Let It Be" (Matt) (C)	
	H-3	Chr-34, 177; Desc-51; Org-53
	S-2	#78-80. Various treatments

Additional Hymn Suggestions

105	"God of Many Names" (Exod)
116	"The God of Abraham Praise" (Exod)
124	"Seek the Lord" (Exod)
126	"Sing Praise to God Who Reigns Above" (Exod)
351	"Pass Me Not, O Gentle Savior" (Exod)
361	"Rock of Ages, Cleft for Me" (Exod)
523	"*Saranam, Saranam*" ("Refuge") (Exod)
700	"Abide with Me" (Exod)
3029	"In the Desert, on God's Mountain" (Exod)
529	"How Firm a Foundation" (Exod, 1 Thess) (C)
66	"Praise, My Soul, the King of Heaven" (Pss)
89	"Joyful, Joyful, We Adore Thee" (Pss)
107	"*La Palabra Del Señor Es Recta*" ("Righteous and Just Is the Word of Our Lord") (Pss)
715	"Rejoice, the Lord Is King" (Pss)
716	"Rejoice, the Lord Is King" (Pss)
717	"The Battle Hymn of the Republic" (Pss)
2009	"O God Beyond All Praising" (Pss)
2177	"Wounded World that Cries for Healing" (Pss)
2183	"Unsettled World" (Pss)
84	"Thank You, Lord" (1 Thess)
537	"Filled with the Spirit's Power" (1 Thess)
566	"Blest Be the Dear Uniting Love" (1 Thess)
2220	"We Are God's People" (1 Thess)
708	"Rejoice in God's Saints" (1 Thess)
170	"O, How I Love Jesus" (1 Thess, Matt)
256	"We Would See Jesus" (Matt)
261	"Lord of the Dance" (Matt)
433	"All Who Love and Serve Your City" (Matt)
441	"What Does the Lord Require" (Matt)
3124	"How Shall I Come Before the Lord" (Matt)

Additional Contemporary Suggestions

S2068	"I Love You, Lord" (Exod)
S2218	"You Are Mine" (Exod)
M38	"In the Secret" ("I Want to Know You") (Exod)
M107	"Show Me Your Ways" (Exod)
UM123	"El-Shaddai" (Exod, Pss)
	S-2 #54 Verses for Vocal Solo
M93	"Rock of Ages" (Exod, Pss)
M126	"Famous One" (Exod, Pss)
M263	"From the Inside Out" (Exod, Pss)
S2040	"Awesome God" (Exod, Pss)
WS3004	"Step by Step" (Exod, Matt)
S2274	"Come, All You People" ("Uyai Mose") (Pss)
SP18	"I Exalt You" (Pss)
S2087	"We Will Glorify" (Pss)
SP78	"I Extol You" (Pss)

M234	"Awesome Is the Lord Most High" (Pss)
S2070	"He Is Exalted" (Pss, Matt)
S2150	"Lord, Be Glorified" (Pss, Matt)
M257	"Came to My Rescue" (1 Thess)
S2065	"More Precious than Silver" (Matt)
S2174	"What Does the Lord Require of You" (Matt)
S2176	"Make Me a Servant" (Matt)
M98	"Take This Life" (Matt, Stewardship)

Vocal Solos

"God, Our Ever Faithful Shepherd" (Exod, Pss)
    V-4   p. 15
"Praise to the Lord, the Almighty" (Pss)
    V-6   p. 18

Anthems

"He Hideth My Soul" (Exod)
Mark Shepperd; MorningStar 50-5010
SATB and piano

"What Does the Lord Require of You?" (Matt)
Robert Hobby; MorningStar 50-8330
SATB with keyboard, flute or oboe

Other Suggestions

Visuals:
O	Rock, cleft rock, hand
P	Earthquake, cloud, footstool
E	Symbols of the Holy Spirit, Trinity
G	Array of coins around an empty offering plate, cross

Call to Worship: S2274. "Come, All You People" ("*Uyai Mose*") (Pss)
Greeting: BOW451 (Pss)
Opening Prayer: BOW459 or BOW462 (Exod)
Prayer of Confession: BOW480 (Exod)
Canticle: UM125. "Canticle of Covenant Faithfulness" (Exod)
Litany: BOW432. Litany for Laity Sunday.
Prayer: BOW518. For Others (1 Thess)
Prayer: BOW524. For Strength (Exod, Pss)
Prayer: BOW525. For Wisdom (Matt)
Prayer: BOW539. For Disciples in the Marketplace (Matt)
Prayer: BOW544. For Leaders (Exod, Matt)
Prayer of Thanksgiving: BOW551 (Exod, Pss, Matt)
Response: UM588. "All Things Come of Thee" (Matt, Stewardship)

Deuteronomy 34:1-12

¹Then Moses went up from the plains of Moab to Mount Nebo, to the top of Pisgah, which is opposite Jericho, and the LORD showed him the whole land: Gilead as far as Dan, ²all Naphtali, the land of Ephraim and Manasseh, all the land of Judah as far as the Western Sea, ³the Negeb, and the Plain—that is, the valley of Jericho, the city of palm trees—as far as Zoar. ⁴The LORD said to him, "This is the land of which I swore to Abraham, to Isaac, and to Jacob, saying, 'I will give it to your descendants'; I have let you see it with your eyes, but you shall not cross over there." ⁵Then Moses, the servant of the LORD, died there in the land of Moab, at the LORD's command. ⁶He was buried in a valley in the land of Moab, opposite Beth-peor, but no one knows his burial place to this day. ⁷Moses was one hundred twenty years old when he died; his sight was unimpaired and his vigor had not abated. ⁸The Israelites wept for Moses in the plains of Moab thirty days; then the period of mourning for Moses was ended.

⁹Joshua son of Nun was full of the spirit of wisdom, because Moses had laid his hands on him; and the Israelites obeyed him, doing as the LORD had commanded Moses.

¹⁰Never since has there arisen a prophet in Israel like Moses, whom the LORD knew face to face. ¹¹He was unequaled for all the signs and wonders that the LORD sent him to perform in the land of Egypt, against Pharaoh and all his servants and his entire land, ¹²and for all the mighty deeds and all the terrifying displays of power that Moses performed in the sight of all Israel.

Psalm 90:1-6, 13-17 (UM809)

¹Lord, you have been our dwelling place
    in all generations.
²Before the mountains were brought forth,
    or ever you had formed the earth and the world,
    from everlasting to everlasting you are God.
³You turn us back to dust,
    and say, "Turn back, you mortals."
⁴For a thousand years in your sight
    are like yesterday when it is past,
    or like a watch in the night.
⁵You sweep them away; they are like a dream,
    like grass that is renewed in the morning;
⁶in the morning it flourishes and is renewed;
    in the evening it fades and withers.
. . . .
¹³Turn, O LORD! How long?
    Have compassion on your servants!
¹⁴Satisfy us in the morning with your steadfast love,
    so that we may rejoice and be glad all our days.
¹⁵Make us glad as many days as you have afflicted us,
    and as many years as we have seen evil.
¹⁶Let your work be manifest to your servants,
    and your glorious power to their children.
¹⁷Let the favor of the Lord our God be upon us,
    and prosper for us the work of our hands—
    O prosper the work of our hands!

1 Thessalonians 2:1-8

¹You yourselves know, brothers and sisters, that our coming to you was not in vain, ²but though we had already suffered and been shamefully mistreated at Philippi, as you know, we had courage in our God to declare to you the gospel of God in spite of great opposition. ³For our appeal does not spring from deceit or impure motives or trickery, ⁴but just as we have been approved by God to be entrusted with the message of the gospel, even so we speak, not to please mortals, but to please God who tests our hearts. ⁵As you know and as God is our witness, we never came with words of flattery or with a pretext for greed; ⁶nor did we seek praise from mortals, whether from you or from others, ⁷though we might have made demands as apostles of Christ. But we were gentle among you, like a nurse tenderly caring for her own children. ⁸So deeply do we care for you that we are determined to share with you not only the gospel of God but also our own selves, because you have become very dear to us.

Matthew 22:34-46

³⁴When the Pharisees heard that he had silenced the Sadducees, they gathered together, ³⁵and one of them, a lawyer, asked him a question to test him. ³⁶"Teacher, which commandment in the law is the greatest?" ³⁷He said to him, "'You shall love the Lord your God with all your heart, and with all your soul, and with all your mind.' ³⁸This is the greatest and first commandment. ³⁹And a second is like it: 'You shall love your neighbor as yourself.' ⁴⁰On these two commandments hang all the law and the prophets."

⁴¹Now while the Pharisees were gathered together, Jesus asked them this question: ⁴²"What do you think of the Messiah? Whose son is he?" They said to him, "The son of David." ⁴³He said to them, "How is it then that David by the Spirit calls him Lord, saying,
⁴⁴'The Lord said to my Lord,
"Sit at my right hand,
    until I put your enemies under your feet"'?
⁴⁵If David thus calls him Lord, how can he be his son?" ⁴⁶No one was able to give him an answer, nor from that day did anyone dare to ask him any more questions.

Primary Hymns and Songs for the Day

117	"O God, Our Help in Ages Past" (Pss) (O)	
	H-3	Hbl-87; Chr-60, 143; Desc-93; Org-132
	S-1	#293–296. Various treatments
402	"Lord, I Want to Be a Christian" (Matt)	
	H-3	Chr-130
2168	"Love the Lord Your God" (Matt)	
3116	"Love the Lord" (Matt)	
453	"More Love to Thee, O Christ" (Matt) (C)	
	H-3	Org-94

Additional Hymn Suggestions

60	"I'll Praise My Maker While I've Breath" (Deut)
108	"God Hath Spoken by the Prophets" (Deut)
448	"Go Down, Moses" (Deut)
	(See especially stanzas 8–11)
524	"Beams of Heaven as I Go" (Deut)
703	"Swing Low, Sweet Chariot" (Deut)
3030	"Eternal God Transcending Time" (Deut)
86	"Mountains Are All Aglow" (Deut, Pss)
2206	"Without Seeing You" (Pss)
66	"Praise, My Soul, the King of Heaven" (Pss, 1 Thess)
115	"How Like a Gentle Spirit" (1 Thess)
118	"The Care the Eagle Gives Her Young" (1 Thess)
463	"Lord, Speak to Me" (1 Thess)
557	"Blest Be the Tie That Binds" (1 Thess) (C)
672	"God Be with You Till We Meet Again" (1 Thess) (C)
673	"God Be with You Till We Meet Again" (1 Thess) (C)
430	"O Master, Let Me Walk with Thee" (1 Thess, Matt) (C)
572	"Pass It On" (1 Thess, Matt)
408	"The Gift of Love" (Matt)
410	"I Want a Principle Within" (Matt)
500	"Spirit of God, Descend upon My Heart" (Matt)
549	"Where Charity and Love Prevail" (Matt)
2213	"Healer of Our Every Ill" (Matt)
2254	"In Remembrance of Me" (Matt, Comm.)
590	"Christ Loves the Church" (Reformation Day)

Additional Contemporary Suggestions

S2139	"Oh, I Know the Lord's Laid His Hands on Me" (Deut)
WS3005	"Fill Us with Your Love, O Lord" (Pss)
SP185	"The Steadfast Love of the Lord" (Pss)
M103	"How Great Are You, Lord" (Pss)
M243	"Beautiful Savior" (Pss)
M250	"Our God Saves" (Pss)
UM432	*Jesu, Jesu* (Matt)
	S-1 #63 Vocal part
S2037	"I Sing Praises to Your Name" (Matt)
S2071	"Jesus, Name above All Names" (Matt)
S2161	"To Know You More" (Matt)
S2167	"More Like You" (Matt)
S2171	"Make Me a Channel of Your Peace" (Matt)
S2188	"The Family Prayer Song" (Matt)
M40	"More Love, More Power" (Matt)
M41	"You're Worthy of My Praise" (Matt)
M49	"Refresh My Heart" (Matt)
M53	"Let It Be Said of Us" (Matt)
M62	"Rise Up and Praise Him" (Matt)
M83	"Just Let Me Say" (Matt)
M98	"Take This Life" (Matt)
SP187	"With All of My Heart" (Matt)
	M86

WS3103	"Purify My Heart" (Matt)	
WS3117	"Rule of Life" (Matt)	

Vocal Solos

"Over Yonder" (Deut)
    V-7   p. 38
"Make Me a Channel of Your Peace" (Matt)
    V-3 (2)   p. 25
    V-3 (3)   p. 28
"The Gift of Love" (Matt)
    V-8   p. 120

Anthems

"Lead, Kindly Light" (Deut, 1 Thess)
Arr. Dan Forrest; Hinshaw HMC2354
SATB divisi with piano

"A Jubilant Song" (Pss)
Allen Pote; Hope F-979
SATB with keyboard, opt. brass and handbells

Other Suggestions

Visuals:

	O	Portrait or bust of Moses, tears
	P	Tall grass, morning/evening, rejoicing, hands at work/praise
	E	Nurturing, caring for children
	G	Images of loving God, neighbor, self, worship, service to others, nurture, Matt 22:37, 38

Greeting: BOW452 (1 Thess) or BOW455 (Deut)
Opening Prayer: BOW462 (Matt)
Prayer of Confession: BOW476 or BOW489 (Matt)
Prayer: UM268. Lent (Deut)
Prayer: BOW518 (Matt)
Response: S2179. "Live in Charity" ("*Ubi Caritas*") (Matt)
Prayers: BOW501-BOW506. For the Church (Reformation)
Canticle: UM646. "Canticle of Love" (Matt) (See S-1, p. 387.)
Scripture Response: UM92, stanza 4. "For the Beauty of the Earth" (Matt)
Offering Prayer: WSL98. "Lord God, let me give" (Matt)
Blessing: WSL177 or BOW560 (Deut, Matt)
Benediction: S2171. "Make Me a Channel of Your Peace" (Matt)

Revelation 7:9-17

[9]After this I looked, and there was a great multitude that no one could count, from every nation, from all tribes and peoples and languages, standing before the throne and before the Lamb, robed in white, with palm branches in their hands. [10]They cried out in a loud voice, saying,

"Salvation belongs to our God who is seated on the throne,
          and to the Lamb!"

[11]And all the angels stood around the throne and around the elders and the four living creatures, and they fell on their faces before the throne and worshiped God, [12]singing,

"Amen! Blessing and glory and wisdom
and thanksgiving and honor
and power and might
be to our God forever and ever! Amen."

[13]Then one of the elders addressed me, saying, "Who are these, robed in white, and where have they come from?" [14]I said to him, "Sir, you are the one that knows." Then he said to me, "These are they who have come out of the great ordeal; they have washed their robes and made them white in the blood of the Lamb.

[15]For this reason they are before the throne of God,
     and worship him day and night within his temple,
     and the one who is seated on the throne will shelter them.
[16]They will hunger no more, and thirst no more;
     the sun will not strike them,
     nor any scorching heat;
[17]for the Lamb at the center of the throne will be their
          shepherd,
     and he will guide them to springs of the water of life,
and God will wipe away every tear from their eyes."

Psalm 34:1-10, 22 (UM769)

[1]I will bless the LORD at all times;
     his praise shall continually be in my mouth.
[2]My soul makes its boast in the LORD;
     let the humble hear and be glad.
[3]O magnify the LORD with me,
     and let us exalt his name together.

[4]I sought the LORD, and he answered me,
     and delivered me from all my fears.
[5]Look to him, and be radiant;
     so your faces shall never be ashamed.
[6]This poor soul cried, and was heard by the LORD,
     and was saved from every trouble.
[7]The angel of the LORD encamps
     around those who fear him, and delivers them.
[8]O taste and see that the LORD is good;
     happy are those who take refuge in him.
[9]O fear the LORD, you his holy ones,
     for those who fear him have no want.
[10]The young lions suffer want and hunger,
     but those who seek the LORD lack no good thing.

. . . .

[22]The LORD redeems the life of his servants;
     none of those who take refuge in him will be condemned.

1 John 3:1-3

[1] See what love the Father has given us, that we should be called children of God; and that is what we are. The reason the world does not know us is that it did not know him. [2]Beloved, we are God's children now; what we will be has not yet been revealed. What we do know is this: when he is revealed, we will be like him, for we will see him as he is. [3]And all who have this hope in him purify themselves, just as he is pure.

Matthew 5:1-12

[1]When Jesus saw the crowds, he went up the mountain; and after he sat down, his disciples came to him. [2]Then he began to speak, and taught them, saying:

[3]"Blessed are the poor in spirit, for theirs is the kingdom of heaven.

[4]"Blessed are those who mourn, for they will be comforted.

[5]"Blessed are the meek, for they will inherit the earth.

[6]"Blessed are those who hunger and thirst for righteousness, for they will be filled.

[7]"Blessed are the merciful, for they will receive mercy.

[8]"Blessed are the pure in heart, for they will see God.

[9]"Blessed are the peacemakers, for they will be called children of God.

[10]"Blessed are those who are persecuted for righteousness' sake, for theirs is the kingdom of heaven.

[11]"Blessed are you when people revile you and persecute you and utter all kinds of evil against you falsely on my account. [12]Rejoice and be glad, for your reward is great in heaven, for in the same way they persecuted the prophets who were before you."

Primary Hymns and Songs for the Day

711	"For All the Saints" (Matt, All Saints) (O)	
	H-3	Hbl-58; Chr-65; Org-152
	S-1	#314-318. Various treatments
2155	"Blest Are They" (Matt)	
2108	"O How He Loves You and Me!" (1 John)	
568	"Christ for the World We Sing" (Matt, All Saints)	
	H-3	Hbl-28, 49, 53; Chr-56; Desc-57; Org-63
	S-1	#185-186. Desc. and Harm.
708	"Rejoice in God's Saints" (Rev, All Saints) (C)	
	H-3	Hbl-90, 105; Chr-221; Desc-49; Org-51
	S-2	#71-74. Intro. and Harm.

Additional Hymn Suggestions

88	"Maker, in Whom We Live" (Rev) (O)
90	"Ye Watchers and Ye Holy Ones" (Rev)
181	"Ye Servants of God" (Rev) (O) or (C)
638	"This Is the Feast of Victory" (Rev, Comm.)
655, 4123	"Fix Me, Jesus" (Rev)
674	"See the Morning Sun Ascending" (Rev)
709	"Come, Let Us Join Our Friends Above" (Rev, All Saints)
732	"Come, We That Love the Lord" (Rev)
733	"Marching to Zion" (Rev)
2264	"Come to the Table" (Rev, Pss, Comm.)
2126	"All Who Hunger" (Rev, Pss, Matt, Comm.)
2261	"Life-Giving Bread" (Pss, Comm.)
2267	"Taste and See" (Pss, Comm.)
3155	"The Lord of Life, a Vine Is He" (Pss)
3170	"What Feast of Love" (Pss, Comm.)
616	"Come, Sinners, to the Gospel Feast" (Pss)
2248	"Baptized in Water" (1 John, Baptism)
2236	"Gather Us In" (Matt) (O)
2140	"Since Jesus Came into My Heart" (Matt)
2190	"Bring Forth the Kingdom" (Matt)
2262	"Let Us Offer to the Father" ("*Te Ofrecemos Padre Nuestro*") (Matt, Comm.)
3103	"Purify My Heart" (Matt)
440	"Let There Be Light" (Matt, All Saints)
547	"O Church of God, United" (Matt, All Saints)
712	"I Sing a Song of the Saints of God" (Matt, All Saints)
3126	"Everything That Has Voice" (Matt)
3157	"Come, Let Us Dream" (Matt)
2168	"Love the Lord Your God" (Matt, All Saints)
2042	"How Lovely, Lord, How Lovely" (All Saints)
2221	"In Unity We Lift Our Song" (All Saints)
2283	"For All the Saints" (All Saints)
614	"For the Bread Which You Have Broken" (All Saints, Comm.)

Additional Contemporary Suggestions

WS3003	"How Great Is Our God" (Rev)
WS3187	"We Fall Down" (Rev, All Saints)
M21	"Blessing, Honour and Glory" (Rev)
M23	"Hallelujah to the Lamb" (Rev)
M27	"We Will Worship the Lamb of Glory" (Rev)
M43	"We Declare Your Majesty" (Rev)
M261	"Overcome" (Rev)
SP60	"To Him Who Sits on the Throne" (Rev)
UM99	"My Tribute" ("To God Be the Glory") (Rev)
	V-8 p. 5. Vocal Solo
S2058	"Shepherd Me, O God" (Rev, All Saints)
S2194	"O Freedom" (Rev)
S2195	"In the Lord I'll Be Ever Thankful" (Rev)
S2210	"Joy Comes with the Dawn" (Rev)

S2272	"Holy Ground" (Rev)
WS3099	"Falling on My Knees" (Rev, Pss)
WS3167	"Feed Us, Lord" (Rev, Pss, Comm.)
S2023	"How Majestic Is Your Name" (Pss)
M60	"Better Is One Day" (Pss)
S2132	"You Who Are Thirsty" (Pss, Matt)
SP50	"Think about His Love" (Pss, 1 John)
SP48	"Behold, What Manner of Love" (1 John)
S2073	"Celebrate Love" (1 John)
S2085	"He Came Down" (1 John)
M265	"I Have a Hope" (1 John)
S2039	"Holy, Holy" (1 John, Matt)
S2086	"Open Our Eyes, Lord" (Matt)
S2036	"Give Thanks" (Matt)
WS3008	"Open the Eyes of My Heart" (Matt)
WS3108	"Tradin' My Sorrows" (Matt, All Saints)

Vocal Solos

"Ye Servants of God" (Rev)
    V-1   p. 41
"Maybe the Rain" (Rev, Matt)
    V-5(2)   p. 27
"In Bright Mansions Above" (All Saints)
    V-4   p. 39
"How Long Train Been Gone" (All Saints)
    V-7   p. 17

Anthems

"And Peace Shall Guard You" (Rev, Pss, Matt)
Michael John Trotta; MorningStar 50-9213
SSATBB, a cappella

"Blessed" (Matt)
Paul D. Weber; MorningStar 50-0565
SATB with organ, opt. congregation

Other Suggestions

These scriptures and ideas may be used on Oct. 29 or Nov. 5.
Visuals:
O	White robe, palm branches
P	"Taste & See," spices to taste, abundance, rejoicing, refuge
E	Images of "saints" of the congregation
G	Images of people living the Beatitudes, mountain

Introit: WS3044, "Make Way" (Matt)
Greeting: BOW414 (All Saints) or BOW449 (Pss)
Affirmation of Faith: WSL83 (Matt)
Prayer: UM392. Prayer for a New Heart (Matt)
Prayer: WSL49 (Matt)
Response: S2277. "Lord, Have Mercy" (Rev)
Prayer: UM713, WSL46, or BOW415 (All Saints Day)
Prayer: BOW512. For Guidance (Rev, 1 John)
Prayer: BOW522. For Purity (1 John)
Memorial Prayer: WSL44, UM461, or BOW548 (All Saints)
Litany and Prayer for Naming of Saints: WSL45 (All Saints)
Response: BOW219 "Beloved, Now We Are the Saints of God" (1 John, All Saints)
Blessing: WSL169. "As you have been fed" (Matt, Comm.)

Joshua 3:7-17

[7]The LORD said to Joshua, "This day I will begin to exalt you in the sight of all Israel, so that they may know that I will be with you as I was with Moses. [8]You are the one who shall command the priests who bear the ark of the covenant, 'When you come to the edge of the waters of the Jordan, you shall stand still in the Jordan.'" [9]Joshua then said to the Israelites, "Draw near and hear the words of the LORD your God." [10]Joshua said, "By this you shall know that among you is the living God who without fail will drive out from before you the Canaanites, Hittites, Hivites, Perizzites, Girgashites, Amorites, and Jebusites: [11]the ark of the covenant of the Lord of all the earth is going to pass before you into the Jordan. [12]So now select twelve men from the tribes of Israel, one from each tribe. [13]When the soles of the feet of the priests who bear the ark of the LORD, the Lord of all the earth, rest in the waters of the Jordan, the waters of the Jordan flowing from above shall be cut off; they shall stand in a single heap."

[14]When the people set out from their tents to cross over the Jordan, the priests bearing the ark of the covenant were in front of the people. [15]Now the Jordan overflows all its banks throughout the time of harvest. So when those who bore the ark had come to the Jordan, and the feet of the priests bearing the ark were dipped in the edge of the water, [16]the waters flowing from above stood still, rising up in a single heap far off at Adam, the city that is beside Zarethan, while those flowing toward the sea of the Arabah, the Dead Sea, were wholly cut off. Then the people crossed over opposite Jericho. [17]While all Israel were crossing over on dry ground, the priests who bore the ark of the covenant of the LORD stood on dry ground in the middle of the Jordan, until the entire nation finished crossing over the Jordan.

Psalm 107:1-7, 33-37 (UM830)

[1]O give thanks to the LORD, for he is good;
 for his steadfast love endures forever.
[2]Let the redeemed of the LORD say so,
 those he redeemed from trouble
[3]and gathered in from the lands,
 from the east and from the west,
 from the north and from the south.
[4]Some wandered in desert wastes,
 finding no way to an inhabited town;
[5]hungry and thirsty,
 their soul fainted within them.
[6]Then they cried to the LORD in their trouble,
 and he delivered them from their distress;
[7]he led them by a straight way,
 until they reached an inhabited town.
. . . .
[33]He turns rivers into a desert,
 springs of water into thirsty ground,
[34]a fruitful land into a salty waste,
 because of the wickedness of its inhabitants.
[35]He turns a desert into pools of water,
 a parched land into springs of water.
[36]And there he lets the hungry live,
 and they establish a town to live in;
[37]they sow fields, and plant vineyards,
 and get a fruitful yield.

1 Thessalonians 2:9-13

[9]You remember our labor and toil, brothers and sisters; we worked night and day, so that we might not burden any of you while we proclaimed to you the gospel of God. [10]You are witnesses, and God also, how pure, upright, and blameless our conduct was toward you believers. [11]As you know, we dealt with each one of you like a father with his children, [12]urging and encouraging you and pleading that you lead a life worthy of God, who calls you into his own kingdom and glory.

[13]We also constantly give thanks to God for this, that when you received the word of God that you heard from us, you accepted it not as a human word but as what it really is, God's word, which is also at work in you believers.

Matthew 23:1-12

[1]Then Jesus said to the crowds and to his disciples, [2]"The scribes and the Pharisees sit on Moses' seat; [3]therefore, do whatever they teach you and follow it; but do not do as they do, for they do not practice what they teach. [4]They tie up heavy burdens, hard to bear, and lay them on the shoulders of others; but they themselves are unwilling to lift a finger to move them. [5]They do all their deeds to be seen by others; for they make their phylacteries broad and their fringes long. [6]They love to have the place of honor at banquets and the best seats in the synagogues, [7]and to be greeted with respect in the marketplaces, and to have people call them rabbi. [8]But you are not to be called rabbi, for you have one teacher, and you are all students. [9]And call no one your father on earth, for you have one Father—the one in heaven. [10]Nor are you to be called instructors, for you have one instructor, the Messiah. [11]The greatest among you will be your servant. [12]All who exalt themselves will be humbled, and all who humble themselves will be exalted."

Primary Hymns and Songs for the Day

127	"Guide Me, O Thou Great Jehovah" (Josh) (O)	
	H-3	Hbl-25, 51, 58; Chr-89; Desc-26; Org-23
	S-1	#76-77. Desc. and Harm.
404	"Every Time I Feel the Spirit" (Josh)	
416	"Come Out the Wilderness" (Josh)	
724	"On Jordan's Stormy Banks I Stand" (Deut)	
	H-3	Chr-155; Org-117
	S-1	#271. Orff Instr. Arr.
		#272. Transposition in D major
581	"Lord, Whose Love Through Humble Service" (Matt)	
	H-3	Hbl-14, 64; Chr-132, 203
	S-2	#22. Desc.
430	"O Master, Let Me Walk with Thee" (Matt) (C)	
	H-3	Hbl-81; Chr-147; Desc-74; Org-87
	S-2	#118. Desc.

Additional Hymn Suggestions

110	"A Mighty Fortress Is Our God" (Josh, Pss) (O)
128	"He Leadeth Me: O Blessed Thought" (Josh)
448	"Go Down, Moses" (Josh)
474	"Precious Lord, Take My Hand" (Josh)
508	"Faith, While Trees Are Still in Blossom" (Josh)
524	"Beams of Heaven as I Go" (Josh)
519	"Lift Every Voice and Sing" (Josh, Pss)
629	"You Satisfy the Hungry Heart" (Pss, Comm.)
631	"O Food to Pilgrims Given" (Pss, Comm.)
2009	"O God Beyond All Praising" (Pss)
2236	"Gather Us In" (Pss) (O)
2264	"Come to the Table" (Pss)
84	"Thank You, Lord" (Pss, 1 Thess)
364	"Because He Lives" (Pss, 1 Thess)
163	"Ask Ye What Great Thing I Know" (1 Thess, Matt)
433	"All Who Love and Serve Your City" (1 Thess, Matt)
558	"We Are the Church" (1 Thess)
601	"Thy Word Is a Lamp" (1 Thess)
649	"How Shall They Hear the Word of God" (1 Thess)
670	"Go Forth for God" (1 Thess) (C)
2153	"I'm Gonna Live So God Can Use Me" (1 Thess, Matt)
432	"*Jesu, Jesu*" (Matt)
	S-1 #63 Vocal part
463	"Lord, Speak to Me" (Matt)
571	"Go, Make of All Disciples" (Matt)
632	"Draw Us in the Spirit's Tether" (Matt, Comm.)
2175	"Together We Serve" (Matt, Comm.)
2268	"As We Gather at Your Table" (Matt, Comm.)

Additional Contemporary Suggestions

S2272	"Holy Ground" (Josh)
M36	"Awesome in This Place" (Josh)
S2132	"You Who Are Thirsty" (Pss)
WS3015	"How Great You Are" (Pss)
WS3023	"Forever" (Pss)
WS3042	"Shout to the North" (Pss)
WS3027	"Hallelujah" ("Your Love Is Amazing") (Pss)
WS3099	"Hungry" ("Falling on My Knees") (Pss)
WS3167	"Feed Us, Lord" (Pss, Comm.)
M159	"All Who Are Thirsty" (Pss)
M189	"Your Love, Oh Lord" (Pss)
M236	"Say So" (Pss)
S2195	"In the Lord I'll Be Ever Thankful" (Pss, 1 Thess)
S2164	"Sanctuary" (1 Thess)
S2031	"We Bring the Sacrifice of Praise" (1 Thess, Matt)
S2222	"The Servant Song" (Matt)
S2176	"Make Me a Servant" (Matt)

S2131	"Humble Thyself in the Sight of the Lord" (Matt)
M40	"More Love, More Power" (Matt)
M227	"I Will Boast" (Matt)

Vocal Solos

"Deep River" (Josh)
  V-3 (1)   p. 4
"Ev'ry Time I Feel De Spirit" (Josh)
  V-7   p. 78
"Take My Life" (Matt)
  V-8   p. 262

Anthems

"On Jordan's Stormy Banks" (Josh)
Arr. Carolyn Hamlin, Alfred 36814
SSATB with keyboard

"A Mighty Fortress" (Josh, Pss)
Arr. Ken Berg; Choristers Guild CGA1324
Unison with piano

Other Suggestions

Today may also be celebrated as All Saints Sunday, using suggestions for Nov. 1.
Daylight Saving Time ends today.
Visuals:
  O   Flowing water
  P   Water, bubbling water, sand, grapes, wheat
  E   Man encouraging child, open Bible
  G   Christ as teacher, servanthood (bowl/pitcher/towel), boxes symbolizing burdens, phylacteries, chair
Greeting: BOW453 (Pss)
Opening Prayer: BOW460 (Matt)
Prayer of Confession: BOW476 (Matt)
Prayer: BOW511. For God's Reign (Matt)
Prayer: BOW540. For Those Who Work (1 Thess)
Prayer: UM353. Ash Wednesday (1 Thess)
Offering Prayer: WSL146 (Matt)
Prayer of Thanksgiving: BOW550 or BOW555 (1 Thess, Matt)
Closing Prayer: BOW567 (Matt)
Benediction: UM672 or UM673, stanza 2. "God Be with You till We Meet Again" (Josh)

Joshua 24:1-3a, 14-25

[1]Then Joshua gathered all the tribes of Israel to Shechem, and summoned the elders, the heads, the judges, and the officers of Israel; and they presented themselves before God. [2]And Joshua said to all the people, "Thus says the LORD, the God of Israel: Long ago your ancestors—Terah and his sons Abraham and Nahor—lived beyond the Euphrates and served other gods. [3a]Then I took your father Abraham from beyond the River and led him through all the land of Canaan and made his offspring many. . . .

[14]"Now therefore revere the LORD, and serve him in sincerity and in faithfulness; put away the gods that your ancestors served beyond the River and in Egypt, and serve the LORD. [15]Now if you are unwilling to serve the LORD, choose this day whom you will serve, whether the gods your ancestors served in the region beyond the River or the gods of the Amorites in whose land you are living; but as for me and my household, we will serve the LORD."

[16]Then the people answered, "Far be it from us that we should forsake the LORD to serve other gods; [17]for it is the LORD our God who brought us and our ancestors up from the land of Egypt, out of the house of slavery, and who did those great signs in our sight. He protected us along all the way that we went, and among all the peoples through whom we passed; [18]and the LORD drove out before us all the peoples, the Amorites who lived in the land. Therefore we also will serve the LORD, for he is our God."

[19]But Joshua said to the people, "You cannot serve the LORD, for he is a holy God. He is a jealous God; he will not forgive your transgressions or your sins. [20]If you forsake the LORD and serve foreign gods, then he will turn and do you harm, and consume you, after having done you good." [21]And the people said to Joshua, "No, we will serve the LORD!" [22]Then Joshua said to the people, "You are witnesses against yourselves that you have chosen the LORD, to serve him." And they said, "We are witnesses."[23]He said, "Then put away the foreign gods that are among you, and incline your hearts to the LORD, the God of Israel." [24]The people said to Joshua, "The LORD our God we will serve, and him we will obey." [25]So Joshua made a covenant with the people that day, and made statutes and ordinances for them at Shechem.

Psalm 78:1-7 (UM799)

[1]Give ear, O my people, to my teaching;
    incline your ears to the words of my mouth.
[2]I will open my mouth in a parable;
    I will utter dark sayings from of old,
[3]things that we have heard and known,
    that our ancestors have told us.
[4]We will not hide them from their children;
    we will tell to the coming generation
the glorious deeds of the LORD, and his might,
    and the wonders that he has done.
[5]He established a decree in Jacob,
    and appointed a law in Israel,
which he commanded our ancestors
    to teach to their children;
[6]that the next generation might know them,
    the children yet unborn,
and rise up and tell them to their children,
[7]   so that they should set their hope in God,
and not forget the works of God,
    but keep his commandments;

1 Thessalonians 4:13-18

[13]But we do not want you to be uninformed, brothers and sisters, about those who have died, so that you may not grieve as others do who have no hope. [14]For since we believe that Jesus died and rose again, even so, through Jesus, God will bring with him those who have died. [15]For this we declare to you by the word of the Lord, that we who are alive, who are left until the coming of the Lord, will by no means precede those who have died. [16]For the Lord himself, with a cry of command, with the archangel's call and with the sound of God's trumpet, will descend from heaven, and the dead in Christ will rise first. [17]Then we who are alive, who are left, will be caught up in the clouds together with them to meet the Lord in the air; and so we will be with the Lord forever.[18]Therefore encourage one another with these words.

Matthew 25:1-13

"Then the kingdom of heaven will be like this. Ten brides-maidstook their lamps and went to meet the bridegroom. [2]Five of them were foolish, and five were wise. [3]When the foolish took their lamps, they took no oil with them; [4]but the wise took flasks of oil with their lamps. [5]As the bridegroom was delayed, all of them became drowsy and slept. [6]But at midnight there was a shout, 'Look! Here is the bridegroom! Come out to meet him.' [7]Then all those bridesmaids got up and trimmed their lamps. [8]The foolish said to the wise, 'Give us some of your oil, for our lamps are going out.' [9]But the wise replied, 'No! there will not be enough for you and for us; you had better go to the dealers and buy some for yourselves.'[10]And while they went to buy it, the bridegroom came, and those who were ready went with him into the wedding banquet; and the door was shut.[11]Later the other bridesmaids came also, saying, 'Lord, lord, open to us.' [12]But he replied, 'Truly I tell you, I do not know you.' [13]Keep awake therefore, for you know neither the day nor the hour.

Primary Hymns and Songs for the Day

662   "Stand Up and Bless the Lord" (Josh) (O)
         H-3   Hbl-79; Chr-141; Desc-95; Org-143
         S-1   #306-308. Various treatments
2188   "The Family Prayer Song" (Josh)
2220   "We Are God's People" (Josh, Matt)
718   "Lo, He Comes with Clouds Descending" (1 Thess)
         H-3   Hbl-93; Chr-129; Desc-50; Org-53
         S-1   #157. Desc.
719   "My Lord, What a Morning" (1 Thess)
         H-3   Chr-139
720   "Wake, Awake, for Night Is Flying" (Matt) (C)
         H-3   Chr-174, 203; Org-172

Additional Hymn Suggestions

116   "The God of Abraham Praise" (Josh) (O)
117   "O God, Our Help in Ages Past" (Josh)
124   "Seek the Lord" (Josh)
391   "O Happy Day, That Fixed My Choice" (Josh)
411   "Dear Lord, Lead Me Day by Day" (Josh)
472   "Near to the Heart of God" (Josh)
717   "The Battle Hymn of the Republic" (Josh, 1 Thess)
551   "Awake, O Sleeper" (Josh, Matt)
2130   "The Summons" (Josh, Matt)
2153   "I'm Gonna Live So God Can Use Me" (Josh, Matt)
2166   "Christ Beside Me" (Josh, Matt)
2175   "Together We Serve" (Josh, Matt)
2242   "Walk with Me" (Josh, Matt)
2245   "Within the Day-to-Day" (Josh, Matt)
701   "When We All Get to Heaven" (1 Thess)
702   "Sing with All the Saints in Glory" (1 Thess)
715   "Rejoice, the Lord Is King" (1 Thess)
716   "Rejoice, the Lord Is King" (1 Thess)
2147   "There Are Some Things I May Not Know" ("Yes, God Is Real") (1 Thess)
3110   "By Grace We Have Been Saved" (1 Thess)
704   "Steal Away to Jesus" (1 Thess, Matt)
440   "Let There Be Light" (Matt)
540   "I Love Thy Kingdom, Lord" (Matt)
722   "I Want to Be Ready" (Matt)
2149   "Living for Jesus" (Matt)

Additional Contemporary Suggestions

UM328   "Surely the Presence of the Lord" (Josh)
          S-2,   #200 Stanzas for soloist
S2161   "To Know You More" (Josh)
S2165   "Cry of My Heart" (Josh)
S2208   "Guide My Feet" (Josh)
S2240   "One God and Father of Us All" (Josh)
S2272   "Holy Ground" (Josh)
WS3004 "Step by Step" (Josh)
M41   "You're Worthy of My Praise" (Josh)
M97   "I Give You My Heart" (Josh)
M122   "Every Move I Make" (Josh)
M263   "From the Inside Out" (Josh, 1 Thess)
S2192   "Freedom Is Coming" (Josh, 1 Thess, Matt)
S2040   "Awesome God" (Pss)
SP158   "The Battle Belongs to the Lord" (1 Thess)
SP151   "Blow the Trumpet in Zion" (1 Thess)
M7   "I Believe in Jesus" (1 Thess)
S2194   "O Freedom" (1 Thess, Matt)
M17   "This Kingdom" (1 Thess, Matt)
M31   "I See the Lord" (1 Thess, Matt)
M111   "The Heavens Shall Declare" (1 Thess, Matt)

M140   "We Will Dance" (1 Thess, Matt)
WS3141 "Holy Darkness" (Matt)

Vocal Solos

"Here I Am" (Josh)
     V-11   p. 19
"Gospel Train" (Josh, 1 Thess)
     V-7   p. 74
"Prepare Thyself, Zion" (Matt)
     V-9   p. 2

Anthems

"Rejoice, the Lord Is King" (1 Thess)
Arr. Joel Raney; Hope C-5483
SATB with piano, opt. handbells

"Keep Your Lamps!" (Matt)
Arr. Andre Thomas; Hinshaw Music HMC-577
SATB with conga drums

Other Suggestions

Visuals:
     O   "Choose this day whom you will serve", "As for me and my household . . . ," servanthood (bowl / pitcher / towel)
     P   Christ as teacher, open Bible
     E   Trumpet, clouds, resurrection, encouragement
     G   Ten lamps, oil, wedding garments, bouquet, clock set at 12:00
Call to Worship: UM719, refrain. "My Lord, What a Morning" (1 Thess)
Act of Congregational Centering: BOW472 (Josh)
Greeting: BOW450 (1 Thess, Matt)
Opening Prayer: BOW468 (Josh)
Call to Prayer: UM704, refrain. "Steal Away to Jesus" (1 Thess)
Prayer of Confession: BOW483 or BOW490 (Josh, Matt)
Prayer: BOW510. For Discernment (Josh)
Prayer: BOW511 or BOW513 (1 Thess, Matt)
Prayer: BOW528. A Prayer of Susanna Wesley (Matt)
Prayer of Thanksgiving: BOW551 (Josh) or BOW556 (Pss)
Blessing: BOW562 (Josh)

Judges 4:1-7

¹ The Israelites again did what was evil in the sight of the LORD, after Ehud died. ²So the LORD sold them into the hand of King Jabin of Canaan, who reigned in Hazor; the commander of his army was Sisera, who lived in Harosheth-ha-goiim. ³Then the Israelites cried out to the LORD for help; for he had nine hundred chariots of iron, and had oppressed the Israelites cruelly twenty years.

⁴At that time Deborah, a prophetess, wife of Lappidoth, was judging Israel. ⁵She used to sit under the palm of Deborah between Ramah and Bethel in the hill country of Ephraim; and the Israelites came up to her for judgment. ⁶She sent and summoned Barak son of Abinoam from Kedesh in Naphtali, and said to him, "The LORD, the God of Israel, commands you, 'Go, take position at Mount Tabor, bringing ten thousand from the tribe of Naphtali and the tribe of Zebulun. ⁷I will draw out Sisera, the general of Jabin's army, to meet you by the Wadi Kishon with his chariots and his troops; and I will give him into your hand.'"

Psalm 123

¹To you I lift up my eyes,
    O you who are enthroned in the heavens!
²As the eyes of servants
    look to the hand of their master,
as the eyes of a maid
    to the hand of her mistress,
so our eyes look to the LORD our God,
    until he has mercy upon us.
³Have mercy upon us, O LORD, have mercy upon us,
    for we have had more than enough of contempt.
⁴Our soul has had more than its fill
    of the scorn of those who are at ease,
    of the contempt of the proud.

1 Thessalonians 5:1-11

¹Now concerning the times and the seasons, brothers and sisters, you do not need to have anything written to you. ²For you yourselves know very well that the day of the Lord will come like a thief in the night. ³When they say, "There is peace and security," then sudden destruction will come upon them, as labor pains come upon a pregnant woman, and there will be no escape! ⁴But you, beloved, are not in darkness, for that day to surprise you like a thief; ⁵for you are all children of light and children of the day; we are not of the night or of darkness. ⁶So then let us not fall asleep as others do, but let us keep awake and be sober; ⁷for those who sleep sleep at night, and those who are drunk get drunk at night. ⁸But since we belong to the day, let us be sober, and put on the breastplate of faith and love, and for a helmet the hope of salvation. ⁹For God has destined us not for wrath but for obtaining salvation through our Lord Jesus Christ, ¹⁰who died for us, so that whether we are awake or asleep we may live with him. ¹¹Therefore encourage one another and build up each other, as indeed you are doing.

Matthew 25:14-30

¹⁴"For it is as if a man, going on a journey, summoned his slaves and entrusted his property to them; ¹⁵to one he gave five talents, to another two, to another one, to each according to his ability. Then he went away. ¹⁶The one who had received the five talents went off at once and traded with them, and made five more talents. ¹⁷In the same way, the one who had the two talents made two more talents. ¹⁸But the one who had received the one talent went off and dug a hole in the ground and hid his master's money. ¹⁹After a long time the master of those slaves came and settled accounts with them. ²⁰Then the one who had received the five talents came forward, bringing five more talents, saying, 'Master, you handed over to me five talents; see, I have made five more talents.' ²¹His master said to him, 'Well done, good and trustworthy slave; you have been trustworthy in a few things, I will put you in charge of many things; enter into the joy of your master.' ²²And the one with the two talents also came forward, saying, 'Master, you handed over to me two talents; see, I have made two more talents.' ²³His master said to him, 'Well done, good and trustworthy slave; you have been trustworthy in a few things, I will put you in charge of many things; enter into the joy of your master.' ²⁴Then the one who had received the one talent also came forward, saying, 'Master, I knew that you were a harsh man, reaping where you did not sow, and gathering where you did not scatter seed; ²⁵so I was afraid, and I went and hid your talent in the ground. Here you have what is yours.' ²⁶But his master replied, 'You wicked and lazy slave! You knew, did you, that I reap where I did not sow, and gather where I did not scatter? ²⁷Then you ought to have invested my money with the bankers, and on my return I would have received what was my own with interest. ²⁸So take the talent from him, and give it to the one with the ten talents. ²⁹For to all those who have, more will be given, and they will have an abundance; but from those who have nothing, even what they have will be taken away. ³⁰As for this worthless slave, throw him into the outer darkness, where there will be weeping and gnashing of teeth.'"

Primary Hymns and Songs for the Day

206	"I Want to Walk as a Child of the Light" (1 Thess) (O)	
	S-2	#91. Desc.
81	"¡Canta, Dèbora, Canta!" (Judg)	
	S-1	#81. Tambourine part
2150	"Lord, Be Glorified" (Matt)	
399	"Take My Life, and Let It Be" (Matt)	
	H-3	Chr-34, 177; Desc-51; Org-53
	S-2	#78-80. Various treatments
413	"A Charge to Keep I Have" (Matt) (C)	
	H-3	Desc-19; Org-14
	S-1	#46. Choral Harm.

Additional Hymn Suggestions

108	"God Hath Spoken By the Prophets" (Judg)
107	"La Palabra Del Señor Es Recta" ("Righteous and Just Is the Word of Our Lord") (Judg)
121	"There's a Wideness in God's Mercy" (Pss)
482	"Lord, Have Mercy" (Pss)
485	"Let Us Pray to the Lord" (Pss)
247	"O Morning Star, How Fair and Bright" (1 Thess)
289	"Ah, Holy Jesus" (1 Thess)
301	"Jesus, Keep Me Near the Cross" (1 Thess)
356	"Pues Si Vivimos" ("When We Are Living") (1 Thess)
551	"Awake, O Sleeper" (1 Thess)
2172	"We Are Called" (1 Thess) (O)
2175	"Together We Serve" (1 Thess, Matt)
2214	"Lead Me, Guide Me" (1 Thess)
2236	"Gather Us In" (1 Thess) (O)
2284	"Joy in the Morning" (1 Thess)
87	"What Gift Can We Bring" (Matt)
150	"God Who Stretched the Spangled Heavens" (Matt)
433	"All Who Love and Serve Your City" (Matt)
508	"Faith, While Trees Are Still in Blossom" (Matt)
581	"Lord, Whose Love Through Humble Service" (Matt) (C)
650	"Give Me the Faith Which Can Remove" (Matt)
2153	"I'm Gonna Live So God Can Use Me" (Matt)

Additional Contemporary Suggestions

UM483	"Kyrie Eleison" ("Lord, Have Mercy") (Pss)
	UM484 (different tunes)
S2192	"Freedom Is Coming" (1 Thess)
S2194	"O Freedom" (1 Thess)
S2204	"Light of the World" (1 Thess)
S2235b	"We Are Marching" ("Siyahamba") (1 Thess)
WS3041	"Praise Him" (1 Thess)
WS3163	"Walking in the Light of God" (1 Thess)
M19	"Shine on Us" (1 Thess)
M64	"Hear Our Praises" (1 Thess)
M150	"Everyday" (1 Thess)
SP144	"Song for the Nations" ("May We Be a Shining Light") (1 Thess)
WS3177	"Here I Am to Worship" (1 Thess)
S2032	"My Life Is in You, Lord" (Matt)
WS3186	"Days of Elijah" (Matt)
M53	"Let It Be Said of Us" (Matt)
M115	"When It's All Been Said and Done" (Matt)
BOW179	"For the Gift of Creation" (Matt)

Vocal Solos

"I Will Lift Up Mine Eyes" (Pss)	
V-11	p. 27
"Let De Heb'n-Light Shine on Me" (1 Thess)	
V-7	p. 66
"Redeeming Grace" (1 Thess, Matt)	
V-4	p. 47
"Take My Life, and Let It Be" (Matt)	
V-8	p. 262
"Fit for a King" (Matt, Stewardship)	
V-10	p. 32

Anthems

"Have Mercy upon Us" (*Miserere nostri, Domine*) (Pss)
G. P. Palestrina; ECS Publishing 1269
SATB a cappella

"Consecration" (Matt)
Arr. Bruce Saylor; Paraclete Press PPM01114
SATB with organ and optional children's choir

Other Suggestions

Today's parable from Matt lends itself well to a stewardship emphasis. Many Nov. 9 suggestions related to 1 Thess are also appropriate with today's reading from 1 Thess
Visuals:

O	Manacles
P	Hand
E	Robber's mask, light/dark, awake/asleep, lantern
G	Three piles of coins (large, medium, small, bank bag, time/talent survey, nos. 1, 2 and 5, (nos. 10, 4, and 1)

Greeting: BOW450 (1 Thess, Matt)
Opening Prayer: BOW460 (1 Thess, Matt)
Prayer of Confession: BOW476, BOW478, or BOW480 (1 Thess, Matt)
Response: S2275. "Kyrie" or S2277. "Lord, Have Mercy" (Pss)
Baptism Response: S2249, BOW175. "God Claims You" (1 Thess)
Prayer: UM403. For True Life (1 Thess, Matt)
Prayer: UM481. Prayer of Saint Francis (Pss)
Prayer: BOW508. Psalm of the Woodlands (Matt)
Prayer: BOW540. For Those Who Work (Matt)
Offering Prayer: WSL112. "With money, time, talents" (Matt)
Response: BOW179. "For the Gift of Creation" (Matt)
Dismissal: BOW559 (1 Thess, Matt)

Deuteronomy 8:7-18

[7]For the LORD your God is bringing you into a good land, a land with flowing streams, with springs and underground waters welling up in valleys and hills, [8]a land of wheat and barley, of vines and fig trees and pomegranates, a land of olive trees and honey, [9]a land where you may eat bread without scarcity, where you will lack nothing, a land whose stones are iron and from whose hills you may mine copper. [10]You shall eat your fill and bless the LORD your God for the good land that he has given you.

[11]Take care that you do not forget the LORD your God, by failing to keep his commandments, his ordinances, and his statutes, which I am commanding you today. [12]When you have eaten your fill and have built fine houses and live in them, [13]and when your herds and flocks have multiplied, and your silver and gold is multiplied, and all that you have is multiplied, [14]then do not exalt yourself, forgetting the LORD your God, who brought you out of the land of Egypt, out of the house of slavery, [15]who led you through the great and terrible wilderness, an arid wasteland with poisonous snakes and scorpions. He made water flow for you from flint rock, [16]and fed you in the wilderness with manna that your ancestors did not know, to humble you and to test you, and in the end to do you good. [17]Do not say to yourself, "My power and the might of my own hand have gotten me this wealth." [18]But remember the LORD your God, for it is he who gives you power to get wealth, so that he may confirm his covenant that he swore to your ancestors, as he is doing today.

Psalm 65 (UM789)

[1]Praise is due to you,
    O God, in Zion;
and to you shall vows be performed,
    [2]O you who answer prayer!
To you all flesh shall come.
[3]When deeds of iniquity overwhelm us,
    you forgive our transgressions.
[4]Happy are those whom you choose and bring near
    to live in your courts.
We shall be satisfied with the goodness of your house,
    your holy temple.
[5]By awesome deeds you answer us with deliverance,
    O God of our salvation;
you are the hope of all the ends of the earth
    and of the farthest seas.
[6]By your strength you established the mountains;
    you are girded with might.
[7]You silence the roaring of the seas,
    the roaring of their waves,
    the tumult of the peoples.
[8]Those who live at earth's farthest bounds are awed by your
            signs;
you make the gateways of the morning and the evening shout
            for joy.
[9]You visit the earth and water it,
    you greatly enrich it;
the river of God is full of water;
    you provide the people with grain,
    for so you have prepared it.
[10]You water its furrows abundantly,
    settling its ridges,
softening it with showers,
    and blessing its growth.

[11]You crown the year with your bounty;
    your wagon tracks overflow with richness.
[12]The pastures of the wilderness overflow,
    the hills gird themselves with joy,
[13]the meadows clothe themselves with flocks,
    the valleys deck themselves with grain,
    they shout and sing together for joy.

2 Corinthians 9:6-15

[6]The point is this: the one who sows sparingly will also reap sparingly, and the one who sows bountifully will also reap bountifully. [7]Each of you must give as you have made up your mind, not reluctantly or under compulsion, for God loves a cheerful giver. [8]And God is able to provide you with every blessing in abundance, so that by always having enough of everything, you may share abundantly in every good work. [9]As it is written,
"He scatters abroad, he gives to the poor;
    his righteousness endures forever."
[10]He who supplies seed to the sower and bread for food will supply and multiply your seed for sowing and increase the harvest of your righteousness. [11]You will be enriched in every way for your great generosity, which will produce thanksgiving to God through us; [12]for the rendering of this ministry not only supplies the needs of the saints but also overflows with many thanksgivings to God. [13]Through the testing of this ministry you glorify God by your obedience to the confession of the gospel of Christ and by the generosity of your sharing with them and with all others, [14]while they long for you and pray for you because of the surpassing grace of God that he has given you. [15]Thanks be to God for his indescribable gift!

Luke 17:11-19

[11]On the way to Jerusalem Jesus was going through the region between Samaria and Galilee. [12]As he entered a village, ten lepers approached him. Keeping their distance, [13]they called out, saying, "Jesus, Master, have mercy on us!" [14]When he saw them, he said to them, "Go and show yourselves to the priests." And as they went, they were made clean. [15]Then one of them, when he saw that he was healed, turned back, praising God with a loud voice. [16]He prostrated himself at Jesus' feet and thanked him. And he was a Samaritan. [17]Then Jesus asked, "Were not ten made clean? But the other nine, where are they? [18]Was none of them found to return and give praise to God except this foreigner?" [19]Then he said to him, "Get up and go on your way; your faith has made you well."

Primary Hymns and Songs for the Day

694   "Come, Ye Thankful People, Come" (2 Cor, Thanks.)
      (O)
      H-3   Hbl-54; Chr-58; Desc-94; Org-137
      S-1   #302-303. Harm. with Desc.

92   "For the Beauty of the Earth" (Deut, Pss, Thanks.)
      H-3   Chr-33, 65; Desc-30; Org-29
      S-1   #93-96. Various treatments

583   *"Sois la Semilla"* ("You Are the Seed") (2 Cor)

2036   "Give Thanks" (2 Cor)

60   "I'll Praise My Maker While I've Breath" (Luke) (C)
      H-3   Chr-109; Org-105
      S-2   #141. Harm.

Additional Hymn Suggestions

139   "Praise to the Lord, the Almighty" (Deut, Thanks.)
      (O)

87   "What Gift Can We Bring" (Deut)

97   "For the Fruits of This Creation" (Deut)

102   "Now Thank We All Our God" (Deut, Thanks.)

586   "Let My People Seek Their Freedom" (Deut)

637   *"Una Espiga"* ("Sheaves of Summer") (Pss, Comm.)

2279   "The Trees of the Field" (Pss) (C)

86   "Mountains Are All Aglow" (Deut, Pss, 1 Cor)

2061   "Praise Our God Above" ("Harvest Song") (Deut, Pss,
      Thanks.)

66   "Praise, My Soul, The King of Heaven" (Luke,
      Thanks.)

263   "When Jesus the Healer Passed Through Galilee"
      (Luke)

273   "Jesus' Hands Were Kind Hands" (Luke)

372   "How Can We Sinners Know" (Luke)

551   "Awake, O Sleeper" (Luke)

2104   "An Outcast among Outcasts" (Luke)

3001   "O For a Thousand Tongues to Sing" (Luke)

3100   "Jesus Paid It All" (Luke)

565   "Father, We Thank You" (Thanks., Comm.)

617   "I Come with Joy" (Thanks., Comm.)

2044   "My Gratitude Now Accept, O God ("*Gracias, Señor*")
      (Thanks.)

2262   "Let Us Offer to the Father" ("*Te Ofrecemos Padre
      Nuestro*") (Thanks., Comm.)

2265   "Time Now to Gather" (Thanks., Comm.)

2283   "For All the Saints" (Thanks.)

Additional Contemporary Suggestions

S2271   "Come! Come! Everybody Worship" (2 Cor)

S2150   "Lord, Be Glorified" (2 Cor)

S2162   "Grace Alone" (2 Cor)

M13   "Be Glorified" (2 Cor)

M37   "He Is Able" (2 Cor)

M152   "Be Glorified" (2 Cor)

S2195   "In the Lord I'll Be Ever Thankful" (2 Cor, Luke)

S2079   "Jesus Be Praised" (Luke)

S2081   "Thank You, Jesus" ("*Tino Tenda, Jesu*") (Luke)

M35   "White as Snow" (Luke)

M244   "Jesus Paid It All" (Luke)

UM84   "Thank You, Lord" (Luke, Thanks.)

UM394   "Something Beautiful" (Luke)

WS3002   "Blessed Be Your Name" (Luke, Thanks.)

WS3037   "I Thank You, Jesus" (Luke)

WS3104   "Amazing Grace" ("My Chains Are Gone") (Luke)

Vocal Solos

"O For a Thousand Tongues to Sing" (Luke)
      V-1   p. 32

"I Just Came to Praise the Lord" (Luke, Thanks.)
      V-8   p. 294

"Now Thank We All Our God" (Thanks.)
      V-6   p. 8

Anthems

"We Plow The Fields" (Deut, Pss, Thanks.)
Donald McCullough; Hinshaw HMC2182
SATB with keyboard and flute

"A Grateful Heart" (Thanks.)
Debra Scroggins; Choristers Guild CGA1336
SATB with organ

Other Suggestions

Visuals:
   O   Flowing water, wheat, barley, figs, etc.
   P   Cornucopia with fruit, vegetables, etc., water, sheep,
         sea, mountains, grain
   E   Seed, bread, people in ministry, 2 Cor 9:15
   G   Nos. 1 and 9, healing, praise, Luke 17:19b

Act of Congregational Centering: BOW471 (Thanks.)
Greeting: BOW417 (Thanks.)
Opening Prayer: BOW464 (Deut, Luke, Thanks.)
Litany of Praise: WSL56. "Come on!" (Luke, Thanks.)
Canticle: UM74. "Canticle of Thanksgiving" (See S-1, p. 374.)
Prayer of Confession: BOW485 or BOW494 (Thanks.)
Response: S2275. "*Kyrie*" (Luke)
Prayer: BOW507. For Creation (Thanks.)
Prayer: BOW521. A Vision of Hope (2 Cor, Thanks.)
Prayer: BOW532 (Luke)
Offering Prayer: WSL118. "O Lord, you know" (Deut)
Prayer of Thanksgiving: BOW418 or BOW557 (Deut)
Response: BOW203, S2081. "Thank You, Jesus (Luke)
Blessing: BOW565 (Deut, Thanks.)

Lead an abundant life, grow as a faithful disciple, and find new avenues to serve.

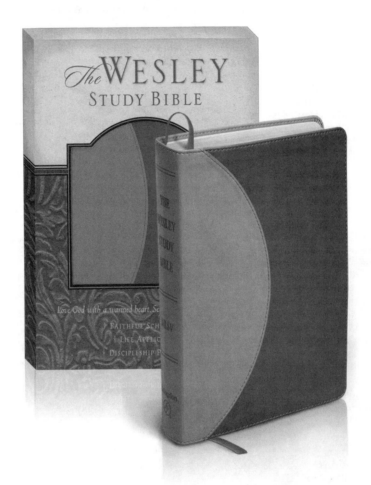

New Revised Standard Version Wesley Study Bible | 9780687645039

Love God with a warmed heart. Serve God with active hands.

As God transforms readers through study, they will be inspired to transform the world. Contributors from across the Wesleyan family join together to help one experience God in fresh ways. The Wesley Study Bible offers easy-to-understand explanations of core terms that cover eternal life, forgiveness, grace, heaven, holiness, justice, and mission. The Bible has extended references to works by John Wesley.

Ezekiel 34:11-16, 20-24

[11]For thus says the Lord GOD: I myself will search for my sheep, and will seek them out. [12]As shepherds seek out their flocks when they are among their scattered sheep, so I will seek out my sheep. I will rescue them from all the places to which they have been scattered on a day of clouds and thick darkness. [13]I will bring them out from the peoples and gather them from the countries, and will bring them into their own land; and I will feed them on the mountains of Israel, by the watercourses, and in all the inhabited parts of the land. [14]I will feed them with good pasture, and the mountain heights of Israel shall be their pasture; there they shall lie down in good grazing land, and they shall feed on rich pasture on the mountains of Israel. [15]I myself will be the shepherd of my sheep, and I will make them lie down, says the Lord GOD. [16]I will seek the lost, and I will bring back the strayed, and I will bind up the injured, and I will strengthen the weak, but the fat and the strong I will destroy. I will feed them with justice. . . .

[20]Therefore, thus says the Lord GOD to them: I myself will judge between the fat sheep and the lean sheep. [21]Because you pushed with flank and shoulder, and butted at all the weak animals with your horns until you scattered them far and wide, [22]I will save my flock, and they shall no longer be ravaged; and I will judge between sheep and sheep.

[23]I will set up over them one shepherd, my servant David, and he shall feed them: he shall feed them and be their shepherd. [24]And I, the LORD, will be their God, and my servant David shall be prince among them; I, the LORD, have spoken.

Psalm 100 (UM821)

[1]Make a joyful noise to the LORD, all the earth.
  [2]Worship the LORD with gladness;
  come into his presence with singing.
[3]Know that the LORD is God.
  It is he that made us, and we are his;
  we are his people, and the sheep of his pasture.
[4]Enter his gates with thanksgiving,
  and his courts with praise.
  Give thanks to him, bless his name.
[5]For the LORD is good;
  his steadfast love endures forever,
  and his faithfulness to all generations.

Ephesians 1:15-23

[15]I have heard of your faith in the Lord Jesus and your love toward all the saints, and for this reason [16]I do not cease to give thanks for you as I remember you in my prayers. [17]I pray that the God of our Lord Jesus Christ, the Father of glory, may give you a spirit of wisdom and revelation as you come to know him, [18]so that, with the eyes of your heart enlightened, you may know what is the hope to which he has called you, what are the riches of his glorious inheritance among the saints, [19]and what is the immeasurable greatness of his power for us who believe, according to the working of his great power. [20]God put this power to work in Christ when he raised him from the dead and seated him at his right hand in the heavenly places, [21]far above all rule and authority and power and dominion, and above every name that is named, not only in this age but also in the age to come. [22]And he has put all things under his feet and has made him the head over all things for the church, [23]which is his body, the fullness of him who fills all in all.

Matthew 25:31-46

[31]"When the Son of Man comes in his glory, and all the angels with him, then he will sit on the throne of his glory. [32]All the nations will be gathered before him, and he will separate people one from another as a shepherd separates the sheep from the goats, [33]and he will put the sheep at his right hand and the goats at the left. [34]Then the king will say to those at his right hand, 'Come, you that are blessed by my Father, inherit the kingdom prepared for you from the foundation of the world; [35]for I was hungry and you gave me food, I was thirsty and you gave me something to drink, I was a stranger and you welcomed me, [36]I was naked and you gave me clothing, I was sick and you took care of me, I was in prison and you visited me.' [37]Then the righteous will answer him, 'Lord, when was it that we saw you hungry and gave you food, or thirsty and gave you something to drink? [38]And when was it that we saw you a stranger and welcomed you, or naked and gave you clothing? [39]And when was it that we saw you sick or in prison and visited you?' [40]And the king will answer them, 'Truly I tell you, just as you did it to one of the least of these who are members of my family, you did it to me.' [41]Then he will say to those at his left hand, 'You that are accursed, depart from me into the eternal fire prepared for the devil and his angels; [42]for I was hungry and you gave me no food, I was thirsty and you gave me nothing to drink, [43]I was a stranger and you did not welcome me, naked and you did not give me clothing, sick and in prison and you did not visit me.' [44]Then they also will answer, 'Lord, when was it that we saw you hungry or thirsty or a stranger or naked or sick or in prison, and did not take care of you?' [45]Then he will answer them, 'Truly I tell you, just as you did not do it to one of the least of these, you did not do it to me.' [46]And these will go away into eternal punishment, but the righteous into eternal life."

Primary Hymns and Songs for the Day

75	"All People That on Earth Do Dwell" (Pss) (O)
	H-3 Hbl-45; Chr-24; Desc-84, 85; Org-107
	S-1 #257-259. Various treatments
	S-2 #140. Desc.
2236	"Gather Us In" (Eze, Matt) (O)
434	*Cuando El Pobre* ("When the Poor Ones") (Matt)
581	"Lord, Whose Love Through Humble Service" (Matt) (C)
	H-3 Hbl-14, 64; Chr-132, 203
	S-2 #22. Desc.

Additional Hymn Suggestions

66	"Praise, My Soul, the King of Heaven" (Eze, Christ the King)
115	"How Like a Gentle Spirit" (Eze)
132	"All My Hope Is Firmly Grounded" (Eze)
2123	"Loving Spirit" (Eze)
2177	"Wounded World that Cries for Healing" (Eze)
2178	"Here Am I" (Eze, Matt)
2180	"Why Stand So Far Away, My God?" (Eze)
2182	"When God Restored Our Common Life" (Eze, Matt)
381	"Savior, Like a Shepherd Lead Us" (Eze, Pss)
61	"Come, Thou Almighty King" (Pss, Eph, Christ the King)
62	"All Creatures of Our God and King" (Pss, Christ the King)
694	"Come, Ye Thankful People, Come" (Pss, Matt, Thanks.)
73	"O Worship the King" (Eph, Christ the King)
79	"Holy God, We Praise Thy Name" (Eph, Christ the King) *(See especially stanzas 1, 5–7)*
96	"Praise the Lord Who Reigns Above" (Eph, Christ the King)
103	"Immortal, Invisible, God Only Wise" (Eph)
175	"Jesus, the Very Thought of Thee" (Eph)
178	"Hope of the World" (Eph)
368	"My Hope Is Built" (Eph)
711	"For All the Saints" (Eph)
2147	"There Are Some Things I May Not Know" ("Yes, God Is Real") (Eph)
2220	"We Are God's People" (Eph)
2276	"Glory to God in the Highest" (Eph, Christ the King)
3035	"Bless Christ Through Whom All Things Are Made" (Eph)
3140	"Give Me Jesus" (Eph)
2269	"Come, Share the Lord" (Eph, Matt, Christ the King, Comm.)
131	"We Gather Together" (Matt, Thanks.) (O)
192	"There's a Spirit in the Air" (Matt)
433	"All Who Love and Serve Your City" (Matt)
591	"Rescue the Perishing" (Matt)
2048	"God Weeps" (Matt)
2094	"Carol of the Epiphany" (Matt)
2126	"All Who Hunger" (Matt, Comm.)
2175	"Together We Serve" (Matt)
2254	"In Remembrance of Me" (Matt, Comm.)
2268	"As We Gather at Your Table" (Matt, Comm.)
3128	"Whatever You Do" (Matt)

Additional Contemporary Suggestions

S2036	"Give Thanks" (Eze, Matt)
S2055	"You Are My Hiding Place" (Eze)
S2058	"Shepherd Me, O God"
M92	"All Things Are Possible" (Eze)
M68	"Forever" (Pss, Eph)
M229	"Forevermore" (Pss)
WS3007	*Laudate Dominum* ("Sing, Praise") (Pss)
WS3027	"Hallelujah" ("Your Love Is Amazing") (Pss)
S2017	"Come, Rejoice in God" ("*Jubilate Servite*") (Pss)
S2035	"Praise, Praise, Praise the Lord" (Pss)
S2270	"I Will Enter His Gates" (Pss)
WS3008	"Open the Eyes of My Heart" (Eph)
WS3105	"In Christ Alone" ("My Hope Is Found") (Eph)
WS3140	"Give Me Jesus" (Eph)
S2244	"People Need the Lord" (Matt)
S2075	"King of Kings" (Christ the King)
WS3130	"Come, Emmanuel" (Christ the King)
WS3190	"Mary Had a Little Lamb" (Christ the King)
M275	"Prepare Ye the Way" ("You Reign on High") (Christ the King)

Vocal Solos

"He Shall Feed His Flock Like a Shepherd" (Eze)
  V-2

"God, Our Ever Faithful Shepherd" (Eze, Matt)
  V-4   p. 15

"Above All" (Eph)
  V-3(2)   p. 17

"Reach Out to Your Neighbor" (Matt)
  V-8   p. 372

"Praise to the Lord, the Almighty" (Christ the King)
  V-6   p. 18

"Crown Him, the Risen King" (Christ the King)
  V-10   p. 55

Anthems

"Rain Down" (Eze, Matt)
Arr. John Carter; Hope A-717
3-part mixed with piano

"Everything Is One" (Christ the King)
Charles Forsberg; Augsburg 9781451482898
SATB with keyboard

Other Suggestions

Visuals:

O	Sheep, good shepherd
P	Instruments, worship, singing
E	Portraits of Christ or local church "saints," church history
G	Christ descending, angels, food, drink, clothes, visitation, medicine bag, prison ministry, Bible, crown, rich fabric, Christ as king.

Call to Worship: S2274 "Come, All You People" (Pss)
Response: UM93. "Let All the World in Every Corner Sing" (Pss)
Greeting: BOW420 (Christ the King)
Greeting: BOW450 or BOW452 (Pss) or BOW454 (Eze)
Opening Prayer: WSL63 or BOW460 (Matt, Christ the King)
Canticle: UM74 or UM91 (Pss)
Prayer of Confession: WSL87, BOW476 or BOW481 (Matt)
Prayer: UM323. Ascension (Eph)
Prayer: UM721 or BOW421 or BOW511 (Christ the King)
Prayer: WSL199, BOW522, BOW529, or BOW546 (Matt)
Prayer of Thanksgiving: BOW555 (Pss, Matt)
Response: UM67. "We, Thy People, Praise Thee" (Pss)
Blessing: BOW564 or WSL169 (Matt)

Isaiah 64:1-9

¹O that you would tear open the heavens and come down,
    so that the mountains would quake at your presence—
    ²as when fire kindles brushwood
    and the fire causes water to boil—
to make your name known to your adversaries,
    so that the nations might tremble at your presence!
³When you did awesome deeds that we did not expect,
    you came down, the mountains quaked at your presence.
⁴From ages past no one has heard,
    no ear has perceived,
no eye has seen any God besides you,
    who works for those who wait for him.
⁵You meet those who gladly do right,
    those who remember you in your ways.
But you were angry, and we sinned;
    because you hid yourself we transgressed.
⁶We have all become like one who is unclean,
    and all our righteous deeds are like a filthy cloth.
We all fade like a leaf,
    and our iniquities, like the wind, take us away.
⁷There is no one who calls on your name,
    or attempts to take hold of you;
for you have hidden your face from us,
    and have delivered us into the hand of our iniquity.
⁸Yet, O LORD, you are our Father;
    we are the clay, and you are our potter;
    we are all the work of your hand.
⁹Do not be exceedingly angry, O LORD,
    and do not remember iniquity forever.
    Now consider, we are all your people.

Psalm 80:1-7, 17-19 (UM801)

¹Give ear, O Shepherd of Israel,
    you who lead Joseph like a flock!
You who are enthroned upon the cherubim, shine forth
    ²before Ephraim and Benjamin and Manasseh.
Stir up your might,
    and come to save us!
³Restore us, O God;
    let your face shine, that we may be saved.
⁴O LORD God of hosts,
    how long will you be angry with your people's prayers?
⁵You have fed them with the bread of tears,
    and given them tears to drink in full measure.
⁶You make us the scorn of our neighbors;
    our enemies laugh among themselves.
⁷Restore us, O God of hosts;
    let your face shine, that we may be saved.
. . . .
¹⁷But let your hand be upon the one at your right hand,
    the one whom you made strong for yourself.
¹⁸Then we will never turn back from you;
    give us life, and we will call on your name.
¹⁹Restore us, O LORD God of hosts;
    let your face shine, that we may be saved.

1 Corinthians 1:3-9

³Grace to you and peace from God our Father and the Lord Jesus Christ.

⁴I give thanks to my God always for you because of the grace of God that has been given you in Christ Jesus, ⁵for in every way you have been enriched in him, in speech and knowledge of every kind— ⁶just as the testimony of Christ has been strengthened among you— ⁷so that you are not lacking in any spiritual gift as you wait for the revealing of our Lord Jesus Christ. ⁸He will also strengthen you to the end, so that you may be blameless on the day of our Lord Jesus Christ. ⁹God is faithful; by him you were called into the fellowship of his Son, Jesus Christ our Lord.

Mark 13:24-37

²⁴"But in those days, after that suffering,
the sun will be darkened,
    and the moon will not give its light,
²⁵and the stars will be falling from heaven,
    and the powers in the heavens will be shaken.
²⁶Then they will see 'the Son of Man coming in clouds' with great power and glory. ²⁷Then he will send out the angels, and gather his elect from the four winds, from the ends of the earth to the ends of heaven.

²⁸"From the fig tree learn its lesson: as soon as its branch becomes tender and puts forth its leaves, you know that summer is near. ²⁹So also, when you see these things taking place, you know that he is near, at the very gates. ³⁰Truly I tell you, this generation will not pass away until all these things have taken place. ³¹Heaven and earth will pass away, but my words will not pass away.

³²"But about that day or hour no one knows, neither the angels in heaven, nor the Son, but only the Father. ³³Beware, keep alert; for you do not know when the time will come. ³⁴It is like a man going on a journey, when he leaves home and puts his slaves in charge, each with his work, and commands the doorkeeper to be on the watch. ³⁵Therefore, keep awake—for you do not know when the master of the house will come, in the evening, or at midnight, or at cockcrow, or at dawn, ³⁶or else he may find you asleep when he comes suddenly. ³⁷And what I say to you I say to all: Keep awake."

Primary Hymns and Songs for the Day
196	"Come, Thou Long-Expected Jesus" (Mark, Pss) (O)
	H-3 Hbl-46; Chr-26, 134; Desc-53; Org-56
	S-1 #168-171. Various treatments
382	"Have Thine Own Way, Lord" (Isa)
	S-2 #2. Instr. Desc.
2152	"Change My Heart, O God" (Isa)
719	"My Lord, What a Morning" (Mark)
	H-3 Chr-139
3048	"View the Present through the Promise" (Mark)
706	"Soon and Very Soon" (Mark) (C)
	S-2 #187. Piano Arr.

Additional Hymn Suggestions
115	"How Like a Gentle Spirit" (Isa)
132	"All My Hope Is Firmly Grounded" (Isa)
518	"O Thou, in Whose Presence" (Isa)
140, 4011	"Great Is Thy Faithfulness" (Pss, 1 Cor)
195	"Send Your Word" (Pss, 1 Cor)
247	"O Morning Star, How Fair and Bright" (Pss, Mark)
373	"Nothing Between" (Pss, 1 Cor)
627	"O the Depth of Love Divine" (Comm., 1 Cor)
714	"I Know Whom I Have Believed" (1 Cor, Mark)
202	"People, Look East" (Mark)
551	"Awake, O Sleeper" (Mark)
718	"Lo, He Comes with Clouds Descending" (Mark)
720	"Wake, Awake, for Night Is Flying" (Mark)
722	"I Want to Be Ready" (Mark)
730	"O Day of God, Draw Nigh" (Mark, Advent)
2210	"Joy Comes with the Dawn" (Mark)
3049	"Wait for the Lord" (Mark, Advent)
626	"Let All Mortal Flesh Keep Silence" (Mark, Comm.)
636	"Christian People, Raise Your Song" (Comm.)
2100	"Thou Didst Leave Thy Throne" (Advent)

Additional Contemporary Suggestions
S2040	"Awesome God" (Isa)
S2086	"Open Our Eyes, Lord" (Isa)
S2253	"Water, River, Spirit, Grace" (Isa, Baptism)
WS3008	"Open the Eyes of My Heart" (Isa)
M26	"The Power of Your Love" (Isa)
M85	"The Potter's Hand" (Isa)
M112	"Jesus, Lover of My Soul" (Isa)
M265	"I Have a Hope" (Isa)
M264	"Song of Hope" ("Heaven Come Down") (Isa, Mark)
S2173	"Shine, Jesus, Shine" (Pss, Advent)
S2163	"He Who Began a Good Work in You" (1 Cor)
M87	"Let the Peace of God Reign" (1 Cor)
UM171	"There's Something About That Name" (Mark)
S2192	"Freedom Is Coming" (Mark)
S2194	"O Freedom" (Mark)
WS3046	"Come, O Redeemer, Come" (Mark, Advent)
WS3141	"Holy Darkness" (Mark)
WS3186	"Days of Elijah" (Mark, Advent)
M1	"Ancient of Days" (Mark)
M25	"No Greater Love" (Mark)
M69	"Did You Feel the Mountains Tremble?" (Mark)

Vocal Solos
"Patiently Have I Waited" (Isa, Advent)
  V-4   p. 24
"But Who May Abide" (Isa, Mark)
  V-2

"Lost in the Night" (Isa, Mark, Advent)
  V-5(1) p. 18
"Then Shall the Righteous Shine Forth" (Isa, Mark)
  V-8   p. 274
"My Lord, What a Mornin'" (Mark)
  V-7   p. 68
"Prepare Thyself, Zion" (Mark)
  V-9   p. 2

Anthems
"Here I Am, Lord" (Isa)
Arr. Mary McDonald; Alfred 42956
SATB with keyboard

"Come, Thou Long-Expected Jesus" (Mark, Pss)
Mark Miller; Choristers Guild CGA1225
SAB with piano

Other Suggestions
Visuals:
O	Fire, volcanic imagery, dirty cloth, leaf, potter, potter's wheel, lump of clay, water
P	Angels, water (tears), dried leaves, rough cloth (burlap), shepherd
E	Portrait of Christ, pile of gifts, 1 Cor 1: 9
G	Eclipse of sun/moon, stars, angels, fig tree, alarm clock, crowing rooster

Introit: WS3048 "View the Present through the Promise" (Advent)
Greeting: BOW243 (Mark)
Advent Wreath Readings: BOW262 (Advent)
Response: S2090. "Light the Advent Candle" (Advent)
Canticle: UM205. Canticle of Light and Darkness (Pss) See S-1, p. 383.
Opening Prayer: WSL1 or BOW254 (Mark, Advent)
Prayer of Confession: BOW486 (Isa, Pss)
Prayers: C19 or F189 (Advent)
Prayer: WSL57 (Isa)
Prayer: BOW500. For Blessing, Mercy, and Courage (Isa, Pss)
Litany: BOW433. "Gracious God, Eternal God" (Student Day)
Offering Prayer: WSL125 (Advent)
Great Thanksgiving for Advent: BOW54
Blessing: BOW560 (Pss)
Benediction: BOW190. "Benediction" (Pss)
See The Abingdon Worship Annual 2017 *for additional ideas.*

Isaiah 40:1-11

[1]Comfort, O comfort my people,
     says your God.
[2]Speak tenderly to Jerusalem,
     and cry to her
that she has served her term,
     that her penalty is paid,
that she has received from the Lord's hand
     double for all her sins.
[3]A voice cries out:
"In the wilderness prepare the way of the LORD,
     make straight in the desert a highway for our God.
[4]Every valley shall be lifted up,
     and every mountain and hill be made low;
the uneven ground shall become level,
     and the rough places a plain.
[5]Then the glory of the LORD shall be revealed,
     and all people shall see it together,
     for the mouth of the LORD has spoken."
[6]A voice says, "Cry out!"
     And I said, "What shall I cry?"
All people are grass,
     their constancy is like the flower of the field.
[7]The grass withers, the flower fades,
     when the breath of the LORD blows upon it;
     surely the people are grass.
[8]The grass withers, the flower fades;
     but the word of our God will stand forever.
[9]Get you up to a high mountain,
     O Zion, herald of good tidings;
lift up your voice with strength,
     O Jerusalem, herald of good tidings,
     lift it up, do not fear;
say to the cities of Judah,
     "Here is your God!"
[10]See, the Lord GOD comes with might,
     and his arm rules for him;
his reward is with him,
     and his recompense before him.
[11]He will feed his flock like a shepherd;
     he will gather the lambs in his arms,
and carry them in his bosom,
     and gently lead the mother sheep.

Psalm 85:1-2, 8-13 (UM806)

[1]LORD, you were favorable to your land;
     you restored the fortunes of Jacob.
[2]You forgave the iniquity of your people;
     you pardoned all their sin. *[Selah]*

. . . .

[8]Let me hear what God the LORD will speak,
     for he will speak peace to his people,
     to his faithful, to those who turn to him in their hearts.
[9]Surely his salvation is at hand for those who fear him,
     that his glory may dwell in our land.
[10]Steadfast love and faithfulness will meet;
     righteousness and peace will kiss each other.
[11]Faithfulness will spring up from the ground,
     and righteousness will look down from the sky.
[12]The LORD will give what is good,
     and our land will yield its increase.
[13]Righteousness will go before him,
     and will make a path for his steps.

2 Peter 3:8-15a

[8]But do not ignore this one fact, beloved, that with the Lord one day is like a thousand years, and a thousand years are like one day. [9]The Lord is not slow about his promise, as some think of slowness, but is patient with you, not wanting any to perish, but all to come to repentance. [10]But the day of the Lord will come like a thief, and then the heavens will pass away with a loud noise, and the elements will be dissolved with fire, and the earth and everything that is done on it will be disclosed.

[11]Since all these things are to be dissolved in this way, what sort of persons ought you to be in leading lives of holiness and godliness, [12]waiting for and hastening the coming of the day of God, because of which the heavens will be set ablaze and dissolved, and the elements will melt with fire? [13]But, in accordance with his promise, we wait for new heavens and a new earth, where righteousness is at home.

[14]Therefore, beloved, while you are waiting for these things, strive to be found by him at peace, without spot or blemish; [15a]and regard the patience of our Lord as salvation.

Mark 1:1-8

[1]The beginning of the good news of Jesus Christ, the Son of God.
     [2]As it is written in the prophet Isaiah,
"See, I am sending my messenger ahead of you,
     who will prepare your way;
     [3]the voice of one crying out in the wilderness:
     'Prepare the way of the Lord, make his paths straight,'"
[4]John the baptizer appeared in the wilderness, proclaiming a baptism of repentance for the forgiveness of sins. [5]And people from the whole Judean countryside and all the people of Jerusalem were going out to him, and were baptized by him in the river Jordan, confessing their sins. [6]Now John was clothed with camel's hair, with a leather belt around his waist, and he ate locusts and wild honey. [7]He proclaimed, "The one who is more powerful than I is coming after me; I am not worthy to stoop down and untie the thong of his sandals. [8]I have baptized you with water; but he will baptize you with the Holy Spirit."

Primary Hymns and Songs for the Day

211	"O Come, O Come, Emmanuel" (Pss, Mark) (O)	
	H-3	Hbl-14, 79; Chr-141; Org-168
	S-1	#342. Handbell accompaniment
207	"Prepare the Way of the Lord" (Isa, Mark)	
171	"There's Something About That Name" (2 Pet, Mark)	
2089	"Wild and Lone the Prophet's Voice" (Mark)	
567	"Heralds of Christ" (Isa, Mark) (C)	
	H-3	Hbl-64; Chr-78; Desc-78; Org-96
	S-2	#131-132. Harm. with Desc.

Additional Hymn Suggestions

202	"People, Look East" (Isa, Advent)
210	*"Toda la Tierra"* ("All Earth Is Waiting") (Isa)
519	"Lift Every Voice and Sing" (Isa)
2142	"Blessed Quietness" (Isa, Advent)
3169	"You Feed Us, Gentle Savior" (Isa, Comm.)
108	"God Hath Spoken by the Prophets" (Isa, Mark) (O)
196	"Come, Thou Long-Expected Jesus" (Isa, Mark) (O)
203	"Hail to the Lord's Anointed" (Isa, Mark)
209	"Blessed Be the God of Israel" (Isa, Mark)
729	"O Day of Peace That Dimly Shines" (Pss)
3126	"Everything That Has Voice" (Pss)
213	"Lift Up Your Heads, Ye Mighty Gates" (Pss, 2 Pet)
725	"Arise, Shine Out, Your Light Has Come" (Pss, 2 Pet, Advent)
117	"O God Our Help in Ages Past" (2 Pet)
233	*"En el Frío Invernal"* ("Cold December Flies Away" (2 Pet, Advent)
383	"This Is a Day of New Beginnings" (2 Pet, Comm.)
384	"Love Divine, All Loves Excelling" (2 Pet)
666	"Shalom to You" (2 Pet) (C)
714	"I Know Whom I Have Believed" (2 Pet)
730	"O Day of God, Draw Nigh" (2 Pet, Advent)
3047	"God Almighty, We Are Waiting" (2 Pet, Advent)
3048	"View the Present through the Promise" (2 Pet, Advent)
220	"Angels from the Realms of Glory" (Mark)
473	"Lead Me, Lord" (Mark)
3045	"Down by the Jordan" (Mark)
619	"Now the Silence" (Comm., Advent)
626	"Let All Mortal Flesh Keep Silence (Comm., Advent)
2255	"In the Singing" (Comm., Advent)

Additional Contemporary Suggestions

UM186	"Alleluia" (Isa, Mark)
	S-2　#3-4
S2006	"Lord God Almighty" (Isa)
S2049	"God Is Here Today" (*"Dios Está Aquí"*) (Isa)
S2143	"O Lord, Your Tenderness" (Isa)
WS3167	"Feed Us, Lord" (Isa, Comm.)
WS3096	"Gentle Shepherd" (Isa)
M4	"Let It Rise" (Isa)
M62	"Rise Up and Praise Him" (Isa)
M103	"How Great Are You, Lord" (Isa, Pss)
M242	"Salvation Is Here" (Isa, Pss)
S2085	"He Came Down" (Isa, Pss, Advent)
WS3044	"Make Way" (Isa, Mark)
SP40	"God Will Make a Way" (Isa, Mark)
M275	"Prepare Ye the Way" ("You Reign on High") (Isa, Mark)
S2192	"Freedom Is Coming" (2 Peter)
S2194	"O Freedom" (2 Peter)
SP130	"While We Are Waiting, Come" (2 Peter, Advent)

S2071	"Jesus, Name above All Names" (Mark)
UM204	"Emmanuel, Emmanuel" (Advent)

Vocal Solos

"Comfort Ye"
"Every Valley"
"O Thou That Tellest Good Tidings to Zion" (Isa)
　　V-2
"He Shall Feed His Flock Like a Shepherd" (Isa)
　　V-2
　　V-8　　p. 334
"Lift Up Your Heads" (2 Pet, Pss)
　　V-10　　p. 38
"My Lord, What a Mornin'" (2 Pet)
　　V-7　　p. 68

Anthems

"Welcome to Our World" (Isa)
Arr. Jack Schrader; Hope C5191
SATB with piano (SAB C5847)

"O Come to Us, Emmanuel" (Isa, Mark)
Joseph M. Martin; Hope C-5778
SATB with piano (also available SAB)

Other Suggestions

Visuals:
O	God's outstretched hand, Bible, straight highway, wilderness, places of solitude, city streets, prairies, mountaintop, shepherd carrying a lamb, sheep
P	Kiss, images of peace, reconciliation
E	Fire, upheaval/peace, calm
G	Wilderness, water, rough fabric, leather, honeycomb, sandals, fire/dove (Holy Spirit)

Introit: UM207 or BOW211. "Prepare the Way" (Mark)
Litany: UM211. Advent Antiphons (Pss, Mark)
Greeting: BOW240 (Pss) or BOW307 (2 Pet)
Greeting: BOW241 or BOW248 (Isa, Mark)
Advent Wreath Readings: BOW262 (Advent)
Response: S2090. "Light the Advent Candle" (Advent)
Opening Prayer: BOW250 (Isa, Mark) or BOW464 (Pss, 2 Pet)
Canticle: UM199. "Canticle of Mary" (Isa) See S-1, p. 382.
Canticle: UM205. "Canticle of Light and Darkness" (Isa) See S-1, p. 383.
Canticle: UM734. "Canticle of Hope" (2 Pet)
Prayer of Confession: BOW478 (1 Pet)
Prayer: UM201. Advent
Prayer: BOW521. A Vision of Hope (Pss, 2 Pet)
Offering Prayer: WSL152 (Mark, Advent)
Great Thanksgiving for Advent: BOW54
Blessing: BOW246 (Isa)

Isaiah 61:1-4, 8-11

[1]The spirit of the Lord God is upon me,
    because the Lord has anointed me;
he has sent me to bring good news to the oppressed,
    to bind up the brokenhearted,
to proclaim liberty to the captives,
    and release to the prisoners;
[2]to proclaim the year of the Lord's favor,
    and the day of vengeance of our God;
    to comfort all who mourn;
[3]to provide for those who mourn in Zion—
    to give them a garland instead of ashes,
the oil of gladness instead of mourning,
    the mantle of praise instead of a faint spirit.
They will be called oaks of righteousness,
    the planting of the Lord, to display his glory.
[4]They shall build up the ancient ruins,
    they shall raise up the former devastations;
they shall repair the ruined cities,
    the devastations of many generations.

. . . .

[8]For I the Lord love justice,
    I hate robbery and wrongdoing;
I will faithfully give them their recompense,
    and I will make an everlasting covenant with them.
[9]Their descendants shall be known among the nations,
    and their offspring among the peoples;
all who see them shall acknowledge
    that they are a people whom the Lord has blessed.
[10]I will greatly rejoice in the Lord,
    my whole being shall exult in my God;
for he has clothed me with the garments of salvation,
    he has covered me with the robe of righteousness,
as a bridegroom decks himself with a garland,
    and as a bride adorns herself with her jewels.
[11]For as the earth brings forth its shoots,
    and as a garden causes what is sown in it to spring up,
so the Lord God will cause righteousness and praise
    to spring up before all the nations.

Psalm 126 (UM847)

[1]When the Lord restored the fortunes of Zion,
    we were like those who dream.
[2]Then our mouth was filled with laughter,
    and our tongue with shouts of joy;
then it was said among the nations,
    "The Lord has done great things for them."
[3]The Lord has done great things for us,
    and we rejoiced.
[4]Restore our fortunes, O Lord,
    like the watercourses in the Negeb.
[5]May those who sow in tears
    reap with shouts of joy.
[6]Those who go out weeping,
    bearing the seed for sowing,
shall come home with shouts of joy,
    carrying their sheaves.

1 Thessalonians 5:16-24

[16]Rejoice always, [17]pray without ceasing, [18]give thanks in all circumstances; for this is the will of God in Christ Jesus for you. [19]Do not quench the Spirit. [20]Do not despise the words of prophets, [21]but test everything; hold fast to what is good; [22]abstain from every form of evil.

[23]May the God of peace himself sanctify you entirely; and may your spirit and soul and body be kept sound and blameless at the coming of our Lord Jesus Christ. [24]The one who calls you is faithful, and he will do this.

John 1:6-8, 19-28

[6]There was a man sent from God, whose name was John. [7]He came as a witness to testify to the light, so that all might believe through him. [8]He himself was not the light, but he came to testify to the light. . . .

[19]This is the testimony given by John when the Jews sent priests and Levites from Jerusalem to ask him, "Who are you?" [20]He confessed and did not deny it, but confessed, "I am not the Messiah." [21]And they asked him, "What then? Are you Elijah?" He said, "I am not." "Are you the prophet?" He answered, "No." [22]Then they said to him, "Who are you? Let us have an answer for those who sent us. What do you say about yourself?" [23]He said,

    "I am the voice of one crying out in the wilderness,
    'Make straight the way of the Lord,'"
as the prophet Isaiah said.

[24]Now they had been sent from the Pharisees. [25]They asked him, "Why then are you baptizing if you are neither the Messiah, nor Elijah, nor the prophet?" [26]John answered them, "I baptize with water. Among you stands one whom you do not know, [27]the one who is coming after me; I am not worthy to untie the thong of his sandal." [28]This took place in Bethany across the Jordan where John was baptizing.

Primary Hymns and Songs for the Day

57	"O For a Thousand Tongues to Sing" (Isa) (O)	
	H-3	Hbl-79; Chr-142; Desc-17; Org-12
	S-1	#33-38. Various Treatments
203	"Hail to the Lord's Anointed" (Isa)	
	H-3	Hbl-16, 22, 68; Chr-101; Desc-37
	S-1	#114. Desc.
		#115. Harm.
670	"Go Forth for God" (1 Thess) (C)	
	S-1	#138-9. Harm. with Desc.
		#140. Harm.
	H-3	Hbl-77; Chr-63; Org-106
240,	"Hark! the Herald Angels Sing" (John) (C)	
4038	H-3	Hbl-26, 67; Chr-91; Desc-75; Org-89
	S-1	#234-6. Harm. and Desc.

Additional Hymn Suggestions

59	"*Mil Voces Para Celebrar*" (Isa)
60	"I'll Praise My Maker While I've Breath" (Isa)
64	"Holy, Holy, Holy! Lord God Almighty" (Isa)
65	"*¡Santo! ¡Santo! ¡Santo!*" (Isa)
196	"Come, Thou Long-Expected Jesus" (Isa)
200	"Tell Out, My Soul" (Isa)
333	"I'm Goin'a Sing When the Spirit Says Sing" (Isa)
573	"O Zion, Haste" (Isa)
2019	"Holy" ("*Santo*") (Isa)
2117	"Spirit of God" (Isa)
2177	"Wounded World that Cries for Healing" (Isa)
2241	"The Spirit Sends Us Forth to Serve" (Isa) (C)
3157	"Come, Let Us Dream" (Isa)
2210	"Joy Comes with the Dawn" (Isa., Pss)
2120	"Spirit of Gentleness" (Isa, Pss, John)
2172	"We Are Called" (Isa, John)
2236	"Gather Us In" (Isa, John) (O)
3047	"God Almighty, We Are Waiting" (Isa, John)
2182	"When God Restored Our Common Life" (Pss)
2279	"The Trees of the Field" (Pss) (C)
160	"Rejoice, Ye Pure in Heart" (Pss, 1 Thess) (O)
161	"Rejoice, Ye Pure in Heart" (Pss, 1 Thess)
2205	"The Fragrance of Christ" (1 Thess)
108	"God Hath Spoken by the Prophets" (John)
173	"Christ, Whose Glory Fills the Skies" (John)
182	"Word of God, Come Down on Earth" (John)
188	"Christ Is the World's Light" (John)
195	"Send Your Word" (John)
206	"I Want to Walk as a Child of the Light" (John)
214	"Savior of the Nations, Come" (John) (C)
473	"Lead Me, Lord" (John)
567	"Heralds of Christ" (John) (O)
2214	"Lead Me, Guide Me" (John)
2089	"Wild and Lone the Prophet's Voice" (John)
3045	"Down by the Jordan" (John)
3051	"A Star Shone Bright" (John, Advent)

Additional Contemporary Suggestions

S2109	"Hosanna! Hosanna!" (Isa)
S2039	"Holy, Holy" (Isa)
S2118	"Holy Spirit, Come to Us" (Isa, Advent)
S2143	"O Lord, Your Tenderness" (Isa)
WS3108	"Tradin' My Sorrows" (Isa, Pss)
WS3130	"Come, Emmanuel" (Isa, Pss, Advent)
WS3152	"Welcome" (Isa, Pss)
M263	"From the Inside Out" (Isa, Pss)
WS3044	"Make Way" (Isa, John, Advent)
S2074	"Shout to the Lord" (Pss)

S2017	"Come, Rejoice in God" (1 Thess)
S2164	"Sanctuary" (1 Thess)
S2186	"Song of Hope" ("*Canto de Esperanza*") (1 Thess)
S2193	"Lord, Listen to Your Children Praying" (1 Thess)
S2195	"In the Lord I'll Be Ever Thankful" (1 Thess)
S2273	"Jesus, We Are Here" (1 Thess)
WS3023	"Forever" (1 Thess)
SP150	"Rejoice" (1 Thess)
UM207	"Prepare the Way of the Lord" (John)
S2005	"Arise, Shine" (John)
S2071	"Jesus, Name above All Names" (John)
S2204	"Light of the World" (John)
SP48	"Behold, What Manner of Love" (John)
SP176	"Arise, Shine, for Your Light Is Come" (John)
M231	"Glory in the Highest" (John)
WS3105	"In Christ Alone" ("*My Hope Is Found*") (John)
WS3163	"Walking in the Light of God" (John)
WS3177	"Here I Am to Worship" (John)

Vocal Solos

"Come, Thou Long-Expected Jesus" (Isa)

V-1	p. 5
V-3(3)	p. 50
V-10	p. 11

"Rejoice Greatly, O Daughter of Zion" (Pss)

V-2	

Anthems

"The Spirit of the Lord" (Isa)
Kevin Siegfried; ECS Publishing 6335
SATB with organ

"Thou Shalt Know Him" (Isa, John)
Hal H. Hopson; Shawnee Press 35023258
SATB a cappella

Other Suggestions

Visuals:

O	Garland, oil, mantel, oak tree, rich garments/jewelry
P	Praise, tears of joy, sheaves of wheat
E	Praying hands, 1 Thess 5:16, 17
G	Water/baptism, light, John 1: 23 (Christ candle)

Introit: S2202. "Come Away with Me" (1 Thess)
Introit: UM202, stanza 3. "People, Look East" (Advent)
Greeting: BOW241 (John)
Greeting: BOW242 or BOW453 (Pss, 1 Thess)
Canticle: UM205. "Canticle of Light and Darkness" (John)
Opening Prayer: BOW252 (Isa, John)
Call to Prayer: S2118. "Holy Spirit, Come to Us" (Isa)
Prayer of Confession: UM201. Advent (Isa, John)
Prayer: UM489. For God's Gifts (John)
Prayer: BOW513. For Justice (Isa)
Prayer for Illumination: WSL75 (John, Advent)
Prayer of Thanksgiving/Intercession: BOW255 (John, Advent)
Response: UM473. "Lead Me, Lord" (John)
Offering Prayer: WSL136 (Advent)
Benediction: WSL165 (1 Thess)

2 Samuel 7:1-11, 16

[1]Now when the king was settled in his house, and the LORD had given him rest from all his enemies around him, [2]the king said to the prophet Nathan, "See now, I am living in a house of cedar, but the ark of God stays in a tent." [3]Nathan said to the king, "Go, do all that you have in mind; for the LORD is with you."

[4]But that same night the word of the LORD came to Nathan: [5]Go and tell my servant David: Thus says the LORD: Are you the one to build me a house to live in? [6]I have not lived in a house since the day I brought up the people of Israel from Egypt to this day, but I have been moving about in a tent and a tabernacle. [7]Wherever I have moved about among all the people of Israel, did I ever speak a word with any of the tribal leaders of Israel, whom I commanded to shepherd my people Israel, saying, "Why have you not built me a house of cedar?" [8]Now therefore thus you shall say to my servant David: Thus says the LORD of hosts: I took you from the pasture, from following the sheep to be prince over my people Israel; [9]and I have been with you wherever you went, and have cut off all your enemies from before you; and I will make for you a great name, like the name of the great ones of the earth. [10]And I will appoint a place for my people Israel and will plant them, so that they may live in their own place, and be disturbed no more; and evildoers shall afflict them no more, as formerly, [11]from the time that I appointed judges over my people Israel; and I will give you rest from all your enemies. Moreover the LORD declares to you that the LORD will make you a house. . . .

[16]Your house and your kingdom shall be made sure forever before me; your throne shall be established forever.

Luke 1:46b-55

[46b]"My soul magnifies the Lord,
[47] and my spirit rejoices in God my Savior,
[48]for he has looked with favor on the lowliness of his servant.
  Surely, from now on all generations will call me blessed;
[49]for the Mighty One has done great things for me,
  and holy is his name.
[50]His mercy is for those who fear him
  from generation to generation.
[51]He has shown strength with his arm;
  he has scattered the proud in the thoughts of their hearts.
[52]He has brought down the powerful from their thrones,
  and lifted up the lowly;
[53]he has filled the hungry with good things,
  and sent the rich away empty.
[54]He has helped his servant Israel,
  in remembrance of his mercy,
[55]according to the promise he made to our ancestors,
  to Abraham and to his descendants forever."

Romans 16:25-27

[25]Now to God who is able to strengthen you according to my gospel and the proclamation of Jesus Christ, according to the revelation of the mystery that was kept secret for long ages [26]but is now disclosed, and through the prophetic writings is made known to all the Gentiles, according to the command of the eternal God, to bring about the obedience of faith— [27]to the only wise God, through Jesus Christ, to whom be the glory forever! Amen.

Luke 1:26-38

[26]In the sixth month the angel Gabriel was sent by God to a town in Galilee called Nazareth, [27]to a virgin engaged to a man whose name was Joseph, of the house of David. The virgin's name was Mary. [28]And he came to her and said, "Greetings, favored one! The Lord is with you." [29]But she was much perplexed by his words and pondered what sort of greeting this might be. [30]The angel said to her, "Do not be afraid, Mary, for you have found favor with God. [31]And now, you will conceive in your womb and bear a son, and you will name him Jesus. [32]He will be great, and will be called the Son of the Most High, and the Lord God will give to him the throne of his ancestor David. [33]He will reign over the house of Jacob forever, and of his kingdom there will be no end." [34]Mary said to the angel, "How can this be, since I am a virgin?" [35]The angel said to her, "The Holy Spirit will come upon you, and the power of the Most High will overshadow you; therefore the child to be born will be holy; he will be called Son of God. [36]And now, your relative Elizabeth in her old age has also conceived a son; and this is the sixth month for her who was said to be barren. [37]For nothing will be impossible with God." [38]Then Mary said, "Here am I, the servant of the Lord; let it be with me according to your word." Then the angel departed from her.

Primary Hymns and Songs for the Day

203	"Hail to the Lord's Anointed" (2 Sam, Luke) (O)	
	H-3	Hbl-16, 22, 68; Chr-101; Desc-37
	S-1	#114. Desc.
		#115. Harm.
198	"My Soul Gives Glory to My God" (Luke)	
215	"To a Maid Engaged to Joseph" (Luke)	
2036	"Give Thanks" (Luke)	
3048	"View the Present through the Promise" (Luke)	
218	"It Came Upon the Midnight Clear" (2 Sam, Luke) (C)	
	H-3	Hbl-72; Chr-113; Desc-22; Org-19
	S-2	#39. Desc.

Additional Hymn Suggestions

209	"Blessed Be the God of Israel" (2 Sam)
211	"O Come, O Come, Emmanuel" (2 Sam)
216	"Lo, How a Rose E'er Blooming" (2 Sam, Luke)
241	"That Boy-Child of Mary" (2 Sam, Luke)
593	"Here I Am, Lord" (2 Sam, Luke)
98	"To God Be the Glory" (Rom)
103	"Immortal, Invisible, God Only Wise" (Rom)
60	"I'll Praise My Maker While I've Breath" (Luke)
196	"Come, Thou Long-Expected Jesus" (Luke) (O)
197	"Ye Who Claim the Faith of Jesus" (Luke)
200	"Tell Out, My Soul" (Luke)
202	"People, Look East" (Luke)
214	"Savior of the Nations, Come" (Luke)
221	"In the Bleak Midwinter" (Luke)
228	"He Is Born" ("*Il Est Né*") (Luke)
234	"O Come, All Ye Faithful" (Luke) (O)
250	"Once in Royal David's City" (Luke)
272	"Sing of Mary, Pure and Lowly" (Luke)
276	"The First One Ever" (Luke)
2093	"The Snow Lay on the Ground" (Luke)
2098	"The Virgin Mary Had a Baby Boy" (Luke)
2099	"Joseph Dearest, Joseph Mine" (Luke)
2120	"Spirit of Gentleness" (Luke)
2122	"She Comes Sailing on the Wind" (Luke)
2151	"I'm So Glad Jesus Lifted Me" (Luke)
2155	"Blest Are They" (Luke)
3059	"Love Has Come" (Luke)
3061	"See Him Lying on a Bed of Straw" (Luke)
3157	"Come, Let Us Dream" (Luke)

Additional Contemporary Suggestions

S2188	"The Family Prayer Song" (2 Sam)
M92	"All Things Are Possible" (2 Sam, Luke)
M37	"He Is Able" (Rom)
2208	"Guide My Feet" (Rom)
SP181	"God Is the Strength of My Heart" (Rom)
WS3040	"You Are My All in All" (Rom, Luke)
S2029	"Praise to the Lord" (Luke)
S2033	"Glory to God" ("*Gloria a Dios*") (Luke)
WS3015	"How Great You Are" (Luke)
WS3042	"Shout to the North" (Luke)
WS3044	"Make Way" (Luke, Advent)
WS3050	"Until Jesus Comes" (Luke, Advent)
WS3057	"Glory in the Highest" ("*Gloria en las Alturas*") (Luke)
WS3106	"Your Grace Is Enough" (Luke)
WS3190	"Mary Had a Little Lamb" (Luke, Advent)
SP4	"Great and Mighty Is He" (Luke)
M17	"This Kingdom" (Luke)
M88	"Holy Spirit, Rain Down" (Luke)

M164	"Good to Me" (Luke)
M237	"My Savior Lives"

Vocal Solos

"Behold, A Virgin Shall Conceive" (Luke)
　　V-2
"Sing of Mary, Pure and Lowly" (Luke)
　　V-5(1)　　p. 21
"Mary Had a Baby" (Luke)
　　V-7　　p. 46
"Nativity Lullaby" (Luke)
　　V-9　　p. 10
"Sleep, Little Baby" (Luke, Christmas)
　　V-10　　p. 27

Anthems

"Mary, Did You Know" (Luke)
Arr. Craig Courtney; Beckenhorst CU1034
SATB with piano

"Lo, How a Rose E'er Blooming" (Luke)
Donald Bailey; Gentry Publications JG2251
SATB divisi, a cappella

Other Suggestions

Visuals:

O	Cedar, crown, tent, ark of the covenant (chest)
G	Luke 1:46b, food, hungry being fed
E	Open Bible, Christ, servant, obedience
G	Luke 1:28 ff, angel, Mary, annunciation, servant imagery, Luke 1:38

Greeting: BOW246 (Luke)
Advent Wreath Readings: BOW262 (Advent)
Response: S2090. "Light the Advent Candle" (Advent)
Opening Prayer: BOW253 (Advent) or BOW473 (Winter)
Canticle: UM208. "Canticle of Zechariah" (2 Sam) (See S-1, p. 384.)
Canticle: UM112, Response 2. "Canticle of Wisdom" (Rom)
Canticle: UM199. "Canticle of Mary" (Luke) (See S-1, p. 382.)
As an alternative to reading the Canticle of Mary (the Magnificat reading), have the choir lead the congregation in singing UM198, "My Soul Gives Glory to My God."
Prayers: WSL6, BOW256 and BOW257 (Luke)
Prayer: BOW527. For the World (2 Sam, Luke)
Offering Prayer: WSL135 or WSL148 (Luke, Advent)
Blessing: BOW563

Isaiah 9:2-7

2 The people who walked in darkness
   have seen a great light;
those who lived in a land of deep darkness—
   on them light has shined.
3 You have multiplied the nation,
   you have increased its joy;
they rejoice before you
   as with joy at the harvest,
   as people exult when dividing plunder.
4 For the yoke of their burden,
   and the bar across their shoulders,
   the rod of their oppressor,
   you have broken as on the day of Midian.
5 For all the boots of the tramping warriors
   and all the garments rolled in blood
   shall be burned as fuel for the fire.
6 For a child has been born for us,
   a son given to us;
authority rests upon his shoulders;
   and he is named
Wonderful Counselor, Mighty God,
   Everlasting Father, Prince of Peace.
7 His authority shall grow continually,
   and there shall be endless peace
for the throne of David and his kingdom.
   He will establish and uphold it
with justice and with righteousness
   from this time onward and forevermore.
The zeal of the LORD of hosts will do this.

Psalm 96 (UM815)

1 O sing to the LORD a new song;
   sing to the LORD, all the earth.
2 Sing to the LORD, bless his name;
   tell of his salvation from day to day.
3 Declare his glory among the nations,
   his marvelous works among all the peoples.
4 For great is the LORD, and greatly to be praised;
   he is to be revered above all gods.
5 For all the gods of the peoples are idols,
   but the LORD made the heavens.
6 Honor and majesty are before him;
   strength and beauty are in his sanctuary.
7 Ascribe to the LORD, O families of the peoples,
   ascribe to the LORD glory and strength.
8 Ascribe to the LORD the glory due his name;
   bring an offering, and come into his courts.
9 Worship the LORD in holy splendor;
   tremble before him, all the earth.
10 Say among the nations, "The LORD is king!
   The world is firmly established; it shall never be moved.
   He will judge the peoples with equity."
11 Let the heavens be glad, and let the earth rejoice;
   let the sea roar, and all that fills it;
12   let the field exult, and everything in it.
Then shall all the trees of the forest sing for joy
13   before the LORD; for he is coming,
   for he is coming to judge the earth.
He will judge the world with righteousness,
   and the peoples with his truth.

Titus 2:11-14

11 For the grace of God has appeared, bringing salvation to all, 12 training us to renounce impiety and worldly passions, and in the present age to live lives that are self-controlled, upright, and godly, 13 while we wait for the blessed hope and the manifestation of the glory of our great God and Savior, Jesus Christ. 14 He it is who gave himself for us that he might redeem us from all iniquity and purify for himself a people of his own who are zealous for good deeds.

Luke 2:1-20

1 In those days a decree went out from Emperor Augustus that all the world should be registered. 2 This was the first registration and was taken while Quirinius was governor of Syria. 3 All went to their own towns to be registered. 4 Joseph also went from the town of Nazareth in Galilee to Judea, to the city of David called Bethlehem, because he was descended from the house and family of David. 5 He went to be registered with Mary, to whom he was engaged and who was expecting a child. 6 While they were there, the time came for her to deliver her child. 7 And she gave birth to her firstborn son and wrapped him in bands of cloth, and laid him in a manger, because there was no place for them in the inn.
8 In that region there were shepherds living in the fields, keeping watch over their flock by night. 9 Then an angel of the Lord stood before them, and the glory of the Lord shone around them, and they were terrified. 10 But the angel said to them, "Do not be afraid; for see—I am bringing you good news of great joy for all the people: 11 to you is born this day in the city of David a Savior, who is the Messiah, the Lord. 12 This will be a sign for you: you will find a child wrapped in bands of cloth and lying in a manger." 13 And suddenly there was with the angel a multitude of the heavenly host, praising God and saying,
14 "Glory to God in the highest heaven,
   and on earth peace among those whom he favors!"
15 When the angels had left them and gone into heaven, the shepherds said to one another, "Let us go now to Bethlehem and see this thing that has taken place, which the Lord has made known to us." 16 So they went with haste and found Mary and Joseph, and the child lying in the manger. 17 When they saw this, they made known what had been told them about this child; 18 and all who heard it were amazed at what the shepherds told them. 19 But Mary treasured all these words and pondered them in her heart. 20 The shepherds returned, glorifying and praising God for all they had heard and seen, as it had been told them.

Primary Hymns and Songs for the Day

234 "O Come, All Ye Faithful" (Isa, Luke) (O)
  (See especially stanzas 1, 3, and 4)
   H-3 Hbl-78; Desc-12; Org-2
   S-1 #7-13. Various treatments

230 "O Little Town of Bethlehem" (Luke)
   H-3 Hbl-81; Chr-145; Desc-95; Org-141
   S-1 #304. Harm.

238 "Angels We Have Heard on High" (Luke) (festive close)
   H-3 Hbl-47; Chr-31; Desc-43; Org-45

239 "Silent Night, Holy Night" (Luke) (quiet close)
   H-3 Hbl-92; Chr-171; Desc-99; Org-159
   S-1 #322. Desc.
     #323. Guitar/Autoharp chords
   S-2 #167. Handbell Arr.

Additional Hymn Suggestions

562 "Jesus, Lord, We Look to Thee" (Isa)
567 "Heralds of Christ" (Isa)
2172 "We Are Called" (Isa)
2236 "Gather Us In" (Isa)
3059 "Love Has Come" (Isa, Luke)
3064 "On Christmas Night" (Isa, Luke)
2001 "We Sing to You, O God" (Pss)
2011 "We Sing of Your Glory" (Pss, Luke)
2255 "In the Singing" (Titus, Comm.)
2266 "Here Is Bread, Here Is Wine" (Titus, Comm.)
217 "Away in a Manger" (Luke)
219 "What Child Is This" (Luke)
224 "Good Christian Friends, Rejoice" (Luke)
227 "The Friendly Beasts" (Luke)
229 "Infant Holy, Infant Lowly" (Luke)
236 "While Shepherds Watched Their Flocks" (Luke)
240, 4038 "Hark! the Herald Angels Sing" (Luke)
242 "Love Came Down at Christmas" (Luke)
245 "The First Noel" (Luke)
248 "On This Day Earth Shall Ring" (Luke)
251 "Go, Tell It on the Mountain" (Luke)
2092 "Like a Child" (Luke)
2093 "The Snow Lay on the Ground" (Luke)
2096 "Rise Up, Shepherd, and Follow" (Luke)
2097 "One Holy Night in Bethlehem" (Luke)
2276 "Glory to God in the Highest" (Luke)
3061 "See Him Lying on a Bed of Straw" (Luke)
3065 "Some Children See Him" (Luke)
3066 "Still, Still, Still" (Luke)

Additional Contemporary Suggestions

UM174 "His Name Is Wonderful" (Isa)
S2075 "King of Kings" (Isa)
S2232 "Come Now, O Prince of Peace" ("*O-So-So*") (Isa)
S2204 "Light of the World" (Isa)
S2023 "How Majestic Is Your Name" (Isa)
S2071 "Jesus, Name above All Names" (Isa)
WS3060 "Jesus, Jesus, Oh, What a Wonderful Child" (Isa, Luke)
S2037 "I Sing Praises to Your Name" (Pss)
S2074 "Shout to the Lord" (Pss)
S2088 "Lord, I Lift Your Name on High" (Luke)
S2072 "Amen, Amen" (Luke)

Vocal Solos

"O Holy Night" (Luke)
 V-8 p. 93
"This Night in David's City" (Luke)
 V-9 p. 8
"Fit for a King" (Luke, Christmas)
 V-10 p. 32
"Sing Noel!" (Christmas)
 V-11 p. 13
"Welcome to Our World" (Luke, Christmas)
 V-5(1) p. 34
 WS3067

Anthems

"Child of Mary" (Luke)
Allen Pote: MorningStar 50-1360
SATB with piano and opt. handbells

"This Silent Night" (Luke)
Arr. Mark Patterson; Hope C-5885
SAB with piano, opt. Horn or C-Instrument

Other Suggestions

Visuals:
 O Joy, praise, Isa 9:6b
 P Musical notes, sea, field, trees, branches upraised, Ps 96:12b
 E Titus 2:11, Christ child, manger
 G Christ child, manger, Mary, Joseph, shepherds/angels, peace, joy, Luke 2:14, 19

Introit: UM244, stanzas 1 and 4 " 'Twas in the Moon of Wintertime" (Luke, Chrsitmas)
Introit: UM72 or S2033. "Gloria" (Luke)
Greeting: BOW271 (Luke) or BOW273 (Titus)
Christ Candle Prayer: BOW277 (Isa, Luke)
Response: S2090. "Light the Advent Candle" (Advent)
Opening Prayer: BOW276 or UM231 (Luke, Christmas)
Response: UM256, stanza 1. "We Would See Jesus" (Luke)
Canticle: UM82 or UM83 "Canticle of God's Glory" (Luke)
Canticle: UM91. "Canticle of Praise to God" (Pss)
Canticle: UM205. "Canticle of Light and Darkness" (Isa)
Prayer of Intercession: BOW279 (Luke)
Response: UM241, stanzas 2 and 5. "That Boy-Child of Mary" (Luke)
Call to Offering: WS3063. "If I Could Visit Bethlehem" (Luke)
Offering Prayer: WSL149. "Gracious God" (Christmas)
Great Thanksgiving for Christmas Eve: BOW56
See The Abingdon Worship Annual 2017 *for additional ideas.*
Alternate lessons for Christmas Day: Isa 52:7-10; Ps 98; Heb 1:1-4(5-12); John 1:1-14

Isaiah 61:10–62:3

[10] I will greatly rejoice in the LORD,
    my whole being shall exult in my God;
for he has clothed me with the garments of salvation,
    he has covered me with the robe of righteousness,
as a bridegroom decks himself with a garland,
    and as a bride adorns herself with her jewels.
[11] For as the earth brings forth its shoots,
    and as a garden causes what is sown in it to spring up,
so the Lord GOD will cause righteousness and praise
    to spring up before all the nations.
62 [1] For Zion's sake I will not keep silent,
    and for Jerusalem's sake I will not rest,
until her vindication shines out like the dawn,
    and her salvation like a burning torch.
[2] The nations shall see your vindication,
    and all the kings your glory;
and you shall be called by a new name
    that the mouth of the LORD will give.
[3] You shall be a crown of beauty in the hand of the LORD,
    and a royal diadem in the hand of your God.

Psalm 148 (UM861)

[1] Praise the LORD!
Praise the LORD from the heavens;
    praise him in the heights!
[2] Praise him, all his angels;
    praise him, all his host!
[3] Praise him, sun and moon;
    praise him, all you shining stars!
[4] Praise him, you highest heavens,
    and you waters above the heavens!
[5] Let them praise the name of the LORD,
    for he commanded and they were created.
[6] He established them forever and ever;
    he fixed their bounds, which cannot be passed.
[7] Praise the LORD from the earth,
    you sea monsters and all deeps,
[8] fire and hail, snow and frost,
    stormy wind fulfilling his command!
[9] Mountains and all hills,
    fruit trees and all cedars!
[10] Wild animals and all cattle,
    creeping things and flying birds!
[11] Kings of the earth and all peoples,
    princes and all rulers of the earth!
[12] Young men and women alike,
    old and young together!
[13] Let them praise the name of the LORD,
    for his name alone is exalted;
    his glory is above earth and heaven.
[14] He has raised up a horn for his people,
    praise for all his faithful,
    for the people of Israel who are close to him.
Praise the LORD!

Galatians 4:4-7

[4] But when the fullness of time had come, God sent his Son, born of a woman, born under the law, [5] in order to redeem those who were under the law, so that we might receive adoption as children. [6] And because you are children, God has sent the Spirit of his Son into our hearts, crying, "Abba! Father!" [7] So you are no longer a slave but a child, and if a child then also an heir, through God.

Luke 2:22-40

[22] When the time came for their purification according to the law of Moses, they brought him up to Jerusalem to present him to the Lord [23] (as it is written in the law of the Lord, "Every firstborn male shall be designated as holy to the Lord"), [24] and they offered a sacrifice according to what is stated in the law of the Lord, "a pair of turtledoves or two young pigeons."

[25] Now there was a man in Jerusalem whose name was Simeon; this man was righteous and devout, looking forward to the consolation of Israel, and the Holy Spirit rested on him. [26] It had been revealed to him by the Holy Spirit that he would not see death before he had seen the Lord's Messiah. [27] Guided by the Spirit, Simeon came into the temple; and when the parents brought in the child Jesus, to do for him what was customary under the law, [28] Simeon took him in his arms and praised God, saying,

[29] "Master, now you are dismissing your servant in peace,
    according to your word;
[30] for my eyes have seen your salvation,
[31]   which you have prepared in the presence of all peoples,
[32] a light for revelation to the Gentiles
    and for glory to your people Israel."

[33] And the child's father and mother were amazed at what was being said about him. [34] Then Simeon blessed them and said to his mother Mary, "This child is destined for the falling and the rising of many in Israel, and to be a sign that will be opposed [35] so that the inner thoughts of many will be revealed—and a sword will pierce your own soul too."

[36] There was also a prophet, Anna the daughter of Phanuel, of the tribe of Asher. She was of a great age, having lived with her husband seven years after her marriage, [37] then as a widow to the age of eighty-four. She never left the temple but worshiped there with fasting and prayer night and day. [38] At that moment she came, and began to praise God and to speak about the child to all who were looking for the redemption of Jerusalem.

[39] When they had finished everything required by the law of the Lord, they returned to Galilee, to their own town of Nazareth. [40] The child grew and became strong, filled with wisdom; and the favor of God was upon him.

Primary Hymns and Songs for the Day

62	"All Creatures of Our God and King" (Pss) (O)
	H-3 Hbl-44; Chr-21; Desc-66; Org-73
	S-1 #198-204. Various treatments
226	"My Master, See, the Time Has Come" (Luke)
	H-3 Chr-139, 145; Desc-77
	S-1 #241-242. Orff Arr. and Desc.
228	"He Is Born" ("*Il Est Né*") (Luke, Christmas)
	H-3 Chr-92
	S-1 #177. Orff Instr. Arr.
249	"There's a Song in the Air" (Luke, Christmas) (C)
	H-3 Chr-194
	S-2 #40. Desc.

Additional Hymn Suggestions

152	"I Sing the Almighty Power of God" (Isa, Gal)
240, 4038	"Hark! the Herald Angels Sing" (Isa, Gal, Christmas) (O)
203	"Hail to the Lord's Anointed" (Isa)
216	"Lo, How a Rose E'er Blooming" (Isa)
612	"Deck Thyself, My Soul, with Gladness" (Isa)
233	"*En el Frío Invernal*" ("Cold December Flies Away") (Isa, Gal)
77	"How Great Thou Art" (Pss)
151	"God Created Heaven and Earth" (Pss)
2008	"Let All Things Now Living" (Pss)
3018	"Creation Sings" (Pss)
2248	"Baptized in Water" (Gal, Baptism)
150	"God Who Stretched the Spangled Heavens" (Gal)
214	"Savior of the Nations, Come" (Gal)
364	"Because He Lives" (Gal)
605	"Wash, O God, Our Sons and Daughters" (Gal)
250	"Once in Royal David's City" (Gal, Luke)
206	"I Want to Walk as a Child of the Light" (Luke)
217	"Away in a Manger" (Luke, Christmas)
219	"What Child Is This" (Luke, Christmas)
237	"Sing We Now of Christmas" (Luke, Christmas)
241	"That Boy-Child of Mary" (Luke, Christmas)
272	"Sing of Mary, Pure and Lowly" (Luke)
447	"Our Parent, by Whose Name" (Luke)
668	"Let Us Now Depart in Thy Peace" (Luke)
2092	"Like a Child" (Luke, Christmas)
2099	"Joseph Dearest, Joseph Mine" (Luke, Christmas)
2197	"Lord of All Hopefulness" (Luke)
2236	"Gather Us In" (Luke)
3058	"Mary Had a Baby" (Luke, Christmas)
3062	"Spirit-Child Jesus" (Luke, Christmas)
671	"Lord, Dismiss Us with Thy Blessing" (Luke) (C)

Additional Contemporary Suggestions

SP237	"Garment of Praise" (Isa)
S2018	"Honor and Praise" (Pss)
M59	"Let Everything That Has Breath" (Pss)
WS3034	"God of Wonders" (Pss)
M231	"Glory in the Highest" (Pss, Christmas)
M238	"Cannons" (Pss)
S2003	"Praise You" (Pss, Luke)
S2039	"Holy, Holy" (Gal, Comm.)
S2088	"Lord, I Lift Your Name on High" (Gal, Luke)
S2069	"All Hail King Jesus" (Luke)
S2071	"Jesus, Name above All Names" (Luke)
S2098	"The Virgin Mary Had a Baby Boy" (Luke, Christmas)
S2173	"Shine, Jesus, Shine" (Luke)
WS3053	"Bethlehem" (Luke, Christmas)

WS3060	"Jesus, Jesus, Oh, What a Wonderful Child" (Luke, Christmas)
WS3162	"Stand in Awe" (Luke)
UM186	"Alleluia" (Luke, Christmas)
UM665	"Go Now in Peace" (Luke)

Vocal Solos

"Sing a Song of Joy" (Pss)
V-4   p. 2
"Gentle Jesus, Meek and Mild" (Luke, Christmas)
V-1   p. 11
"Glory Hallelujah to de New-Born King" (Luke, Christmas)
V-7   p. 80
"Sing for Christ Is Born" (Luke, Christmas)
V-10   p. 16

Anthems

"Jesus, Oh, What a Wonderful Child" (Luke, Christmas)
Arr. Lloyd Larson; Hope C-5898
Two-part mixed with piano

"Christmas Is the Harvest Time of Love" (Christmas)
Helen Kemp; Choristers Guild CGA1317
Unison/two-part with piano

Other Suggestions

Today may also be celebrated as Epiphany Sunday, using January 6 scriptures and ideas.
Alternately, you may choose to use Watch Night scriptures.
Visuals:

O	Wedding garments, crown, garland, Spring garden,
P	Celestial imagery, nature imagery, all ages of people praising
E	Clock, open manacles, children's toys
G	Baby, elderly man/woman, Christ candle

Introit: UM244, stanzas 2 and 4. "'Twas in the Moon of Wintertime" (Christmas)
Introit: BOW213. "Christ Is Born" (Gal)
Greeting: BOW274 (Isa, Pss) or BOW275 (Luke)
Opening Prayer: BOW277 (Luke) or BOW463 (Gal)
Canticle: UM225. "Canticle of Simeon" (Luke) See S-1, p. 386.
Response: 2276. "Glory to God in the Highest" (Luke)
Prayer of Confession: WSL43. "We often act" (Gal)
Prayer: WSL69. "Creator God, how great" (Pss)
Prayer: UM231 (Gal)
Prayer: BOW316. Presentation of Jesus (Luke)
Prayer: BOW524. For Strength (Luke)
Sung Benediction: WS3182. "Benediction Hymn" (Luke)
See Christmas Eve/Day for additional Christmas carols.

Ecclesiastes 3:1-13

[1]For everything there is a season, and a time for every matter under heaven:

[2]a time to be born, and a time to die;

a time to plant, and a time to pluck up what is planted;

[3]a time to kill, and a time to heal;

a time to break down, and a time to build up;

[4]a time to weep, and a time to laugh;

a time to mourn, and a time to dance;

[5]a time to throw away stones, and a time to gather stones together;

a time to embrace, and a time to refrain from embracing;

[6]a time to seek, and a time to lose;

a time to keep, and a time to throw away;

[7]a time to tear, and a time to sew;

a time to keep silence, and a time to speak;

[8]a time to love, and a time to hate;

a time for war, and a time for peace.

[9]What gain have the workers from their toil? [10]I have seen the business that God has given to everyone to be busy with. [11]He has made everything suitable for its time; moreover he has put a sense of past and future into their minds, yet they cannot find out what God has done from the beginning to the end. [12]I know that there is nothing better for them than to be happy and enjoy themselves as long as they live; [13]moreover, it is God's gift that all should eat and drink and take pleasure in all their toil.

Psalm 8 (UM743)

[1]O LORD, our Sovereign,

how majestic is your name in all the earth!

You have set your glory above the heavens.

[2]Out of the mouths of babes and infants

you have founded a bulwark because of your foes,

to silence the enemy and the avenger.

[3]When I look at your heavens, the work of your fingers,

the moon and the stars that you have established;

[4]what are human beings that you are mindful of them,

mortals that you care for them?

[5]Yet you have made them a little lower than God,

and crowned them with glory and honor.

[6]You have given them dominion over the works of your hands;

you have put all things under their feet,

[7]all sheep and oxen,

and also the beasts of the field,

[8]the birds of the air, and the fish of the sea,

whatever passes along the paths of the seas.

[9]O LORD, our Sovereign,

how majestic is your name in all the earth!

Revelation 21:1-6a

[1]Then I saw a new heaven and a new earth; for the first heaven and the first earth had passed away, and the sea was no more. [2]And I saw the holy city, the new Jerusalem, coming down out of heaven from God, prepared as a bride adorned for her husband. [3]And I heard a loud voice from the throne saying,

"See, the home of God is among mortals.

He will dwell with them as their God;

they will be his peoples,

and God himself will be with them;

[4]he will wipe every tear from their eyes.

Death will be no more;

mourning and crying and pain will be no more,

for the first things have passed away."

[5]And the one who was seated on the throne said, "See, I am making all things new." Also he said, "Write this, for these words are trustworthy and true." [6a]Then he said to me, "It is done! I am the Alpha and the Omega, the beginning and the end.

Matthew 25:31-46

[31]"When the Son of Man comes in his glory, and all the angels with him, then he will sit on the throne of his glory. [32]All the nations will be gathered before him, and he will separate people one from another as a shepherd separates the sheep from the goats, [33]and he will put the sheep at his right hand and the goats at the left. [34]Then the king will say to those at his right hand, 'Come, you that are blessed by my Father, inherit the kingdom prepared for you from the foundation of the world; [35]for I was hungry and you gave me food, I was thirsty and you gave me something to drink, I was a stranger and you welcomed me, [36]I was naked and you gave me clothing, I was sick and you took care of me, I was in prison and you visited me.' [37]Then the righteous will answer him, 'Lord, when was it that we saw you hungry and gave you food, or thirsty and gave you something to drink? [38]And when was it that we saw you a stranger and welcomed you, or naked and gave you clothing? [39]And when was it that we saw you sick or in prison and visited you?' [40]And the king will answer them, 'Truly I tell you, just as you did it to one of the least of these who are members of my family, you did it to me.' [41]Then he will say to those at his left hand, 'You that are accursed, depart from me into the eternal fire prepared for the devil and his angels; [42]for I was hungry and you gave me no food, I was thirsty and you gave me nothing to drink, [43]I was a stranger and you did not welcome me, naked and you did not give me clothing, sick and in prison and you did not visit me.' [44]Then they also will answer, 'Lord, when was it that we saw you hungry or thirsty or a stranger or naked or sick or in prison, and did not take care of you?' [45]Then he will answer them, 'Truly I tell you, just as you did not do it to one of the least of these, you did not do it to me.' [46]And these will go away into eternal punishment, but the righteous into eternal life."

Primary Hymns and Songs for the Day
707   "Hymn of Promise" (Eccl) (O)
      H-3   Chr-112; Org-117
      S-1   #270. Desc.
2023   "How Majestic Is Your Name" (Pss)
383   "This Is a Day of New Beginnings" (Rev, Comm.)
      H-3   Chr-196
192   "There's a Spirit in the Air" (Matt)
      S-2   #144. Orff Instr. Arr.
569   "We've a Story to Tell to the Nations" (Rev, Matt) (C)
      H-3   Chr-210; Org-91

Additional Hymn Suggestions
117   "O God, Our Help in Ages Past" (Eccl) (O) or (C)
524   "Beams of Heaven as I Go" (Eccl, Rev)
77   "How Great Thou Art" (Pss)
384   "Love Divine, All Loves Excelling" (Rev)
388   "O Come and Dwell in Me" (Rev)
510   "Come, Ye Disconsolate" (Rev)
533   "We Shall Overcome" (Rev)
722   "I Want to Be Ready" (Rev)
726   "O Holy City, Seen of John" (Rev)
727   "O What Their Joy and Their Glory Must Be" (Rev)
2142   "Blessed Quietness" (Rev)
2210   "Joy Comes with the Dawn" (Rev)
2284   "Joy in the Morning" (Rev)
428   "For the Healing of the Nations" (Rev)
2126   "All Who Hunger" (Rev, Matt, Comm.)
203   "Hail to the Lord's Anointed" (Matt)
434   "*Cuando El Pobre*" ("When the Poor Ones") (Matt)
591   "Rescue the Perishing" (Matt)
629   "You Satisfy the Hungry Heart" (Matt, Comm.)
634   "Now Let Us from This Table Rise" (Matt, Comm.)
2048   "God Weeps" (Matt)
2094   "Carol of the Epiphany" (Matt)
2095   "Star-Child" (Matt, New Year)
2126   "All Who Hunger" (Matt, Comm.)
2175   "Together We Serve" (Matt, Covenant Renewal)
2178   "Here Am I" (Matt)
3128   "Whatever You Do" (Matt)
2254   "In Remembrance of Me" (Matt, Comm.)
2268   "As We Gather at Your Table" (Matt, Comm.)
3167   "Feed Us, Lord" (Matt, Comm.)
3169   "You Feed Us, Gentle Savior" (Matt, Comm.)

Additional Contemporary Suggestions
S2203   "In His Time" (Eccl)
M63   "I Could Sing of Your Love Forever" (Eccl)
M152   "Be Glorified" (Eccl, Matt)
M165   "Friend of God" (Pss, Matt)
M178   "Majestic" (Pss)
M252   "God with Us" (Pss)
WS3027   "Hallelujah" ("Your Love Is Amazing") (Pss)
WS3034   "God of Wonders" (Pss)
WS3032   "Across the Lands" (Pss)
UM706   "Soon and Very Soon" (Rev)
S2087   "We Will Glorify" (Pss, Rev)
S2194   "O Freedom" (Rev)
UM347   "Spirit Song" (Rev)
UM171   "There's Something About That Name" (Rev)
M21   "Blessing, Honor and Glory" (Rev)
M23   "Hallelujah to the Lamb" (Rev)
M27   "We Will Worship the Lamb of Glory" (Rev)
M32   "Holy and Anointed One" (Rev)
M55   "Jehovah Reigns" (Rev)

M69   "Did You Feel the Mountains Tremble?" (Rev)
M31   "I See the Lord" (Rev, Matt)
SP60   "To Him Who Sits on the Throne" (Rev, Matt)
S2132   "You Who Are Thirsty" (Rev, Matt)
S2244   "People Need the Lord" (Matt)

Vocal Solos
"I Will Sing of Thy Great Mercies" (Eccl)
      V-4   p. 43
"My Lord, What a Mornin'" (Rev)
      V-7   p. 68
"Reach Out to Your Neighbor" (Matt)
      V-8   p. 372
"A Covenant Prayer" (New Year, Covenant Service)
      V-11   p. 6

Anthems
"Soon and Very Soon" (Rev)
Arr. Lloyd Larson; Lorenz 10/4639L
SATB with piano, opt instrumental ensemble

"Creation of Peace" (Rev)
Mark Miller; Abingdon Press 9790300601939
SATB with piano and opt. solo

Other Suggestions
These scriptures may also be used on Sunday morning, December 31.
Visuals:
    O   Clock, many images from text
    P   Infants, all ages, outer space, nature
    E   Butterfly, chrysalis, bride, portrait of Christ
    G   Shepherd, sheep, goats, ministries to others
Covenant Renewal Service: BOW288
Greeting: BOW294 (New Year)
Opening Prayer: WSL64 (Pss, Covenant Renewal)
Canticle: UM734. "Canticle of Hope" (Rev)
Prayer of Confession: WSL87 or BOW494 (Matt)
Prayer: UM607. A Covenant Prayer in the Wesleyan Tradition
    (New Year)
Prayer: BOW294 (New Year)
Prayer: BOW510. For Discernment (Eccl)
Prayer: UM639. Bread and Justice (Matt)
Prayer: BOW519. For Others (Matt)
Litany: BOW508. Psalm of the Woodlands (Pss, Matt)
Prayer of Thanksgiving: BOW556 (Pss)
Great Thanksgiving for New Year: BOW58
Blessing: BOW564 (Rev, Matt)
Benediction or Sending Words: WSL169 (Matt)
Sung Benediction: UM383, stanza 4. "This Is a Day of New
    Beginnings" (Rev)

Isaiah 60:1-6

[1]Arise, shine; for your light has come,
  and the glory of the LORD has risen upon you.
[2]For darkness shall cover the earth,
  and thick darkness the peoples;
but the LORD will arise upon you,
  and his glory will appear over you.
[3]Nations shall come to your light,
  and kings to the brightness of your dawn.
[4]Lift up your eyes and look around;
  they all gather together, they come to you;
your sons shall come from far away,
  and your daughters shall be carried on their nurses' arms.
[5]Then you shall see and be radiant;
  your heart shall thrill and rejoice,
because the abundance of the sea shall be brought to you,
  the wealth of the nations shall come to you.
[6]A multitude of camels shall cover you,
  the young camels of Midian and Ephah;
  all those from Sheba shall come.
They shall bring gold and frankincense,
  and shall proclaim the praise of the LORD.

Psalm 72:1-7, 10-14 (UM795)

[1]Give the king your justice, O God,
  and your righteousness to a king's son.
[2]May he judge your people with righteousness,
  and your poor with justice.
[3]May the mountains yield prosperity for the people,
  and the hills, in righteousness.
[4]May he defend the cause of the poor of the people,
  give deliverance to the needy,
  and crush the oppressor.
[5]May he live while the sun endures,
  and as long as the moon, throughout all generations.
[6]May he be like rain that falls on the mown grass,
  like showers that water the earth.
[7]In his days may righteousness flourish
  and peace abound, until the moon is no more.
. . . .
[10]May the kings of Tarshish and of the isles
  render him tribute,
may the kings of Sheba and Seba bring gifts.
[11]May all kings fall down before him,
  all nations give him service.
[12]For he delivers the needy when they call,
  the poor and those who have no helper.
[13]He has pity on the weak and the needy,
  and saves the lives of the needy.
[14]From oppression and violence he redeems their life;
  and precious is their blood in his sight.

Ephesians 3:1-12

[1]This is the reason that I Paul am a prisoner for Christ Jesus for the sake of you Gentiles— [2]for surely you have already heard of the commission of God's grace that was given me for you, [3]and how the mystery was made known to me by revelation, as I wrote above in a few words, [4]a reading of which will enable you to perceive my understanding of the mystery of Christ. [5]In former generations this mystery was not made known to humankind, as it has now been revealed to his holy apostles and prophets by the Spirit: [6]that is, the Gentiles have become fellow heirs, members of the same body, and sharers in the promise in Christ Jesus through the gospel.

[7]Of this gospel I have become a servant according to the gift of God's grace that was given me by the working of his power. [8]Although I am the very least of all the saints, this grace was given to me to bring to the Gentiles the news of the boundless riches of Christ, [9]and to make everyone see what is the plan of the mystery hidden for ages in God who created all things; [10]so that through the church the wisdom of God in its rich variety might now be made known to the rulers and authorities in the heavenly places. [11]This was in accordance with the eternal purpose that he has carried out in Christ Jesus our Lord, [12]in whom we have access to God in boldness and confidence through faith in him.

Matthew 2:1-12

[1]In the time of King Herod, after Jesus was born in Bethlehem of Judea, wise men from the East came to Jerusalem, [2]asking, "Where is the child who has been born king of the Jews? For we observed his star at its rising, and have come to pay him homage." [3]When King Herod heard this, he was frightened, and all Jerusalem with him; [4]and calling together all the chief priests and scribes of the people, he inquired of them where the Messiah was to be born. [5]They told him, "In Bethlehem of Judea; for so it has been written by the prophet:
[6]'And you, Bethlehem, in the land of Judah,
  are by no means least among the rulers of Judah;
for from you shall come a ruler
  who is to shepherd my people Israel.'"
[7]Then Herod secretly called for the wise men and learned from them the exact time when the star had appeared. [8]Then he sent them to Bethlehem, saying, "Go and search diligently for the child; and when you have found him, bring me word so that I may also go and pay him homage." [9]When they had heard the king, they set out; and there, ahead of them, went the star that they had seen at its rising, until it stopped over the place where the child was. [10]When they saw that the star had stopped, they were overwhelmed with joy. [11]On entering the house, they saw the child with Mary his mother; and they knelt down and paid him homage. Then, opening their treasure chests, they offered him gifts of gold, frankincense, and myrrh. [12]And having been warned in a dream not to return to Herod, they left for their own country by another road

Primary Hymns and Songs for the Day
220   "Angels from the Realms of Glory" (Matt) (O)
     H-3   Chr-30, 48, 62; Desc-89; Org-121
     S-1   #280. Desc. and Harm.
219   "What Child Is This" (Matt)
     H-3   Hbl-102; Chr-210; Desc-46; Org-47
     S-1   #150. Guitar chords
254   "We Three Kings" (Matt)
     H-3   Chr-208; Org-65
245   "The First Noel" (Matt) (C)
     H-3   Hbl-95; Chr-182; Desc-100; Org-161
     S-1   #328-330. Various treatments

Additional Hymn Suggestions
187   "Rise, Shine, You People" (Isa)
223   "Break Forth, O Beauteous Heavenly Light" (Isa)
585   "This Little Light of Mine" (Isa)
725   "Arise, Shine Out, Your Light Has Come" (Isa)
2236   "Gather Us In" (Isa)
2172   "We Are Called" (Isa, Pss)
247   "O Morning Star, How Fair and Bright" (Isa, Matt)
157   "Jesus Shall Reign" (Pss)
203   "Hail to the Lord's Anointed" (Pss)
2177   "Wounded World that Cries for Healing" (Pss)
2178   "Here Am I" (Pss)
2182   "When God Restored Our Common Life" (Pss)
103   "Immortal, Invisible, God Only Wise" (Eph)
421   "Make Me a Captive, Lord" (Eph)
251   "Go, Tell It on the Mountain" (Eph, Matt) (C)
216   "Lo, How a Rose E'er Blooming" (Matt)
237   "Sing We Now of Christmas" (Matt)
243   *De Tierra Lejana Venimos* ("From a Distant Home") (Matt)
248   "On This Day Earth Shall Ring" (Matt)
256   "We Would See Jesus" (Matt)
383   "This Is a Day of New Beginnings" (New Year, Comm.)
2094   "Carol of the Epiphany" (Matt)
2095   "Star-Child" (Matt)
2096   "Rise Up, Shepherd, and Follow" (Matt)
2098   "The Virgin Mary Had a Baby Boy" (Matt)
3051   "A Star Shone Bright" (Matt)
3061   "See Him Lying on a Bed of Straw" (Matt)
3062   "Spirit-Child Jesus" (Matt)
3063   "If I Could Visit Bethlehem" (Matt)
3149   "A Place at the Table" (Matt, Comm.)

Additional Contemporary Suggestions
S2005   "Arise, Shine" (Isa)
S2173   "Shine, Jesus, Shine" (Isa, Epiphany)
     SP142; V-3(2)   p. 48 Vocal Solo
WS3038   "Mighty to Save" (Isa)
WS3056   "Jesus, the Light of the World" (Isa, Epiphany)
WS3177   "Here I Am to Worship" (Isa, Epiphany)
SP176   "Arise, Shine" (Isa)
M4   "Let It Rise" (Isa)
M19   "Shine on Us" (Isa, Epiphany)
UM63   "Blessed Be the Name" (Pss)
     S2034 (different tune)
M235   "Sing, Sing, Sing" (Pss, Matt)
S2162   "Grace Alone" (Eph)
S2018   "Honor and Praise" (Matt, Epiphany)
S2069   "All Hail King Jesus" (Matt, Epiphany)
WS3062   "Spirit-Child Jesus" (Matt, New Year)
SP103   "We Worship and Adore You" (Matt)
M18   "Come and Behold Him" (Matt)

UM186   "Alleluia" (Matt, Epiphany)
     S-2   #3-4

Vocal Solos
"O Thou That Tellest Good Tidings to Zion" (Isa)
"The People That Walked in Darkness" (Isa)
     V-2
"Behold That Star!" (Matt, Epiphany)
     V-3 (1)   p. 34
"A Scottish Christmas Song" (Matt)
     V-4   p. 4
"Jesus, What a Wonderful Child" (Matt, Epiphany)
(with "Go, Tell It on the Mountain")
     V-5(1)   p. 48
"The Kings" (Matt)
     V-9   p. 13

Anthems
"Arise, Shine; for Your Light has Come" (Isa., Matt)
Robert A. Hobby; MorningStar 50-2008
SATB with organ

"Go, Tell It on the Mountain" (Eph, Matt)
Robert A. Hobby; MorningStar 50-1958
SATRB with keyboard

Other Suggestions
Visuals:
     O   Light, gold, frankincense, crown
     P   Deliverance, poor and needy being helped, sun, moon, rain, kings, gifts
     E   Manacles, towel, bowl/pitcher (servant)
     G   Kings, gold, frankincense, myrrh (gifts), star
Introit: BOW216. "Arise, Shine" (Isa)
Introit: S2118. "Holy Spirit, Come to Us" (Pss)
Introit: UM244, stanzas 3 and 4. "'Twas in the Moon of Wintertime" (Matt)
Greeting: BOW296 (Epiphany), BOW304 (Isa,) or BOW455 (Matt)
Opening Prayer: BOW313 or BOW315 (Matt)
Centering Words: BOW472 (Matt, 1 Cor, Epiphany)
Canticle: UM225. Canticle of Simeon (Matt) See S-1, p. 386.
Prayer of Confession: BOW482 (Matt)
Prayer: UM255 or BOW297 (Epiphany, Matt)
Prayer: BOW510, BOW522, or BOW525 (Matt)
Great Thanksgiving for Epiphany: BOW58
Blessing: BOW562 (Matt, Epiphany)
For additional ideas, see *The Abingdon Worship Annual 2018.*
Alternate lessons for the 2nd Sunday after Christmas: Jer 31:7-14; Pss 147:12-20; Eph 1:3-14; John 1:(1-9), 10-16. See 2013–2014 edition for related suggestions.

Genesis 1:1-5

[1]In the beginning when God created the heavens and the earth, [2]the earth was a formless void and darkness covered the face of the deep, while a wind from God swept over the face of the waters. [3]Then God said, "Let there be light"; and there was light. [4]And God saw that the light was good; and God separated the light from the darkness. [5]God called the light Day, and the darkness he called Night. And there was evening and there was morning, the first day.

Psalm 29 (UM761)

[1]Ascribe to the LORD, O heavenly beings,
  ascribe to the LORD glory and strength.
[2]Ascribe to the LORD the glory of his name;
  worship the LORD in holy splendor.
[3]The voice of the LORD is over the waters;
  the God of glory thunders,
  the LORD, over mighty waters.
[4]The voice of the LORD is powerful;
  the voice of the LORD is full of majesty.
[5]The voice of the LORD breaks the cedars;
  the LORD breaks the cedars of Lebanon.
[6]He makes Lebanon skip like a calf,
  and Sirion like a young wild ox.
[7]The voice of the LORD flashes forth flames of fire.
[8]The voice of the LORD shakes the wilderness;
  the LORD shakes the wilderness of Kadesh.
[9]The voice of the LORD causes the oaks to whirl,
  and strips the forest bare;
  and in his temple all say, "Glory!"
[10]The LORD sits enthroned over the flood;
  the LORD sits enthroned as king forever.
[11]May the LORD give strength to his people!
May the LORD bless his people with peace!

Acts 19:1-7

[1]While Apollos was in Corinth, Paul passed through the interior regions and came to Ephesus, where he found some disciples. [2]He said to them, "Did you receive the Holy Spirit when you became believers?" They replied, "No, we have not even heard that there is a Holy Spirit." [3]Then he said, "Into what then were you baptized?" They answered, "Into John's baptism." [4]Paul said, "John baptized with the baptism of repentance, telling the people to believe in the one who was to come after him, that is, in Jesus." [5]On hearing this, they were baptized in the name of the Lord Jesus. [6]When Paul had laid his hands on them, the Holy Spirit came upon them, and they spoke in tongues and prophesied—[7]altogether there were about twelve of them.

Mark 1:4-11

[4]John the baptizer appeared in the wilderness, proclaiming a baptism of repentance for the forgiveness of sins. [5]And people from the whole Judean countryside and all the people of Jerusalem were going out to him, and were baptized by him in the river Jordan, confessing their sins. [6]Now John was clothed with camel's hair, with a leather belt around his waist, and he ate locusts and wild honey. [7]He proclaimed, "The one who is more powerful than I is coming after me; I am not worthy to stoop down and untie the thong of his sandals. [8]I have baptized you with water; but he will baptize you with the Holy Spirit."

[9]In those days Jesus came from Nazareth of Galilee and was baptized by John in the Jordan. [10]And just as he was coming up out of the water, he saw the heavens torn apart and the Spirit descending like a dove on him. [11]And a voice came from heaven, "You are my Son, the Beloved; with you I am well pleased."

Primary Hymns and Songs for the Day
152 "I Sing the Almighty Power of God" (Gen, Pss) (O)
       H-3   Hbl-44; Chr-21; Desc-40; Org-40
       S-1   #131-132. Intro. and Desc.
252 "When Jesus Came to Jordan" (Mark)
       H-3   Chr-211
347 "Spirit Song" (Mark)
2250 "I've Just Come from the Fountain" (Acts, Mark, Baptism) (C)

Additional Hymn Suggestions
122 "God of the Sparrow, God of the Whale" (Gen)
145 "Morning Has Broken" (Gen)
151 "God Created Heaven and Earth" (Gen)
543 "O Breath of Life" (Gen)
       WS3146
443 "O God Who Shaped Creation" (Gen)
538 "Wind Who Makes All Winds That Blow" (Gen)
688 "God, That Madest Earth and Heaven" (Gen, Evening)
2046 "Womb of Life" (Gen)
2050 "Mothering God, You Gave Me Birth" (Gen, Baptism)
2060 "God the Sculptor of the Mountains" (Gen)
3017 "Come, Join the Dance of Trinity" (Gen)
2117 "Spirit of God" (Gen, Mark)
2120 "Spirit, Spirit of Gentleness" (Gen, Mark)
2122 "She Comes Sailing on the Wind" (Gen, Mark)
2123 "Loving Spirit" (Gen, Mark, Baptism)
3035 "Bless Christ Through Whom All Things Are Made" (Gen)
77   "How Great Thou Art" (Pss)
89   "Joyful, Joyful, We Adore Thee" (Pss)
604 "Praise and Thanksgiving Be to God" (Pss, Acts, Mark, Baptism)
2076 "O Blessed Spring" (Pss, Baptism)
331 "Holy Spirit, Come, Confirm Us" (Acts)
605 "Wash, O God, Our Sons and Daughters" (Acts)
606 "Come, Let Us Use the Grace Divine" (Acts)
608 "This Is the Spirit's Entry Now" (Acts, Mark)
651 "Come, Holy Ghost, Our Souls Inspire" (Acts, Mark)
2247 "Wonder of Wonders" (Acts, Mark, Baptism)
2248 "Baptized in Water" (Acts, Mark, Baptism)
193 "Jesus! The Name High over All" (Mark)
209 "Blessed Be the God of Israel" (Mark)
267 "O Love, How Deep" (Mark)
609 "You Have Put on Christ" (Mark, Baptism)
723 "Shall We Gather at the River" (Mark, Baptism)
2089 "Wild and Lone the Prophet's Voice" (Mark)
2114 "At the Font We Start Our Journey" (Mark)
3045 "Down by the Jordan" (Mark)
3164 "Down to the River to Pray" (Mark, Baptism)

Additional Contemporary Suggestions
WS3032 "Across the Lands" (Gen)
S2041 "Thou Art Worthy" (Gen, Mark)
S2118 "Holy Spirit, Come to Us" (Gen, Baptism)
SP2   "Ah, Lord God" (Gen)
M229   "Forevermore" (Gen)
WS3034 "God of Wonders" (Gen, Pss)
S2139 "Oh, I Know the Lord's Laid His Hands on Me" (Acts, Mark)
S2154 "Please Enter My Heart, Hosanna" (Acts)
S2229 "We Are One in Christ Jesus" (Acts)
S2273 "Jesus, We Are Here" ("*Yesu Tawa Pano*") (Acts)
S2071 "Jesus, Name above All Names" (Mark)

S2107 "Wade in the Water" (Mark)
S2253 "Water, River, Spirit, Grace" (Mark)
WS3165 "Take Me to the Water" (Mark, Baptism)
SP4   "Great and Mighty Is He" (Mark)
M88   "Holy Spirit, Rain Down" (Mark)

Vocal Solos
"Spirit of Faith Come Down" (Mark)
     V-1   p. 43
"Brighter than the Sun" (Mark, Baptism)
     V-5(1) p. 57
"Waterlife" (Mark, Baptism)
     V-5(3) p. 17
"This Is De Healin' Water" (Baptism)
     V-7   p. 52

Anthems
"We Sing the Mighty Power of God" (Gen, Pss)
Arr. Anna Laura Page: Alfred 44572
SATB with keyboard

"Take Me to the Water" (Mark, Baptism)
Arr. David M. Cherwien; MorningStar 50-5332
SATB divisi, a cappella

Other Suggestions
This is an excellent day to celebrate baptisms or baptism renewal using Baptismal Covenant IV, p. 50 in UM. See BOW, pp. 81–114 for a full range of baptismal covenant possibilities.
Visuals:
     O   Light/darkness, water, wind, evening/morning
     P   Ps 29:2b, 11ab; water, cedar, skipping calf, wind (bent trees)
     E   Dove, symbols of the Holy Spirit, water, baptism
     G   Sandals, water, dove, 1:8, 11b
Introit: UM145, stanza 1. "Morning Has Broken" (Gen)
Greeting: BOW300 (Baptism, Pss) or BOW458 (Gen)
Opening Prayer: WSL42 or BOW459 (Gen, Baptism)
Litany: BOW507. For Creation (Gen)
Call to Prayer: S2125. "Come, Holy Spirit" (Gen)
Prayer of Confession: BOW487 (Gen)
Prayer: WSL12. "Great God of waves" (Mark, Baptism)
Prayer: WSL50. "O God whose love" (Gen, Mark, Baptism)
Prayer: UM146, UM253, or BOW301 (Baptism, Mark)
Call to Baptism: S2252, BOW173. "Come, Be Baptized"
Baptism Response: UM609. "You Have Put On Christ" (Acts)
Response: UM334. "Sweet, Sweet Spirit." (Acts, Mark)
Prayer of Thanksgiving: BOW556 (Gen)
Response: BOW179. "For the Gift of Creation" (Gen)
Blessing: BOW561 (Acts, Mark)

1 Samuel 3:1-10, (11-20)

[1]Now the boy Samuel was ministering to the Lord under Eli. The word of the Lord was rare in those days; visions were not widespread.

[2]At that time Eli, whose eyesight had begun to grow dim so that he could not see, was lying down in his room; [3]the lamp of God had not yet gone out, and Samuel was lying down in the temple of the Lord, where the ark of God was. [4]Then the Lord called, "Samuel! Samuel!" and he said, "Here I am!" [5]and ran to Eli, and said, "Here I am, for you called me." But he said, "I did not call; lie down again." So he went and lay down. [6]The Lord called again, "Samuel!" Samuel got up and went to Eli, and said, "Here I am, for you called me." But he said, "I did not call, my son; lie down again." [7]Now Samuel did not yet know the Lord, and the word of the Lord had not yet been revealed to him. [8]The Lord called Samuel again, a third time. And he got up and went to Eli, and said, "Here I am, for you called me." Then Eli perceived that the Lord was calling the boy. [9]Therefore Eli said to Samuel, "Go, lie down; and if he calls you, you shall say, 'Speak, Lord, for your servant is listening.'" So Samuel went and lay down in his place.

[10]Now the Lord came and stood there, calling as before, "Samuel! Samuel!" And Samuel said, "Speak, for your servant is listening." ([11]Then the Lord said to Samuel, "See, I am about to do something in Israel that will make both ears of anyone who hears of it tingle. [12]On that day I will fulfill against Eli all that I have spoken concerning his house, from beginning to end. [13]For I have told him that I am about to punish his house forever, for the iniquity that he knew, because his sons were blaspheming God, and he did not restrain them. [14]Therefore I swear to the house of Eli that the iniquity of Eli's house shall not be expiated by sacrifice or offering forever."

[15]Samuel lay there until morning; then he opened the doors of the house of the Lord. Samuel was afraid to tell the vision to Eli. [16]But Eli called Samuel and said, "Samuel, my son." He said, "Here I am." [17]Eli said, "What was it that he told you? Do not hide it from me. May God do so to you and more also, if you hide anything from me of all that he told you." [18]So Samuel told him everything and hid nothing from him. Then he said, "It is the Lord; let him do what seems good to him."

[19]As Samuel grew up, the Lord was with him and let none of his words fall to the ground. [20]And all Israel from Dan to Beer-sheba knew that Samuel was a trustworthy prophet of the Lord.)

Psalm 139:1-6, 13-18 (UM854)

[1]O Lord, you have searched me and known me.
[2]You know when I sit down and when I rise up;
    you discern my thoughts from far away.
[3]You search out my path and my lying down,
    and are acquainted with all my ways.
[4]Even before a word is on my tongue,
    O Lord, you know it completely.
[5]You hem me in, behind and before,
    and lay your hand upon me.
[6]Such knowledge is too wonderful for me;
    it is so high that I cannot attain it.
. . . .
[13]For it was you who formed my inward parts;
    you knit me together in my mother's womb.
[14]I praise you, for I am fearfully and wonderfully made.
    Wonderful are your works;
that I know very well.
    [15]My frame was not hidden from you,
when I was being made in secret,
    intricately woven in the depths of the earth.

[16]Your eyes beheld my unformed substance.
In your book were written
    all the days that were formed for me,
    when none of them as yet existed.
[17]How weighty to me are your thoughts, O God!
    How vast is the sum of them!
[18]I try to count them—they are more than the sand;
    I come to the end—I am still with you.

1 Corinthians 6:12-20

[12]"All things are lawful for me," but not all things are beneficial. "All things are lawful for me," but I will not be dominated by anything. [13]"Food is meant for the stomach and the stomach for food," and God will destroy both one and the other. The body is meant not for fornication but for the Lord, and the Lord for the body. [14]And God raised the Lord and will also raise us by his power. [15]Do you not know that your bodies are members of Christ? Should I therefore take the members of Christ and make them members of a prostitute? Never! [16]Do you not know that whoever is united to a prostitute becomes one body with her? For it is said, "The two shall be one flesh." [17]But anyone united to the Lord becomes one spirit with him. [18]Shun fornication! Every sin that a person commits is outside the body; but the fornicator sins against the body itself. [19]Or do you not know that your body is a temple of the Holy Spirit within you, which you have from God, and that you are not your own? [20]For you were bought with a price; therefore glorify God in your body.

John 1:43-51

[43]The next day Jesus decided to go to Galilee. He found Philip and said to him, "Follow me." [44]Now Philip was from Bethsaida, the city of Andrew and Peter. [45]Philip found Nathanael and said to him, "We have found him about whom Moses in the law and also the prophets wrote, Jesus son of Joseph from Nazareth." [46]Nathanael said to him, "Can anything good come out of Nazareth?" Philip said to him, "Come and see." [47]When Jesus saw Nathanael coming toward him, he said of him, "Here is truly an Israelite in whom there is no deceit!" [48]Nathanael asked him, "Where did you get to know me?" Jesus answered, "I saw you under the fig tree before Philip called you." [49]Nathanael replied, "Rabbi, you are the Son of God! You are the King of Israel!" [50]Jesus answered, "Do you believe because I told you that I saw you under the fig tree? You will see greater things than these." [51]And he said to him, "Very truly, I tell you, you will see heaven opened and the angels of God ascending and descending upon the Son of Man."

Primary Hymns and Songs for the Day

454   "Open My Eyes, That I May See" (1 Sam) (O)
      H-3   Chr-157; Org-108
419   "I Am Thine, O Lord" (1 Sam, John)
2052   "The Lone, Wild Bird" (Pss)
2127   "Come and See" ("*Kyrie*") (John)
463   "Lord, Speak to Me" (1 Sam, John) (C)
      H-3   Hbl-75; Chr-131; Desc-22; Org-18
      S-1   #52. Desc.

Additional Hymn Suggestions

400   "Come, Thou Fount of Every Blessing" (1 Sam)
593   "Here I Am, Lord" (1 Sam)
451   "Be Thou My Vision" (1 Sam, 1 Cor, John)
508   "Faith, While Trees Are Still in Blossom" (1 Sam, John)
582   "Whom Shall I Send?" (1 Sam, John)
584   "Lord, You Give the Great Commission" (1 Sam, John) (C)
579   "Lord God, Your Love Has Called Us Here" (1 Cor) (O)
139   "Praise to the Lord, the Almighty" (Pss) (O)
411   "Dear Lord, Lead Me Day by Day" (Pss)
474   "Precious Lord, Take My Hand" (Pss, MLK Day)
2046   "Womb of Life" (Pss)
2050   "Mothering God, You Gave Me Birth" (Pss)
2051   "I Was There to Hear Your Borning Cry" (Pss)
2117   "Spirit of God" (Pss)
2123   "Loving Spirit" (Pss)
2208   "Guide My Feet" (Pss, MLK Day)
2214   "Lead Me, Guide Me" (Pss)
3011   "All My Days" (Pss)
3019   "Bidden, Unbidden" (Pss)
430   "O Master, Let Me Walk with Thee" (Pss, 1 Cor, John)
98   "To God Be the Glory" (1 Cor)
382   "Have Thine Own Way, Lord" (1 Cor)
413   "A Charge to Keep I Have" (1 Cor)
2084   "Come, Let Us with Our Lord Arise" (1 Cor)
3100   "Jesus Paid It All" (1 Cor)
3147   "Built on a Rock" (1 Cor)
128   "He Leadeth Me: O Blessed Thought" (John) (C)
256   "We Would See Jesus" (John)
300   "O The Lamb" (John)
714   "I Know Whom I Have Believed" (John) (C)
2101   "Two Fishermen" (John)
2137   "Would I Have Answered When You Called" (John)
3161   "Gracious Creator of Sea and of Land" (John)
733   "Marching to Zion" (Human Relations Day)
2135   "When Cain Killed Abel" (Human Relations)
2170   "God Made from One Blood" (MLK Day)
2181   "We Need a Faith" (Human Relations, MLK Day)

Additional Contemporary Suggestions

S2139   "Oh, I Know the Lord's Laid His Hands on Me" (1 Sam, Pss, MLK Day)
WS3113   "A Wilderness Wandering People" (1 Sam, MLK Day, Human Relations Day)
WS3025   "God Is Speaking" (1 Sam, John 1)
WS3095   "Somebody's Knockin' at Your Door" (1 Sam, John)
M105   "Let My Words Be Few" (1 Sam)
M108   "Lead Me, Lord" (1 Sam, John)
M109   "He Knows My Name" (1 Sam, Pss)
WS3015   "How Great You Are" (Pss)
M38   "In the Secret" ("I Want to Know You") (Pss)
M85   "The Potter's Hand" (Pss)

M101   "These Hands" (Pss)
S2164   "Sanctuary" (1 Cor)
S2150   "Lord, Be Glorified" (1 Cor)
WS3132   "House of God" (1 Cor)
M13   "Be Glorified" (1 Cor)
M152   "Be Glorified" (1 Cor)
S2165   "Cry of My Heart" (John)
S2218   "You Are Mine" (John)
M47   "Come Just As You Are" (John)
M255   "Just to Be with You" (John)
WS3004   "Step by Step" (John)
WS3160   "We Will Follow" ("*Somlandela*") (John)

Vocal Solos

"Be Thou My Vision" (1 Sam, 1 Cor, John)
     V-6   p. 13
"Chosen of the Lord" (1 Sam, John)
     V-8   p. 34
"Here I Am" (1 Sam, John)
     V-11   p. 19
"Gospel Train" (John)
     V-7   p. 74

Anthems

"Here I Am, Lord" (1 Sam)
Arr. Ovid Young; Augsburg 9780800656058
SATB with keyboard

"Come Just As You Are" (John)
Arr. Benjamin Harlan; Alfred 44578
SATB with piano

Other Suggestions

Visuals:
   O   Listening, service to others, 3:4b, 5b, 9b
   P   Hand, newborn child, hour glass
   E   Unity, various body shapes and sizes, circle of hands, 1 Cor 6:19
   G   John 1:43c, "Come and see," invitation, fig tree, mission

Introit: WS3150. "Father, We Have Heard You Calling" (1 Sam, John)
Greeting: BOW307 (Human Relations, Epiphany)
Opening Prayer: BOW313 (1 Sam) or BOW315 (Human Relations)
Opening Litany: BOW423 (Human Relations Day)
Call to Prayer: BOW196. "Call to Prayer" (Pss)
Prayer of Confession: BOW478 (1 Sam) or BOW480 (Pss)
Prayer of Confession: BOW492 (Human Relations)
Prayer: UM403. For True Life (1 Sam)
Prayer: UM570. Prayer of Ignatius (Human Relations)
Prayer: BOW435 or BOW544 (John, MLK Day)
Prayer: BOW510. For Discernment (1 Sam)
Prayer: WSL51 (1 Sam, Pss)
Prayer: BOW519, BOW526, or BOW547 (Human Relations)
Responsive Prayer: WSL77 (John, MLK Day, Human Relations)
Response: S2072. "Amen, Amen" (John, MLK Day)

Jonah 3:1-5, 10

[1]The word of the LORD came to Jonah a second time, saying, [2]"Get up, go to Nineveh, that great city, and proclaim to it the message that I tell you." [3]So Jonah set out and went to Nineveh, according to the word of the LORD. Now Nineveh was an exceedingly large city, a three days' walk across. [4]Jonah began to go into the city, going a day's walk. And he cried out, "Forty days more, and Nineveh shall be overthrown!" [5]And the people of Nineveh believed God; they proclaimed a fast, and everyone, great and small, put on sackcloth. . . .

[10]When God saw what they did, how they turned from their evil ways, God changed his mind about the calamity that he had said he would bring upon them; and he did not do it.

Psalm 62:5-12 (UM787)

[5]For God alone my soul waits in silence,
    for my hope is from him.
[6]He alone is my rock and my salvation,
    my fortress; I shall not be shaken.
[7]On God rests my deliverance and my honor;
    my mighty rock, my refuge is in God.
[8]Trust in him at all times, O people;
    pour out your heart before him;
    God is a refuge for us. *[Selah]*
[9]Those of low estate are but a breath,
    those of high estate are a delusion;
in the balances they go up;
    they are together lighter than a breath.
[10]Put no confidence in extortion,
    and set no vain hopes on robbery;
    if riches increase, do not set your heart on them.
[11]Once God has spoken;
    twice have I heard this:
that power belongs to God,
    [12]and steadfast love belongs to you, O Lord.
For you repay to all
    according to their work.

1 Corinthians 7:29-31

[29]I mean, brothers and sisters, the appointed time has grown short; from now on, let even those who have wives be as though they had none, [30]and those who mourn as though they were not mourning, and those who rejoice as though they were not rejoicing, and those who buy as though they had no possessions, [31]and those who deal with the world as though they had no dealings with it. For the present form of this world is passing away.

Mark 1:14-20

[14]Now after John was arrested, Jesus came to Galilee, proclaiming the good news of God, [15]and saying, "The time is fulfilled, and the kingdom of God has come near; repent, and believe in the good news."

[16]As Jesus passed along the Sea of Galilee, he saw Simon and his brother Andrew casting a net into the sea—for they were fishermen. [17]And Jesus said to them, "Follow me and I will make you fish for people." [18]And immediately they left their nets and followed him. [19]As he went a little farther, he saw James son of Zebedee and his brother John, who were in their boat mending the nets. [20]Immediately he called them; and they left their father Zebedee in the boat with the hired men, and followed him.

Primary Hymns and Songs for the Day

261	"Lord of the Dance" (Mark) (O)	
	H-3	Chr-106; Org-81
344	"*Tú Has Venido a la Orilla*" ("Lord, You Have Come to the Lakeshore") (Mark)	
	H-3	Chr-133; Org-114
358	"Dear Lord and Father of Mankind" (Jonah, Mark) (Alternate Text "Parent of Us All")	
	H-3	Hbl-56; Chr-61; Org-124
	S-2	#151. Intro.
		#152. Violin Desc.
2101	"Two Fishermen" (Mark)	
2129	"I Have Decided to Follow Jesus" (Mark)	
398	"Jesus Calls Us" (Mark) (C)	
	H-3	Chr-115
	S-2	#65. Harm.

Additional Hymn Suggestions

120	"Your Love, O God" (Jonah)
365	"Grace Greater than Our Sin" (Jonah)
428	"For the Healing of the Nations" (Jonah)
2009	"O God Beyond All Praising" (Jonah)
361	"Rock of Ages, Cleft for Me" (Jonah, Pss)
467	"Trust and Obey" (Jonah, Pss)
352	"It's Me, It's Me, O Lord" (Jonah, 1 Cor)
2267	"Taste and See" (Pss, Comm.)
209	"Blessed Be the God of Israel" (Jonah, Mark) (O)
350	"Come, All of You" (Jonah, Mark)
355	"Depth of Mercy" (Jonah, Mark)
3097	"Depth of Mercy" (Jonah, Mark)
578	"God of Love and God of Power" (Jonah, Mark)
579	"Lord God, Your Love Has Called Us Here" (Jonah, Mark)
110	"A Mighty Fortress Is Our God" (Pss)
178	"Hope of the World" (Pss)
523	"*Saranam, Saranam*" ("Refuge") (Pss)
411	"Dear Lord, Lead Me Day by Day" (1 Cor)
732	"Come, We That Love the Lord" (1 Cor)
577	"God of Grace and God of Glory" (1 Cor, Mark) (O)
438	"Forth in Thy Name, O Lord" (1 Cor, Mark) (C)
256	"We Would See Jesus" (Mark)
348	"Softly and Tenderly Jesus Is Calling" (Mark)
396	"O Jesus, I Have Promised" (Mark)
582	"Whom Shall I Send" (Mark)
712	"I Sing a Song of the Saints of God" (Mark)
2127	"Come and See" ("*Kyrie*") (Mark)
2130	"The Summons" (Mark)
2137	"Would I Have Answered When You Called" (Mark)
3161	"Gracious Creator of Sea and of Land" (Mark)

Additional Contemporary Suggestions

S2002	"I Will Call Upon the Lord" (Jonah, Pss)
M257	"Came to My Rescue" (Jonah)
WS3041	"Praise Him" (Pss)
WS3135	"In God Alone" (Pss)
M28	"Who Can Satisfy My Soul Like You?" (Pss)
M93	"Rock of Ages" (Pss)
M271	"Psalm 62" ("My Soul Finds Rest") (Pss)
M272	"None but Jesus" (Pss)
S2036	"Give Thanks" (Pss)
S2066	"Praise the Name of Jesus" (Pss, Mark)
S2072	"Amen, Amen" (Mark)
S2218	"You Are Mine" (Mark)
S2165	"Cry of My Heart" (Mark)
M41	"You're Worthy of My Praise" (Mark)

WS3004	"Step by Step" (Mark)
WS3160	"We Will Follow" ("*Somlandela*") (Mark)
M72	"Jesus, Lover of My Soul" ("It's All about You") (Mark)
M108	"Lead Me, Lord" (Mark)
M122	"Every Move I Make" (Mark)
M150	"Everyday" (Mark)

Vocal Solos

"Keep A-Inchin' Along" (Jonah, Mark)
   V-7   p. 32
Here I Am" (Jonah, Mark)
   V-11   p. 19

Anthems

"God of Grace and God of Glory" (1 Cor, Mark)
Arr. Michael Burkhardt; MorningStar 60-8015
SATH with Organ and opt. brass

"Lord of the Dance" (Mark)
Arr. John Rutter; Hope C-5166
SATB with keyboard

Other Suggestions

Visuals:

O	Sackcloth, empty plate, no. 40
P	Large rock, refuge, symbols of power, Ps 62:11
E	Ticking alarm clock
G	Sackcloth, fish/net, fishing, nets left behind, discipling, multiple images of people

Introit: WS3150. "Father, We Have Heard You Calling" (Jonah, Mark)

Call to Confession: UM366. For Guidance.

Offering Prayer: WSL113. "Loving God, faithful and gracious" (Jonah, Mark)

Response: UM587. "Bless Thou the Gifts" (Jonah, Mark)

Sung Benediction: WS3180. "As We Part for the Towns and Cities" (Jonah, Mark)

See The Abingdon Worship Annual 2018 *for additional worship resources.*

Deuteronomy 18:15-20

[15]The LORD your God will raise up for you a prophet like me from among your own people; you shall heed such a prophet. [16]This is what you requested of the LORD your God at Horeb on the day of the assembly when you said: "If I hear the voice of the LORD my God any more, or ever again see this great fire, I will die." [17]Then the LORD replied to me: "They are right in what they have said. [18]I will raise up for them a prophet like you from among their own people; I will put my words in the mouth of the prophet, who shall speak to them everything that I command. [19]Anyone who does not heed the words that the prophet shall speak in my name, I myself will hold accountable. [20]But any prophet who speaks in the name of other gods, or who presumes to speak in my name a word that I have not commanded the prophet to speak—that prophet shall die."

Psalm 111 (UM832)

[1]Praise the LORD!
I will give thanks to the LORD with my whole heart,
    in the company of the upright, in the congregation.
[2]Great are the works of the LORD,
    studied by all who delight in them.
[3]Full of honor and majesty is his work,
    and his righteousness endures forever.
[4]He has gained renown by his wonderful deeds;
    the LORD is gracious and merciful.
[5]He provides food for those who fear him;
    he is ever mindful of his covenant.
[6]He has shown his people the power of his works,
    in giving them the heritage of the nations.
[7]The works of his hands are faithful and just;
    all his precepts are trustworthy.
[8]They are established forever and ever,
    to be performed with faithfulness and uprightness.
[9]He sent redemption to his people;
    he has commanded his covenant forever.
    Holy and awesome is his name.
[10]The fear of the LORD is the beginning of wisdom;
    all those who practice it have a good understanding.
    His praise endures forever.

1 Corinthians 8:1-13

[1]Now concerning food sacrificed to idols: we know that "all of us possess knowledge." Knowledge puffs up, but love builds up. [2]Anyone who claims to know something does not yet have the necessary knowledge; [3]but anyone who loves God is known by him.

[4]Hence, as to the eating of food offered to idols, we know that "no idol in the world really exists," and that "there is no God but one." [5]Indeed, even though there may be so-called gods in heaven or on earth—as in fact there are many gods and many lords—[6]yet for us there is one God, the Father, from whom are all things and for whom we exist, and one Lord, Jesus Christ, through whom are all things and through whom we exist.

[7]It is not everyone, however, who has this knowledge. Since some have become so accustomed to idols until now, they still think of the food they eat as food offered to an idol; and their conscience, being weak, is defiled. [8]"Food will not bring us close to God." We are no worse off if we do not eat, and no better off if we do. [9]But take care that this liberty of yours does not somehow become a stumbling block to the weak. [10]For if others see you, who possess knowledge, eating in the temple of an idol, might they not, since their conscience is weak, be encouraged to the point of eating food sacrificed to idols? [11]So by your knowledge those weak believers for whom Christ died are destroyed. [12]But when you thus sin against members of your family, and wound their conscience when it is weak, you sin against Christ. [13]Therefore, if food is a cause of their falling, I will never eat meat, so that I may not cause one of them to fall.

Mark 1:21-28

[21]They went to Capernaum; and when the sabbath came, he entered the synagogue and taught. [22]They were astounded at his teaching, for he taught them as one having authority, and not as the scribes. [23]Just then there was in their synagogue a man with an unclean spirit, [24]and he cried out, "What have you to do with us, Jesus of Nazareth? Have you come to destroy us? I know who you are, the Holy One of God." [25]But Jesus rebuked him, saying, "Be silent, and come out of him!" [26]And the unclean spirit, convulsing him and crying with a loud voice, came out of him. [27]They were all amazed, and they kept on asking one another, "What is this? A new teaching—with authority! He commands even the unclean spirits, and they obey him." [28]At once his fame began to spread throughout the surrounding region of Galilee.

Primary Hymns and Songs for the Day

463	"Lord, Speak to Me" (Deut) (O)
561	"Jesus, United by Thy Grace" (1 Cor)
	H-3 Hbl-66, 73; Chr-90; Desc-92; Org-131
	S-1 #291-292. Desc. and Harm.
264	"Silence, Frenzied, Unclean Spirit" (Mark)
	Alternate Tunes: EBENEZER or BEACH SPRING
	H-3 Chr-171
557	"Blest Be the Tie That Binds" (1 Cor) (C)
	H-3 Hbl-49; Chr-14; Desc-27; Org-25

Additional Hymn Suggestions

108	"God Hath Spoken By the Prophets" (Deut) (O)
127	"Guide Me, O Thou Great Jehovah" (Deut) (O)
2001	"We Sing to You, O God" (Deut)
2011	"We Sing of Your Glory" (Deut)
67	"We, Thy People, Praise Thee" (Pss)
96	"Praise the Lord Who Reigns Above" (Pss)
62	"All Creatures of Our God and King" (1 Cor) (O)
85	"We Believe in One True God" (1 Cor)
188	"Christ Is the World's Light" (1 Cor)
390	"Forgive Our Sins as We Forgive" (1 Cor)
451	"Be Thou My Vision" (1 Cor)
554	"All Praise to Our Redeeming Lord" (1 Cor)
560	"Help Us Accept Each Other" (1 Cor)
562	"Jesus, Lord, We Look to Thee" (1 Cor)
616	"Come, Sinners, to the Gospel Feast" (1 Cor, Comm.)
2170	"God Made from One Blood" (1 Cor)
2175	"Together We Serve" (1 Cor)
2187	"Now It Is Evening" (1 Cor, Evening)
2228	"Sacred the Body" (1 Cor)
2248	"Baptized in Water" (1 Cor, Baptism)
3156	"One Is the Body" (1 Cor, Comm.)
2117	"Spirit of God" (1 Cor, Mark)
2213	"Healer of Our Every Ill" (1 Cor, Mark)
265	"O Christ, the Healer" (1 Cor, Mark)
632	"Draw Us in the Spirit's Tether" (1 Cor, Comm.)
173	"Christ, Whose Glory Fills the Skies" (Mark)
187	"Rise, Shine, You People" (Mark)
262	"Heal Me, Hands of Jesus" (Mark)
263	"When Jesus the Healer Passed Through Galilee" (Mark)
267	"O Love, How Deep" (Mark)
458	"Dear Lord, for All in Pain" (Mark)
2104	"An Outcast among Outcasts" (Mark)
2177	"Wounded World that Cries for Healing" (Mark)
3072	"Cast Out, O Christ" (Mark)
629	"You Satisfy the Hungry Heart" (Comm.)

Additional Contemporary Suggestions

S2040	"Awesome God" (Deut, Pss, Mark)
UM176	"Majesty" (Deut, Mark)
UM84	"Thank You, Lord" (Pss)
S2022	"Great Is the Lord" (Pss)
S2023	"How Majestic Is Your Name" (Pss)
S2195	"In the Lord I'll Be Ever Thankful" (Pss)
M126	"Famous One" (Pss)
M224	"Because of Your Love" (Pss)
M262	"Desert Song" (Pss)
S2021	"What a Mighty God We Serve" (Pss, Mark)
UM507	"Through It All" (Pss, Mark)
S2224	"Make Us One" (1 Cor)
S2226	"Bind Us Together" (1 Cor)
S2244	"People Need the Lord" (Mark)
WS3038	"Mighty to Save" (Mark)

WS3073	"We Walk His Way" (Mark)
M3	"Jesus, Your Name" (Mark)
M104	"There Is None Like You" (Mark)
M164	"Good to Me" (Mark)
M266	"You Have Saved Us" (Mark)

Vocal Solos

"Where Shall My Wondering Soul Begin?" (Mark)
   V-1   p. 59
"Jesus Is Lord of All" (Mark)
   V-8   p. 254
"In Jesus' Name" (Mark)
   V-8   p. 188

Anthems

"We Believe" (1 Cor)
Dan Forrest; Beckenhorst BP2052
SATB with keyboard, opt. brass quintet

"Christ Is the World's Light" (1 Cor)
Arr. Lloyd Larsen; Hope C5797
SATB with keyboard and opt. brass

Other Suggestions

Visuals:

O	Bust or painting of Moses, fire, prophets, pulpit, open Bible
P	Praise, food, hands, justice, Ps 111:9c, 10a, c
E	Building, no. 1 (God, Lord), 1 Cor 8:1b, food, stumbling blocks, books, healing, Christ, love
G	Christ sitting and teaching, healing, others teaching, healing, Mark 1:24b, open Bible

Greeting: BOW303 or BOW451 (Pss, Epiphany)
Opening Prayer: BOW308 (Mark, Epiphany)
Prayer of Confession: BOW477 (1 Cor)
Prayer: UM564, WSL43, or WSL53 (1 Cor)
Prayer: BOW312, BOW500, BOW518, or BOW546 (Mark, 1 Cor)
Prayer: BOW525. For Wisdom (Pss)
Song of Preparation: UM264. "Silence, Frenzied, Unclean Spirit." For congregational singing, consider alternate tunes in 87.87D meter, such as EBENEZER or HYMN TO JOY (Mark)
Prayer of Thanksgiving: BOW551 (Deut, Pss)
Response: UM84. "Thank You, Lord" (Pss)
Blessing: BOW564 (Pss, 1 Cor)

Isaiah 40:21-31

21Have you not known? Have you not heard?
　　Has it not been told you from the beginning?
　　Have you not understood from the foundations of the earth?
22It is he who sits above the circle of the earth,
　　and its inhabitants are like grasshoppers;
who stretches out the heavens like a curtain,
　　and spreads them like a tent to live in;
23who brings princes to naught,
　　and makes the rulers of the earth as nothing.
24Scarcely are they planted, scarcely sown,
　　scarcely has their stem taken root in the earth,
when he blows upon them, and they wither,
　　and the tempest carries them off like stubble.
25To whom then will you compare me,
　　or who is my equal? says the Holy One.
26Lift up your eyes on high and see:
　　Who created these?
He who brings out their host and numbers them,
　　calling them all by name;
because he is great in strength,
　　mighty in power,
　　not one is missing.
27Why do you say, O Jacob,
　　and speak, O Israel,
"My way is hidden from the Lord,
　　and my right is disregarded by my God"?
28Have you not known? Have you not heard?
The Lord is the everlasting God,
　　the Creator of the ends of the earth.
He does not faint or grow weary;
　　his understanding is unsearchable.
29He gives power to the faint,
　　and strengthens the powerless.
30Even youths will faint and be weary,
　　and the young will fall exhausted;
31but those who wait for the Lord shall renew their strength,
　　they shall mount up with wings like eagles,
they shall run and not be weary,
　　they shall walk and not faint.

Psalm 147:1-11, 20c (UM859)

1Praise the Lord!
How good it is to sing praises to our God;
　　for he is gracious, and a song of praise is fitting.
2The Lord builds up Jerusalem;
　　he gathers the outcasts of Israel.
3He heals the brokenhearted,
　　and binds up their wounds.
4He determines the number of the stars;
　　he gives to all of them their names.
5Great is our Lord, and abundant in power;
　　his understanding is beyond measure.
6The Lord lifts up the downtrodden;
　　he casts the wicked to the ground.
7Sing to the Lord with thanksgiving;
　　make melody to our God on the lyre.
8He covers the heavens with clouds,
　　prepares rain for the earth,
　　makes grass grow on the hills.
9He gives to the animals their food,
　　and to the young ravens when they cry.
10His delight is not in the strength of the horse,
　　nor his pleasure in the speed of a runner;
11but the Lord takes pleasure in those who fear him,
　　in those who hope in his steadfast love.
. . . .
20cPraise the Lord!

1 Corinthians 9:16-23

16If I proclaim the gospel, this gives me no ground for boasting, for an obligation is laid on me, and woe to me if I do not proclaim the gospel! 17For if I do this of my own will, I have a reward; but if not of my own will, I am entrusted with a commission. 18What then is my reward? Just this: that in my proclamation I may make the gospel free of charge, so as not to make full use of my rights in the gospel.

19For though I am free with respect to all, I have made myself a slave to all, so that I might win more of them. 20To the Jews I became as a Jew, in order to win Jews. To those under the law I became as one under the law (though I myself am not under the law) so that I might win those under the law. 21To those outside the law I became as one outside the law (though I am not free from God's law but am under Christ's law) so that I might win those outside the law. 22To the weak I became weak, so that I might win the weak. I have become all things to all people, that I might by all means save some. 23I do it all for the sake of the gospel, so that I may share in its blessings.

Mark 1:29-39

29As soon as they left the synagogue, they entered the house of Simon and Andrew, with James and John. 30Now Simon's mother-in-law was in bed with a fever, and they told him about her at once. 31He came and took her by the hand and lifted her up. Then the fever left her, and she began to serve them. 32That evening, at sundown, they brought to him all who were sick or possessed with demons. 33And the whole city was gathered around the door. 34And he cured many who were sick with various diseases, and cast out many demons; and he would not permit the demons to speak, because they knew him.

35In the morning, while it was still very dark, he got up and went out to a deserted place, and there he prayed. 36And Simon and his companions hunted for him. 37When they found him, they said to him, "Everyone is searching for you." 38He answered, "Let us go on to the neighboring towns, so that I may proclaim the message there also; for that is what I came out to do." 39And he went throughout Galilee, proclaiming the message in their synagogues and casting out demons.

Primary Hymns and Songs for the Day

139   "Praise to the Lord, the Almighty" (Isa, Pss) (O)
       H-3   Hbl-89; Chr-163; Desc-69; Org-79
       S-1   #218-222. Various treatments
263   "When Jesus the Healer Passed Through Galilee" (Mark)
       S-2   #76. Flute/recorder Desc.
375   "There Is a Balm in Gilead" (Mark, Black History)
474   "Precious Lord, Take My Hand" (Mark, Black History)
       H-3   Chr-164; Org-116
421   "Make Me a Captive, Lord" (1 Cor) (C)
       H-3   Hbl-61; Chr-71; Desc-93; Org-133

Additional Hymn Suggestions

709   "Come, Let Us Join Our Friends Above" (Isa, Comm.)
2001   "We Sing to You, O God" (Isa)
2077   "You Alone Are Holy" ("*Sólo Tú Eres Santo*") (Isa)
2117   "Spirit of God" (Isa, Comm.)
2121   "O Holy Spirit, Root of Life" (Isa)
2238   "In the Midst of New Dimensions" (Isa)
126   "Sing Praise to God Who Reigns Above" (Isa, Pss) (O)
132   "All My Hope Is Firmly Grounded" (Isa, Pss)
57   "O For a Thousand Tongues to Sing" (Pss) (O)
160   "Rejoice, Ye Pure in Heart" (Pss) (C)
161   "Rejoice, Ye Pure in Heart" (Pss)
200   "Tell Out, My Soul" (Pss)
333   "I'm Goin'a Sing When the Spirit Says Sing" (Pss, Black History)
3010   "Sing of the Lord's Goodness" (Pss)
3012   "When Words Alone Cannot Express" (Pss)
410   "I Want a Principle Within" (1 Cor)
413   "A Charge to Keep I Have" (1 Cor)
568   "Christ for the World We Sing" (1 Cor)
573   "O Zion, Haste" (1 Cor)
578   "God of Love and God of Power" (1 Cor) (O)
261   "Lord of the Dance" (1 Cor, Mark)
569   "We've a Story to Tell to the Nations" (1 Cor, Mark) (C)
262   "Heal Me, Hands of Jesus" (Mark)
265   "O Christ, the Healer" (Mark)
266   "Heal Us, Emmanuel, Hear Our Prayer" (Mark)
267   "O Love, How Deep" (Mark)
367   "He Touched Me" (Mark)
395   "Take Time to Be Holy" (Mark)
2151   "I'm So Glad Jesus Lifted Me" (Mark, Black History)
3072   "Cast Out, O Christ" (Mark)

Additional Contemporary Suggestions

UM143   "On Eagle's Wings" (Isa)
       S-2   #143. Stanzas for soloist
WS3021 "Everlasting God" (Isa)
WS3042 "Shout to the North" (Isa)
WS3040 "You Are My All in All" (Isa)
WS3134 "Still" (Isa)
M26   "The Power of Your Love" (Isa)
M158   "Eagle's Wings" (Isa)
M189   "Your Love, Oh Lord" (Isa)
M229   "Forevermore" (Isa)
M260   "I Will Rise" (Isa)
SP4   "Great and Mighty Is He" (Isa, Pss)
SP102   "Great Are You, Lord" (Isa, Pss)
M103   "How Great Are You, Lord" (Isa, Pss)
M164   "Good To Me" (Isa, Mark)
S2244   "People Need the Lord" (Isa, Mark)
S2022   "Great Is the Lord" (Pss)

S2144   "Someone Asked the Question" (Pss, Black History)
M234   "Awesome Is the Lord Most High" (Pss)
M266   "You Have Saved Us" (Pss, Mark)
S2064   "Oh Lord, You're Beautiful" (Mark)
S2072   "Amen, Amen" (Mark, Black History)
S2139   "Oh, I Know the Lord's Laid His Hands on Me" (Mark, Black History)
S2266   "Here Is Bread, Here Is Wine" (Mark, Comm.)
WS3073 "We Walk His Way" (Mark)
M3   "Jesus, Your Name" (Mark)
M73   "My Redeemer Lives" (Mark)
M104   "There Is None Like You" (Mark)
UM349   "Turn Your Eyes upon Jesus" (Mark)

Vocal Solos

"Wings Like Eagles" (Isa)
       V-11   p. 9
"On Eagle's Wings" (Isa)
       V-3(2)   p. 2
"O For a Thousand Tongues to Sing" (Pss)
       V-1   p. 32
"Sing a Song of Joy" (Pss)
       V-4   p. 2
"A Song of Joy" (Pss)
       V-11   p. 2

Anthems

"Have You Not Known?" (Isa)
Robert A. Hobby; MorningStar 50-0024
SATB with organ

"Jesus, Lover of My Soul" (Isa, Mark)
Arr. David Huntsinger; Alfred 29371
SATB with keyboard

Other Suggestions

February is Black History Month, which can be reflected in your choice of music and liturgy.
Visuals:
    O   Helping the powerless, exhausted youth, Isa 40:31
    P   Praising, singing, healing, stars, stringed instruments (lyre), rain clouds, grass, birds, love
    E   Proclamation, ordination certificate, manacles (slave)
    G   Helping older woman up, healing, sundown/early dawn
Greeting: BOW307 (Mark)
Opening Prayer: UM466. An Invitation to Christ (Mark)
Call to Prayer: UM265, stanza 1. O Christ, the Healer (Mark)
Intercessory Prayer: UM457. For the Sick (Mark)
Prayer: BOW314 (1 Cor) or BOW524 (Isa)
Scripture Response: UM382, stanza 3. "Have Thine Own Way, Lord" (Pss, Mark)
Service of Healing: BOW615 (Mark)
Response: S2067, BOW177. "Amen, We Praise Your Name, O God" ("*Amen Siakudumisa*") (Pss, Black History)
Benediction: S2281. "May You Run and Not Be Weary" (Isa)

2 Kings 2:1-12

[1]Now when the LORD was about to take Elijah up to heaven by a whirlwind, Elijah and Elisha were on their way from Gilgal. [2]Elijah said to Elisha, "Stay here; for the LORD has sent me as far as Bethel." But Elisha said, "As the LORD lives, and as you yourself live, I will not leave you." So they went down to Bethel. [3]The company of prophets who were in Bethel came out to Elisha, and said to him, "Do you know that today the LORD will take your master away from you?" And he said, "Yes, I know; keep silent."

[4]Elijah said to him, "Elisha, stay here; for the LORD has sent me to Jericho." But he said, "As the LORD lives, and as you yourself live, I will not leave you." So they came to Jericho. [5]The company of prophets who were at Jericho drew near to Elisha, and said to him, "Do you know that today the LORD will take your master away from you?" And he answered, "Yes, I know; be silent."

[6]Then Elijah said to him, "Stay here; for the LORD has sent me to the Jordan." But he said, "As the LORD lives, and as you yourself live, I will not leave you." So the two of them went on. [7]Fifty men of the company of prophets also went, and stood at some distance from them, as they both were standing by the Jordan. [8]Then Elijah took his mantle and rolled it up, and struck the water; the water was parted to the one side and to the other, until the two of them crossed on dry ground.

[9]When they had crossed, Elijah said to Elisha, "Tell me what I may do for you, before I am taken from you." Elisha said, "Please let me inherit a double share of your spirit." [10]He responded, "You have asked a hard thing; yet, if you see me as I am being taken from you, it will be granted you; if not, it will not." [11]As they continued walking and talking, a chariot of fire and horses of fire separated the two of them, and Elijah ascended in a whirlwind into heaven. [12]Elisha kept watching and crying out, "Father, father! The chariots of Israel and its horsemen!" But when he could no longer see him, he grasped his own clothes and tore them in two pieces.

Psalm 50:1-6 (UM783)

[1]The mighty one, God the LORD,
      speaks and summons the earth
      from the rising of the sun to its setting.
[2]Out of Zion, the perfection of beauty,
      God shines forth.
[3]Our God comes and does not keep silence,
      before him is a devouring fire,
      and a mighty tempest all around him.
[4]He calls to the heavens above
      and to the earth, that he may judge his people:
[5]"Gather to me my faithful ones,
      who made a covenant with me by sacrifice!"
[6]The heavens declare his righteousness,
      for God himself is judge.

[Selah]

2 Corinthians 4:3-6

[3]And even if our gospel is veiled, it is veiled to those who are perishing. [4]In their case the god of this world has blinded the minds of the unbelievers, to keep them from seeing the light of the gospel of the glory of Christ, who is the image of God. [5]For we do not proclaim ourselves; we proclaim Jesus Christ as Lord and ourselves as your slaves for Jesus' sake. [6]For it is the God who said, "Let light shine out of darkness," who has shone in our hearts to give the light of the knowledge of the glory of God in the face of Jesus Christ.

Mark 9:2-9

[2]Six days later, Jesus took with him Peter and James and John, and led them up a high mountain apart, by themselves. And he was transfigured before them, [3]and his clothes became dazzling white, such as no one on earth could bleach them. [4]And there appeared to them Elijah with Moses, who were talking with Jesus. [5]Then Peter said to Jesus, "Rabbi, it is good for us to be here; let us make three dwellings, one for you, one for Moses, and one for Elijah." [6]He did not know what to say, for they were terrified. [7]Then a cloud overshadowed them, and from the cloud there came a voice, "This is my Son, the Beloved; listen to him!" [8]Suddenly when they looked around, they saw no one with them any more, but only Jesus.

[9]As they were coming down the mountain, he ordered them to tell no one about what they had seen, until after the Son of Man had risen from the dead.

Primary Hymns and Songs for the Day
173 "Christ, Whose Glory Fills the Skies" (Mark) (O)
    H-3 Hbl-51; Chr-206; Desc-89; Org-120
    S-1 #278-279. Harm.
258 "O Wondrous Sight! O Vision Fair" (Mark)
    H-3 Hbl-93; Chr-84; Desc-102; Org-175
    S-2 #191. Harm.
2103 "We Have Come at Christ's Own Bidding" (Mark)
    H-3 Hbl-46; Chr-26, 134; Desc-53; Org-56
    S-1 #168-171. Various treatments
2173 "Shine, Jesus, Shine" (2 Cor, Mark)
    H-3 Chr-171
703 "Swing Low, Sweet Chariot" (2 Kgs, Black History) (C)
    H-3 Chr-177

Additional Hymn Suggestions
113 "Source and Sovereign, Rock and Cloud" (2 Kgs, Pss, 2 Cor, Mark)
203 "Hail to the Lord's Anointed" (2 Kgs, Mark) (O)
704 "Steal Away to Jesus" (2 Kgs, Mark, Black History)
124 "Seek the Lord" (Pss)
206 "I Want to Walk as a Child of the Light" (2 Cor)
451 "Be Thou My Vision" (2 Cor)
454 "Open My Eyes, That I May See" (2 Cor)
585 "This Little Light of Mine" (2 Cor)
2166 "Christ Beside Me" (2 Cor)
2204 "Light of the World" (2 Cor)
2218 "You Are Mine" (2 Cor)
2237 "As a Fire Is Meant for Burning" (2 Cor)
188 "Christ Is the World's Light" (2 Cor, Mark) (C)
157 "Jesus Shall Reign" (Mark)
260 "Christ, Upon the Mountain Peak" (Mark)
371 "I Stand Amazed in the Presence" (Mark)
636 "Christian People, Raise Your Song" (Mark, Comm.)
638 "This Is the Feast of Victory" (Mark, Comm.)
717 "Mine Eyes Have Seen the Glory" (Mark, Transfig.)
2077 "You Alone Are Holy" (Mark)
2084 "Come, Let Us with Our Lord Arise" (Mark)
2102 "Swiftly Pass the Clouds of Glory" (Mark)
2202 "Come Away with Me" (Mark)
2268 "As We Gather at Your Table" (Mark, Comm.)
3157 "Come, Let Us Dream" (Mark)
3043 "You, Lord, Are Both Lamb and Shepherd" (Transfig.)

Additional Contemporary Suggestions
WS3186 "Days of Elijah" (2 Kgs)
S2029 "Praise to the Lord" (Pss)
S2024 "From the Rising of the Sun" (Pss)
S2049 "God Is Here Today" (Pss, Transfig.)
WS3023 "Forever" (Pss)
WS3016 "What a Mighty God We Serve" (Pss)
    SP3; S2021, SF2021 alternate tune
M211 "I Will Not Forget You" (Pss)
M19 "Shine on Us" (2 Cor)
WS3038 "Mighty to Save" (2 Cor)
WS3105 "In Christ Alone" (2 Cor)
WS3163 "Walking in the Light of God" (2 Cor)
UM349 "Turn Your Eyes upon Jesus" (Mark)
S2273 "Jesus, We Are Here" ("*Yesu Tawa Pano*") (Mark)
S2272 "Holy Ground" (Mark)
SP20 "Oh, the Glory of Your Presence" (Mark, Transfig.)
SP71 "When I Look Into Your Holiness" (Mark, Transfig.)
M43 "We Declare Your Majesty" (Mark, Transfig.)
S2070 "He Is Exalted" (Mark, Transfig.)
S2086 "Open Our Eyes, Lord" (Mark, Transfig.)

S2018 "Honor and Praise" (Transfig.)
S2069 "All Hail King Jesus" (Transfig.)
WS3056 "Jesus, the Light of the World" (Transfig.)
SP4 "Great and Mighty Is He" (Transfig.)
M36 "Awesome in This Place" (Transfig.)

Vocal Solos
"Shine, Jesus, Shine" (2 Cor, Transfig.)
    V-3(2) p. 48
"I Saw the Lord, and All Beside Was Darkness" (Mark)
    V-8 p. 268

Anthems
"This Little Light of Mine" (2 Cor)
Arr. David L. Bone; Hinshaw HMC1966
SATB divisi, a cappella

"Holy Ground" (Mark)
Ken Medema; Hope GC 980
SATB with piano

Other Suggestions
Visuals:
  O Light, whirlwind, fire, mantel/stole, generations
  P Sunrise/set, fire, scales of justice, Ps 50:6a
  E Manacles, light/darkness, Christ
  G White robe, cloud, transfigured Christ, Elijah, Moses
Introit: S2005, BOW216. "Arise, Shine" (2 Kgs, Mark)
Greeting: BOW306 (2 Cor) or BOW318 (2 Kgs, Mark)
Opening Prayer: BOW308 or BOW310 (Mark)
Canticle: UM652. "Canticle of Remembrance" (1 Kgs)
Call to Prayer: S2202. "Come Away with Me" (Mark)
Prayer of Confession: BOW478 (Mark)
Words of Assurance: BOW476 (2 Cor)
Prayer: BOW436 (Scouting Sunday)
Prayer: UM259. Transfig. (2 Cor, Mark)
Prayer: UM489 or BOW525 (2 Cor)
Prayer: BOW319, BOW500, or BOW529 (1 Kgs, Mark)
Prayer of Thanksgiving: BOW556 (Transfig.)
Closing Prayer: WSL13 (Transfig.)
Blessing: BOW560 (Transfig.)

Joel 2:1-2, 12-17

¹Blow the trumpet in Zion;
　sound the alarm on my holy mountain!
Let all the inhabitants of the land tremble,
　for the day of the LORD is coming, it is near—
²a day of darkness and gloom,
　a day of clouds and thick darkness!
Like blackness spread upon the mountains
　a great and powerful army comes;
their like has never been from of old,
　nor will be again after them
　in ages to come.
. . . .

¹²Yet even now, says the LORD,
　return to me with all your heart,
with fasting, with weeping, and with mourning;
　¹³rend your hearts and not your clothing.
Return to the LORD, your God,
　for he is gracious and merciful,
slow to anger, and abounding in steadfast love,
　and relents from punishing.
¹⁴Who knows whether he will not turn and relent,
　and leave a blessing behind him,
a grain offering and a drink offering
　for the LORD, your God?
¹⁵Blow the trumpet in Zion;
　sanctify a fast;
call a solemn assembly;
　¹⁶gather the people.
Sanctify the congregation;
　assemble the aged;
gather the children,
　even infants at the breast.
Let the bridegroom leave his room,
　and the bride her canopy.
¹⁷Between the vestibule and the altar
　let the priests, the ministers of the LORD, weep.
Let them say, "Spare your people, O LORD,
　and do not make your heritage a mockery,
　a byword among the nations.
Why should it be said among the peoples,
　'Where is their God?'"

Psalm 51:1-17 [G423, N657, P195/196, UM785]

¹Have mercy on me, O God,
　according to your steadfast love;
according to your abundant mercy
　blot out my transgressions.
²Wash me thoroughly from my iniquity,
　and cleanse me from my sin.
³For I know my transgressions,
　and my sin is ever before me.
⁴Against you, you alone, have I sinned,
　and done what is evil in your sight,
so that you are justified in your sentence
　and blameless when you pass judgment.
⁵Indeed, I was born guilty,
　a sinner when my mother conceived me.
⁶You desire truth in the inward being;
　therefore teach me wisdom in my secret heart.
⁷Purge me with hyssop, and I shall be clean;
　wash me, and I shall be whiter than snow.
⁸Let me hear joy and gladness;
　let the bones that you have crushed rejoice.
⁹Hide your face from my sins,
　and blot out all my iniquities.
¹⁰Create in me a clean heart, O God,
　and put a new and right spirit within me.

¹¹Do not cast me away from your presence,
　and do not take your holy spirit from me.
¹²Restore to me the joy of your salvation,
　and sustain in me a willing spirit.
¹³Then I will teach transgressors your ways,
　and sinners will return to you.
¹⁴Deliver me from bloodshed, O God,
　O God of my salvation,
　and my tongue will sing aloud of your deliverance.
¹⁵O Lord, open my lips,
　and my mouth will declare your praise.
¹⁶For you have no delight in sacrifice;
　if I were to give a burnt offering, you would not be pleased.
¹⁷The sacrifice acceptable to God is a broken spirit;
　a broken and contrite heart, O God, you will not despise.

2 Corinthians 5:20b–6:10

²⁰ᵇ[W]e entreat you on behalf of Christ, be reconciled to God. ²¹For our sake he made him to be sin who knew no sin, so that in him we might become the righteousness of God.

6 As we work together with him, we urge you also not to accept the grace of God in vain. ²For he says,
　"At an acceptable time I have listened to you,
　　and on a day of salvation I have helped you."
See, now is the acceptable time; see, now is the day of salvation! ³We are putting no obstacle in anyone's way, so that no fault may be found with our ministry, ⁴but as servants of God we have commended ourselves in every way: through great endurance, in afflictions, hardships, calamities, ⁵beatings, imprisonments, riots, labors, sleepless nights, hunger; ⁶by purity, knowledge, patience, kindness, holiness of spirit, genuine love, ⁷truthful speech, and the power of God; with the weapons of righteousness for the right hand and for the left; ⁸in honor and dishonor, in ill repute and good repute. We are treated as impostors, and yet are true; ⁹as unknown, and yet are well known; as dying, and see—we are alive; as punished, and yet not killed; ¹⁰as sorrowful, yet always rejoicing; as poor, yet making many rich; as having nothing, and yet possessing everything.

Matthew 6:1-6, 16-21

¹"Beware of practicing your piety before others in order to be seen by them; for then you have no reward from your Father in heaven.

²"So whenever you give alms, do not sound a trumpet before you, as the hypocrites do in the synagogues and in the streets, so that they may be praised by others. Truly I tell you, they have received their reward. ³But when you give alms, do not let your left hand know what your right hand is doing, ⁴so that your alms may be done in secret; and your Father who sees in secret will reward you.

⁵"And whenever you pray, do not be like the hypocrites; for they love to stand and pray in the synagogues and at the street corners, so that they may be seen by others. Truly I tell you, they have received their reward. ⁶But whenever you pray, go into your room and shut the door and pray to your Father who is in secret; and your Father who sees in secret will reward you. . . .

¹⁶"And whenever you fast, do not look dismal, like the hypocrites, for they disfigure their faces so as to show others that they are fasting. Truly I tell you, they have received their reward. ¹⁷But when you fast, put oil on your head and wash your face, ¹⁸so that your fasting may be seen not by others but by your Father who is in secret; and your Father who sees in secret will reward you.

¹⁹"Do not store up for yourselves treasures on earth, where moth and rust consume and where thieves break in and steal; ²⁰but store up for yourselves treasures in heaven, where neither moth nor rust consumes and where thieves do not break in and steal. ²¹For where your treasure is, there your heart will be also."

Primary Hymns and Songs for the Day

269 "Lord, Who Throughout These Forty Days" (Matt) (O)
        H-3   Chr-106; Desc-65; Org-72
        S-2   #105. Flute/violin Desc.
                 #106. Harm.
453 "More Love to Thee, O Christ" (Matt)
        H-3   Org-94
2128 "Come and Find the Quiet Center" (Matt)
2138 "Sunday's Palms Are Wednesday's Ashes" (Ash Wed.)
        H-3   Hbl-14, 64; Chr-132, 203
        S-2   #22. Desc.
(Note that 2128 and 2138 use the same tune.)
3098 "Dust and Ashes" (Ash Wed.)
402 "Lord, I Want to Be a Christian" (Joel, Matt) (C)
        H-3   Chr-130

Additional Hymn Suggestions

121 "There's a Wideness in God's Mercy" (Joel)
296 "Sing My Tongue, the Glorious Battle" (Joel)
379 "Blow Ye the Trumpet, Blow" (Joel)
2206 "Without Seeing You" (Joel, Ash Wed.)
2236 "Gather Us In" (Joel, Comm.)
2265 "Time Now to Gather" (Joel, Comm.)
355 "Depth of Mercy" (Pss, Lent)
3097 "Depth of mercy" (Pss, Lent)
3103 "Purify My Heart" (Pss)
3140 "Give Me Jesus" (Pss, Black History)
2133 "Give Me a Clean Heart" (Pss)
2134 "Forgive Us, Lord" ("*Perdón, Señor*") (Pss)
292 "What Wondrous Love Is This" (2 Cor)
294 "Alas! and Did My Savior Bleed" (2 Cor)
359 "Alas! and Did My Savior Bleed" (2 Cor)
450 "Creator of the Earth and Skies" (2 Cor)
580 "Lead On, O King Eternal" (2 Cor)
627 "O the Depth of Love Divine" (2 Cor, Comm.)
2234 "Lead On, O Cloud of Presence" (2 Cor, Lent)
2255 "In the Singing" (2 Cor, Comm.)
384 "Love Divine, All Loves Excelling" (2 Cor, Matt)
352 "It's Me, It's Me, O Lord" (Matt, Black History)
357 "Just as I Am, Without One Plea" (Matt)
395 "Take Time to Be Holy" (Matt)
472 "Near to the Heart of God" (Matt)
492 "Prayer Is the Soul's Sincere Desire" (Matt)
496 "Sweet Hour of Prayer" (Matt)
2140 "Since Jesus Came into My Heart" (Matt)
2202 "Come Away with Me" (Matt)
2205 "The Fragrance of Christ" (Matt)
2262 "Let Us Offer to the Father" (Matt)
2278 "The Lord's Prayer" (Matt)
3068 "The Lord's Prayer" (Matt, Lent)

Additional Contemporary Suggestions

WS3176 "Come, Now Is the Time to Worship" (Joel) (O)
M224 "Because of Your Love" (Joel, Pss)
S2086 "Open Our Eyes, Lord" (Pss)
S2133 "Give Me a Clean Heart" (Pss)
S2152 "Change My Heart, O God" (Pss)
S2154 "Please Enter My Heart, Hosanna" (Pss)
S2157 "Come and Fill Our Hearts" (Pss)
S2277 "Lord, Have Mercy" (Pss)
WS3008 "Open the Eyes of My Heart" (Pss)
WS3103 "Purify My Heart" (Pss)
WS3188 "Hosanna" (Pss)
M50 "Refiner's Fire" (Pss)

M26 "The Power of Your Love" (Pss)
M35 "White as Snow" (Pss)
M97 "I Give You My Heart" (Pss)
M153 "Give Us Clean Hands" (Pss)
M251 "Grace Like Rain" (Pss)
M277 "How Great Is the Love" (Pss)
S2055 "You Are My Hiding Place" (Pss, Matt)
SP158 "The Battle Belongs to the Lord" (2 Cor)
M94 "That's Why We Praise Him" (2 Cor)
S2193 "Lord, Listen to Your Children Praying" (Matt)
M38 "I Want to Know You" ("In the Secret") (Matt)
M115 "When It's All Been Said and Done" (Matt)
WS3040 "You Are My All in All" (Matt)
WS3069 "The Lord's Prayer" (Matt, Lent)

Vocal Solos

"If with All Your Hearts" (recitative & aria from *Elijah*) (Joel)
    V-8   p. 277
"A Contrite Heart" (Pss)
    V-4   p. 10
"Give Me Jesus" (Pss, Matt, Lent)
    V-3(1)   p. 53
    V-8   p. 256

Anthems

"O God, Have Mercy" (Pss)
Arr. Lloyd Pfautsch; Hinshaw HMC1875
SATB a cappella

"The Lord's Prayer" (Matt)
Mark A. Miller; Abingdon Press 0687491444
SATB with piano

Other Suggestions

Visuals:
    O   Black cloth, grain, wine, trumpet, empty plate
    P   Water, snow, rejoicing, Ps 51:10, 15, 17, heart
    E   Clock, calendar with today's date, rejoicing, black/gold
    G   Praying hands, oil/water, closed door, empty plate, rust
Introit: S2273, BOW187. "Jesus, We Are Here" (Matt)
Greeting: BOW321 or BOW328 (Joel) or BOW243 (2 Cor)
Opening Prayer: BOW460 (Matt)
Call to Prayer: S2200. "O Lord, Hear My Prayer" (Matt)
Prayer of Confession: WSL14 (Ash Wed., Lent)
Prayer of Confession: BOW475 or WSL15 (Pss)
Response: S2275. "*Kyrie*" (Pss)
Words of Assurance: BOW158. Words of Grace (Ash Wed.)
Prayer: UM353. Ash Wednesday (Pss)
Response: BOW217 "Remember that You Are Dust" (Joel, Ash Wed.)
Offering Prayer: WSL123. "Gracious God" (Matt)
Prayer of Thanksgiving: BOW552 (Joel)

Genesis 9:8-17

[8]Then God said to Noah and to his sons with him, [9]"As for me, I am establishing my covenant with you and your descendants after you, [10]and with every living creature that is with you, the birds, the domestic animals, and every animal of the earth with you, as many as came out of the ark. [11]I establish my covenant with you, that never again shall all flesh be cut off by the waters of a flood, and never again shall there be a flood to destroy the earth." [12]God said, "This is the sign of the covenant that I make between me and you and every living creature that is with you, for all future generations: [13]I have set my bow in the clouds, and it shall be a sign of the covenant between me and the earth. [14]When I bring clouds over the earth and the bow is seen in the clouds, [15]I will remember my covenant that is between me and you and every living creature of all flesh; and the waters shall never again become a flood to destroy all flesh. [16]When the bow is in the clouds, I will see it and remember the everlasting covenant between God and every living creature of all flesh that is on the earth." [17]God said to Noah, "This is the sign of the covenant that I have established between me and all flesh that is on the earth."

Psalm 25:1-10 (UM756)

[1]To you, O LORD, I lift up my soul.
[2]O my God, in you I trust;
    do not let me be put to shame;
    do not let my enemies exult over me.
[3]Do not let those who wait for you be put to shame;
    let them be ashamed who are wantonly treacherous.
[4]Make me to know your ways, O LORD;
    teach me your paths.
[5]Lead me in your truth, and teach me,
    for you are the God of my salvation;
    for you I wait all day long.
[6]Be mindful of your mercy, O LORD, and of your steadfast love,
    for they have been from of old.
[7]Do not remember the sins of my youth or my transgressions;
    according to your steadfast love remember me,
    for your goodness' sake, O LORD!
[8]Good and upright is the LORD;
    therefore he instructs sinners in the way.
[9]He leads the humble in what is right,
    and teaches the humble his way.
[10]All the paths of the LORD are steadfast love and faithfulness,
    for those who keep his covenant and his decrees.

1 Peter 3:18-22

[18]For Christ also suffered for sins once for all, the righteous for the unrighteous, in order to bring you to God. He was put to death in the flesh, but made alive in the spirit, [19]in which also he went and made a proclamation to the spirits in prison, [20]who in former times did not obey, when God waited patiently in the days of Noah, during the building of the ark, in which a few, that is, eight persons, were saved through water. [21]And baptism, which this prefigured, now saves you—not as a removal of dirt from the body, but as an appeal to God for a good conscience, through the resurrection of Jesus Christ, [22]who has gone into heaven and is at the right hand of God, with angels, authorities, and powers made subject to him.

Mark 1:9-15

[9]In those days Jesus came from Nazareth of Galilee and was baptized by John in the Jordan. [10]And just as he was coming up out of the water, he saw the heavens torn apart and the Spirit descending like a dove on him. [11]And a voice came from heaven, "You are my Son, the Beloved; with you I am well pleased."

[12]And the Spirit immediately drove him out into the wilderness. [13]He was in the wilderness forty days, tempted by Satan; and he was with the wild beasts; and the angels waited on him.

[14]Now after John was arrested, Jesus came to Galilee, proclaiming the good news of God, [15]and saying, "The time is fulfilled, and the kingdom of God has come near; repent, and believe in the good news."

Primary Hymns and Songs for the Day

269   "Lord, Who Throughout These Forty Days" (Mark)
     (O)
        H-3   Chr-106; Desc-65; Org-72
        S-2   #105. Flute/violin Desc.
                 #106. Harm.
2165   "Cry of My Heart" (Pss)
252   "When Jesus Came to Jordan" (Mark)
        H-3   Chr-211
347   "Spirit Song" (1 Pet, Mark)
2238   "In the Midst of New Dimensions" (Gen) (C)

Additional Hymn Suggestions

122   "God of the Sparrow" (Gen)
443   "O God Who Shaped Creation" (Gen)
480   "O Love That Wilt Not Let Me Go" (Gen)
508   "Faith, While Trees Are Still in Blossom" (Gen)
2046   "Womb of Life" (Gen)
2170   "God Made from One Blood" (Gen)
2237   "As a Fire Is Meant for Burning" (Gen)
3031   "God Leads Us Along" (Gen, Mark)
2123   "Loving Spirit" (Gen, Mark, Baptism)
502   "Thy Holy Wings, O Savior" (Gen, 1 Pet)
411   "Dear Lord, Lead Me Day by Day" (Pss) (O)
467   "Trust and Obey" (Pss) (C)
473   "Lead Me, Lord" (Pss)
2214   "Lead Me, Guide Me" (Pss)
2254   "In Remembrance of Me" (Pss, Comm.)
3167   "Feed Us, Lord" (Pss, Mark, Comm.)
289   "Ah, Holy Jesus" (1 Pet)
325   "Hail, Thou Once Despised Jesus" (1 Pet)
61   "Come, Thou Almighty King" (1 Pet, Mark) (O)
193   "Jesus! The Name High over All" (1 Pet, Mark)
2247   "Wonder of Wonders" (1 Pet, Mark, Baptism)
2248   "Baptized in Water" (1 Pet, Mark, Baptism)
178   "Hope of the World" (Mark)
267   "O Love, How Deep" (Mark)
525   "We'll Understand It Better By and By" (Mark)
616   "Come, Sinners, to the Gospel Feast" (Mark, Comm.)
723   "Shall We Gather at the River" (Mark, Baptism)
2089   "Wild and Lone the Prophet's Voice" (Mark, Lent)
2105   "Jesus, Tempted in the Desert" (Mark)
2112   "Jesus Walked This Lonesome Valley" (Mark)
2114   "At the Font We Start Our Journey" (Mark, Baptism)
2122   "She Comes Sailing on the Wind" (Mark)
3045   "Down by the Jordan" (Mark)

Additional Contemporary Suggestions

UM488   "Jesus, Remember Me" (Gen)
S2253   "Water, River, Spirit, Grace" (Gen, Mark, Baptism)
S2022   "Great Is the Lord" (Pss)
S2161   "To Know You More" (Pss)
S2167   "More Like You" (Pss)
S2277   "Lord, Have Mercy" (Pss)
M38   "I Want to Know You" ("In the Secret") (Pss)
M63   "I Could Sing of Your Love Forever" (Pss)
WS3023   "Forever" (Pss)
WS3099   "Hungry" ("Falling on My Knees") (Pss, Lent)
M107   "Show Me Your Ways" (Pss)
M108   "Lead Me, Lord" (Pss)
M113   "In the Presence of Jehovah" (Pss)
M277   "How Great Is the Love" (Pss, Lent)
WS3096   "Gentle Shepherd" (Pss, Mark, Lent)
SP40   "God Will Make a Way" (Pss, Mark)
M30   "Knowing You" (Pss, Mark)

S2071   "Jesus, Name above All Names" (1 Pet, Mark)
S2250   "I've Just Come from the Fountain" (1 Pet, Mark)
S2107   "Wade in the Water" (Mark)
S2117   "Spirit of God" (Mark)
S2272   "Holy Ground" (Mark, Lent)
WS3073   "We Walk His Way" (Mark)
WS3164   "Down to the River to Pray" (Mark)

Vocal Solos

"This Is De Healin' Water" (Gen, Mark, Baptism)
    V-7   p. 52
"God Will Make a Way" (with "He Leadeth Me") (Pss, Lent)
    V-3(2)   p. 9
"Ah, Holy Jesus" (1 Pet)
    V-6   p. 24

Anthems

"Jesus Is a Rock in a Weary Land" (Mark, Lent)
Kyle Johnson; MorningStar 50-6104
SATB with piano

"Prayer for Guidance" (Pss)
Allen Pote; Hinshaw HMC2330
SAB with keyboard

Other Suggestions

Visuals:
    O   Water, Noah's ark, animals, rainbow
    P   Praying hands, Ps 25:1, 9a
    E   Baptism, cross, resurrection, open Bible, see (Gen), prison
    G   Rocks, sand, bones, Holy Spirit, no. 40, wild animals, angels, dove
Introit: UM292, stanza 1. "What Wondrous Love Is This"
Greeting: BOW326 (Pss) or BOW329 (Mark)
Opening Prayer: BOW464 (Gen)
Prayer of Confession: WSL14 (Lent)
Prayer of Confession: BOW490 (Mark)
Response: S2275. "Kyrie" (Pss)
Prayer: WSL16, UM253 or BOW333 (Mark)
Prayer: BOW509 or BOW399. Week 3 (Gen)
Prayer: UM493 or UM705 (Pss, Lent)
Scripture Response: UM368, stanza 3. "My Hope Is Built" (Gen)
Call to Baptism: S2050, stanza 1. "Mothering God, You Gave Me Birth" (Gen, Mark)
Blessing: BOW566 (Lent)

Genesis 17:1-7, 15-16

¹When Abram was ninety-nine years old, the LORD appeared to Abram, and said to him, "I am God Almighty; walk before me, and be blameless. ²And I will make my covenant between me and you, and will make you exceedingly numerous." ³Then Abram fell on his face; and God said to him, ⁴"As for me, this is my covenant with you: You shall be the ancestor of a multitude of nations. ⁵No longer shall your name be Abram, but your name shall be Abraham; for I have made you the ancestor of a multitude of nations. ⁶I will make you exceedingly fruitful; and I will make nations of you, and kings shall come from you. ⁷I will establish my covenant between me and you, and your offspring after you throughout their generations, for an everlasting covenant, to be God to you and to your offspring after you." . . .

¹⁵God said to Abraham, "As for Sarai your wife, you shall not call her Sarai, but Sarah shall be her name. ¹⁶I will bless her, and moreover I will give you a son by her. I will bless her, and she shall give rise to nations; kings of peoples shall come from her."

Psalm 22:23-31 (UM752)

²³You who fear the LORD, praise him!
    All you offspring of Jacob, glorify him;
    stand in awe of him, all you offspring of Israel!
²⁴For he did not despise or abhor
    the affliction of the afflicted;
he did not hide his face from me,
    but heard when I cried to him.
²⁵From you comes my praise in the great congregation;
    my vows I will pay before those who fear him.
²⁶The poor shall eat and be satisfied;
    those who seek him shall praise the LORD.
    May your hearts live forever!
²⁷All the ends of the earth shall remember
    and turn to the LORD;
and all the families of the nations
    shall worship before him.
²⁸For dominion belongs to the LORD,
    and he rules over the nations.
²⁹To him, indeed, shall all who sleep in the earth bow down;
    before him shall bow all who go down to the dust,
    and I shall live for him.
³⁰Posterity will serve him;
    future generations will be told about the Lord,
³¹and proclaim his deliverance to a people yet unborn,
    saying that he has done it.

Romans 4:13-25

¹³For the promise that he would inherit the world did not come to Abraham or to his descendants through the law but through the righteousness of faith. ¹⁴If it is the adherents of the law who are to be the heirs, faith is null and the promise is void. ¹⁵For the law brings wrath; but where there is no law, neither is there violation.

¹⁶For this reason it depends on faith, in order that the promise may rest on grace and be guaranteed to all his descendants, not only to the adherents of the law but also to those who share the faith of Abraham (for he is the father of all of us, ¹⁷as it is written, "I have made you the father of many nations")—in the presence of the God in whom he believed, who gives life to the dead and calls into existence the things that do not exist. ¹⁸Hoping against hope, he believed that he would become "the father of many nations," according to what was said, "So numerous shall your descendants be." ¹⁹He did not weaken in faith when he considered his own body, which was already as good as dead (for he was about a hundred years old), or when he considered the barrenness of Sarah's womb. ²⁰No distrust made him waver concerning the promise of God, but he grew strong in his faith as he gave glory to God, ²¹being fully convinced that God was able to do what he had promised. ²²Therefore his faith "was reckoned to him as righteousness." ²³Now the words, "it was reckoned to him," were written not for his sake alone, ²⁴but for ours also. It will be reckoned to us who believe in him who raised Jesus our Lord from the dead, ²⁵who was handed over to death for our trespasses and was raised for our justification.

Mark 8:31-38

³¹Then he began to teach them that the Son of Man must undergo great suffering, and be rejected by the elders, the chief priests, and the scribes, and be killed, and after three days rise again. ³²He said all this quite openly. And Peter took him aside and began to rebuke him. ³³But turning and looking at his disciples, he rebuked Peter and said, "Get behind me, Satan! For you are setting your mind not on divine things but on human things."

³⁴He called the crowd with his disciples, and said to them, "If any want to become my followers, let them deny themselves and take up their cross and follow me. ³⁵For those who want to save their life will lose it, and those who lose their life for my sake, and for the sake of the gospel, will save it. ³⁶For what will it profit them to gain the whole world and forfeit their life? ³⁷Indeed, what can they give in return for their life? ³⁸Those who are ashamed of me and of my words in this adulterous and sinful generation, of them the Son of Man will also be ashamed when he comes in the glory of his Father with the holy angels."

Primary Hymns and Songs for the Day

116	"The God of Abraham Praise" (Gen, Pss, Mark) (O)	
	H-3	Hbl-62, 95; Chr-59; Org-77
	S-1	#211. Harm.
508	"Faith, While Trees Are Still in Blossom" (Gen, Rom)	
	H-3	Chr-67
	S-2	#63-64. Desc. and Harm.
415	"Take Up Thy Cross" (Mark)	
424	"Must Jesus Bear the Cross Alone" (Mark)	
2129	"I Have Decided to Follow Jesus" (Mark)	
338	"Where He Leads Me" (Mark) (C)	

Additional Hymn Suggestions

100	"God, Whose Love Is Reigning o'er Us" (Gen) (O)
2246	"Deep in the Shadows of the Past" (Gen)
451	"Be Thou My Vision" (Gen, Rom)
589	"The Church of Christ, in Every Age" (Gen, Rom)
629	"You Satisfy the Hungry Heart" (Pss, Comm.)
2180	"Why Stand So Far Away, My God?" (Pss)
2267	"Taste and See" (Pss, Comm.)
3142	"I Love the Lord" (Pss)
178	"Hope of the World" (Rom)
374	"Standing on the Promises" (Rom)
385	"Let Us Plead for Faith Alone" (Rom)
507	"Through It All" (Rom)
541	"See How Great a Flame Aspires" (Rom)
710	"Faith of Our Fathers" (Rom)
2147	"There Are Some Things I May Not Know" (Rom)
2196	"We Walk by Faith" (Rom)
2211	"Faith Is Patience in the Night" (Rom)
2255	"In the Singing" (Rom, Comm.)
261	"Lord of the Dance" (Mark)
297	"Beneath the Cross of Jesus" (Mark)
438	"Forth in Thy Name, O Lord" (Mark) (C)
442	"Weary of All Trumpeting" (Mark)
553	"And Are We Yet Alive" (Mark)
589	"The Church of Christ, in Every Age" (Mark)
2083	"My Song Is Love Unknown" (Mark, Lent)
2102	"Swiftly Pass the Clouds of Glory" (Mark)
2137	"Would I Have Answered When You Called" (Mark)
2149	"Living for Jesus" (Mark)

Additional Contemporary Suggestions

WS3004	"Step by Step" (Gen)	
UM123	"El-Shaddai" (Gen)	
	S-2	#54 Verses for Vocal Solo
S2036	"Give Thanks" (Pss)	
WS3162	"Stand in Awe" (Pss)	
UM99	"My Tribute" ("To God Be the Glory") (Rom)	
	V-8	p. 5. Vocal Solo
S2108	"O How He Loves You and Me!" (Rom)	
S2186	"Song of Hope" (Rom) (C)	
S2258	"Sing Alleluia to the Lord" (Rom)	
S2264	"Come to the Table" (Rom, Comm.)	
S2266	"Here Is Bread, Here Is Wine" (Rom, Comm.)	
SP111	"There Is a Redeemer" (Rom, Lent)	
M251	"Grace Like Rain" (Rom)	
WS3073	"We Walk His Way" (Mark)	
WS3160	"We Will Follow" ("*Somlandela*") (Mark)	
M30	"Knowing You" ("All I Once Held Dear") (Mark, Lent)	
M53	"Let It Be Said of Us" (Mark)	
M76	"The Wonderful Cross" (Mark, Lent)	
M79	"I Stand Amazed" (Mark, Lent)	
M98	"Take This Life" (Mark, Lent)	
M106	"I Come to the Cross" (Mark, Lent)	

M122	"Every Move I Make" (Mark)
M150	"Everyday" (Mark)
M248	"One Way" (Mark)
M255	"Just to Be with You" (Mark, Lent)

Vocal Solos

"Redeeming Grace" (Rom)
　　V-4　　p. 47
"Christ Living Within You" (Mark)
　　V-8　　p. 177
"Lead Me to Calvary" (Mark, Lent)
　　V-8　　p. 226

Anthems

"Be Thou My Vision" (Gen, Rom)
Arr. Dan Forrest; Brookfield Press 08745013
SATB with piano

"Take Up Your Cross" (Mark)
Arr. Anthony Giamanco; Augsburg 9780800678968
2-part mixed with piano

Other Suggestions

Visuals:
O	Elderly man/woman, people of all nations, covenant
P	Praising, hungry being fed, people of all nations, deliverance
E	Elderly person holding a child, all nations, resurrection
G	Wooden cross, crucifix, resurrection, sandals (follow)

Introit: 292, stanza 1. "What Wondrous Love Is This." (John)
Greeting: BOW343 (Mark)
Opening Prayer: BOW467 or BOW469 (Gen)
Prayer of Confession: WSL90 or BOW476 (Mark)
Prayer of Confession: BOW483 (Gen, Rom)
Response: S2277. "Lord, Have Mercy" (Mark, Lent)
Prayer: UM268 or UM403 (Mark)
Prayer: BOW336 (Mark) or BOW511 (Pss)
Prayer of Thanksgiving: BOW551 (Gen, Mark)
Benediction or Sending Words: WSL164 (Gen)
Benediction: BOW189. "May This Mind Be in Us" (Rom)
Benediction: WS3183. "As We Go" (Mark)

Exodus 20:1-17

[1]Then God spoke all these words: [2]I am the LORD your God, who brought you out of the land of Egypt, out of the house of slavery; [3]you shall have no other gods before me.

[4]You shall not make for yourself an idol, whether in the form of anything that is in heaven above, or that is on the earth beneath, or that is in the water under the earth. [5]You shall not bow down to them or worship them; for I the LORD your God am a jealous God, punishing children for the iniquity of parents, to the third and the fourth generation of those who reject me, [6]but showing steadfast love to the thousandth generation of those who love me and keep my commandments.

[7]You shall not make wrongful use of the name of the LORD your God, for the LORD will not acquit anyone who misuses his name.

[8]Remember the sabbath day, and keep it holy. [9]Six days you shall labor and do all your work. [10]But the seventh day is a sabbath to the LORD your God; you shall not do any work—you, your son or your daughter, your male or female slave, your livestock, or the alien resident in your towns. [11]For in six days the LORD made heaven and earth, the sea, and all that is in them, but rested the seventh day; therefore the LORD blessed the sabbath day and consecrated it.

[12]Honor your father and your mother, so that your days may be long in the land that the LORD your God is giving you.

[13]You shall not murder.

[14]You shall not commit adultery.

[15]You shall not steal.

[16]You shall not bear false witness against your neighbor.

[17]You shall not covet your neighbor's house; you shall not covet your neighbor's wife, or male or female slave, or ox, or donkey, or anything that belongs to your neighbor.

Psalm 19 (UM750)

[1]The heavens are telling the glory of God;
    and the firmament proclaims his handiwork.
[2]Day to day pours forth speech,
    and night to night declares knowledge.
[3]There is no speech, nor are there words;
    their voice is not heard;
[4]yet their voice goes out through all the earth,
    and their words to the end of the world.
In the heavens he has set a tent for the sun,
[5]which comes out like a bridegroom from his wedding canopy,
    and like a strong man runs its course with joy.
[6]Its rising is from the end of the heavens,
    and its circuit to the end of them;
    and nothing is hid from its heat.
[7]The law of the LORD is perfect,
    reviving the soul;
the decrees of the LORD are sure,
    making wise the simple;
[8]the precepts of the LORD are right,
    rejoicing the heart;
the commandment of the LORD is clear,
    enlightening the eyes;
[9]the fear of the LORD is pure,
    enduring forever;
the ordinances of the LORD are true
    and righteous altogether.
[10]More to be desired are they than gold,
    even much fine gold;
sweeter also than honey,
    and drippings of the honeycomb.

[11]Moreover by them is your servant warned;
    in keeping them there is great reward.
[12]But who can detect their errors?
    Clear me from hidden faults.
[13]Keep back your servant also from the insolent;
    do not let them have dominion over me.
Then I shall be blameless,
    and innocent of great transgression.
[14]Let the words of my mouth and the meditation of my heart
    be acceptable to you,
    O LORD, my rock and my redeemer.

1 Corinthians 1:18-25

[18]For the message about the cross is foolishness to those who are perishing, but to us who are being saved it is the power of God. [19]For it is written,

    "I will destroy the wisdom of the wise,
        and the discernment of the discerning I will thwart."

[20]Where is the one who is wise? Where is the scribe? Where is the debater of this age? Has not God made foolish the wisdom of the world? [21]For since, in the wisdom of God, the world did not know God through wisdom, God decided, through the foolishness of our proclamation, to save those who believe. [22]For Jews demand signs and Greeks desire wisdom, [23]but we proclaim Christ crucified, a stumbling block to Jews and foolishness to Gentiles, [24]but to those who are the called, both Jews and Greeks, Christ the power of God and the wisdom of God. [25]For God's foolishness is wiser than human wisdom, and God's weakness is stronger than human strength.

John 2:13-22

[13]The Passover of the Jews was near, and Jesus went up to Jerusalem. [14]In the temple he found people selling cattle, sheep, and doves, and the money changers seated at their tables. [15]Making a whip of cords, he drove all of them out of the temple, both the sheep and the cattle. He also poured out the coins of the money changers and overturned their tables. [16]He told those who were selling the doves, "Take these things out of here! Stop making my Father's house a marketplace!" [17]His disciples remembered that it was written, "Zeal for your house will consume me." [18]The Jews then said to him, "What sign can you show us for doing this?" [19]Jesus answered them, "Destroy this temple, and in three days I will raise it up." [20]The Jews then said, "This temple has been under construction for forty-six years, and will you raise it up in three days?" [21]But he was speaking of the temple of his body. [22]After he was raised from the dead, his disciples remembered that he had said this; and they believed the scripture and the word that Jesus had spoken.

Primary Hymns and Songs for the Day

77	"How Great Thou Art" (Pss) (O)	
	H-3	Chr-103; Org-105
	S-1	#163. Harm.
295	"In the Cross of Christ I Glory" (1 Cor)	
	H-3	Hbl-72; Chr-113; Desc-89; Org-119
	S-1	#276-277. Harm. with Desc.
2112	"Jesus Walked This Lonesome Valley" (John)	
504	"The Old Rugged Cross" (1 Cor) (C)	
	H-3	Chr-190; Org-163

Additional Hymn Suggestions

211	"O Come, O Come, Emmanuel" (Exod)
	(See especially stanzas 2 and 3.)
390	"Forgive Our Sins as We Forgive" (Exod)
404	"Every Time I Feel the Spirit" (Exod)
417	"O For a Heart to Praise My God" (Exod)
2077	"You Alone Are Holy" (Exod)
2120	"Spirit, Spirit of Gentleness" (Exod)
2168	"Love the Lord Your God" (Exod)
3029	"In the Desert, on God's Mountain" (Exod)
529	"How Firm a Foundation" (Exod, Pss, John)
395	"Take Time to Be Holy" (Exod, John)
410	"I Want a Principle Within" (Exod, John) (C)
149	*"Cantemos al Señor"* ("Let's Sing unto the Lord") (Pss)
685	"Now on Land and Sea Descending" (Pss)
2012	"Let Us with a Joyful Mind" (Pss)
425	"O Crucified Redeemer" (Pss, John)
2004	"Praise the Source of Faith and Learning" (Pss, 1 Cor, John)
132	"All My Hope Is Firmly Grounded" (1 Cor)
160	"Rejoice, Ye Pure in Heart" (1 Cor)
296	"Sing, My Tongue, the Glorious Battle" (1 Cor)
577	"God of Grace and God of Glory" (1 Cor)
627	"O the Depth of Love Divine" (1 Cor)
2266	"Here Is Bread, Here Is Wine" (1 Cor, Comm.)
3075	"Glory in the Cross" (1 Cor, Lent)
3122	"Christ Has Broken Down the Wall" (1 Cor)
265	"O Christ, the Healer" (1 Cor, John)
297	"Beneath the Cross of Jesus" (1 Cor, John)
552	"Here, O Lord, Your Servants Gather" (1 Cor, John, Comm.)
261	"Lord of the Dance" (John)
267	"O Love, How Deep" (John)
269	"Lord, Who Throughout These Forty Days" (John)
289	"Ah, Holy Jesus" (John)
427	"Where Cross the Crowded Ways of Life" (John)
433	"All Who Love and Serve Your City" (John)
614	"For the Bread Which You Have Broken" (John, Comm.)
624	"Bread of the World" (John, Comm.)
2060	"God the Sculptor of the Mountains" (John)
2089	"Wild and Lone the Prophet's Voice" (John)

Additional Contemporary Suggestions

UM404	"Every Time I Feel the Spirit" (Exod)
S2018	"Honor and Praise" (Exod)
M229	"Forevermore" (Exod)
WS3116	"Love the Lord" (Exod)
WS3028	"Holy Is the Lord" (Exod, Pss)
S2002	"I Will Call Upon the Lord" (Pss)
S2066	"Praise the Name of Jesus" (Pss)
WS3034	"God of Wonders" (Pss)
M58	"All Heaven Declares" (Pss)
M111	"The Heavens Shall Declare" (Pss)

M235	"Sing, Sing, Sing" (Pss)
M243	"Beautiful Savior" (Pss, 1 Cor)
M93	"Rock of Ages" (Pss, John)
S2065	"More Precious than Silver" (Pss, John)
WS3042	"Shout to the North" (1 Cor)
M76	"The Wonderful Cross" (1 Cor)
M53	"Let It Be Said of Us" (1 Cor)
M164	"Good to Me" (1 Cor)
M227	"I Will Boast" (1 Cor)
WS3040	"You Are My All in All" (1 Cor, John)
S2164	"Sanctuary" (John)
M71	"The Heart of Worship" (John)

Vocal Solos

"The Heavens Declare His Glory" (Pss)
  V-8   p. 248
"Ah, Holy Jesus" (John)
  V-6   p. 24

Anthems

"At the Cross" (1 Cor)
Arr. Joel Raney; Hope C-5275
SATB with piano, opt. oboe and cello

"Expectans expectavi" (John)
Charles Wood: Free download at www.CPDL.org
SATB with organ

Other Suggestions

Visuals:

O	Tablet/ten commandments, open manacles
P	Celestial images, tent, wedding canopy, bridegroom, runner
E	Wooden cross, clown or jester, (stumbling) block
G	Animals, whip, overturned table, spilled coins, cross,

Introit: S2271. "Come! Come! Everybody Worship" (Exod)
Act of Congregational Centering: BOW470 (1 Cor)
Greeting: BOW330 (1 Cor)
Opening Prayer: BOW460 (John)
Canticle: UM112. "Canticle of Wisdom" (1 Cor)
Prayer of Confession: BOW479 (Exod)
Litany: BOW496. The Ten Commandments (Exod)
Prayer for Illumination: WSL71 (Exod, Pss)
Prayer: UM268. Lent (Exod)
Prayer: UM429. For Our Country (1 Cor, John)
Prayer: BOW335, BOW510, or BOW525 (1 Cor)
Response: BOW193. "Prayer for Wisdom" (1 Cor)
Prayer: BOW501 or BOW514 (John)
Response: BOW191. "May This Mind Be in Us" (John)

Numbers 21:4-9

[4]From Mount Hor they set out by the way to the Red Sea, to go around the land of Edom; but the people became impatient on the way. [5]The people spoke against God and against Moses, "Why have you brought us up out of Egypt to die in the wilderness? For there is no food and no water, and we detest this miserable food." [6]Then the LORD sent poisonous serpents among the people, and they bit the people, so that many Israelites died. [7]The people came to Moses and said, "We have sinned by speaking against the LORD and against you; pray to the LORD to take away the serpents from us." So Moses prayed for the people. [8]And the LORD said to Moses, "Make a poisonous serpent, and set it on a pole; and everyone who is bitten shall look at it and live." [9]So Moses made a serpent of bronze, and put it upon a pole; and whenever a serpent bit someone, that person would look at the serpent of bronze and live.

Psalm 107:1-3, 17-22 (UM830)

[1]O give thanks to the LORD, for he is good;
    for his steadfast love endures forever.
[2]Let the redeemed of the LORD say so,
    those he redeemed from trouble
[3]and gathered in from the lands,
    from the east and from the west,
    from the north and from the south.
. . . .
[17]Some were sick through their sinful ways,
    and because of their iniquities endured affliction;
[18]they loathed any kind of food,
    and they drew near to the gates of death.
[19]Then they cried to the LORD in their trouble,
    and he saved them from their distress;
[20]he sent out his word and healed them,
    and delivered them from destruction.
[21]Let them thank the LORD for his steadfast love,
    for his wonderful works to humankind.
[22]And let them offer thanksgiving sacrifices,
    and tell of his deeds with songs of joy.

Ephesians 2:1-10

[1]You were dead through the trespasses and sins [2]in which you once lived, following the course of this world, following the ruler of the power of the air, the spirit that is now at work among those who are disobedient. [3]All of us once lived among them in the passions of our flesh, following the desires of flesh and senses, and we were by nature children of wrath, like everyone else. [4]But God, who is rich in mercy, out of the great love with which he loved us [5]even when we were dead through our trespasses, made us alive together with Christ—by grace you have been saved—[6]and raised us up with him and seated us with him in the heavenly places in Christ Jesus, [7]so that in the ages to come he might show the immeasurable riches of his grace in kindness toward us in Christ Jesus. [8]For by grace you have been saved through faith, and this is not your own doing; it is the gift of God—[9]not the result of works, so that no one may boast. [10]For we are what he has made us, created in Christ Jesus for good works, which God prepared beforehand to be our way of life.

John 3:14-21

[14]"And just as Moses lifted up the serpent in the wilderness, so must the Son of Man be lifted up, [15]that whoever believes in him may have eternal life.

[16]"For God so loved the world that he gave his only Son, so that everyone who believes in him may not perish but may have eternal life.

[17]"Indeed, God did not send the Son into the world to condemn the world, but in order that the world might be saved through him. [18]Those who believe in him are not condemned; but those who do not believe are condemned already, because they have not believed in the name of the only Son of God. [19]And this is the judgment, that the light has come into the world, and people loved darkness rather than light because their deeds were evil. [20]For all who do evil hate the light and do not come to the light, so that their deeds may not be exposed. [21]But those who do what is true come to the light, so that it may be clearly seen that their deeds have been done in God."

Primary Hymns and Songs for the Day

108	"God Hath Spoken by the Prophets" (Num, John) (O)	
	H-3	Chr-53; Org-33
	S-1	#109-10. Desc. and Harm.
S2036	"Give Thanks" (Num, Pss)	
378,	"Amazing Grace" (Eph, Comm.)	
4091	H-3	Hbl-14, 46; Chr-27; Desc-14; Org-4
	S-2	#5-7. Various treatments
2162	"Grace Alone" (Eph)	
206	"I Want to Walk as a Child of the Light" (John) (O)	
292	"What Wondrous Love Is This" (John) (C)	
	H-3	Hbl-102; Chr-212; Org-185
	S-1	#347. Harm.

Additional Hymn Suggestions

142	"If Thou But Suffer God to Guide Thee" (Num)
3029	"In the Desert, on God's Mountain" (Num)
102	"Now Thank We All Our God" (Pss)
2009	"O God Beyond All Praising" (Pss)
2172	"We Are Called" (Pss, John) (O)
3142	"I Love the Lord" (Pss)
121	"There's a Wideness in God's Mercy" (Eph)
355	"Depth of Mercy" (Eph)
3097	"Depth of Mercy" (Eph)
357	"Just as I Am, Without One Plea (Eph)
361	"Rock of Ages, Cleft for Me" (Eph)
363	"And Can It Be that I Should Gain" (Eph)
381	"Savior, Like a Shepherd Lead Us" (Eph)
385	"Let Us Plead for Faith Alone" (Eph)
579	"Lord God, Your Love Has Called Us Here" (Eph)
2196	"We Walk by Faith" (Eph)
2211	"Faith Is Patience in the Night" (Eph)
2255	"In the Singing" (Eph, Comm.)
3110	"By Grace We Have Been Saved" (Eph)
365	"Grace Greater than Our Sin" (Eph, John)
98	"To God Be the Glory" (John)
184	"Of the Father's Love Begotten" (John)
185	"When Morning Gilds the Skies" (John)
188	"Christ Is the World's Light" (John)
194	"Morning Glory, Starlit Sky" (John)
267	"O Love, How Deep" (John)
287	"O Love Divine, What Hast Thou Done" (John)
364	"Because He Lives" (John)
2084	"Come, Let Us with Our Lord Arise" (John)
2121	"O Holy Spirit, Root of Life" (John)
2149	"Living for Jesus" (John)
2259	"Victim Divine" (John, Lent)
434	*Cuando El Pobre* (UMCOR)

Additional Contemporary Suggestions

S2031	"We Bring the Sacrifice of Praise" (Pss)
WS3023	"Forever" (Pss)
WS3042	"Shout to the North" (Pss)
WS3014	"You Are Good" (Pss)
WS3015	"How Great You Are" (Pss)
WS3027	"Hallelujah" ("Your Love Is Amazing") (Ps, Eph, John)
WS3187	"We Fall Down" (Eph)
WS3026	"God Is Good All the Time" (Eph)
UM176	"Majesty" (Eph)
M251	"Grace Like Rain" (Eph)
S2073	"Celebrate Love" (Eph, John)
S2258	"Sing Alleluia to the Lord" (Eph, John)
S2085	"He Came Down" (John)
S2088	"Lord, I Lift Your Name on High" (John, Lent)
S2108	"O How He Loves You and Me!" (John)

SP111	"There Is a Redeemer" (John)
WS3040	"You Are My All in All" (John)
M25	"No Greater Love" (John)
M63	"I Could Sing of Your Love Forever" (John)
WS3102	"You Are My King" ("Amazing Love") (John)
WS3105	"In Christ Alone" ("My Hope Is Found") (John)
M106	"I Come to the Cross" (John, Lent)

Vocal Solos

"And Can It Be that I Should Gain" (Eph)
  V-1   p. 29
"Redeeming Grace" (Eph)
  V-4   p. 47
"Above All" (John)
  V-3(2)   p. 17

Anthems

"Cherokee Amazing Grace" (Eph, Comm.)
Arr. Huff and Green; Hinshaw HMC2341
SATB and soloists with flute and percussion

"God So Loved the World" (John)
Katherine K. Davis; ECS Publishing 1.2214
SATB a cappella

Other Suggestions

Visuals:

O	Bronze serpent on a pole, wilderness, empty bowl/cup
P	Ps 107:2, map or globe, praying hands, thanksgiving, singing
E	Death (black), resurrection, gift, life preserver (salvation)
G	Light/darkness, wooden cross, crucifix, John 3:16, life preserver

Greeting: BOW326 (Eph) or BOW424 (UMCOR)
Opening Prayer: BOW251 (John)
Prayer of Confession: BOW480 (Num, Eph)
Response: S2275. "*Kyrie*" (Eph)
Song of Assurance: S2141. "There's a Song" (Eph)
Prayer: WSL17. "A wilderness beckons" (Num, Lent)
Prayer: UM456. For Courage to Do Justice (UMCOR)
Prayer: BOW334 (Num, Pss, Eph) or BOW336 (John)
Prayer: BOW500. For Blessing, Mercy, and Courage (Pss)
Poem: UM58 or UM342 (Eph)
Offering Prayer: WSL110 (John)
Prayer of Thanksgiving: BOW551 (Pss, Eph)
Blessing: BOW563 (Eph, John)

Jeremiah 31:31-34

[31]The days are surely coming, says the LORD, when I will make a new covenant with the house of Israel and the house of Judah. [32]It will not be like the covenant that I made with their ancestors when I took them by the hand to bring them out of the land of Egypt—a covenant that they broke, though I was their husband, says the LORD. [33]But this is the covenant that I will make with the house of Israel after those days, says the LORD: I will put my law within them, and I will write it on their hearts; and I will be their God, and they shall be my people. [34]No longer shall they teach one another, or say to each other, "Know the LORD," for they shall all know me, from the least of them to the greatest, says the LORD; for I will forgive their iniquity, and remember their sin no more.

Psalm 51:1-12 (UM785)

[1]Have mercy on me, O God,
    according to your steadfast love;
according to your abundant mercy
    blot out my transgressions.
[2]Wash me thoroughly from my iniquity,
    and cleanse me from my sin.
[3]For I know my transgressions,
    and my sin is ever before me.
[4]Against you, you alone, have I sinned,
    and done what is evil in your sight,
so that you are justified in your sentence
    and blameless when you pass judgment.
[5]Indeed, I was born guilty,
    a sinner when my mother conceived me.
[6]You desire truth in the inward being;
    therefore teach me wisdom in my secret heart.
[7]Purge me with hyssop, and I shall be clean;
    wash me, and I shall be whiter than snow.
[8]Let me hear joy and gladness;
    let the bones that you have crushed rejoice.
[9]Hide your face from my sins,
    and blot out all my iniquities.
[10]Create in me a clean heart, O God,
    and put a new and right spirit within me.
[11]Do not cast me away from your presence,
    and do not take your holy spirit from me.
[12]Restore to me the joy of your salvation,
    and sustain in me a willing spirit.

Hebrews 5:5-10

[5]So also Christ did not glorify himself in becoming a high priest, but was appointed by the one who said to him,
    "You are my Son,
        today I have begotten you";
[6]as he says also in another place,
    "You are a priest forever,
        according to the order of Melchizedek."
[7]In the days of his flesh, Jesus offered up prayers and supplications, with loud cries and tears, to the one who was able to save him from death, and he was heard because of his reverent submission. [8]Although he was a Son, he learned obedience through what he suffered; [9]and having been made perfect, he became the source of eternal salvation for all who obey him, [10]having been designated by God a high priest according to the order of Melchizedek.

John 12:20-33

[20]Now among those who went up to worship at the festival were some Greeks. [21]They came to Philip, who was from Bethsaida in Galilee, and said to him, "Sir, we wish to see Jesus." [22]Philip went and told Andrew; then Andrew and Philip went and told Jesus. [23]Jesus answered them, "The hour has come for the Son of Man to be glorified. [24]Very truly, I tell you, unless a grain of wheat falls into the earth and dies, it remains just a single grain; but if it dies, it bears much fruit. [25]Those who love their life lose it, and those who hate their life in this world will keep it for eternal life. [26]Whoever serves me must follow me, and where I am, there will my servant be also. Whoever serves me, the Father will honor.

[27]"Now my soul is troubled. And what should I say—'Father, save me from this hour'? No, it is for this reason that I have come to this hour. [28]Father, glorify your name." Then a voice came from heaven, "I have glorified it, and I will glorify it again." [29]The crowd standing there heard it and said that it was thunder. Others said, "An angel has spoken to him." [30]Jesus answered, "This voice has come for your sake, not for mine. [31]Now is the judgment of this world; now the ruler of this world will be driven out. [32]And I, when I am lifted up from the earth, will draw all people to myself." [33]He said this to indicate the kind of death he was to die.

Primary Hymns and Songs for the Day
157 "Jesus Shall Reign" (Heb, John) (O)
    H-3 Hbl-29; Chr-117; Desc-31; Org-31
    S-1   #100-103. Various treatments.
383 "This Is a Day of New Beginnings" (Jer, John)
2133 "Give Me a Clean Heart" (Jer, Pss)
2152 "Change My Heart, O God" (Jer, Pss)
2083 "My Song Is Love Unknown" (Heb)
2129 "I Have Decided to Follow Jesus" (John) (C)
413 "A Charge to Keep I Have" (John) (C)
    H-3 Desc-19; Org-14
    S-1   #46. Choral Harm.

Additional Hymn Suggestions
420 "Breathe on Me, Breath of God" (Jer)
480 "O Love That Wilt Not Let Me Go" (Jer)
593 "Here I Am, Lord" (Jer)
606 "Come, Let Us Use the Grace Divine" (Jer)
2140 "Since Jesus Came into My Heart" (Jer, Pss)
2060 "God the Sculptor of the Mountains" (Jer, Comm.)
2247 "Wonder of Wonders" (Jer, Baptism)
410 "I Want a Principle Within" (Jer, Pss)
417 "O For a Heart to Praise My God" (Pss)
2134 "Forgive Us, Lord" ("*Perdón, Señor*") (Pss)
282 "'Tis Finished! The Messiah Dies" (Heb)
289 "Ah, Holy Jesus" (Heb)
300 "O the Lamb" (Heb)
325 "Hail, Thou Once Despised Jesus" (Heb)
2149 "Living for Jesus" (Heb)
2259 "Victim Divine" (Heb, Comm., Lent)
168 "At the Name of Jesus" (Heb, John)
287 "O Love Divine, What Hast Thou Done" (Heb, John)
159 "Lift High the Cross" (John)
165 "Hallelujah! What a Savior" (John)
256 "We Would See Jesus" (John)
290 "Go to Dark Gethsemane" (John)
297 "Beneath the Cross of Jesus" (John)
311 "Now the Green Blade Riseth" (John)
338 "Where He Leads Me" (John)
396 "O Jesus, I Have Promised" (John)
398 "Jesus Calls Us" (John)
415 "Take Up Thy Cross" (John) (C)
424 "Must Jesus Bear the Cross Alone" (John)
553 "And Are We Yet Alive" (John) (O)
2050 "Mothering God, You Gave Me Birth" (John)
2137 "Would I Have Answered When You Called" (John)
2213 "Healer of Our Every Ill" (John)
3155 "The Lord of Life, a Vine Is He" (John)
3174 "Christ, We Are Blest" (John)

Additional Contemporary Suggestions
M85 "The Potter's Hand" (Jer)
M65 "Before the Throne of God Above" (Jer, Heb)
M266 "You Have Saved Us" (Jer, Heb)
M49 "Refresh My Heart" (Jer, Pss)
M89 "Purified" (Jer, Pss)
M97 "I Give You My Heart" (Jer, Pss)
S2154 "Please Enter My Heart, Hosanna" (Jer, Pss, John)
S2157 "Come and Fill Our Hearts" (Jer, John)
WS3097 "Depth of Mercy" (Pss)
WS3103 "Purify My Heart" (Pss)
WS3188 "Hosanna" (Pss)
M26 "The Power of Your Love" (Pss)
M38 "In the Secret" ("I Want to Know You") (Pss)
M50 "Refiner's Fire" (Pss)

M153 "Give Us Clean Hands" (Pss)
M224 "Because of Your Love" (Pss)
WS3140 "Give Me Jesus" (Pss, John)
M91 "Take My Life" (Pss, John)
M94 "That's Why We Praise Him" (Heb)
S2016 "Glorify Thy Name" (John)
S2086 "Open Our Eyes, Lord" (Pss, John)
S2085 "He Came Down" (John)
S2088 "Lord, I Lift Your Name on High" (John, Lent)
S2176 "Make Me a Servant" (John)
S2222 "The Servant Song" (John)
M67 "We Want to See Jesus Lifted High" (John)

Vocal Solos
"A Contrite Heart" (Pss)
   V-4   p. 10
"Turn My Heart to You" (Pss)
   V-5(2) p. 14
"Clean Before My Lord" (Pss)
   V-8   p. 233

Anthems
"Turn Thy Face From My Sins" (Pss)
Arthur S. Sullivan; ECS Publishing 0377
SATB with organ

"*Agnus Dei*" (John)
Jason McCoy; Choristers Guild CGA1329
Three-part treble with piano

Other Suggestions
Visuals:
  O   Heart, Exodus, open Bible, love at work
  P   Water, bones, Ps 51:7b, 10; rejoicing
  E   Miter/chasuble, praying hands, crucifix, cross
  G   Clock or hourglass, Crucifixion, bowl/pitcher/towel (service)
Introit: UM292, stanza 1. "What Wondrous Love Is This."
Greeting: BOW329 (Heb) or BOW343 (John)
Opening Prayer: BOW447. The Collect (Pss)
Prayer: UM353. Ash Wednesday (Jer, Pss)
Prayer of Confession: BOW475 (Pss) or BOW488 (Jer)
Response: S2277. "Lord, Have Mercy" (Jer, Lent)
Prayer: BOW337 (Heb, John) or BOW514 (Heb)
Prayer: BOW518, BOW522, or BOW530 (Jer, Pss)
Scripture Response: UM479, stanza 4. "Jesus, Lover of My Soul" (Jer)
Prayer of Thanksgiving: BOW550 (Jer, Pss)
Blessing: BOW566. Sarum Blessing (Jer)

PALM TEXTS

Mark 11:1-11

[1]When they were approaching Jerusalem, at Bethphage and Bethany, near the Mount of Olives, he sent two of his disciples [2]and said to them, "Go into the village ahead of you, and immediately as you enter it, you will find tied there a colt that has never been ridden; untie it and bring it. [3]If anyone says to you, 'Why are you doing this?' just say this, 'The Lord needs it and will send it back here immediately.'" [4]They went away and found a colt tied near a door, outside in the street. As they were untying it, [5]some of the bystanders said to them, "What are you doing, untying the colt?" [6]They told them what Jesus had said; and they allowed them to take it. [7]Then they brought the colt to Jesus and threw their cloaks on it; and he sat on it. [8]Many people spread their cloaks on the road, and others spread leafy branches that they had cut in the fields. [9]Then those who went ahead and those who followed were shouting,

"Hosanna!
Blessed is the one who comes in the name of the Lord!
[10]Blessed is the coming kingdom of our ancestor David!
Hosanna in the highest heaven!"

[11]Then he entered Jerusalem and went into the temple; and when he had looked around at everything, as it was already late, he went out to Bethany with the twelve.

Psalm 118:1-2, 19-29 (UM839)

[1]O give thanks to the LORD, for he is good;
  his steadfast love endures forever!
[2]Let Israel say,
  "His steadfast love endures forever."
. . . .
[19]Open to me the gates of righteousness,
  that I may enter through them
  and give thanks to the LORD.
[20]This is the gate of the LORD;
  the righteous shall enter through it.
[21]I thank you that you have answered me
  and have become my salvation.
[22]The stone that the builders rejected
  has become the chief cornerstone.
[23]This is the Lord's doing;
  it is marvelous in our eyes.
[24]This is the day that the LORD has made;
  let us rejoice and be glad in it.
[25]Save us, we beseech you, O LORD!
  O LORD, we beseech you, give us success!
[26]Blessed is the one who comes in the name of the LORD.
  We bless you from the house of the LORD.
[27]The LORD is God,
  and he has given us light.
Bind the festal procession with branches,
  up to the horns of the altar.
[28]You are my God, and I will give thanks to you;
  you are my God, I will extol you.
[29]O give thanks to the LORD, for he is good,
  for his steadfast love endures forever.

PASSION TEXTS

Isaiah 50:4-9a

[4]The Lord GOD has given me
  the tongue of a teacher,
that I may know how to sustain
the weary with a word.
Morning by morning he wakens—
  wakens my ear
  to listen as those who are taught.
[5]The Lord GOD has opened my ear,
  and I was not rebellious,
  I did not turn backward.
[6]I gave my back to those who struck me,
  and my cheeks to those who pulled out the beard;
I did not hide my face
  from insult and spitting.
[7]The Lord GOD helps me;
  therefore I have not been disgraced;
therefore I have set my face like flint,
  and I know that I shall not be put to shame;
  [8]he who vindicates me is near.
Who will contend with me?
  Let us stand up together.
Who are my adversaries?
  Let them confront me.
[9a]It is the Lord GOD who helps me;
  who will declare me guilty?

Psalm 31:9-16 (UM764)

[9]Be gracious to me, O LORD, for I am in distress;
  my eye wastes away from grief,
  my soul and body also.
[10]For my life is spent with sorrow,
  and my years with sighing;
my strength fails because of my misery,
  and my bones waste away.
[11]I am the scorn of all my adversaries,
  a horror to my neighbors,
an object of dread to my acquaintances;
  those who see me in the street flee from me.
[12]I have passed out of mind like one who is dead;
  I have become like a broken vessel.
[13]For I hear the whispering of many—
  terror all around!—
as they scheme together against me,
  as they plot to take my life.
[14]But I trust in you, O LORD;
  I say, "You are my God."
[15]My times are in your hand;
  deliver me from the hand of my enemies and persecutors.
[16]Let your face shine upon your servant;
  save me in your steadfast love.

Philippians 2:5-11

[5]Let the same mind be in you that was in Christ Jesus,
[6]who, though he was in the form of God,
  did not regard equality with God
  as something to be exploited,
[7]but emptied himself,
  taking the form of a slave,
  being born in human likeness.
And being found in human form,
  [8]he humbled himself
  and became obedient to the point of death—
  even death on a cross.
[9]Therefore God also highly exalted him
  and gave him the name
  that is above every name,
[10]so that at the name of Jesus
  every knee should bend,

in heaven and on earth and under the earth,
¹¹and every tongue should confess
    that Jesus Christ is Lord,
    to the glory of God the Father.

Mark 14:1–15:47

¹It was two days before the Passover and the festival of Unleavened Bread. The chief priests and the scribes were looking for a way to arrest Jesus by stealth and kill him; ²for they said, "Not during the festival, or there may be a riot among the people."

³While he was at Bethany in the house of Simon the leper, as he sat at the table, a woman came with an alabaster jar of very costly ointment of nard, and she broke open the jar and poured the ointment on his head. ⁴But some were there who said to one another in anger, "Why was the ointment wasted in this way? ⁵For this ointment could have been sold for more than three hundred denarii, and the money given to the poor." And they scolded her. ⁶But Jesus said, "Let her alone; why do you trouble her? She has performed a good service for me. ⁷For you always have the poor with you, and you can show kindness to them whenever you wish; but you will not always have me. ⁸She has done what she could; she has anointed my body beforehand for its burial. ⁹Truly I tell you, wherever the good news is proclaimed in the whole world, what she has done will be told in remembrance of her."

¹⁰Then Judas Iscariot, who was one of the twelve, went to the chief priests in order to betray him to them. ¹¹When they heard it, they were greatly pleased, and promised to give him money. So he began to look for an opportunity to betray him.

¹²On the first day of Unleavened Bread, when the Passover lamb is sacrificed, his disciples said to him, "Where do you want us to go and make the preparations for you to eat the Passover?" ¹³So he sent two of his disciples, saying to them, "Go into the city, and a man carrying a jar of water will meet you; follow him, ¹⁴and wherever he enters, say to the owner of the house, 'The Teacher asks, Where is my guest room where I may eat the Passover with my disciples?' ¹⁵He will show you a large room upstairs, furnished and ready. Make preparations for us there." ¹⁶So the disciples set out and went to the city, and found everything as he had told them; and they prepared the Passover meal.

¹⁷When it was evening, he came with the twelve. ¹⁸And when they had taken their places and were eating, Jesus said, "Truly I tell you, one of you will betray me, one who is eating with me." ¹⁹They began to be distressed and to say to him one after another, "Surely, not I?" ²⁰He said to them, "It is one of the twelve, one who is dipping bread into the bowl with me. ²¹For the Son of Man goes as it is written of him, but woe to that one by whom the Son of Man is betrayed! It would have been better for that one not to have been born."

²²While they were eating, he took a loaf of bread, and after blessing it he broke it, gave it to them, and said, "Take; this is my body." ²³Then he took a cup, and after giving thanks he gave it to them, and all of them drank from it. ²⁴He said to them, "This is my blood of the covenant, which is poured out for many. ²⁵Truly I tell you, I will never again drink of the fruit of the vine until that day when I drink it new in the kingdom of God."

²⁶When they had sung the hymn, they went out to the Mount of Olives. ²⁷And Jesus said to them, "You will all become deserters; for it is written,

'I will strike the shepherd,
    and the sheep will be scattered.'

²⁸But after I am raised up, I will go before you to Galilee." ²⁹Peter said to him, "Even though all become deserters, I will not." ³⁰Jesus said to him, "Truly I tell you, this day, this very night, before the cock crows twice, you will deny me three times." ³¹But he said vehemently, "Even though I must die with you, I will not deny you." And all of them said the same.

³²They went to a place called Gethsemane; and he said to his disciples, "Sit here while I pray." ³³He took with him Peter and James and John, and began to be distressed and agitated. ³⁴And he said to them, "I am deeply grieved, even to death; remain here, and keep awake." ³⁵And going a little farther, he threw himself on the ground and prayed that, if it were possible, the hour might pass from him. ³⁶He said, "Abba, Father, for you all things are possible; remove this cup from me; yet, not what I want, but what you want." ³⁷He came and found them sleeping; and he said to Peter, "Simon, are you asleep? Could you not keep awake one hour? ³⁸Keep awake and pray that you may not come into the time of trial; the spirit indeed is willing, but the flesh is weak." ³⁹And again he went away and prayed, saying the same words. ⁴⁰And once more he came and found them sleeping, for their eyes were very heavy; and they did not know what to say to him. ⁴¹He came a third time and said to them, "Are you still sleeping and taking your rest? Enough! The hour has come; the Son of Man is betrayed into the hands of sinners. ⁴²Get up, let us be going. See, my betrayer is at hand."

⁴³Immediately, while he was still speaking, Judas, one of the twelve, arrived; and with him there was a crowd with swords and clubs, from the chief priests, the scribes, and the elders. ⁴⁴Now the betrayer had given them a sign, saying, "The one I will kiss is the man; arrest him and lead him away under guard." ⁴⁵So when he came, he went up to him at once and said, "Rabbi!" and kissed him. ⁴⁶Then they laid hands on him and arrested him. ⁴⁷But one of those who stood near drew his sword and struck the slave of the high priest, cutting off his ear. ⁴⁸Then Jesus said to them, "Have you come out with swords and clubs to arrest me as though I were a bandit? ⁴⁹Day after day I was with you in the temple teaching, and you did not arrest me. But let the scriptures be fulfilled." ⁵⁰All of them deserted him and fled.

⁵¹A certain young man was following him, wearing nothing but a linen cloth. They caught hold of him, ⁵²but he left the linen cloth and ran off naked.

⁵³They took Jesus to the high priest; and all the chief priests, the elders, and the scribes were assembled. ⁵⁴Peter had followed him at a distance, right into the courtyard of the high priest; and he was sitting with the guards, warming himself at the fire. ⁵⁵Now the chief priests and the whole council were looking for testimony against Jesus to put him to death; but they found none. ⁵⁶For many gave false testimony against him, and their testimony did not agree. ⁵⁷Some stood up and gave false testimony against him, saying, ⁵⁸"We heard him say, 'I will destroy this temple that is made with hands, and in three days I will build another, not made with hands.'" ⁵⁹But even on this point their testimony did not agree. ⁶⁰Then the high priest stood up before them and asked Jesus, "Have you no answer? What is it that they testify against you?" ⁶¹But he was silent and did not answer. Again the high priest asked him, "Are you the Messiah, the Son of the Blessed One?" ⁶²Jesus said, "I am; and

'you will see the Son of Man
    seated at the right hand of the Power,'
    and 'coming with the clouds of heaven.'"

⁶³Then the high priest tore his clothes and said, "Why do we still need witnesses? ⁶⁴You have heard his blasphemy! What is your decision?" All of them condemned him as deserving death. ⁶⁵Some began to spit on him, to blindfold him, and to strike him, saying to him, "Prophesy!" The guards also took him over and beat him.

[66]While Peter was below in the courtyard, one of the servant-girls of the high priest came by. [67]When she saw Peter warming himself, she stared at him and said, "You also were with Jesus, the man from Nazareth." [68]But he denied it, saying, "I do not know or understand what you are talking about." And he went out into the forecourt. Then the cock crowed. [69]And the servant-girl, on seeing him, began again to say to the bystanders, "This man is one of them." [70]But again he denied it. Then after a little while the bystanders again said to Peter, "Certainly you are one of them; for you are a Galilean." [71]But he began to curse, and he swore an oath, "I do not know this man you are talking about." [72]At that moment the cock crowed for the second time. Then Peter remembered that Jesus had said to him, "Before the cock crows twice, you will deny me three times." And he broke down and wept.

15 As soon as it was morning, the chief priests held a consultation with the elders and scribes and the whole council. They bound Jesus, led him away, and handed him over to Pilate. [2]Pilate asked him, "Are you the King of the Jews?" He answered him, "You say so." [3]Then the chief priests accused him of many things. [4]Pilate asked him again, "Have you no answer? See how many charges they bring against you." [5]But Jesus made no further reply, so that Pilate was amazed.

[6]Now at the festival he used to release a prisoner for them, anyone for whom they asked. [7]Now a man called Barabbas was in prison with the rebels who had committed murder during the insurrection. [8]So the crowd came and began to ask Pilate to do for them according to his custom. [9]Then he answered them, "Do you want me to release for you the King of the Jews?" [10]For he realized that it was out of jealousy that the chief priests had handed him over. [11]But the chief priests stirred up the crowd to have him release Barabbas for them instead. [12]Pilate spoke to them again, "Then what do you wish me to do with the man you call the King of the Jews?" [13]They shouted back, "Crucify him!" [14]Pilate asked them, "Why, what evil has he done?" But they shouted all the more, "Crucify him!" [15]So Pilate, wishing to satisfy the crowd, released Barabbas for them; and after flogging Jesus, he handed him over to be crucified.

[16]Then the soldiers led him into the courtyard of the palace (that is, the governor's headquarters); and they called together the whole cohort. [17]And they clothed him in a purple cloak; and after twisting some thorns into a crown, they put it on him. [18]And they began saluting him, "Hail, King of the Jews!" [19]They struck his head with a reed, spat upon him, and knelt down in homage to him. [20]After mocking him, they stripped him of the purple cloak and put his own clothes on him. Then they led him out to crucify him.

[21]They compelled a passer-by, who was coming in from the country, to carry his cross; it was Simon of Cyrene, the father of Alexander and Rufus. [22]Then they brought Jesus to the place called Golgotha (which means the place of a skull). [23]And they offered him wine mixed with myrrh; but he did not take it. [24]And they crucified him, and divided his clothes among them, casting lots to decide what each should take.

[25]It was nine o'clock in the morning when they crucified him. [26]The inscription of the charge against him read, "The King of the Jews." [27]And with him they crucified two bandits, one on his right and one on his left. [29]Those who passed by derided him, shaking their heads and saying, "Aha! You who would destroy the temple and build it in three days, [30]save yourself, and come down from the cross!" [31]In the same way the chief priests, along with the scribes, were also mocking him among themselves and saying, "He saved others; he cannot save himself. [32]Let the Messiah, the King of Israel, come down from the cross now, so that we may see and believe." Those who were crucified with him also taunted him.

[33]When it was noon, darkness came over the whole land until three in the afternoon. [34]At three o'clock Jesus cried out with a loud voice, "Eloi, Eloi, lema sabachthani?" which means, "My God, my God, why have you forsaken me?" [35]When some of the bystanders heard it, they said, "Listen, he is calling for Elijah." [36]And someone ran, filled a sponge with sour wine, put it on a stick, and gave it to him to drink, saying, "Wait, let us see whether Elijah will come to take him down." [37]Then Jesus gave a loud cry and breathed his last. [38]And the curtain of the temple was torn in two, from top to bottom. [39]Now when the centurion, who stood facing him, saw that in this way he breathed his last, he said, "Truly this man was God's Son!"

[40]There were also women looking on from a distance; among them were Mary Magdalene, and Mary the mother of James the younger and of Joses, and Salome. [41]These used to follow him and provided for him when he was in Galilee; and there were many other women who had come up with him to Jerusalem.

[42]When evening had come, and since it was the day of Preparation, that is, the day before the sabbath, [43]Joseph of Arimathea, a respected member of the council, who was also himself waiting expectantly for the kingdom of God, went boldly to Pilate and asked for the body of Jesus. [44]Then Pilate wondered if he were already dead; and summoning the centurion, he asked him whether he had been dead for some time. [45]When he learned from the centurion that he was dead, he granted the body to Joseph. [46]Then Joseph bought a linen cloth, and taking down the body, wrapped it in the linen cloth, and laid it in a tomb that had been hewn out of the rock. He then rolled a stone against the door of the tomb. [47]Mary Magdalene and Mary the mother of Joses saw where the body was laid.

Primary Hymns and Songs for the Day

278   "Hosanna, Loud Hosanna" (Palms Gospel) (O)
        H-3   Hbl-16, 22, 68; Chr-101; Desc-37
        S-1   #115. Harm.
280   "All Glory, Laud, and Honor" (Palms Gospel)
        H-3   Hbl-45; Chr-22; Desc-96; Org-144
        S-1   #309-310. Harm. with Desc.
3079   "Hosanna" (Palms Gospel)
3082   "Who Is He" (Palms Gospel)
        H-3   Hbl-25, 74; Chr-120; Desc-54; Org-58
        S-1   #173-176. Various treatments
296   "Sing, My Tongue, the Glorious Battle" (Passion)
298   "When I Survey the Wondrous Cross" (Passion) (C)
        H-3   Hbl-6, 102; Chr-213; Desc-49; Org-49
        S-1   #155. Desc.
299   "When I Survey the Wondrous Cross" (Passion) (C)
        H-3   Hbl-47; Chr-76; Desc-90; Org-127
        S-1   #288. Transposition to E-flat major

Additional Hymn Suggestions

277   "Tell Me the Stories of Jesus" (Palms Gospel)
279   *Mantos y Palmas* ("Filled with Excitement") (Palms Gospel)
638   "This Is the Feast of Victory" (Palms, Comm.)
2083   "My Song Is Love Unknown" (Palm Sunday)
2256   "Holy, Holy, Holy Lord" (Palms Gospel)
291   "He Never Said a Mumbalin' Word" (Isa, Passion)
166   "All Praise to Thee, for Thou, O King Divine" (Phil, Passion Gospel)
168   "At the Name of Jesus" (Phil)
193   "Jesus! the Name High Over All" (Phil)
536   "Precious Name" (Phil)
561   "Jesus, United by Thy Grace" (Phil)
2100   "Thou Didst Leave Thy Throne" (Phil)
2111   "We Sang Our Glad Hosannas" (Palms and Passion)
159   "Lift High the Cross" (Passion Gospel) (O) or (C)
267   "O Love, How Deep" (Passion Gospel)
285   "To Mock Your Reign, O Dearest Lord" (Passion)
286   "O Sacred Head, Now Wounded" (Passion Gospel)
287   "O Love Divine, What Hast Thou Done" (Passion)
288   "Were You There" (Passion Gospel)
581   "Lord, Whose Love Through Humble Service" (Passion)
633   "The Bread of Life for All Is Broken" (Passion, Comm.)
2104   "An Outcast among Outcasts" (Passion Gospel)
2110   "Why Has God Forsaken Me?" (Passion Gospel)
2263   "Broken for Me" (Passion, Comm.)

Additional Contemporary Suggestions

WS3008   "Open the Eyes of My Heart" (Isa, Phil)
UM657   "This Is the Day" (Ps 118) (O)
S2270   "I Will Enter His Gates" (Ps 118) (O)
S2069   "All Hail King Jesus" (Palms Gospel)
S2075   "King of Kings" (Palm Sunday)
S2091   "The King of Glory Comes" (Palm Sunday)
2S109   "Hosanna! Hosanna!" (Palms Gospel)
S2154   "Please Enter My Heart, Hosanna" (Palms Gospel)
WS3078   "Hosanna" (Palms Gospel)
WS3188   "Hosanna" (Palms Gospel)
WS3083   "We Adore You, Jesus Christ" ("*Adoremus te Christe*") (Palm/Passion)
WS3023   "Forever" (Ps 118)
WS3044   "Make Way" (Ps 118)
S2070   "He Is Exalted" (Phil)

S2071   "Jesus, Name above All Names" (Phil)
UM177   "He Is Lord" (Phil)
SP234   "At the Name of Jesus" (Phil)
WS3176   "Come, Now Is the Time to Worship" (Phil) (O)
M77   "Above All" (Passion Gospel)
UM261   "Lord of the Dance" (Passion Gospel)
S2198   "Stay with Me" ("*Nohu pu*") (Passion Gospel)
WS3085   "The Power of the Cross" (Passion, Holy Week)

Vocal Solos

"Ride On, Jesus" (Palm Sunday)
    V-7   p. 8
"The Palms" (Palm/Passion Sunday)
    V-8   p. 206
"Ride On, Ride On in Majesty!" (Palms Gospel)
    V-5(2)   p. 57

Anthems

"Sing a Glad Hosanna!" (Palms Gospel)
Lee Dengler; Jubilate 44224
SATB with keyboard

"*O Vos Omnes*" (Mark, Passion)
Pablo Casals; Broude AB 128
SATB a cappella

Other Suggestions

Visuals:

Palms	Colt, palms, cloaks, Hosanna
Ps 118	Gates, cornerstone, Ps 118:24, 26a, 29
O	Jesus teaching, Christ's passion, flint
Ps 13	Praying hands, grief, broken pottery
E	Manacles, wooden cross, crucifix, resurrection, Phil 2:9, 10
Passion	
G	Perfume bottle, water jar, cup/bread/wine, cock crowing, sword, bowl of water, wooden cross, placard, purple cloak, sponge/vinegar, torn curtain, shroud, hour glass

Introit: UM658. "This Is the Day" (Ps 118)
Greeting: BOW245 (Palms) or BOW450 (Ps 118)
Call to Worship: WSL21 (Palms)
Opening Prayer: BOW468 (Passion Sunday)
Canticle: UM167. "Canticle of Christ's Obedience" (Phil) (See S-1, p. 381.)
Prayer: UM281. Passion/Palm Sunday
Prayer: BOW336 or BOW348 (Passion Gospel)
Prayer of Confession: BOW482 (Mark)
Response: BOW189. "May This Mind Be in Us" (Phil)
Responses: S2257. "Communion Setting"

Exodus 12:1-4, (5-10), 11-14

[1]The LORD said to Moses and Aaron in the land of Egypt: [2]This month shall mark for you the beginning of months; it shall be the first month of the year for you. [3]Tell the whole congregation of Israel that on the tenth of this month they are to take a lamb for each family, a lamb for each household. [4]If a household is too small for a whole lamb, it shall join its closest neighbor in obtaining one; the lamb shall be divided in proportion to the number of people who eat of it. ([5]Your lamb shall be without blemish, a year-old male; you may take it from the sheep or from the goats. [6]You shall keep it until the fourteenth day of this month; then the whole assembled congregation of Israel shall slaughter it at twilight. [7]They shall take some of the blood and put it on the two doorposts and the lintel of the houses in which they eat it. [8]They shall eat the lamb that same night; they shall eat it roasted over the fire with unleavened bread and bitter herbs. [9]Do not eat any of it raw or boiled in water, but roasted over the fire, with its head, legs, and inner organs. [10]You shall let none of it remain until the morning; anything that remains until the morning you shall burn.) [11]This is how you shall eat it: your loins girded, your sandals on your feet, and your staff in your hand; and you shall eat it hurriedly. It is the passover of the LORD. [12]For I will pass through the land of Egypt that night, and I will strike down every firstborn in the land of Egypt, both human beings and animals; on all the gods of Egypt I will execute judgments: I am the LORD. [13]The blood shall be a sign for you on the houses where you live: when I see the blood, I will pass over you, and no plague shall destroy you when I strike the land of Egypt.

[14]This day shall be a day of remembrance for you. You shall celebrate it as a festival to the LORD; throughout your generations you shall observe it as a perpetual ordinance.

Psalm 116:1-4, 12-19 (UM116)

[1]I love the LORD, because he has heard
　　my voice and my supplications.
[2]Because he inclined his ear to me,
　　therefore I will call on him as long as I live.
[3]The snares of death encompassed me;
　　the pangs of Sheol laid hold on me;
　　I suffered distress and anguish.
[4]Then I called on the name of the LORD:
　　"O LORD, I pray, save my life!"

. . . .

[12]What shall I return to the LORD
　　for all his bounty to me?
[13]I will lift up the cup of salvation
　　and call on the name of the LORD,
[14]I will pay my vows to the LORD
　　in the presence of all his people.
[15]Precious in the sight of the LORD
　　is the death of his faithful ones.
[16]O LORD, I am your servant;
　　I am your servant, the child of your serving girl.
　　You have loosed my bonds.
[17]I will offer to you a thanksgiving sacrifice
　　and call on the name of the LORD.
[18]I will pay my vows to the LORD
　　in the presence of all his people,
[19]in the courts of the house of the LORD,
　　in your midst, O Jerusalem.
Praise the LORD!

1 Corinthians 11:23-26

[23]For I received from the Lord what I also handed on to you, that the Lord Jesus on the night when he was betrayed took a loaf of bread, [24]and when he had given thanks, he broke it and said, "This is my body that is for you. Do this in remembrance of me." [25]In the same way he took the cup also, after supper, saying, "This cup is the new covenant in my blood. Do this, as often as you drink it, in remembrance of me." [26]For as often as you eat this bread and drink the cup, you proclaim the Lord's death until he comes.

John 13:1-17, 31b-35

[1]Now before the festival of the Passover, Jesus knew that his hour had come to depart from this world and go to the Father. Having loved his own who were in the world, he loved them to the end. [2]The devil had already put it into the heart of Judas son of Simon Iscariot to betray him. And during supper [3]Jesus, knowing that the Father had given all things into his hands, and that he had come from God and was going to God, [4]got up from the table, took off his outer robe, and tied a towel around himself. [5]Then he poured water into a basin and began to wash the disciples' feet and to wipe them with the towel that was tied around him. [6]He came to Simon Peter, who said to him, "Lord, are you going to wash my feet?" [7]Jesus answered, "You do not know now what I am doing, but later you will understand." [8]Peter said to him, "You will never wash my feet." Jesus answered, "Unless I wash you, you have no share with me." [9]Simon Peter said to him, "Lord, not my feet only but also my hands and my head!" [10]Jesus said to him, "One who has bathed does not need to wash, except for the feet, but is entirely clean. And you are clean, though not all of you." [11]For he knew who was to betray him; for this reason he said, "Not all of you are clean."

[12]After he had washed their feet, had put on his robe, and had returned to the table, he said to them, "Do you know what I have done to you? [13]You call me Teacher and Lord—and you are right, for that is what I am. [14]So if I, your Lord and Teacher, have washed your feet, you also ought to wash one another's feet. [15]For I have set you an example, that you also should do as I have done to you. [16]Very truly, I tell you, servants are not greater than their master, nor are messengers greater than the one who sent them. [17]If you know these things, you are blessed if you do them. . . .

[31b]"Now the Son of Man has been glorified, and God has been glorified in him. [32]If God has been glorified in him, God will also glorify him in himself and will glorify him at once. [33]Little children, I am with you only a little longer. You will look for me; and as I said to the Jews so now I say to you, 'Where I am going, you cannot come.' [34]I give you a new commandment, that you love one another. Just as I have loved you, you also should love one another. [35]By this everyone will know that you are my disciples, if you have love for one another."

Primary Hymns and Songs for the Day

292   "What Wondrous Love Is This" (John) (O)
      H-3   Hbl-102; Chr-212; Org-185
      S-1   #347. Harm.
614   "For the Bread Which You Have Broken" (1 Cor)
      H-3   Chr-67
      S-2   #63-64. Desc. and Harm.
2254   "In Remembrance of Me" (1 Cor, Comm.)
2263   "Broken for Me" (1 Cor, Comm.)
432   *"Jesu, Jesu"* (John) (C)
      S-1   #63 Vocal part

Additional Hymn Suggestions

448   "Go Down, Moses" (Exod)
586   "Let My People Seek Their Freedom" (Exod)
2060   "God the Sculptor of the Mountains" (Exod, Comm.)
2246   "Deep in the Shadows of the Past" (Exod)
523   *"Saranam, Saranam"* ("Refuge") (Exod, Pss)
3142   "I Love the Lord" (Pss)
615   "For the Bread Which You Have Broken" (1 Cor)
616   "Come, Sinners, to the Gospel Feast" (1 Cor, Comm.) (O)
618   "Let Us Break Bread Together" (1 Cor, Comm.)
2050   "Mothering God, You Gave Me Birth" (1 Cor, Comm.)
2261   "Life-Giving Bread" (1 Cor, Comm.)
637   *"Una Espiga"* ("Sheaves of Summer") (1 Cor, John, Comm.)
624   "Bread of the World" (John, Comm.)
267   "O Love, How Deep" (John)
286   "O Sacred Head, Now Wounded" (John)
287   "O Love Divine, What Hast Thou Done" (John)
396   "O Jesus, I Have Promised" (John)
430   "O Master, Let Me Walk with Thee" (John)
549   "Where Charity and Love Prevail" (John)
579   "Lord God, Your Love Has Called Us Here" (John)
581   "Lord, Whose Love Through Humble Service" (John)
2111   "We Sang Our Glad Hosannas" (Holy Thursday)
2175   "Together We Serve" (John)
2177   "Wounded World that Cries for Healing" (John)
2213   "Healer of Our Every Ill" (John)
2268   "As We Gather at Your Table" (John, Comm.)
3075   "Glory in the Cross" (John, Holy Week)
3128   "Whatever You Do" (John)
3150   "Father, We Have Heard You Calling" (John)
3152   "Welcome" (John)
3169   "You Feed Us, Gentle Savior" (John, Comm.)

Additional Contemporary Suggestions

UM123   "El-Shaddai" (Exod)
      S-2   #54 Verses for Vocal Solo
WS3093   "Fill My Cup, Lord" (Pss, Comm.)
      UM641 (refrain only)
S2002   "I Will Call Upon the Lord" (Pss)
S2031   "We Bring the Sacrifice of Praise" (Pss)
S2068   "I Love You, Lord" (Pss)
M79   "I Stand Amazed" (Pss, Lent)
M211   "I Will Not Forget You" (Pss)
M243   "Beautiful Savior" (Pss, Holy Week)
M252   "God with Us" (Pss, Holy Week)
UM640   "Take Our Bread" (1 Cor, Comm.)
M203   "Communion" (1 Cor, Comm.)
M253   "Jesus Messiah" (1 Cor, Holy Week, Comm.)
S2176   "Make Me a Servant" (John)
S2179   "Live in Charity" ("Ubi Caritas") (John)
S2222   "The Servant Song" (John)

S2223   "They'll Know We Are Christians" (John)
S2198   "Stay with Me" ("Nohu pu") (Holy Thursday)
WS3074   "Jesus Is a Rock in a Weary Land" (John)
UM620   "One Bread, One Body" (Comm.)

Vocal Solos

"In Remembrance" (1 Cor, John, Comm.)
    V-5(2)   p. 7
"Wondrous Love" (John)
    V-6   p. 47
"O the Deep, Deep Love of Jesus" (John, Comm.)
    V-8   p. 247
"This Is My Commandment" (John)
    V-8   p. 284
"He Breaks the Bread, He Pours the Wine" (John, Comm.)
    V-10   p. 43

Anthems

"In Remembrance of Me" (1 Cor, Comm.)
Arr. Lloyd Larson; Hope C-5722
SAB with piano (other voicings available)

"Seek to Serve" (John)
Lloyd Pfautsch; Hope APM 003
Two-part mixed with keyboard

Other Suggestions

Visuals:
    O   Lamb, sandals, staff, Passover meal
    P   Cup or goblet, open manacles
    E   Bread/wine/pottery chalice, Passover meal
    G   Passover meal, outer garment, towel/basin/water/pitcher, 12 disciples, Last Supper, sripping of the altar, darkness

Suggested Service of Worship: BOW351 (Holy Thur.)
Introit: WS3152. "Welcome" (John)
Greeting: BOW344 or BOW455 (1 Cor, John)
Opening Prayer: BOW460 (John)
Prayer of Confession: BOW491 (John)
Prayer: BOW349 or BOW511 (John)
Prayer: UM283. Holy Thursday (John, 1 Cor)
Prayer: UM639. Bread and Justice (John)
Response: BOW187. "Jesus, We Are Here" (John)
Offering Prayer: WSL154 (John)
Great Thanksgiving for Holy Thursday: BOW64-65
Blessing: BOW563 (John)
Blessing: John 13:34

Isaiah 52:13–53:12

[13]See, my servant shall prosper;
  he shall be exalted and lifted up,
  and shall be very high.
[14]Just as there were many who were astonished at him
  —so marred was his appearance, beyond human semblance,
  and his form beyond that of mortals—
[15]so he shall startle many nations;
  kings shall shut their mouths because of him;
for that which had not been told them they shall see,
  and that which they had not heard they shall contemplate.
53Who has believed what we have heard?
  And to whom has the arm of the LORD been revealed?
[2]For he grew up before him like a young plant,
  and like a root out of dry ground;
he had no form or majesty that we should look at him,
  nothing in his appearance that we should desire him.
[3]He was despised and rejected by others;
  a man of suffering and acquainted with infirmity;
and as one from whom others hide their faces
  he was despised, and we held him of no account.
[4]Surely he has borne our infirmities
  and carried our diseases;
yet we accounted him stricken,
  struck down by God, and afflicted.
[5]But he was wounded for our transgressions,
  crushed for our iniquities;
upon him was the punishment that made us whole,
  and by his bruises we are healed.
[6]All we like sheep have gone astray;
  we have all turned to our own way,
and the LORD has laid on him
  the iniquity of us all.
[7]He was oppressed, and he was afflicted,
  yet he did not open his mouth;
like a lamb that is led to the slaughter,
  and like a sheep that before its shearers is silent,
  so he did not open his mouth.
[8]By a perversion of justice he was taken away.
  Who could have imagined his future?
For he was cut off from the land of the living,
  stricken for the transgression of my people.
[9]They made his grave with the wicked
  and his tomb with the rich,
although he had done no violence,
  and there was no deceit in his mouth.
[10]Yet it was the will of the LORD to crush him with pain.
When you make his life an offering for sin,
  he shall see his offspring, and shall prolong his days;
through him the will of the LORD shall prosper.
  [11]Out of his anguish he shall see light;
he shall find satisfaction through his knowledge.
  The righteous one, my servant, shall make many righteous,
  and he shall bear their iniquities.
[12]Therefore I will allot him a portion with the great,
  and he shall divide the spoil with the strong;
because he poured out himself to death,
  and was numbered with the transgressors;
yet he bore the sin of many,
  and made intercession for the transgressors.

Psalm 22 (UM752)

[1]My God, my God, why have you forsaken me?
  Why are you so far from helping me, from the words of my
   groaning?

[2]O my God, I cry by day, but you do not answer;
  and by night, but find no rest.
[3]Yet you are holy,
  enthroned on the praises of Israel.
[4]In you our ancestors trusted;
  they trusted, and you delivered them.
[5]To you they cried, and were saved;
  in you they trusted, and were not put to shame.
[6]But I am a worm, and not human;
  scorned by others, and despised by the people.
[7]All who see me mock at me;
  they make mouths at me, they shake their heads;
[8]"Commit your cause to the LORD; let him deliver—
  let him rescue the one in whom he delights!"
[9]Yet it was you who took me from the womb;
  you kept me safe on my mother's breast.
[10]On you I was cast from my birth,
  and since my mother bore me you have been my God.
[11]Do not be far from me,
  for trouble is near
  and there is no one to help.
[12]Many bulls encircle me,
  strong bulls of Bashan surround me;
[13]they open wide their mouths at me,
  like a ravening and roaring lion.
[14]I am poured out like water,
  and all my bones are out of joint;
my heart is like wax;
  it is melted within my breast;
[15]my mouth is dried up like a potsherd,
  and my tongue sticks to my jaws;
  you lay me in the dust of death.
[16]For dogs are all around me;
  a company of evildoers encircles me.
My hands and feet have shriveled;
[17]I can count all my bones.
They stare and gloat over me;
[18]they divide my clothes among themselves,
  and for my clothing they cast lots.
[19]But you, O LORD, do not be far away!
  O my help, come quickly to my aid!
[20]Deliver my soul from the sword,
  my life from the power of the dog!
  [21]Save me from the mouth of the lion!
From the horns of the wild oxen you have rescued me.
[22]I will tell of your name to my brothers and sisters;
  in the midst of the congregation I will praise you:
[23]You who fear the LORD, praise him!
  All you offspring of Jacob, glorify him;
  stand in awe of him, all you offspring of Israel!
[24]For he did not despise or abhor
  the affliction of the afflicted;
he did not hide his face from me,
  but heard when I cried to him.
[25]From you comes my praise in the great congregation;
  my vows I will pay before those who fear him.
[26]The poor shall eat and be satisfied;
  those who seek him shall praise the LORD.
  May your hearts live forever!
[27]All the ends of the earth shall remember
  and turn to the LORD;
and all the families of the nations
  shall worship before him.
[28]For dominion belongs to the LORD,
  and he rules over the nations.

29To him, indeed, shall all who sleep in the earth bow down;
  before him shall bow all who go down to the dust,
  and I shall live for him.
30Posterity will serve him;
  future generations will be told about the Lord,
31and proclaim his deliverance to a people yet unborn,
  saying that he has done it.

Hebrews 10:16-25

16This is the covenant that I will make with them
  after those days, says the Lord:
I will put my laws in their hearts,
  and I will write them on their minds.
17he also adds,
I will remember their sins and their lawless deeds no more.
18Where there is forgiveness of these, there is no longer any offering for sin.

19Therefore, my friends, since we have confidence to enter the sanctuary by the blood of Jesus, 20by the new and living way that he opened for us through the curtain (that is, through his flesh), 21and since we have a great priest over the house of God, 22let us approach with a true heart in full assurance of faith, with our hearts sprinkled clean from an evil conscience and our bodies washed with pure water. 23Let us hold fast to the confession of our hope without wavering, for he who has promised is faithful. 24And let us consider how to provoke one another to love and good deeds, 25not neglecting to meet together, as is the habit of some, but encouraging one another, and all the more as you see the Day approaching.

John 18:1–19:42

After Jesus had spoken these words, he went out with his disciples across the Kidron valley to a place where there was a garden, which he and his disciples entered. 2Now Judas, who betrayed him, also knew the place, because Jesus often met there with his disciples. 3So Judas brought a detachment of soldiers together with police from the chief priests and the Pharisees, and they came there with lanterns and torches and weapons. 4Then Jesus, knowing all that was to happen to him, came forward and asked them, "Whom are you looking for?" 5They answered, "Jesus of Nazareth." Jesus replied, "I am he." Judas, who betrayed him, was standing with them. 6When Jesus said to them, "I am he," they stepped back and fell to the ground. 7Again he asked them, "Whom are you looking for?" And they said, "Jesus of Nazareth." 8Jesus answered, "I told you that I am he. So if you are looking for me, let these men go." 9This was to fulfill the word that he had spoken, "I did not lose a single one of those whom you gave me." 10Then Simon Peter, who had a sword, drew it, struck the high priest's slave, and cut off his right ear. The slave's name was Malchus. 11Jesus said to Peter, "Put your sword back into its sheath. Am I not to drink the cup that the Father has given me?"

12So the soldiers, their officer, and the Jewish police arrested Jesus and bound him. 13First they took him to Annas, who was the father-in-law of Caiaphas, the high priest that year. 14Caiaphas was the one who had advised the Jews that it was better to have one person die for the people.

15Simon Peter and another disciple followed Jesus. Since that disciple was known to the high priest, he went with Jesus into the courtyard of the high priest, 16but Peter was standing outside at the gate. So the other disciple, who was known to the high priest, went out, spoke to the woman who guarded the gate, and brought Peter in. 17The woman said to Peter, "You are not also one of this man's disciples, are you?" He said, "I am not." 18Now the slaves and the police had made a charcoal fire because it was cold, and they were standing around it and warming themselves. Peter also was standing with them and warming himself.

19Then the high priest questioned Jesus about his disciples and about his teaching. 20Jesus answered, "I have spoken openly to the world; I have always taught in synagogues and in the temple, where all the Jews come together. I have said nothing in secret. 21Why do you ask me? Ask those who heard what I said to them; they know what I said." 22When he had said this, one of the police standing nearby struck Jesus on the face, saying, "Is that how you answer the high priest?" 23Jesus answered, "If I have spoken wrongly, testify to the wrong. But if I have spoken rightly, why do you strike me?" 24Then Annas sent him bound to Caiaphas the high priest.

25Now Simon Peter was standing and warming himself. They asked him, "You are not also one of his disciples, are you?" He denied it and said, "I am not." 26One of the slaves of the high priest, a relative of the man whose ear Peter had cut off, asked, "Did I not see you in the garden with him?" 27Again Peter denied it, and at that moment the cock crowed.

28Then they took Jesus from Caiaphas to Pilate's headquarters. It was early in the morning. They themselves did not enter the headquarters, so as to avoid ritual defilement and to be able to eat the Passover. 29So Pilate went out to them and said, "What accusation do you bring against this man?" 30They answered, "If this man were not a criminal, we would not have handed him over to you." 31Pilate said to them, "Take him yourselves and judge him according to your law." The Jews replied, "We are not permitted to put anyone to death." 32(This was to fulfill what Jesus had said when he indicated the kind of death he was to die.)

33Then Pilate entered the headquarters again, summoned Jesus, and asked him, "Are you the King of the Jews?" 34Jesus answered, "Do you ask this on your own, or did others tell you about me?" 35Pilate replied, "I am not a Jew, am I? Your own nation and the chief priests have handed you over to me. What have you done?" 36Jesus answered, "My kingdom is not from this world. If my kingdom were from this world, my followers would be fighting to keep me from being handed over to the Jews. But as it is, my kingdom is not from here." 37Pilate asked him, "So you are a king?" Jesus answered, "You say that I am a king. For this I was born, and for this I came into the world, to testify to the truth. Everyone who belongs to the truth listens to my voice." 38Pilate asked him, "What is truth?"

After he had said this, he went out to the Jews again and told them, "I find no case against him. 39But you have a custom that I release someone for you at the Passover. Do you want me to release for you the King of the Jews?" 40They shouted in reply, "Not this man, but Barabbas!" Now Barabbas was a bandit.

19 Then Pilate took Jesus and had him flogged. 2And the soldiers wove a crown of thorns and put it on his head, and they dressed him in a purple robe. 3They kept coming up to him, saying, "Hail, King of the Jews!" and striking him on the face. 4Pilate went out again and said to them, "Look, I am bringing him out to you to let you know that I find no case against him." 5So Jesus came out, wearing the crown of thorns and the purple robe. Pilate said to them, "Here is the man!" 6When the chief priests and the police saw him, they shouted, "Crucify him! Crucify him!" Pilate said to them, "Take him yourselves and crucify him; I find no case against him." 7The Jews answered him, "We have a law, and according to that law he ought to die because he has claimed to be the Son of God."

8Now when Pilate heard this, he was more afraid than ever. 9He entered his headquarters again and asked Jesus, "Where are you from?" But Jesus gave him no answer. 10Pilate therefore said to him, "Do you refuse to speak to me? Do you not know that

I have power to release you, and power to crucify you?" [11]Jesus answered him, "You would have no power over me unless it had been given you from above; therefore the one who handed me over to you is guilty of a greater sin." [12]From then on Pilate tried to release him, but the Jews cried out, "If you release this man, you are no friend of the emperor. Everyone who claims to be a king sets himself against the emperor."

[13]When Pilate heard these words, he brought Jesus outside and sat on the judge's bench at a place called The Stone Pavement, or in Hebrew Gabbatha. [14]Now it was the day of Preparation for the Passover; and it was about noon. He said to the Jews, "Here is your King!" [15]They cried out, "Away with him! Away with him! Crucify him!" Pilate asked them, "Shall I crucify your King?" The chief priests answered, "We have no king but the emperor." [16]Then he handed him over to them to be crucified.

So they took Jesus; [17]and carrying the cross by himself, he went out to what is called The Place of the Skull, which in Hebrew is called Golgotha. [18]There they crucified him, and with him two others, one on either side, with Jesus between them. [19]Pilate also had an inscription written and put on the cross. It read, "Jesus of Nazareth, the King of the Jews." [20]Many of the Jews read this inscription, because the place where Jesus was crucified was near the city; and it was written in Hebrew, in Latin, and in Greek. [21]Then the chief priests of the Jews said to Pilate, "Do not write, 'The King of the Jews,' but, 'This man said, I am King of the Jews.'" [22]Pilate answered, "What I have written I have written." [23]When the soldiers had crucified Jesus, they took his clothes and divided them into four parts, one for each soldier. They also took his tunic; now the tunic was seamless, woven in one piece from the top. [24]So they said to one another, "Let us not tear it, but cast lots for it to see who will get it." This was to fulfill what the scripture says,

"They divided my clothes among themselves,
and for my clothing they cast lots."

[25]And that is what the soldiers did.

Meanwhile, standing near the cross of Jesus were his mother, and his mother's sister, Mary the wife of Clopas, and Mary Magdalene. [26]When Jesus saw his mother and the disciple whom he loved standing beside her, he said to his mother, "Woman, here is your son." [27] Then he said to the disciple, "Here is your mother." And from that hour the disciple took her into his own home.

[28]After this, when Jesus knew that all was now finished, he said (in order to fulfill the scripture), "I am thirsty." [29]A jar full of sour wine was standing there. So they put a sponge full of the wine on a branch of hyssop and held it to his mouth. [30]When Jesus had received the wine, he said, "It is finished." Then he bowed his head and gave up his spirit.

[31]Since it was the day of Preparation, the Jews did not want the bodies left on the cross during the sabbath, especially because that sabbath was a day of great solemnity. So they asked Pilate to have the legs of the crucified men broken and the bodies removed. [32]Then the soldiers came and broke the legs of the first and of the other who had been crucified with him. [33]But when they came to Jesus and saw that he was already dead, they did not break his legs. [34]Instead, one of the soldiers pierced his side with a spear, and at once blood and water came out. [35](He who saw this has testified so that you also may believe. His testimony is true, and he knows that he tells the truth.) [36]These things occurred so that the scripture might be fulfilled, "None of his bones shall be broken." [37]And again another passage of scripture says, "They will look on the one whom they have pierced."

[38]After these things, Joseph of Arimathea, who was a disciple of Jesus, though a secret one because of his fear of the Jews, asked Pilate to let him take away the body of Jesus. Pilate gave him permission; so he came and removed his body. [39]Nicodemus, who had at first come to Jesus by night, also came, bringing a mixture of myrrh and aloes, weighing about a hundred pounds. [40]They took the body of Jesus and wrapped it with the spices in linen cloths, according to the burial custom of the Jews. [41]Now there was a garden in the place where he was crucified, and in the garden there was a new tomb in which no one had ever been laid. [42]And so, because it was the Jewish day of Preparation, and the tomb was nearby, they laid Jesus there.

Primary Hymns and Songs for the Day

288	"Were You There" (John) (O)	
	H-3	Hbl-101; Chr-209
	S-2	#195-196. Desc. and Harm.
165	"Hallelujah! What a Savior" (Isa)	
	H-3	Chr-134
286	"O Sacred Head, Now Wounded" (John)	
	H-3	Hbl-82; Chr-148; Desc-86; Org-111
298	"When I Survey the Wondrous Cross" (John) (C)	
	H-3	Hbl-6, 102; Chr-213; Desc-49; Org-49
	S-1	#155. Desc.
299	"When I Survey the Wondrous Cross" (John) (C)	
	H-3	Hbl-47; Chr-76; Desc-90; Org-127
	S-1	#288. Transposition to E-flat major

Additional Hymn Suggestions

3043	"You, Lord, Are Both Lamb and Shepherd" (Isa)
291	"He Never Said a Mumbalin' Word" (Isa, John)
2180	"Why Stand So Far Away, My God?" (Pss, John)
289	"Ah, Holy Jesus" (Heb)
419	"I Am Thine, O Lord" (Heb)
472	"Near to the Heart of God" (Heb)
640	"Take Our Bread" (Heb, Comm.)
2140	"Since Jesus Came into My Heart" (Heb)
2259	"Victim Divine" (Heb, Comm.)
274	"Woman in the Night" (John)
282	"'Tis Finished! The Messiah Dies" (John)
285	"To Mock Your Reign, O Dearest Lord" (John)
287	"O Love Divine, What Hast Thou Done" (John)
290	"Go to Dark Gethsemane" (John)
294	"Alas! and Did My Savior Bleed" (John) (O)
359	"Alas! and Did My Savior Bleed" (John) (O)
295	"In the Cross of Christ I Glory" (John) (C)
470	"My God, I Love Thee" (John)
633	"The Bread of Life for All Is Broken" (John, Comm.)
2083	"My Song Is Love Unknown" (John, Good Friday)
2100	"Thou Didst Leave Thy Throne" (John)
2106	"When Jesus Wept" (John)
2110	"Why Has God Forsaken Me?" (John)
2111	"We Sang Our Glad Hosannas" (John)
2263	"Broken for Me" (John, Good Friday, Comm.)
2219	"Goodness Is Stronger than Evil" (Good Friday)
3080	"Lord, Is It I?" (Good Friday)
3084	"O Christ, You Hang upon a Cross" (Good Friday)

Additional Contemporary Suggestions

WS3085	"The Power of the Cross" (Isa, John)
SP64	"Our God Reigns" (Isa)
M35	"White as Snow" (Isa)
M239	"Wholly Yours" (Isa)
M247	"The Stand" (Isa, John)
M65	"Before the Throne of God Above" (Heb)
M224	"Because of Your Love" (Heb)
M251	"Grace Like Rain" (Heb)
M81	"Amazing Love" (Heb, John)
M76	"The Wonderful Cross" (Heb, John, Good Friday)
WS3102	"You Are My King" ("Amazing Love") (Heb, John)
M106	"I Come to the Cross" (Heb, John)
WS3105	"In Christ Alone" ("My Hope Is Found") (Heb, John)
SP111	"There Is a Redeemer" (Heb, John, Good Friday)
S2108	"O How He Loves You and Me!" (John)
S2209	"How Long, O Lord" (John, Good Friday)
UM261	"Lord of the Dance" (John)
UM488	"Jesus, Remember Me" (John)
M24	"Jesus, We Crown You with Praise" (John)
M77	"Above All" (John)
M128	"You Are God Alone" (John)
S2113	"Lamb of God" (Good Friday)

Vocal Solos

"He Was Despised" from *Messiah* (Isa)
"He was Cut Off Out of the Land of the Living" (recitative)
"But Thou Didst Not Leave His Soul in Hell" (aria)
    V-2
"Ah, Holy Jesus" (Isa, John)
    V-6   p. 24
"'Tis Finished! The Messiah Dies" (John)
    V-1   p. 63
"Were You There?" (John)
    V-7   p. 60
"They Led Him Away" (John)
    V-8   p. 245
"The Shepherd Became a Lamb" (John)
    V-10   p. 48
"Lamb of God" (Good Friday)
    V-5(2)   p. 5

Anthems

"When I Survey the Wondrous Cross" (John)
Arr. Howard Helvy; Jubilate 44234
SATB with keyboard

"O Sacred Head, Now Wounded" (John, Good Friday)
Brahms, Arr. David Cherwien; MorningStar 50-5655
Unison with piano and optional cello

Other Suggestions

Visuals:
Black draping the cross, black paraments, or none

O	Plant, root, suffering, crucifix, lamb, darkness/light,
P	Exodus, mother breastfeeding, water, bones, sword, dog
E	Heb 10:16b, crucifix
G	Sword, charcoal fire, cock crowing, whip, purple robe, rugged cross, tunic, crucifix, nails, crown of thorns, ladder, sponge on branch, spear, shroud

Introit: S2199. "Stay with Us" (John)
Greeting: BOW329 (Heb)
Prayer of Confession: BOW491 (John)
Response: S2113. "Lamb of God" (John)
Prayer: UM284 or BOW335 or BOW337 (John)
Reading of Seven Last Words: BOW365
Suggestions for Way of the Cross: BOW366
Reading: UM293. "Behold the Savior of Mankind" (John)
Scripture Response: UM290. "Go to Dark Gethsemane." Use this hymn to supplement the reading from John. Sing stanza 1 before beginning 18:1, stanza 2 after 19:3, stanza 3 after 19:30. Sing UM288 stanza 5 at the conclusion of the reading.
Offering Prayer: WSL155 (Good Friday)
Dismissal: BOW559 (John)

Acts 10:34-43

[34] Then Peter began to speak to them: "I truly understand that God shows no partiality, [35] but in every nation anyone who fears him and does what is right is acceptable to him. [36] You know the message he sent to the people of Israel, preaching peace by Jesus Christ—he is Lord of all. [37] That message spread throughout Judea, beginning in Galilee after the baptism that John announced: [38] how God anointed Jesus of Nazareth with the Holy Spirit and with power; how he went about doing good and healing all who were oppressed by the devil, for God was with him. [39] We are witnesses to all that he did both in Judea and in Jerusalem. They put him to death by hanging him on a tree; [40] but God raised him on the third day and allowed him to appear, [41] not to all the people but to us who were chosen by God as witnesses, and who ate and drank with him after he rose from the dead. [42] He commanded us to preach to the people and to testify that he is the one ordained by God as judge of the living and the dead. [43] All the prophets testify about him that everyone who believes in him receives forgiveness of sins through his name."

Psalm 118:1-2, 14-24 (UM839)

[1] O give thanks to the LORD, for he is good;
   his steadfast love endures forever!
[2] Let Israel say,
   "His steadfast love endures forever."
. . . .
[14] The LORD is my strength and my might;
   he has become my salvation.
[15] There are glad songs of victory in the tents of the righteous:
"The right hand of the LORD does valiantly;
   [16] the right hand of the LORD is exalted;
   the right hand of the LORD does valiantly."
[17] I shall not die, but I shall live,
   and recount the deeds of the LORD.
[18] The LORD has punished me severely,
   but he did not give me over to death.
[19] Open to me the gates of righteousness,
   that I may enter through them
   and give thanks to the LORD.
[20] This is the gate of the LORD;
   the righteous shall enter through it.
[21] I thank you that you have answered me
   and have become my salvation.
[22] The stone that the builders rejected
   has become the chief cornerstone.
[23] This is the Lord's doing;
   it is marvelous in our eyes.
[24] This is the day that the LORD has made;
   let us rejoice and be glad in it.

1 Corinthians 15:1-11

[1] Now I would remind you, brothers and sisters, of the good news that I proclaimed to you, which you in turn received, in which also you stand, [2] through which also you are being saved, if you hold firmly to the message that I proclaimed to you—unless you have come to believe in vain.

[3] For I handed on to you as of first importance what I in turn had received: that Christ died for our sins in accordance with the scriptures, [4] and that he was buried, and that he was raised on the third day in accordance with the scriptures, [5] and that he appeared to Cephas, then to the twelve. [6] Then he appeared to more than five hundred brothers and sisters at one time, most of whom are still alive, though some have died. [7] Then he appeared to James, then to all the apostles. [8] Last of all, as to one untimely born, he appeared also to me. [9] For I am the least of the apostles, unfit to be called an apostle, because I persecuted the church of God. [10] But by the grace of God I am what I am, and his grace toward me has not been in vain. On the contrary, I worked harder than any of them—though it was not I, but the grace of God that is with me. [11] Whether then it was I or they, so we proclaim and so you have come to believe.

John 20:1-18

[1] Early on the first day of the week, while it was still dark, Mary Magdalene came to the tomb and saw that the stone had been removed from the tomb. [2] So she ran and went to Simon Peter and the other disciple, the one whom Jesus loved, and said to them, "They have taken the Lord out of the tomb, and we do not know where they have laid him." [3] Then Peter and the other disciple set out and went toward the tomb. [4] The two were running together, but the other disciple outran Peter and reached the tomb first. [5] He bent down to look in and saw the linen wrappings lying there, but he did not go in. [6] Then Simon Peter came, following him, and went into the tomb. He saw the linen wrappings lying there, [7] and the cloth that had been on Jesus' head, not lying with the linen wrappings but rolled up in a place by itself. [8] Then the other disciple, who reached the tomb first, also went in, and he saw and believed; [9] for as yet they did not understand the scripture, that he must rise from the dead. [10] Then the disciples returned to their homes.

[11] But Mary stood weeping outside the tomb. As she wept, she bent over to look into the tomb; [12] and she saw two angels in white, sitting where the body of Jesus had been lying, one at the head and the other at the feet. [13] They said to her, "Woman, why are you weeping?" She said to them, "They have taken away my Lord, and I do not know where they have laid him." [14] When she had said this, she turned around and saw Jesus standing there, but she did not know that it was Jesus. [15] Jesus said to her, "Woman, why are you weeping? Whom are you looking for?" Supposing him to be the gardener, she said to him, "Sir, if you have carried him away, tell me where you have laid him, and I will take him away." [16] Jesus said to her, "Mary!" She turned and said to him in Hebrew, "Rabbouni!" (which means Teacher). [17] Jesus said to her, "Do not hold on to me, because I have not yet ascended to the Father. But go to my brothers and say to them, 'I am ascending to my Father and your Father, to my God and your God.'" [18] Mary Magdalene went and announced to the disciples, "I have seen the Lord"; and she told them that he had said these things to her.

Primary Hymns and Songs for the Day

302   "Christ the Lord Is Risen Today" (1 Cor, John) (O)
         H-3   Hbl-8, 51; Chr-49; Desc-31; Org-32
         S-1   #104-108. Various treatments
310   "He Lives" (1 Cor, John)
2115   "Christ Has Risen" (1 Cor, John)
3090   "The Easter Song" (John, Mark, Easter)
327   "Crown Him with Many Crowns" (John) (C)
         H-3   Hbl-55; Chr-60; Desc-30; Org-27
         S-1   #86-88. Various treatments

Additional Hymn Suggestions

257   "We Meet You, O Christ" (Acts)
610   "We Know That Christ Is Raised" (Acts, Baptism)
2043   "Alleluia" (Pss)
2084   "Come, Let Us with Our Lord Arise" (Pss, John)
2267   "Taste and See" (Pss, Comm.)
306   "The Strife Is O'er, the Battle Done" (1 Cor)
394   "Something Beautiful" (1 Cor)
702   "Sing with All the Saints in Glory" (1 Cor) (C)
303   "The Day of Resurrection" (1 Cor, John)
304   "Easter People, Raise Your Voices" (1 Cor, John)
307   "Christ Is Risen" (1 Cor, John, Comm.)
310   "He Lives" (1 Cor, John)
313   "*Cristo Vive*" ("Christ Is Risen") (1 Cor, John)
134   "O Mary, Don't You Weep" (John)
308   "Thine Be the Glory" (John)
309   "On the Day of Resurrection" (John)
314   "In the Garden" (John)
2111   "We Sang Our Glad Hosannas" (John)
2116   "Christ the Lord Is Risen" (John)
274   "Woman in the Night" (John, Mark)
317   "O Sons and Daughters, Let Us Sing" (John, Mark)
2242   "Walk with Me" (John, Mark)
318   "Christ Is Alive" (Mark)
319   "Christ Jesus Lay in Death's Strong Bands" (Mark)
322   "Up from the Grave He Arose" (Mark)
364   "Because He Lives" (Mark)
2077   "You Alone Are Holy" ("*Sólo Tú Eres Santo*") (Easter)
3088   "Easter Alleluia" (Easter)

Additional Contemporary Suggestions

UM204   "Emmanuel, Emmanuel" (Acts)
M24   "Jesus, We Crown You with Praise" (Acts, Easter)
M32   "Holy and Anointed One" (Acts)
M252   "God with Us" (Acts)
WS3023   "Forever" (Pss)
UM84   "Thank You, Lord" (Pss)
S2270   "I Will Enter His Gates" (Pss)
S2162   "Grace Alone" (1 Cor)
S2088   "Lord, I Lift Your Name on High" (1 Cor, John)
S2116   "Christ the Lord Is Risen" (John, Mark)
S2258   "Sing Alleluia to the Lord" (John, Mark, Easter)
WS3105   "In Christ Alone" ("My Hope Is Found") (John)
3143   "Jesus, You Are the New Day" (John, Mark)
SP64   "Our God Reigns" (John)
SP121   "Celebrate Jesus" (John)
M20   "Jesus Is Alive" (John)
UM186   "Alleluia" (Easter)
         S-2   #3-4
S2026.   "Halle, Halle, Halleluja" (Easter)
S2072   "Amen, Amen" (Easter)
S2078   "Alleluia" (Easter)
S2219   "Goodness Is Stronger than Evil" (Easter)
M21   "Blessing, Honor and Glory" (Easter)

M94   "That's Why We Praise Him" (Easter)
M73   "My Redeemer Lives" (Easter)
M201   "Alive Forever, Amen" (Easter)
M221   "Happy Day" (Easter)
M259   "See What a Morning" ("Resurrection Hymn")

Vocal Solos

"Jesus Christ Is Risen Today" (John)
     V-1   p. 50
"I Know That My Redeemer Liveth" (Easter)
     V-2
"I Know That My Redeemer Lives" (Easter)
     V-5(2)   p. 22
"Crown Him, the Risen King" (Easter)
     V-10   p. 55

Anthems

"Christ the Lord Is Risen Again" (John, Easter)
Philip Stopford; MorningStar 50-8210
SATB divisi with organ

"Forth He Came at Easter" (John)
Allen Pote; Hope C5804
SATB with keyboard and opt. brass

Other Suggestions

Visuals:
O (Acts)   Crucifixion/Resurrection, Acts 10:39a
     P   Cornerstone
     E   Butterfly, empty tomb, open Bible, empty cross
     G   Basket, spices, stone, angels, shroud, risen Christ
Introit: WS3130. "Come, Emmanuel" (Acts, John)
Introit: UM324. "Hail Thee, Festival Day" (Mark)
Greeting: BOW386 or WSL31 (John)
Call to Worship: Psalm 118:19
Opening Prayer: BOW394 (1 Cor)
Affirmation of Faith: WSL29, WSL33 or UM888 (1 Cor)
Response: S2039, stanza 5. "Holy, Holy" (Easter)
Prayer of Intercession: BOW399, Week 1 (Easter)
Prayer of Thanksgiving and Intercession: BOW395 (John)
Great Thanksgiving for Easter Day: BOW66
Response: S2081, BOW203. "Thank You, Jesus" (Pss)
Dismissal with Blessing: BOW376 (John)
Hymns Appropriate for Sunrise Service with Guitar:
    "Morning Has Broken" (UM145) (Easter)
    "Lord of the Dance" (UM261) (Acts)
    "The First One Ever" (UM276) (John)
    "This Is the Day" (UM657, SP236) (Pss)
    "Spirit Song" (UM347, SP134) (Acts, John)
    "O Living God" (WS3089) (John, Easter)

Acts 4:32-35

³²Now the whole group of those who believed were of one heart and soul, and no one claimed private ownership of any possessions, but everything they owned was held in common. ³³With great power the apostles gave their testimony to the resurrection of the Lord Jesus, and great grace was upon them all. ³⁴There was not a needy person among them, for as many as owned lands or houses sold them and brought the proceeds of what was sold. ³⁵They laid it at the apostles' feet, and it was distributed to each as any had need.

Psalm 133 (UM850)

¹How very good and pleasant it is
    when kindred live together in unity!
²It is like the precious oil on the head,
    running down upon the beard,
on the beard of Aaron,
    running down over the collar of his robes.
³It is like the dew of Hermon,
    which falls on the mountains of Zion.
For there the LORD ordained his blessing,
    life forevermore.

1 John 1:1–2:2

¹We declare to you what was from the beginning, what we have heard, what we have seen with our eyes, what we have looked at and touched with our hands, concerning the word of life—²this life was revealed, and we have seen it and testify to it, and declare to you the eternal life that was with the Father and was revealed to us—³we declare to you what we have seen and heard so that you also may have fellowship with us; and truly our fellowship is with the Father and with his Son Jesus Christ. ⁴We are writing these things so that our joy may be complete.

⁵This is the message we have heard from him and proclaim to you, that God is light and in him there is no darkness at all. ⁶If we say that we have fellowship with him while we are walking in darkness, we lie and do not do what is true; ⁷but if we walk in the light as he himself is in the light, we have fellowship with one another, and the blood of Jesus his Son cleanses us from all sin. ⁸If we say that we have no sin, we deceive ourselves, and the truth is not in us. ⁹If we confess our sins, he who is faithful and just will forgive us our sins and cleanse us from all unrighteousness. ¹⁰If we say that we have not sinned, we make him a liar, and his word is not in us.

2 My little children, I am writing these things to you so that you may not sin. But if anyone does sin, we have an advocate with the Father, Jesus Christ the righteous; ²and he is the atoning sacrifice for our sins, and not for ours only but also for the sins of the whole world.

John 20:19-31

¹⁹When it was evening on that day, the first day of the week, and the doors of the house where the disciples had met were locked for fear of the Jews, Jesus came and stood among them and said, "Peace be with you." ²⁰After he said this, he showed them his hands and his side. Then the disciples rejoiced when they saw the Lord. ²¹Jesus said to them again, "Peace be with you. As the Father has sent me, so I send you." ²²When he had said this, he breathed on them and said to them, "Receive the Holy Spirit. ²³If you forgive the sins of any, they are forgiven them; if you retain the sins of any, they are retained."

²⁴But Thomas (who was called the Twin), one of the twelve, was not with them when Jesus came. ²⁵So the other disciples told him, "We have seen the Lord." But he said to them, "Unless I see the mark of the nails in his hands, and put my finger in the mark of the nails and my hand in his side, I will not believe."

²⁶A week later his disciples were again in the house, and Thomas was with them. Although the doors were shut, Jesus came and stood among them and said, "Peace be with you." ²⁷Then he said to Thomas, "Put your finger here and see my hands. Reach out your hand and put it in my side. Do not doubt but believe." ²⁸Thomas answered him, "My Lord and my God!" ²⁹Jesus said to him, "Have you believed because you have seen me? Blessed are those who have not seen and yet have come to believe."

³⁰Now Jesus did many other signs in the presence of his disciples, which are not written in this book. ³¹But these are written so that you may come to believe that Jesus is the Messiah, the Son of God, and that through believing you may have life in his name.

Primary Hymns and Songs for the Day

307   "Christ Is Risen" (John) (O)
      H-3   Chr-113; Desc-102; Org-171
      S-1   #345. Handbell/keyboard Arr.
2231   "*¡Miren Qué Bueno!*" ("O Look and Wonder") (Pss)
420   "Breathe on Me, Breath of God" (John)
      H-3   Hbl-49; Chr-45; Desc-101; Org-166
2196   "We Walk by Faith" (John)
      H-3   Chr-21
2206   "Without Seeing You" (John)
206   "I Want to Walk as a Child of the Light" (1 John)
      S-2   #91. Desc.
467   "Trust and Obey" (1 John) (C)
      H-3   Chr-202
      S-1   #336. Harm.

Additional Hymn Suggestions

547   "O Church of God, United" (Acts)
552   "Here, O Lord, Your Servants Gather" (Acts)
554   "All Praise to Our Redeeming Lord" (Acts)
555   "Forward Through the Ages" (Acts)
557   "Blest Be the Tie That Binds" (Acts) (C)
560   "Help Us Accept Each Other" (Acts)
561   "Jesus, United by Thy Grace" (Acts)
562   "Jesus, Lord, We Look to Thee" (Acts)
566   "Blest Be the Dear Uniting Love" (Acts)
2269   "Come, Share the Lord" (Acts, Pss)
407   "Close to Thee" (1 John)
605   "Wash, O God, Our Sons and Daughters" (1 John)
608   "This Is the Spirit's Entry Now" (1 John, Baptism)
632   "Draw Us in the Spirit's Tether" (1 John, Comm.)
2149   "Living for Jesus" (1 John)
2158   "Just a Closer Walk with Thee" (1 John)
2172   "We Are Called" (1 John)
2214   "Lead Me, Guide Me" (1 John)
2242   "Walk with Me" (1 John, John)
2259   "Victim Divine" (1 John, Comm.)
336   "Of All the Spirit's Gifts to Me" (John)
355   "Depth of Mercy" (John)
3097   "Depth of Mercy" (John)
384   "Love Divine, All Loves Excelling" (John)
420   "Breathe on Me, Breath of God" (John)
462   "'Tis So Sweet to Trust in Jesus" (John)
465   "Holy Spirit, Truth Divine" (John)
475   "Come Down, O Love Divine" (John)
503   "Let It Breathe on Me" (John)
543   "O Breath of Life" (John)
      WS3146
623   "Here, O My Lord, I See Thee" (John, Comm.)
636   "Christian People, Raise Your Song" (John, Comm.)
2046   "Womb of Life" (John)
2114   "At the Font We Start Our Journey" (John, Baptism)
2115   "Christ Has Risen" (John)
2117   "Spirit of God" (John)
2187   "Now It Is Evening" (John)
2211   "Faith Is Patience in the Night" (John)
3179   "The Risen Christ" (John)

Additional Contemporary Suggestions

UM558   "We Are the Church" (Acts)
S2162   "Grace Alone" (Acts)
S2223   "They'll Know We Are Christians" (Acts, Pss)
S2224   "Make Us One" (Pss)
S2204   "Light of the World" (1 John)
WS3177   "Here I Am to Worship" (1 John)

S2039   "Holy, Holy" (1 John)
S2073   "Celebrate Love" (1 John, Easter)
S2235b   "We Are Marching" ("*Siyahamba*"/"*Caminando*")
      (1 John)
WS3102   "You Are My King" ("Amazing Love") (1 John)
M150   "Everyday" (1 John)
M228   "Stronger" (1 John, Easter)
M237   "My Savior Lives" (1 John, Easter)
S2086   "Open Our Eyes, Lord" (John)
S2119   "Where the Spirit of the Lord Is" (John)
M26   "The Power of Your Love" (John)
UM328   "Surely the Presence of the Lord" (John)
      S-2   #200 Stanzas for soloist
UM376   "*Dona Nobis Pacem*" (John)
WS3026   "God Is Good, All the Time" (John)
WS3145   "Breath of God, Breath of Peace" (John)

Vocal Solos

"Just a Closer Walk with Thee" (1 John)
      V-8   p. 323
"I Know That My Redeemer Liveth" (John, Easter)
      V-2

Anthems

"Oh, How Good It Is" (Psalm)
Arr. Joey Hoelscher; Alfred 44235
SATB with keyboard, opt. violin

"I Know That My Redeemer Lives" (John, Easter)
Arr. Hal H. Hopson; Alfred 44251
SATB a cappella

Other Suggestions

Visuals:
O (Acts)   Offering plates filled with money
   P   Oil, clasped hands, dew
   E   Light/darkness, water (cleansing), briefcase
         (advocate), 1 John 2:1b
   G   Lock, wind (breath) (Holy Spirit), risen Christ,
         question mark, dove, peace
Introit: WS3086, stanza 2. "Day of Arising" (John)
Greeting: BOW390 (Acts)
Opening Prayer: BOW392 (1 John)
Litany: UM556 or BOW495 (Acts, Pss)
Canticle: UM205. "Canticle of Light and Darkness" (1 John).
   See S-1, p. 383.
Prayer: UM639. Bread and Justice (Acts, Pss)
Prayer: BOW503 or BOW518 (Acts, John)
Prayer: WSL30. Sanctifier of time (1 John)
Response: UM503. "Let It Breathe on Me" (John)
Prayer of Intercession: BOW399, Week 2 (Easter)
Prayer of Thanksgiving and Intercession: BOW396 (John)
Blessing: BOW560 (John)
See The Abingdon Worship Annual 2018 *for more ideas.*

Acts 3:12-19

[12]When Peter saw it, he addressed the people, "You Israelites, why do you wonder at this, or why do you stare at us, as though by our own power or piety we had made him walk? [13]The God of Abraham, the God of Isaac, and the God of Jacob, the God of our ancestors has glorified his servant Jesus, whom you handed over and rejected in the presence of Pilate, though he had decided to release him. [14]But you rejected the Holy and Righteous One and asked to have a murderer given to you, [15]and you killed the Author of life, whom God raised from the dead. To this we are witnesses. [16]And by faith in his name, his name itself has made this man strong, whom you see and know; and the faith that is through Jesus has given him this perfect health in the presence of all of you.

[17]"And now, friends, I know that you acted in ignorance, as did also your rulers. [18]In this way God fulfilled what he had foretold through all the prophets, that his Messiah would suffer. [19]Repent therefore, and turn to God so that your sins may be wiped out."

Psalm 4 (UM741)

[1]Answer me when I call, O God of my right!
    You gave me room when I was in distress.
    Be gracious to me, and hear my prayer.
[2]How long, you people, shall my honor suffer shame?
    How long will you love vain words, and seek after lies?
                                [Selah]
[3]But know that the LORD has set apart the faithful for himself;
    the LORD hears when I call to him.
[4]When you are disturbed, do not sin;
    ponder it on your beds, and be silent. *[Selah]*
[5]Offer right sacrifices,
    and put your trust in the LORD.
[6]There are many who say, "O that we might see some good!
    Let the light of your face shine on us, O LORD!"
[7]You have put gladness in my heart
    more than when their grain and wine abound.
[8]I will both lie down and sleep in peace;
    for you alone, O LORD, make me lie down in safety.

1 John 3:1-7

[1]See what love the Father has given us, that we should be called children of God; and that is what we are. The reason the world does not know us is that it did not know him. [2]Beloved, we are God's children now; what we will be has not yet been revealed. What we do know is this: when he is revealed, we will be like him, for we will see him as he is. [3]And all who have this hope in him purify themselves, just as he is pure.

[4] Everyone who commits sin is guilty of lawlessness; sin is lawlessness. [5]You know that he was revealed to take away sins, and in him there is no sin. [6]No one who abides in him sins; no one who sins has either seen him or known him. [7]Little children, let no one deceive you. Everyone who does what is right is righteous, just as he is righteous.

Luke 24:36b-48

[36b]Jesus himself stood among them and said to them, "Peace be with you." [37]They were startled and terrified, and thought that they were seeing a ghost. [38]He said to them, "Why are you frightened, and why do doubts arise in your hearts? [39]Look at my hands and my feet; see that it is I myself. Touch me and see; for a ghost does not have flesh and bones as you see that I have." [40]And when he had said this, he showed them his hands and his feet. [41]While in their joy they were disbelieving and still wondering, he said to them, "Have you anything here to eat?" [42]They gave him a piece of broiled fish, [43]and he took it and ate in their presence.

[44]Then he said to them, "These are my words that I spoke to you while I was still with you—that everything written about me in the law of Moses, the prophets, and the psalms must be fulfilled." [45]Then he opened their minds to understand the scriptures, [46]and he said to them, "Thus it is written, that the Messiah is to suffer and to rise from the dead on the third day, [47]and that repentance and forgiveness of sins is to be proclaimed in his name to all nations, beginning from Jerusalem. [48]You are witnesses of these things."

Primary Hymns and Songs for the Day

308	"Thine Be the Glory" (Luke) (O)	
	H-3	Hbl-98; Chr-195; Desc-59
	S-1	#190. Arr. for choir and Instr.
	S-2	#95. Various treatments
473	"Lead Me, Lord" (Pss)	
2108	"O How He Loves You and Me!" (1 John)	
2115	"Christ Has Risen" (Luke)	
	H-3	Chr-80; Desc-52
	S-1	#160-162. Various treatments
	S-2	#87-88. Brass/timpani intro. and arr.
318	"Christ Is Alive" (Acts, Luke) (C)	
	H-3	Hbl-50; Chr-47; Desc-101; Org-167
	S-1	#334-5. Desc. and Harm.

Additional Hymn Suggestions

108	"God Hath Spoken by the Prophets" (Acts)
339	"Come, Sinners, to the Gospel Feast" (Acts) (O)
340	"Come, Ye Sinners, Poor and Needy" (Acts)
363	"And Can It Be that I Should Gain" (Acts)
577	"God of Grace and God of Glory" (Acts)
616	"Come, Sinners, to the Gospel Feast" (Acts)
698	"God of the Ages" (Acts)
3166	"Author of Life Divine" (Acts)
310	"He Lives" (Acts, Luke)
2214	"Lead Me, Guide Me" (Pss)
306	"The Strife Is O'er, the Battle Done" (1 John)
2085	"He Came Down" (1 John)
2147	"There Are Some Things I May Not Know" (1 John)
2248	"Baptized in Water" (1 John, Baptism)
175	"Jesus, the Very Thought of Thee" (1 John, Luke)
267	"O Love, How Deep (1 John, Luke)
3022	"Peace of Our Praying" (1 John, Luke)
78	"Heleluyan" (Luke, Native American)
148	"Many and Great, O God" (Luke, Native American)
257	"We Meet You, O Christ" (Luke)
304	"Easter People, Raise Your Voices" (Luke) (O)
309	"On the Day of Resurrection" (Luke)
315	"Come, Ye Faithful, Raise the Strain" (Luke)
367	"He Touched Me" (Luke)
462	"'Tis So Sweet to Trust in Jesus" (Luke)
596	"Blessed Jesus, at Thy Word" (Luke)
623	"Here, O My Lord, I See Thee" (Luke, Comm.)
635	"Because Thou Hast Said" (Luke, Comm.)
2117	"Spirit of God" (Luke)
2184	"Sent Out in Jesus' Name" (Luke)
2199	"Stay with Us" (Luke)
2213	"Healer of Our Every Ill" (Luke)
2241	"The Spirit Sends Us Forth to Serve" (Luke)
2269	"Come, Share the Lord" (Luke, Comm.)
2059	"I Am Your Mother" (Native American)
3086	"Day of Arising" (Luke)
3158	"Go to the World" (Luke)

Additional Contemporary Suggestions

S2031	"We Bring the Sacrifice of Praise" (Pss)
S2154	"Please Enter My Heart, Hosanna" (Pss)
M49	"Refresh My Heart" (Pss)
M108	"Lead Me, Lord" (Pss)
S2039	"Holy, Holy" (1 John)
S2073	"Celebrate Love" (1 John)
SP48	"Behold, What Manner of Love" (1 John)
M77	"Above All" (1 John, Luke, Easter)
WS3008	"Open the Eyes of My Heart" (Luke)
SP121	"Celebrate Jesus" (Luke, Easter)

M20	"Jesus Is Alive" (Luke, Easter)
S2006	"Lord God Almighty" (Luke)
S2086	"Open Our Eyes, Lord" (Luke)
S2157	"Come and Fill Our Hearts" (Luke)
S2273	"Jesus, We Are Here" (Luke)
UM349	"Turn Your Eyes upon Jesus" (Luke)
UM666	"Shalom to You" (Luke)
WS3088	"Easter Alleluia" (Luke)

Vocal Solos

"Author of Life Divine" (Acts)
    V-1   p. 39
"I Walked Today Where Jesus Walked" (Luke, Easter)
    V-8   p. 14

Anthems

"I Then Shall Live" (1 John)
Arr. Jay Rouse; PraiseGathering.com 13965
TTBB with piano

"*O Sacrum Convivium*" (Luke)
Howard Helvey; MorningStar 50-3470
SATB a cappella (TTBB 50-3485)

Other Suggestions

Visuals:

O	(Acts)	Portrait of Christ crucified, risen, names given to Jesus, eraser (forgiveness)
	P	Praying hands, person pondering, light, rejoicing
	E	Children, risen Christ, 1 John 3:1
	G	Risen Christ, fear, broiled fish, open Bible, Luke 24:36c, 48, witnessing

Introit: S2273, BOW187. "Jesus, We Are Here" (Luke)
Act of Centering: BOW470 (Native American)
Response: BOW197. Shawnee Traveling Song (Native American)
Greeting: BOW379 or BOW425 or BOW458 (Easter, Native American)
Call to Worship: WSL29. "Christ is risen" (Luke)
Opening Prayer: BOW455 (Native American)
Canticle: UM646. "Canticle of Love" (Pss, 1 John)
Call to Prayer: S2193. "Lord, Listen to Your Children" (Pss)
Prayer of Confession: BOW487 (Native American)
Prayer: UM329. Prayer to the Holy Spirit (Luke, Native American)
Prayer: BOW512. For Guidance (1 John)
Prayers: S2201. "Prayers of the People" (Pss)
Prayer of Intercession: BOW399, Week 3 (Easter)
Response: S2200. "O Lord, Hear My Prayer" (Pss)
Response: UM116, stanza 1. "The God of Abraham Praise" (Acts)
Prayer of Thanksgiving: UM553 (Acts) or BOW396 (Luke)
Blessing: BOW560 (Pss)

Acts 4:5-12

[5]The next day their rulers, elders, and scribes assembled in Jerusalem, [6]with Annas the high priest, Caiaphas, John, and Alexander, and all who were of the high-priestly family. [7]When they had made the prisoners stand in their midst, they inquired, "By what power or by what name did you do this?" [8]Then Peter, filled with the Holy Spirit, said to them, "Rulers of the people and elders, [9]if we are questioned today because of a good deed done to someone who was sick and are asked how this man has been healed, [10]let it be known to all of you, and to all the people of Israel, that this man is standing before you in good health by the name of Jesus Christ of Nazareth, whom you crucified, whom God raised from the dead. [11]This Jesus is

the stone that was rejected by you, the builders;
it has become the cornerstone.

[12]There is salvation in no one else, for there is no other name under heaven given among mortals by which we must be saved."

Psalm 23 (UM754)

[1]The Lord is my shepherd, I shall not want.
[2]He makes me lie down in green pastures;
he leads me beside still waters;
[3]he restores my soul.
He leads me in right paths
for his name's sake.
[4]Even though I walk through the darkest valley,
I fear no evil;
for you are with me;
your rod and your staff—
they comfort me.
[5]You prepare a table before me
in the presence of my enemies;
you anoint my head with oil;
my cup overflows.
[6]Surely goodness and mercy shall follow me
all the days of my life,
and I shall dwell in the house of the Lord
my whole life long.

1 John 3:16-24

[16]We know love by this, that he laid down his life for us—and we ought to lay down our lives for one another. [17]How does God's love abide in anyone who has the world's goods and sees a brother or sister in need and yet refuses help?

[18]Little children, let us love, not in word or speech, but in truth and action. [19]And by this we will know that we are from the truth and will reassure our hearts before him [20]whenever our hearts condemn us; for God is greater than our hearts, and he knows everything. [21]Beloved, if our hearts do not condemn us, we have boldness before God; [22]and we receive from him whatever we ask, because we obey his commandments and do what pleases him.

[23]And this is his commandment, that we should believe in the name of his Son Jesus Christ and love one another, just as he has commanded us. [24]All who obey his commandments abide in him, and he abides in them. And by this we know that he abides in us, by the Spirit that he has given us.

John 10:11-18

[11]"I am the good shepherd. The good shepherd lays down his life for the sheep. [12]The hired hand, who is not the shepherd and does not own the sheep, sees the wolf coming and leaves the sheep and runs away—and the wolf snatches them and scatters them. [13]The hired hand runs away because a hired hand does not care for the sheep. [14]I am the good shepherd. I know my own and my own know me, [15]just as the Father knows me and I know the Father. And I lay down my life for the sheep. [16]I have other sheep that do not belong to this fold. I must bring them also, and they will listen to my voice. So there will be one flock, one shepherd. [17]For this reason the Father loves me, because I lay down my life in order to take it up again. [18]No one takes it from me, but I lay it down of my own accord. I have power to lay it down, and I have power to take it up again. I have received this command from my Father."

Primary Hymns and Songs for the Day

546	"The Church's One Foundation" (Acts) (O)	
	H-3	Hbl-94; Chr-180; Desc-16; Org-9
	S-1	#25-26. Desc. and Harm.
138	"The King of Love My Shepherd Is" (Pss, 1 John, John)	
	H-3	Hbl-96; Chr-188; Desc-93; Org-135
	S-1	#298-299. Harm.
381	"Savior, Like a Shepherd Lead Us" (Pss, John)	
	H-3	Chr-167; Org-15
	S-2	#29. Harm.
2214	"Lead Me, Guide Me" (Pss)	
2058	"Shepherd Me, O God" (Pss, John)	
559	"Christ Is Made the Sure Foundation" (Acts) (C)	
	H-3	Chr-49; Desc-103; Org-180
	S-1	#346. Desc.

Additional Hymn Suggestions

168	"At the Name of Jesus" (Acts)
2220	"We Are God's People" (Acts)
2213	"Healer of Our Every Ill" (Acts, 1 John)
444	"O Young and Fearless Prophet" (Acts, John)
3147	"Built on a Rock" (Acts, John)
128	"He Leadeth Me: O Blessed Thought" (Pss) (O)
136	"The Lord's My Shepherd, I'll Not Want" (Pss)
407	"Close to Thee (Pss)
474	"Precious Lord, Take My Hand" (Pss)
497	"Send Me, Lord" (Pss)
2112	"Jesus Walked This Lonesome Valley" (Pss)
2206	"Without Seeing You" (Pss)
3031	"God Leads Us Along" (Pss)
3088	"Easter Alleluia" (Pss, Easter)
518	"O Thou, in Whose Presence" (Pss, John)
700	"Abide with Me" (Pss, 1 John, John) (C)
3169	"You Feed Us, Gentle Savior" (Pss, 1 John)
408	"The Gift of Love" (1 John)
434	*Cuando El Pobre* ("When the Poor Ones") (1 John)
549	"Where Charity and Love Prevail" (1 John)
566	"Blest Be the Dear Uniting Love" (1 John)
2083	"My Song Is Love Unknown" (1 John)
2178	"Here Am I" (1 John)
2223	"They'll Know We Are Christians" (1 John)
2260	"Let Us Be Bread" (1 John, Comm.)
2245	"Within the Day-to-Day" (1 John)
115	"How Like a Gentle Spirit" (John)
289	"Ah, Holy Jesus" (John)
419	"I Am Thine, O Lord" (John)
650	"Give Me the Faith Which Can Remove" (John)

Additional Contemporary Suggestions

S2066	"Praise the Name of Jesus" (Acts)
S2162	"Grace Alone" (Acts)
SP177	"Cornerstone" (Acts)
WS3105	"In Christ Alone" ("My Hope Is Found") (Acts)
S2054	"Nothing Can Trouble" ("*Nada Te Turbe*") (Pss)
S2113	"Lamb of God" (Pss)
WS3026	"God Is Good All the Time" (Pss)
WS3096	"Gentle Shepherd" (Pss, John)
WS3106	"Your Grace Is Enough" (Pss)
WS3167	"Feed Us, Lord" (Pss, Comm.)
SP40	"God Will Make a Way" (Pss)
M258	"You Never Let Go" (Pss)
M265	"I Have a Hope" (Pss)
S2038	"Father, I Adore You" (1 John)
S2159	"Jesus, Draw Me Close" (1 John)

S2179	"Live in Charity" (1 John)
S2224	"Make Us One" (1 John)
S2226	"Bind Us Together" (1 John)
M53	"Let It Be Said of Us" (1 John)
M63	"I Could Sing of Your Love Forever" (1 John)
UM174	"His Name Is Wonderful" (1 John)
S2244	"People Need the Lord" (1 John, John)

Vocal Solos

"How Firm a Foundation" (Acts)
V-6   p. 31
"The Lord Is My Shepherd" (Pss)
V-5(3)   p. 30
"My Shepherd Will Supply My Need" (Pss)
V-10   p. 4
"God, Our Ever Faithful Shepherd" (Pss, 1 John)
V-4   p. 15

Anthems

"The Lord Is My Shepherd" (Pss)
Neil Harmon; MorningStar 50-5860
SATB with keyboard

"The Lamb" (Pss, John)
Jackson Henry; Choristers Guild CGA1341
SATB with piano and opt. oboe

Other Suggestions

Visuals:

O (Acts)		Stone, cornerstone
	P	Shepherd, Christ as a shepherd, sheep, water, path
	E	Cross, people sacrificing for others, pitcher/bowl/ towel
	G	Christ the Shepherd, sheep, wolf, crucifix, John 10:11

Greeting: BOW381 (John) or BOW456 (Acts)
Opening Prayer: BOW393 or BOW460 (Acts, Pss, John)
Canticle: UM646. "Canticle of Love" (1 John) See S-1, p. 387.
Psalter: UM137. Psalm 23.
Prayer: UM457 (Acts) or UM460 (Pss)
Prayer: BOW506. For the Church (Acts)
Prayer: BOW518. For Others (1 John)
Prayer: BOW529. A Prayer of Saint Patrick (Pss, John)
Prayer: BOW399 Week 4 or BOW398 (Pss, John)
Dismissal with a Blessing: BOW376 (Acts, Easter)
For more ideas, see The Abingdon Worship Annual 2018.

Acts 8:26-40

[26]Then an angel of the Lord said to Philip, "Get up and go toward the south to the road that goes down from Jerusalem to Gaza." (This is a wilderness road.) [27]So he got up and went. Now there was an Ethiopian eunuch, a court official of the Candace, queen of the Ethiopians, in charge of her entire treasury. He had come to Jerusalem to worship [28]and was returning home; seated in his chariot, he was reading the prophet Isaiah. [29]Then the Spirit said to Philip, "Go over to this chariot and join it." [30]So Philip ran up to it and heard him reading the prophet Isaiah. He asked, "Do you understand what you are reading?" [31]He replied, "How can I, unless someone guides me?" And he invited Philip to get in and sit beside him. [32]Now the passage of the scripture that he was reading was this:

Like a sheep he was led to the slaughter,
and like a lamb silent before its shearer,
so he does not open his mouth.
[33]In his humiliation justice was denied him.
Who can describe his generation?
For his life is taken away from the earth.

[34]The eunuch asked Philip, "About whom, may I ask you, does the prophet say this, about himself or about someone else?" [35]Then Philip began to speak, and starting with this scripture, he proclaimed to him the good news about Jesus. [36]As they were going along the road, they came to some water; and the eunuch said, "Look, here is water! What is to prevent me from being baptized?" [38]He commanded the chariot to stop, and both of them, Philip and the eunuch, went down into the water, and Philip baptized him. [39]When they came up out of the water, the Spirit of the Lord snatched Philip away; the eunuch saw him no more, and went on his way rejoicing. [40]But Philip found himself at Azotus, and as he was passing through the region, he proclaimed the good news to all the towns until he came to Caesarea.

Psalm 22:25-31 (UM752)

[25]From you comes my praise in the great congregation;
my vows I will pay before those who fear him.
[26]The poor shall eat and be satisfied;
those who seek him shall praise the LORD.
May your hearts live forever!
[27]All the ends of the earth shall remember
and turn to the LORD;
and all the families of the nations
shall worship before him.
[28]For dominion belongs to the LORD,
and he rules over the nations.
[29]To him, indeed, shall all who sleep in the earth bow down;
before him shall bow all who go down to the dust,
and I shall live for him.
[30]Posterity will serve him;
future generations will be told about the Lord,
[31]and proclaim his deliverance to a people yet unborn,
saying that he has done it.

1 John 4:7-21

[7]Beloved, let us love one another, because love is from God; everyone who loves is born of God and knows God. [8]Whoever does not love does not know God, for God is love. [9]God's love was revealed among us in this way: God sent his only Son into the world so that we might live through him. [10]In this is love, not that we loved God but that he loved us and sent his Son to be the atoning sacrifice for our sins. [11]Beloved, since God loved us so much, we also ought to love one another. [12]No one has ever seen God; if we love one another, God lives in us, and his love is perfected in us.

[13]By this we know that we abide in him and he in us, because he has given us of his Spirit. [14]And we have seen and do testify that the Father has sent his Son as the Savior of the world. [15]God abides in those who confess that Jesus is the Son of God, and they abide in God. [16]So we have known and believe the love that God has for us.

God is love, and those who abide in love abide in God, and God abides in them. [17]Love has been perfected among us in this: that we may have boldness on the day of judgment, because as he is, so are we in this world. [18]There is no fear in love, but perfect love casts out fear; for fear has to do with punishment, and whoever fears has not reached perfection in love. [19]We love because he first loved us. [20]Those who say, "I love God," and hate their brothers or sisters, are liars; for those who do not love a brother or sister whom they have seen, cannot love God whom they have not seen. [21]The commandment we have from him is this: those who love God must love their brothers and sisters also.

John 15:1-8

[1]"I am the true vine, and my Father is the vinegrower. [2]He removes every branch in me that bears no fruit. Every branch that bears fruit he prunes to make it bear more fruit. [3]You have already been cleansed by the word that I have spoken to you. [4]Abide in me as I abide in you. Just as the branch cannot bear fruit by itself unless it abides in the vine, neither can you unless you abide in me. [5]I am the vine, you are the branches. Those who abide in me and I in them bear much fruit, because apart from me you can do nothing. [6]Whoever does not abide in me is thrown away like a branch and withers; such branches are gathered, thrown into the fire, and burned. [7]If you abide in me, and my words abide in you, ask for whatever you wish, and it will be done for you. [8]My Father is glorified by this, that you bear much fruit and become my disciples."

Primary Hymns and Songs for the Day

662   "Stand Up, and Bless the Lord" (Pss, 1 John) (O)
       H-3   Hbl-79; Chr-141; Desc-95; Org-143
       S-1   #306-308. Various treatments
610   "We Know That Christ Is Raised" (Acts, Baptism)
       H-3   Hbl-100; Chr-214; Desc-38 ; Org-37
       S-1   #118-127. Various treatments
397   "I Need Thee Every Hour" (John)
       H-3   Chr-107
2076   "O Blessed Spring" (John)
529   "How Firm a Foundation" (John) (C)
       H-3   Hbl-27, 69; Chr-102; Desc-41; Org-41
       S-1   #133. Harm.
             #134. Performance note

Additional Hymn Suggestions

165   "Hallelujah! What a Savior" (Acts)
287   "O Love Divine, What Hast Thou Done" (Acts)
289   "Ah, Holy Jesus" (Acts)
571   "Go, Make of All Disciples" (Acts) (C)
703   "Swing Low, Sweet Chariot" (Acts)
2123   "Loving Spirit" (Acts)
2246   "Deep in the Shadows of the Past" (Acts)
2247   "Wonder of Wonders" (Acts, Baptism)
2248   "Baptized in Water" (Acts, Baptism)
2251   "We Were Baptized in Christ Jesus" (Acts, Baptism)
3045   "Down by the Jordan" (Acts, Baptism)
3164   "Down to the River to Pray" (Acts, Baptism)
433   "All Who Love and Serve Your City" (Acts, Pss)
578   "God of Love and God of Power" (Acts, 1 John)
92   "For the Beauty of the Earth" (1 John)
98   "To God Be the Glory" (1 John)
121   "There's a Wideness in God's Mercy" (1 John)
172   "My Jesus, I Love Thee" (1 John)
183   "Jesu, Thy Boundless Love to Me" (1 John)
184   "Of the Father's Love Begotten" (1 John)
292   "What Wondrous Love Is This" (1 John)
305   "*Camina, Pueblo de Dios*" (Walk On, O People of God)
        (1 John, Easter)
332   "Spirit of Faith, Come Down" (1 John)
549   "Where Charity and Love Prevail" (1 John)
645   "O Perfect Love" (1 John)
647   "Your Love, O God, Has Called Us Here" (1 John)
2110   "Why Has God Forsaken Me?" (1 John)
2135   "When Cain Killed Abel" (1 John)
2213   "Healer of Our Every Ill" (1 John)
2259   "Victim Divine" (1 John)
3157   "Come, Let Us Dream" (1 John)
3169   "You Feed Us, Gentle Savior" (1 John, John, Comm.)
111   "How Can We Name a Love" (1 John, John)
113   "Source and Sovereign, Rock and Cloud" (1 John, John)
124   "Seek the Lord" (1 John, John)
700   "Abide with Me" (1 John, John)
544   "Like the Murmur of the Dove's Song" (John)
2050   "Mothering God, You Gave Me Birth" (John)
2060   "God the Sculptor of the Mountains" (John)
2261   "Life-Giving Bread" (John, Comm.)
2262   "Let Us Offer to the Father" ("*Te Ofrecemos Padre Nuestro*") (John, Comm.)
3155   "The Lord of Life, a Vine Is He" (John)

Additional Contemporary Suggestions

S2250   "I've Just Come from the Fountain" (Acts, Baptism)
S2267   "Taste and See" (Pss, Comm.)

WS3165   "Take Me To the Water" (Acts, Baptism)
WS3176   "Come, Now Is the Time to Worship" (Pss)
WS3162   "Stand in Awe" (Pss)
M1   "Ancient of Days" (Pss)
M235   "Sing, Sing, Sing" (Pss)
S2022   "Great Is the Lord" (1 John)
S2073   "Celebrate Love" (1 John)
S2179   "Live in Charity" ("*Ubi Caritas*") (1 John)
S2223   "They'll Know We Are Christians" (1 John)
S2224   "Make Us One" (1 John)
S2226   "Bind Us Together" (1 John)
S2260   "Let Us Be Bread" (1 John, Comm.)
M25   "No Greater Love" (1 John)
M63   "I Could Sing of Your Love Forever" (1 John)
WS3102   "You Are My King" ("*Amazing Love*") (1 John)
WS3188   "Hosanna" (John)
S2150   "Lord, Be Glorified" (John)
M13   "Be Glorified" (John)
M152   "Be Glorified" (John)

Vocal Solos

"Wash, O God, Our Sons and Daughters" (Acts, Baptism)
    V-5(1)   p. 64
"Wondrous Love" (1 John)
    V-6   p. 47
"I Am the Vine" (John)
    V-8   p. 280

Anthems

"Down in the River to Pray" (Acts)
David L. Mennicke; MorningStar 50-5902
SATB a cappella

"Let Us Love One Another" (1 John)
Arnold Sherman; Lorenz S5781
Two-part with keyboard and optional C-Instrument

Other Suggestions

Visuals:
O (Acts)   Open scroll/Bible open to Isaiah, water (baptism)
   P   Poor being fed, globe, flags of nations, earth from space
   E   Cross, sacrificial love, Christ, 1 John 4:16b, 18a
   G   Grape vine, grapes, pruned branches, fire, John 15:5
Greeting: BOW381 (John), BOW411 (1 John) or BOW451 (Pss)
Opening Prayer: BOW392 (Acts)
Prayer: UM401. For Holiness of Heart (1 John)
Prayer: WSL28. "Eternal God" (John)
Prayer of Intercession: BOW399, Week 5 (Easter)
Call to Baptism: BOW173. "Come Be Baptized" (Acts)
Baptism Prayer: WSL212. "Deep, flowing mystery" (Acts)
Baptism Response: BOW174 or BOW175. (Acts)
Prayer of Thanksgiving: BOW553 (John)

Acts 10:44-48

[44]While Peter was still speaking, the Holy Spirit fell upon all who heard the word. [45]The circumcised believers who had come with Peter were astounded that the gift of the Holy Spirit had been poured out even on the Gentiles, [46]for they heard them speaking in tongues and extolling God. Then Peter said, [47]"Can anyone withhold the water for baptizing these people who have received the Holy Spirit just as we have?" [48]So he ordered them to be baptized in the name of Jesus Christ. Then they invited him to stay for several days.

Psalm 98 (UM818)

[1]O sing to the Lord a new song,
　　for he has done marvelous things.
His right hand and his holy arm
　　have gotten him victory.
[2]The Lord has made known his victory;
　　he has revealed his vindication in the sight of the nations.
[3]He has remembered his steadfast love and faithfulness
　　to the house of Israel.
All the ends of the earth have seen
　　the victory of our God.
[4]Make a joyful noise to the Lord, all the earth;
　　break forth into joyous song and sing praises.
[5]Sing praises to the Lord with the lyre,
　　with the lyre and the sound of melody.
[6]With trumpets and the sound of the horn
　　make a joyful noise before the King, the Lord.
[7]Let the sea roar, and all that fills it;
　　the world and those who live in it.
[8]Let the floods clap their hands;
　　let the hills sing together for joy
[9]at the presence of the Lord, for he is coming
　　to judge the earth.
He will judge the world with righteousness,
　　and the peoples with equity.

1 John 5:1-6

[1]Everyone who believes that Jesus is the Christ has been born of God, and everyone who loves the parent loves the child. [2]By this we know that we love the children of God, when we love God and obey his commandments. [3]For the love of God is this, that we obey his commandments. And his commandments are not burdensome, [4]for whatever is born of God conquers the world. And this is the victory that conquers the world, our faith. [5]Who is it that conquers the world but the one who believes that Jesus is the Son of God?

[6]This is the one who came by water and blood, Jesus Christ, not with the water only but with the water and the blood. And the Spirit is the one that testifies, for the Spirit is the truth.

John 15:9-17

[9]"As the Father has loved me, so I have loved you; abide in my love. [10]If you keep my commandments, you will abide in my love, just as I have kept my Father's commandments and abide in his love. [11]I have said these things to you so that my joy may be in you, and that your joy may be complete.

[12]"This is my commandment, that you love one another as I have loved you. [13]No one has greater love than this, to lay down one's life for one's friends. [14]You are my friends if you do what I command you. [15]I do not call you servants any longer, because the servant does not know what the master is doing; but I have called you friends, because I have made known to you everything that I have heard from my Father. [16]You did not choose me but I chose you. And I appointed you to go and bear fruit, fruit that will last, so that the Father will give you whatever you ask him in my name. [17]I am giving you these commands so that you may love one another."

Primary Hymns and Songs for the Day

139	"Praise to the Lord, the Almighty" (Pss) (O)
	H-3 Hbl-89; Chr-163; Desc-69; Org-79
	S-1 #218-222. Various treatments
393	"Spirit of the Living God" (Acts)
	H-3 Chr-176
	S-1 #212. Vocal Desc. idea
2045	"Sing a New Song to the Lord" (Pss)
557	"Blest Be the Tie That Binds" (Acts, John) (C)

Additional Hymn Suggestions

332	"Spirit of Faith, Come Down" (Acts)
544	"Like the Murmur of the Dove's Song" (Acts)
2114	"At the Font We Start Our Journey" (Acts)
2247	"Wonder of Wonders" (Acts, Baptism)
2248	"Baptized in Water" (Acts, Baptism)
2251	"We Were Baptized in Christ Jesus" (Acts, Baptism)
3045	"Down by the Jordan" (Acts, Baptism)
3164	"Down to the River to Pray" (Acts, Baptism)
3001	"O For a Thousand Tongues to Sing" (Acts, Pss)
57	"O For a Thousand Tongues to Sing" (Acts, Pss)
59	*Mil Voces Para Celebrar* (Acts, Pss)
475	"Come Down, O Love Divine" (Acts, John)
537	"Filled with the Spirit's Power" (Acts, John)
548	"In Christ There Is No East or West" (Acts, John)
552	"Here, O Lord, Your Servants Gather" (Acts, John)
560	"Help Us Accept Each Other" (Acts, John)
96	"Praise the Lord Who Reigns Above" (Pss)
246	"Joy to the World" (Pss)
98	"To God Be the Glory" (Pss, 1 John)
370	"Victory in Jesus" (Pss, 1 John)
369	"Blessed Assurance" (1 John)
372	"How Can We Sinners Know" (1 John)
428	"For the Healing of the Nations" (1 John)
442	"Weary of All Trumpeting" (1 John)
447	"Our Parent, by Whose Name" (1 John)
2111	"We Sang Our Glad Hosannas" (1 John)
395	"Take Time to Be Holy" (John)
443	"O God Who Shaped Creation" (John)
526	"What a Friend We Have in Jesus" (John)
617	"I Come with Joy" (John, Comm.)
659	"Jesus Our Friend and Brother" (John)
2142	"Blessed Quietness" (John)
2213	"Healer of Our Every Ill" (John)
2260	"Let Us Be Bread" (John, Comm.)
3155	"The Lord of Life, a Vine Is He" (John)
3169	"You Feed Us, Gentle Savior" (John, Comm.)

Additional Contemporary Suggestions

WS3165	"Take Me to the Water" (Acts, Baptism)
S2250	"I've Just Come from the Fountain" (Acts, Baptism)
S2028	"Clap Your Hands" (Pss)
S2074	"Shout to the Lord" (Pss)
S2144	"Someone Asked the Question" (Pss)
WS3007	*Laudate Dominum* ("Sing, Praise") (Pss)
SP23	"Sing unto the Lord a New Song" (Pss)
SP147	"I Will Celebrate" (Pss)
UM99	"To God Be the Glory" (Pss, 1 John)
	V-8 p. 5. Vocal Solo
S2159	"Jesus, Draw Me Close" (1 John)
S2204	"Light of the World" (1 John)
S2219	"Goodness Is Stronger than Evil" (1 John)
M53	"Let It Be Said of Us" (1 John, John)
M40	"More Love, More Power" (1 John, John)
S2223	"They'll Know We Are Christians" (John)

S2226	"Bind Us Together" (John)
S2224	"Make Us One" (John)
S2179	"Live in Charity" ("*Ubi Caritas*") (John)
M25	"No Greater Love" (John)
M63	"I Could Sing of Your Love Forever" (John)
M154	"Dwell" (John)

Vocal Solos

"Praise to the Lord, the Almighty" (Pss)
     V-6   p. 18
"Shout to the Lord" (with "All Creatures of Our God and King") (Pss)
     V-3(2)   p. 32
"In Remembrance" (John, Comm.)
     V-5(2)   p. 7
"This Is My Commandment" (John)
     V-8   p. 284

Anthems

"A New Song" (Pss)
Bob Kauflin, Arr. Hayes; Lorenz 10/3660M
SATB with piano

"So Have I Loved You" (John)
Carlyle Sharpe; ECS Publishing 7128
SATB a cappella

Other Suggestions

Visuals:

O (Acts)	Dove/flames (Holy Spirit), water (baptism)
P	Lyre, sheet music, trumpet, sea, floods, hills, scales of justice
E	Water, wine, symbols of the Holy Spirit
G	Sacrificial love, cross, friendship, fruit (love enacted), John 15:9c

Introit: BOW181. "Sing to the Lord a New Song" (Pss)
Greeting: BOW303 (Pss) or BOW382 (John)
Greeting: Psalm 98:1. Sing to the Lord.
Opening Prayer: UM335 or WSL52 (Acts)
Opening Prayer: BOW394 (1 John)
Prayer of Intercession: BOW399, Week 6 (Easter)
Prayer of Thanksgiving/Intercession: BOW397 (1 John)
Prayer: WSL62. "Wondrous God, our hearts" (Pss)
Prayer: WSL28. "Eternal God, rock and refuge" (John)
Prayer: UM481 or BOW518 (1 John, John)
Canticle: UM646. "Canticle of Love" (John). See S-1, p. 387
Baptism Prayer: WSL212. "Deep, flowing mystery" (Acts)

Acts 1:1-11

[1] In the first book, Theophilus, I wrote about all that Jesus did and taught from the beginning [2] until the day when he was taken up to heaven, after giving instructions through the Holy Spirit to the apostles whom he had chosen. [3] After his suffering he presented himself alive to them by many convincing proofs, appearing to them during forty days and speaking about the kingdom of God. [4] While staying with them, he ordered them not to leave Jerusalem, but to wait there for the promise of the Father. "This," he said, "is what you have heard from me; [5] for John baptized with water, but you will be baptized with the Holy Spirit not many days from now."

[6] So when they had come together, they asked him, "Lord, is this the time when you will restore the kingdom to Israel?" [7] He replied, "It is not for you to know the times or periods that the Father has set by his own authority. [8] But you will receive power when the Holy Spirit has come upon you; and you will be my witnesses in Jerusalem, in all Judea and Samaria, and to the ends of the earth." [9] When he had said this, as they were watching, he was lifted up, and a cloud took him out of their sight. [10] While he was going and they were gazing up toward heaven, suddenly two men in white robes stood by them. [11] They said, "Men of Galilee, why do you stand looking up toward heaven? This Jesus, who has been taken up from you into heaven, will come in the same way as you saw him go into heaven."

Psalm 47 (UM781)

[1] Clap your hands, all you peoples;
　　shout to God with loud songs of joy.
[2] For the LORD, the Most High, is awesome,
　　a great king over all the earth.
[3] He subdued peoples under us,
　　and nations under our feet.
[4] He chose our heritage for us,
　　the pride of Jacob whom he loves. *[Selah]*
[5] God has gone up with a shout,
　　the LORD with the sound of a trumpet.
[6] Sing praises to God, sing praises;
　　sing praises to our King, sing praises.
[7] For God is the king of all the earth;
　　sing praises with a psalm.
[8] God is king over the nations;
　　God sits on his holy throne.
[9] The princes of the peoples gather
　　as the people of the God of Abraham.
For the shields of the earth belong to God;
　　he is highly exalted.

Ephesians 1:15-23

[15] I have heard of your faith in the Lord Jesus and your love toward all the saints, and for this reason [16] I do not cease to give thanks for you as I remember you in my prayers. [17] I pray that the God of our Lord Jesus Christ, the Father of glory, may give you a spirit of wisdom and revelation as you come to know him, [18] so that, with the eyes of your heart enlightened, you may know what is the hope to which he has called you, what are the riches of his glorious inheritance among the saints, [19] and what is the immeasurable greatness of his power for us who believe, according to the working of his great power. [20] God put this power to work in Christ when he raised him from the dead and seated him at his right hand in the heavenly places, [21] far above all rule and authority and power and dominion, and above every name that is named, not only in this age but also in the age to come. [22] And he has put all things under his feet and has made him the head over all things for the church, [23] which is his body, the fullness of him who fills all in all.

Luke 24:44-53

[44] Then he said to them, "These are my words that I spoke to you while I was still with you—that everything written about me in the law of Moses, the prophets, and the psalms must be fulfilled." [45] Then he opened their minds to understand the scriptures, [46] and he said to them, "Thus it is written, that the Messiah is to suffer and to rise from the dead on the third day, [47] and that repentance and forgiveness of sins is to be proclaimed in his name to all nations, beginning from Jerusalem. [48] You are witnesses of these things. [49] And see, I am sending upon you what my Father promised; so stay here in the city until you have been clothed with power from on high."

[50] Then he led them out as far as Bethany, and, lifting up his hands, he blessed them. [51] While he was blessing them, he withdrew from them and was carried up into heaven. [52] And they worshiped him, and returned to Jerusalem with great joy; [53] and they were continually in the temple blessing God.

Primary Hymns and Songs for the Day

312   "Hail the Day That Sees Him Rise" (Acts, Luke) (O)
       H-3   Hbl-72; Chr-50; Desc-69; Org-78
       S-1   #213. Desc.
327   "Crown Him with Many Crowns" (Pss, Eph, Luke)
       H-3   Hbl-55; Chr-60; Desc-30; Org-27
       S-1   #86-88. Various treatments
2074   "Shout to the Lord" (Pss)
       V-3(2) p. 32 Vocal Solo
157   "Jesus Shall Reign" (Pss, Eph) (C)
       H-3   Hbl-29; Chr-117; Desc-31; Org-31
       S-1   #100-103. Various treatments.

Additional Hymn Suggestions

541   "See How Great a Flame Aspires" (Acts)
703   "Swing Low, Sweet Chariot" (Acts)
711   "For All the Saints" (Acts, Eph) (O)
163   "Ask Ye What Great Thing I Know" (Acts, Luke)
173   "Christ, Whose Glory Fills the Skies" (Acts, Luke)
302   "Christ the Lord Is Risen Today" (Acts, Luke) (O)
304   "Easter People, Raise Your Voices" (Acts, Luke)
307   "Christ Is Risen" (Acts, Luke)
308   "Thine Be the Glory" (Acts, Luke) (C)
310   "He Lives" (Acts, Luke)
318   "Christ Is Alive" (Acts, Luke)
319   "Christ Jesus Lay in Death's Strong Bands" (Acts, Luke)
322   "Up from the Grave He Arose" (Acts, Luke)
324   "Hail Thee, Festival Day" (Acts, Luke)
718   "Lo, He Comes with Clouds Descending" (Acts, Luke, Ascension)
3156   "One is the Body" (Acts, Luke, Eph, Comm.)
2279   "The Trees of the Field" (Pss)
2276   "Glory to God in the Highest" (Pss, Eph)
168   "At the Name of Jesus" (Eph)
175   "Jesus, the Very Thought of Thee" (Eph)
178   "Hope of the World" (Eph)
368   "My Hope Is Built" (Eph)
2147   "There Are Some Things I May Not Know" (Eph)
2220   "We Are God's People" (Eph)
2261   "Life-Giving Bread" (Eph, Comm.)
2269   "Come, Share the Lord" (Eph, Comm.)
3035   "Bless Christ Through Whom All Things Are Made" (Eph)
2077   "You Alone Are Holy" (Luke)
2114   "At the Font We Start Our Journey" (Luke, Baptism)
2115   "Christ Has Risen" (Luke)
2117   "Spirit of God" (Luke)
2184   "Sent Out in Jesus' Name" (Luke) (C)
2199   "Stay with Us" (Luke)
2239   "Go Ye, Go Ye into the World" (Luke) (C)
2268   "As We Gather at Your Table" (Luke, Comm.)
2282   "I'll Fly Away" (Luke, Ascension)
3087   "O Christ, When You Ascended" (Luke)
3158   "Go to the World" (Luke)

Additional Contemporary Suggestions

S2118   "Holy Spirit, Come to Us" (Acts)
S2125   "Come, Holy Spirit" (Acts)
UM494   *Kum Ba Yah* ("Come By Here") (Acts)
M88   "Holy Spirit, Rain Down" (Acts, Eph)
WS3140   "Give Me Jesus" (Eph)
M120   "Lord Most High" (Pss)
M234   "Awesome Is the Lord Most High" (Pss, Ascension)
M279   "Glorious Day" (Pss, Ascension)

S2028   "Clap Your Hands" (Pss)
S2040   "Awesome God" (Pss)
S2070   "He Is Exalted" (Pss, Ascension)
WS3008   "Open the Eyes of My Heart" (Eph)
WS3023   "Forever" (Eph)
WS3105   "In Christ Alone" (Eph, Ascension)
M77   "Above All" (Pss, Eph, Ascension)
S2006   "Lord God Almighty" (Luke)
S2078   "Alleluia" (Luke)
S2088   "Lord, I Lift Your Name on High" (Ascension)
S2116   "Christ the Lord Is Risen" (Luke, Ascension)
M259   "See What a Morning" ("Resurrection Hymn") (Luke, Ascension)
M260   "I Will Rise" (Luke Ascension)
M228   "Stronger" (Ascension, Easter)

Vocal Solos

"Jesus Christ Is Risen Today" (Acts, Luke)
    V-1   p. 50
"In the First Light" (Ascension)
    V-5(1)   p. 28
"Rejoice Now, My Spirit" (Ascension)
    V-9   p. 30

Anthems

"How Great Thou Art and Majesty" (Acts, Eph, Luke)
Arr. Joel Raney; Hope C-5108
SATB with piano, opt. piano 4-hand

"Angels Visit When We Sing" (Acts, Eph, Luke)
K. Lee Scott; MorningStar 50-9220
SATB with piano and optional strings

Other Suggestions

These ideas may be used on May 13 as Ascension Sunday.
Visuals:
O (Acts)   Water, dove, flames, shell (baptism)
     P   Clapping hands, feet, trumpet, singing, shield
     E   Witnessing, Ascension, risen Christ, saints
     G   Bible, risen Christ, map or globe, Ascension, Luke 24:48
Introit: S2273, BOW187. "Jesus, We Are Here" (Acts)
Greeting: BOW389 or BOW402 (Acts, Luke, Eph)
Call to Worship: WSL35. "Let us gather" (Luke)
Prayer: BOW393 and BOW403 (Acts, Luke, Eph)
Prayer: UM323. The Ascension (Acts, Luke, Eph)
Prayer: UM542. Day of Pentecost (Acts)
Prayer of Intercession: BOW399, Week 7 (Easter)
Response: S2276, "Glory to God in the Highest" (Pss)
Benediction for Pentecost: BOW218 (Acts, Luke)

Acts 1:15-17, 21-26

[15]In those days Peter stood up among the believers (together the crowd numbered about one hundred twenty persons) and said, [16]"Friends, the scripture had to be fulfilled, which the Holy Spirit through David foretold concerning Judas, who became a guide for those who arrested Jesus—[17]for he was numbered among us and was allotted his share in this ministry.". . .

[21]"So one of the men who have accompanied us during all the time that the Lord Jesus went in and out among us, [22]beginning from the baptism of John until the day when he was taken up from us—one of these must become a witness with us to his resurrection." [23]So they proposed two, Joseph called Barsabbas, who was also known as Justus, and Matthias. [24]Then they prayed and said, "Lord, you know everyone's heart. Show us which one of these two you have chosen [25]to take the place in this ministry and apostleship from which Judas turned aside to go to his own place." [26]And they cast lots for them, and the lot fell on Matthias; and he was added to the eleven apostles.

Psalm 1 (UM738)

[1]Happy are those
    who do not follow the advice of the wicked,
or take the path that sinners tread,
    or sit in the seat of scoffers;
[2]but their delight is in the law of the LORD,
    and on his law they meditate day and night.
[3]They are like trees
    planted by streams of water,
which yield their fruit in its season,
    and their leaves do not wither.
In all that they do, they prosper.
[4]The wicked are not so,
    but are like chaff that the wind drives away.
[5]Therefore the wicked will not stand in the judgment,
    nor sinners in the congregation of the righteous;
[6]for the LORD watches over the way of the righteous,
    but the way of the wicked will perish.

1 John 5:9-13

[9]If we receive human testimony, the testimony of God is greater; for this is the testimony of God that he has testified to his Son. [10]Those who believe in the Son of God have the testimony in their hearts. Those who do not believe in God have made him a liar by not believing in the testimony that God has given concerning his Son. [11]And this is the testimony: God gave us eternal life, and this life is in his Son. [12]Whoever has the Son has life; whoever does not have the Son of God does not have life.

[13]I write these things to you who believe in the name of the Son of God, so that you may know that you have eternal life.

John 17:6-19

[6]"I have made your name known to those whom you gave me from the world. They were yours, and you gave them to me, and they have kept your word. [7]Now they know that everything you have given me is from you; [8]for the words that you gave to me I have given to them, and they have received them and know in truth that I came from you; and they have believed that you sent me. [9]I am asking on their behalf; I am not asking on behalf of the world, but on behalf of those whom you gave me, because they are yours. [10]All mine are yours, and yours are mine; and I have been glorified in them. [11]And now I am no longer in the world, but they are in the world, and I am coming to you. Holy Father, protect them in your name that you have given me, so that they may be one, as we are one. [12]While I was with them, I protected them in your name that you have given me. I guarded them, and not one of them was lost except the one destined to be lost, so that the scripture might be fulfilled. [13]But now I am coming to you, and I speak these things in the world so that they may have my joy made complete in themselves. [14]I have given them your word, and the world has hated them because they do not belong to the world, just as I do not belong to the world. [15]I am not asking you to take them out of the world, but I ask you to protect them from the evil one. [16]They do not belong to the world, just as I do not belong to the world. [17]Sanctify them in the truth; your word is truth. [18]As you have sent me into the world, so I have sent them into the world. [19]And for their sakes I sanctify myself, so that they also may be sanctified in truth."

Primary Hymns and Songs for the Day

599	"Break Thou the Bread of Life" (John) (O)	
494	"*Kum Ba Yah*" ("Come by Here") (1 John)	
526	"What a Friend We Have in Jesus" (1 John)	
463	"Lord, Speak to Me" (Acts) (C)	
	H-3	Hbl-75; Chr-131; Desc-22; Org-18
	S-1	#52. Desc.

Additional Hymn Suggestions

369	"Blessed Assurance" (Acts)
454	"Open My Eyes, That I May See" (Acts)
648	"God the Spirit, Guide and Guardian" (Acts)
726	"O Holy City, Seen of John" (Acts)
2117	"Spirit of God" (Acts)
85	"We Believe in One True God" (1 John)
98	"To God Be the Glory" (1 John, John)
356	"*Pues Si Vivimos*" ("When We Are Living") (1 John)
372	"How Can We Sinners Know" (1 John)
714	"I Know Whom I Have Believed" (1 John)
2121	"O Holy Spirit, Root of Life" (1 John)
2149	"Living for Jesus" (1 John)
2147	"There Are Some Things I May Not Know" (1 John)
2084	"Come, Let Us with Our Lord Arise" (1 John, John)
178	"Hope of the World" (John)
395	"Take Time to Be Holy" (John)
521	"I Want Jesus to Walk with Me" (John)
526	"What a Friend We Have in Jesus" (John)
547	"O Church of God, United" (John)
550	"Christ, from Whom All Blessings Flow" (John)
551	"Awake, O Sleeper" (John)
2189	"A Mother Lined a Basket" (Mother's Day)
445	"Happy the Home When God Is There" (Christian Home)

Additional Contemporary Suggestions

S2139	"Oh, I Know the Lord's Laid His Hands on Me" (Acts)
SP111	"There Is a Redeemer" (Acts)
S2032	"My Life Is in You, Lord" (1 John)
S2039	"Holy, Holy" (1 John)
WS3040	"You Are My All in All" (1 John)
WS3102	"You Are My King" ("Amazing Love") (1 John)
WS3105	"In Christ Alone" (1 John)
M7	"I Believe in Jesus" (1 John)
WS3153	"O God in Whom We Live" (1 John, John)
S2150	"Lord, Be Glorified" (John)
S2224	"Make Us One" (John)
S2226	"Bind Us Together" (John)
M13	"Be Glorified" (John)
M63	"I Could Sing of Your Love Forever" (John)
M152	"Be Glorified" (John)
S2188	"The Family Prayer Song" (Christian Home)

Vocal Solos

"Above All" (1 John, John)
  V-3 (2)   p. 17
"That's Why We Are Beautiful" (John)
  V-8   p. 160

Anthems

"Oh, How Good It Is" (John)
Arr. Joey Hoelscher; Alfred 44235
SATB with keyboard, opt. violin

"My Mother's Love" (Mother's Day)
Tom Shelton; Hinshaw HMC2352
Unison Children and Adult Women with piano

Other Suggestions

Today may also be celebrated as Ascension Sunday using the ideas for May 10.

Visuals:
O (Acts)	Peter, open Bible, Judas, 2 men, lots
P	Path, trees/water/fruit, chaff/wind, scales
E	Open Bible, hearts/people, 5:11b, 12a
G	Jesus praying, praying hands

Opening Prayer: BOW463 or BOW466 (Mother's Day)
Prayer: WSL62 (Mother's Day, Christian Home)
Prayer: WSL201. "God our Creator" (Mother's Day)
Prayer of Intercession: BOW438 (Mother's Day)
Prayer: BOW437 (Festival of the Christian Home)

Acts 2:1-21

[1]When the day of Pentecost had come, they were all together in one place. [2]And suddenly from heaven there came a sound like the rush of a violent wind, and it filled the entire house where they were sitting. [3]Divided tongues, as of fire, appeared among them, and a tongue rested on each of them. [4]All of them were filled with the Holy Spirit and began to speak in other languages, as the Spirit gave them ability.

[5]Now there were devout Jews from every nation under heaven living in Jerusalem. [6]And at this sound the crowd gathered and was bewildered, because each one heard them speaking in the native language of each. [7]Amazed and astonished, they asked, "Are not all these who are speaking Galileans? [8]And how is it that we hear, each of us, in our own native language? [9]Parthians, Medes, Elamites, and residents of Mesopotamia, Judea and Cappadocia, Pontus and Asia, [10]Phrygia and Pamphylia, Egypt and the parts of Libya belonging to Cyrene, and visitors from Rome, both Jews and proselytes, [11]Cretans and Arabs—in our own languages we hear them speaking about God's deeds of power." [12]All were amazed and perplexed, saying to one another, "What does this mean?" [13]But others sneered and said, "They are filled with new wine."

[14]But Peter, standing with the eleven, raised his voice and addressed them, "Men of Judea and all who live in Jerusalem, let this be known to you, and listen to what I say. [15]Indeed, these are not drunk, as you suppose, for it is only nine o'clock in the morning. [16]No, this is what was spoken through the prophet Joel:

[17]'In the last days it will be, God declares,
that I will pour out my Spirit upon all flesh,
    and your sons and your daughters shall prophesy,
and your young men shall see visions,
    and your old men shall dream dreams.
[18]Even upon my slaves, both men and women,
    in those days I will pour out my Spirit;
        and they shall prophesy.
[19]And I will show portents in the heaven above
    and signs on the earth below,
        blood, and fire, and smoky mist.
[20]The sun shall be turned to darkness
    and the moon to blood,
        before the coming of the Lord's great and glorious day.
[21]Then everyone who calls on the name of the Lord shall be
        saved.'

Psalm 104:24-34, 35b (UM826)

[24]O Lord, how manifold are your works!
    In wisdom you have made them all;
        the earth is full of your creatures.
[25]Yonder is the sea, great and wide,
    creeping things innumerable are there,
        living things both small and great.
[26]There go the ships,
    and Leviathan that you formed to sport in it.
[27]These all look to you
    to give them their food in due season;
[28]when you give to them, they gather it up;
    when you open your hand, they are filled with good things.
[29]When you hide your face, they are dismayed;
    when you take away their breath, they die
        and return to their dust.
[30]When you send forth your spirit, they are created;
    and you renew the face of the ground.

[31]May the glory of the Lord endure forever;
    may the Lord rejoice in his works–
[32]who looks on the earth and it trembles,
    who touches the mountains and they smoke.
[33]I will sing to the Lord as long as I live;
    I will sing praise to my God while I have being.
[34]May my meditation be pleasing to him,
    for I rejoice in the Lord. . . .
[35b]Bless the Lord, O my soul.
Praise the Lord!

Romans 8:22-27

[22]We know that the whole creation has been groaning in labor pains until now; [23]and not only the creation, but we ourselves, who have the first fruits of the Spirit, groan inwardly while we wait for adoption, the redemption of our bodies. [24]For in hope we were saved. Now hope that is seen is not hope. For who hopes for what is seen? [25]But if we hope for what we do not see, we wait for it with patience.

[26]Likewise the Spirit helps us in our weakness; for we do not know how to pray as we ought, but that very Spirit intercedes with sighs too deep for words. [27]And God, who searches the heart, knows what is the mind of the Spirit, because the Spirit intercedes for the saints according to the will of God.

John 15:26-27; 16:4b-15

[26]"When the Advocate comes, whom I will send to you from the Father, the Spirit of truth who comes from the Father, he will testify on my behalf. [27]You also are to testify because you have been with me from the beginning." . . .

16 [4b]"I did not say these things to you from the beginning, because I was with you. [5]But now I am going to him who sent me; yet none of you asks me, 'Where are you going?' [6]But because I have said these things to you, sorrow has filled your hearts. [7]Nevertheless, I tell you the truth: it is to your advantage that I go away, for if I do not go away, the Advocate will not come to you; but if I go, I will send him to you. [8]And when he comes, he will prove the world wrong about sin and righteousness and judgment: [9]about sin, because they do not believe in me; [10]about righteousness, because I am going to the Father and you will see me no longer; [11]about judgment, because the ruler of this world has been condemned.

[12]"I still have many things to say to you, but you cannot bear them now. [13]When the Spirit of truth comes, he will guide you into all the truth; for he will not speak on his own, but will speak whatever he hears, and he will declare to you the things that are to come. [14]He will glorify me, because he will take what is mine and declare it to you. [15]All that the Father has is mine. For this reason I said that he will take what is mine and declare it to you."

Primary Hymns and Songs for the Day

332	"Spirit of Faith, Come Down" (Acts) (O)
347	"Spirit Song" (Acts, John)
393	"Spirit of the Living God" (Acts, John)
	H-3 Chr-176
	S-1 #212. Vocal Desc. idea
539	"O Spirit of the Living God" (Acts) (C)
	H-3 Hbl-44; Chr-21; Desc-40; Org-40
	S-1 #131-132. Intro. and Desc.

Additional Hymn Suggestions

2236	"Gather Us In" (Acts, Comm.) (O)
324	"Hail Thee, Festival Day" (Acts)
334	"Sweet, Sweet Spirit" (Acts)
420	"Breathe on Me, Breath of God" (Acts)
422	"Jesus, Thine All-Victorious Love" (Acts)
590	"Christ Loves the Church" (Acts) (C)
537	"Filled with the Spirit's Power" (Acts)
538	"Wind Who Makes All Winds that Blow" (Acts)
541	"See How Great a Flame Aspires" (Acts)
543	"O Breath of Life" (Acts)
544	"Like the Murmur of the Dove's Song" (Acts)
547	"O Church of God, United" (Acts)
640	"Take Our Bread" (Acts, Comm.)
3017	"Come, Join the Dance of Trinity" (Acts)
3109	"Living Spirit, Holy Fire" (Acts, Pentecost)
2077	"You Alone Are Holy" (Acts)
2027	"Now Praise the Hidden God of Love" (Acts)
2117	"Spirit of God" (Acts)
2122	"She Comes Sailing on the Wind" (Acts)
2123	"Loving Spirit" (Acts, Pentecost)
2237	"As a Fire Is Meant for Burning" (Acts)
2238	"In the Midst of New Dimensions" (Acts, Pentecost)
2246	"Deep in the Shadows of the Past" (Acts)
2269	"Come, Share the Lord" (Acts, Comm.)
2120	"Spirit, Spirit of Gentleness" (Acts, Rom)
368	"My Hope Is Built" (Acts, Rom)
500	"Spirit of God, Descend upon My Heart" (Acts, Rom)
475	"Come Down, O Love Divine" (Acts, John)
651	"Come, Holy Ghost, Our Souls Inspire" (Acts, John)
2213	"Healer of Our Every Ill" (Acts, John)
3150	"Father, We Have Heard You Calling" (Acts, John)
73	"O Worship the King" (Pss) (O) or (C)
148	"Many and Great, O God" (Pss)
404	"Every Time I Feel the Spirit" (Rom)
2019	"Holy" ("Santo") (Rom)
2121	"O Holy Spirit, Root of Life" (Rom)
3115	"Covenant Prayer" (Rom)
3020	"God of the Bible" (Rom, Pentecost)
454	"Open My Eyes, That I May See" (John)

Additional Contemporary Suggestions

S2002	"I Will Call Upon the Lord" (Acts)
S2039	"Holy, Holy" (Acts)
S2049	"God Is Here Today" ("Dios Está Aquí") (Acts)
S2118	"Holy Spirit, Come to Us" ("Veni Sancte Spiritus") (Acts)
S2119	"Where the Spirit of the Lord Is" (Acts)
S2124	"Come, O Holy Spirit, Come" ("Wa Wa Wa Emimimo") (Acts, Pentecost)
S2272	"Holy Ground" (Acts)
WS3092	"Come, Holy Spirit" (Acts, Pentecost)
SP240	"As We Gather" (Acts)
WS3008	"Open the Eyes of My Heart" (Acts)
WS3042	"Shout to the North" (Acts, Rom)

M88	"Holy Spirit, Rain Down" (Acts, John)
UM328	"Surely the Presence of the Lord" (Acts, John)
	S-2, #200 Stanzas for soloist
UM333	"I'm Goin'a Sing When the Spirit Says Sing" (Acts, John)
M4	"Let It Rise" (Pss)
M69	"Did You Feel the Mountains Tremble?" (Pss)
SP32	"Bless the Lord, O My Soul" (Pss)
S2152	"Change My Heart, O God" (Rom)
S2165	"Cry of My Heart" (Rom)
M154	"Dwell" (Pentecost)

Vocal Solos

"Spirit of Faith Come Down" (Acts, Pentecost)
    V-1   p. 43
"Ev'ry Time I Feel De Spirit" (Acts, Pentecost)
    V-7   p. 78
"New Wind Blowin'" (Acts, Pentecost)
    V-8   p. 192
"A Covenant Prayer" (Rom)
    V-11   p. 6

Anthems

"There's a Spirit of Love in This Place" (Acts)
Mark A. Miller; Abingdon Press 9780687644629
SATB with piano (opt. solo)

"I Will Pour Our My Spirit" (Roms)
Allen Pote; Hinshaw HMC2441
SATB with piano

Other Suggestions

Visuals:
O (Acts) Wind, tongues of fire, praising, all races of people
    P   Sea/ships, whales, dove, volcano, singing, Ps 104:35b
    E   Praying hands, Holy Spirit (flames, descending dove)
    G   Briefcase (Advocate), Trinity (triangle, trefoil, others)
Introit: S2125. "Come, Holy Spirit" (Acts)
Greeting: BOW390 or BOW406 (Acts) or BOW382 (Rom)
Opening Prayer: BOW464 (Rom)
Canticle: UM406. "Canticle of Prayer" (Rom)
Call to Prayer: BOW214. "Spirit of God" (Acts)
Prayer of Confession: BOW482 or BOW489 (Acts)
Prayer: WSL39, UM329, UM542, or UM574 (Acts, Pentecost)
Prayer: BOW404, BOW407, or BOW408 (Acts, John)
Prayer: BOW440 or BOW542 (Memorial Day)
Hymn: BOW223. "O Holy Spirit" (Acts)
Offering Prayer: WSL132 (Acts, Pentecost)
Great Thanksgiving for Pentecost: BOW68
Benediction Response: S2241. "The Spirit Sends Us Forth to
    Serve" (Acts, Pentecost)

Isaiah 6:1-8

[1]In the year that King Uzziah died, I saw the Lord sitting on a throne, high and lofty; and the hem of his robe filled the temple. [2]Seraphs were in attendance above him; each had six wings: with two they covered their faces, and with two they covered their feet, and with two they flew. [3]And one called to another and said:

"Holy, holy, holy is the LORD of hosts;
the whole earth is full of his glory."

[4]The pivots on the thresholds shook at the voices of those who called, and the house filled with smoke. [5]And I said: "Woe is me! I am lost, for I am a man of unclean lips, and I live among a people of unclean lips; yet my eyes have seen the King, the LORD of hosts!"

[6]Then one of the seraphs flew to me, holding a live coal that had been taken from the altar with a pair of tongs. [7]The seraph touched my mouth with it and said: "Now that this has touched your lips, your guilt has departed and your sin is blotted out." [8]Then I heard the voice of the Lord saying, "Whom shall I send, and who will go for us?" And I said, "Here am I; send me!"

Psalm 29 (UM761)

[1]Ascribe to the LORD, O heavenly beings,
ascribe to the LORD glory and strength.
[2]Ascribe to the LORD the glory of his name;
worship the LORD in holy splendor.
[3]The voice of the LORD is over the waters;
the God of glory thunders,
the LORD, over mighty waters.
[4]The voice of the LORD is powerful;
the voice of the LORD is full of majesty.
[5]The voice of the LORD breaks the cedars;
the LORD breaks the cedars of Lebanon.
[6]He makes Lebanon skip like a calf,
and Sirion like a young wild ox.
[7]The voice of the LORD flashes forth flames of fire.
[8]The voice of the LORD shakes the wilderness;
the LORD shakes the wilderness of Kadesh.
[9]The voice of the LORD causes the oaks to whirl,
and strips the forest bare;
and in his temple all say, "Glory!"
[10]The LORD sits enthroned over the flood;
the LORD sits enthroned as king forever.
[11]May the LORD give strength to his people!
May the LORD bless his people with peace!

Romans 8:12-17

[12]So then, brothers and sisters, we are debtors, not to the flesh, to live according to the flesh— [13]for if you live according to the flesh, you will die; but if by the Spirit you put to death the deeds of the body, you will live. [14]For all who are led by the Spirit of God are children of God. [15]For you did not receive a spirit of slavery to fall back into fear, but you have received a spirit of adoption. When we cry, "Abba! Father!" [16]it is that very Spirit bearing witness with our spirit that we are children of God, [17]and if children, then heirs, heirs of God and joint heirs with Christ— if, in fact, we suffer with him so that we may also be glorified with him.

John 3:1-17

Now there was a Pharisee named Nicodemus, a leader of the Jews. [2]He came to Jesus by night and said to him, "Rabbi, we know that you are a teacher who has come from God; for no one can do these signs that you do apart from the presence of God." [3]Jesus answered him, "Very truly, I tell you, no one can see the kingdom of God without being born from above." [4]Nicodemus said to him, "How can anyone be born after having grown old? Can one enter a second time into the mother's womb and be born?" [5]Jesus answered, "Very truly, I tell you, no one can enter the kingdom of God without being born of water and Spirit. [6]What is born of the flesh is flesh, and what is born of the Spirit is spirit. [7]Do not be astonished that I said to you, 'You must be born from above.' [8]The wind blows where it chooses, and you hear the sound of it, but you do not know where it comes from or where it goes. So it is with everyone who is born of the Spirit." [9]Nicodemus said to him, "How can these things be?" [10]Jesus answered him, "Are you a teacher of Israel, and yet you do not understand these things?

[11]"Very truly, I tell you, we speak of what we know and testify to what we have seen; yet you do not receive our testimony. [12]If I have told you about earthly things and you do not believe, how can you believe if I tell you about heavenly things? [13]No one has ascended into heaven except the one who descended from heaven, the Son of Man. [14]And just as Moses lifted up the serpent in the wilderness, so must the Son of Man be lifted up, [15]that whoever believes in him may have eternal life.

[16]"For God so loved the world that he gave his only Son, so that everyone who believes in him may not perish but may have eternal life. [17]Indeed, God did not send the Son into the world to condemn the world, but in order that the world might be saved through him."

Primary Hymns and Songs for the Day

64   "Holy, Holy, Holy! Lord God Almighty" (Isa, Trinity) (O)
       H-3   Hbl-68; Chr-99; Desc-80; Org-97
       S-1   #245-248. Various treatments.
2019   "Holy" ("*Santo*") (Isa)
3028   "Holy Is the Lord" (Isa)
159   "Lift High the Cross" (John)
331   "Holy Spirit, Come, Confirm Us" (Trinity) (C)
       H-3   Chr-67
       S-2   #63-64. Desc. and Harm.
662   "Stand Up and Bless the Lord" (Isa) (C)
       H-3   Hbl-79; Chr-141; Desc-95; Org-143
       S-1   #306-308. Various treatments

Additional Hymn Suggestions

65   "*¡Santo! ¡Santo! ¡Santo!*" (Isa, Trinity) (O)
85   "We Believe in One True God" (Isa, Trinity)
88   "Maker, in Whom We Live" (Isa, Trinity)
90   "Ye Watchers and Ye Holy Ones" (Isa, Trinity)
436   "The Voice of God Is Calling" (Isa)
497   "Send Me, Lord" (Isa)
508   "Faith, While Trees Are Still in Blossom" (Isa)
582   "Whom Shall I Send" (Isa)
593   "Here I Am, Lord" (Isa)
626   "Let All Mortal Flesh Keep Silence" (Isa, Comm.)
638   "This Is the Feast of Victory" (Isa, Comm.)
2256   "Holy, Holy, Holy Lord" ("Sanctus") (Isa, Comm.)
3150   "Father, We Have Heard You Calling" (Isa, Trinity)
717   "Mine Eyes Have Seen the Glory" (Isa, Pss)
3126   "Everything That Has Voice" (Isa, Pss)
109   "Creating God, Your Fingers Trace" (Rom, Trinity)
332   "Spirit of Faith, Come Down" (Rom)
356   "*Pues Si Vivimos*" ("When We Are Living") (Rom)
404   "Every Time I Feel the Spirit" (Rom)
414   "Thou Hidden Love of God" (Rom)
2052   "The Lone, Wild Bird" (Rom)
2248   "Baptized in Water" (Rom, Baptism)
2050   "Mothering God, You Gave Me Birth" (Rom, John)
372   "How Can We Sinners Know" (Rom, John)
98   "To God Be the Glory" (John)
184   "Of the Father's Love Begotten" (John, Trinity)
267   "O Love, How Deep" (John, Trinity)
605   "Wash, O God, Our Sons and Daughters" (John, Baptism)
610   "We Know That Christ Is Raised" (John, Baptism)
2046   "Womb of Life" (John, Trinity)
2084   "Come, Let Us with Our Lord Arise" (John)
2085   "He Came Down" (John)
2220   "We Are God's People" (John)
2236   "Gather Us In" (John)
3146   "O Breath of Life" (John)
2121   "O Holy Spirit, Root of Life" (John, Trinity)
3017   "Come, Join the Dance of Trinity" (Trinity)
2174   "What Does the Lord Require of You" (Peace with Justice)
3124   "How Shall I Come Before the Lord" (Peace with Justice)

Additional Contemporary Suggestions

M77   "Above All" (Isa, John)
S2007   "*Santo, Santo, Santo*" ("Holy, Holy, Holy") (Isa.)
WS3013 "Sing the Praise of God Our Maker" (Isa, Trinity)
SP91   "Holy Is the Lord" (Isa)
WS3040 "You Are My All in All" (Isa, John)
S2039   "Holy, Holy" (Isa, Rom)
UM393   "Spirit of the Living God" (Rom)
       S-1   #212 Vocal Desc.
WS3102 "You Are My King" ("Amazing Love") (Rom, John)
M247   "The Stand" (Rom)
S2223   "They'll Know We Are Christians" (Rom, Trinity)
S2108   "O How He Loves You and Me!" (John)
S2073   "Celebrate Love" (John)
WS3102 "You Are My King" ("Amazing Love") (John)
WS3105 "In Christ Alone" (John)
M7   "I Believe in Jesus" (John, Trinity)
M94   "That's Why We Praise Him" (John, Easter)
SP111   "There Is a Redeemer" (John, Trinity)
S2006   "Lord God Almighty" (Trinity)
WS3003 "How Great Is Our God" (Trinity)
M250   "Our God Saves" (Trinity)
S2171   "Make Me a Channel of Your Peace" (Peace with Justice)

Vocal Solos

"Alleluia" (Isa, Trinity)
       V-8   p. 358
"The Gospel of Grace" (John)
       V-3 (1)   p.44
"Wash Me in Your Water" (John, Baptism)
       V-5(2)   p. 18

Anthems

"Here I Am, Lord" (Isa)
Arr. Mary McDonald; Alfred 42956
SATB with keyboard

"Lift High the Cross" (John)
Arr. Paul Leddington Wright; Hope C5802
SATB with organ and opt. brass

Other Suggestions

Visuals:
    O   Seraphs, incense, glowing coals
    P   Storm, flames, lightning, wind, skipping calf
    E   Crown (heirs), open manacles (handcuffs)
    G   wind, white garment, water, flame/dove (Holy Spirit)
Call to Worship: UM234, stanzas 2 and 3. "O Come, All Ye Faithful" (John, Trinity)
Greeting: BOW391 or BOW411 (Trinity) or BOW300 (Pss)
Opening Prayer: BOW392 (John)
Prayer of Confession: WSL91 (Isa, Trinity)
Prayer: BOW412 (Trinity Sunday)
Prayers: WSL60, BOW428, BOW513 (Peace with Justice)
Canticle: UM80. "Canticle of the Holy Trinity"
Affirmation of Faith: UM880. The Nicene Creed (Trinity)
Communion Responses: WS3172. "Communion Setting" (Isa)
Offering Response: BOW182. "Doxology" (John)
Closing Prayer: WSL172. "Holy Trinity" (Trinity)
Blessing: BOW563 (Trinity) or BOW521 (Peace with Justice)

1 Samuel 3:1-20

[1] Now the boy Samuel was ministering to the LORD under Eli. The word of the LORD was rare in those days; visions were not widespread.

[2] At that time Eli, whose eyesight had begun to grow dim so that he could not see, was lying down in his room; [3] the lamp of God had not yet gone out, and Samuel was lying down in the temple of the LORD, where the ark of God was. [4] Then the LORD called, "Samuel! Samuel!" and he said, "Here I am!" [5] and ran to Eli, and said, "Here I am, for you called me." But he said, "I did not call; lie down again." So he went and lay down. [6] The LORD called again, "Samuel!" Samuel got up and went to Eli, and said, "Here I am, for you called me." But he said, "I did not call, my son; lie down again." [7] Now Samuel did not yet know the LORD, and the word of the LORD had not yet been revealed to him. [8] The LORD called Samuel again, a third time. And he got up and went to Eli, and said, "Here I am, for you called me." Then Eli perceived that the LORD was calling the boy. [9] Therefore Eli said to Samuel, "Go, lie down; and if he calls you, you shall say, 'Speak, LORD, for your servant is listening.'" So Samuel went and lay down in his place.

[10] Now the LORD came and stood there, calling as before, "Samuel! Samuel!" And Samuel said, "Speak, for your servant is listening." [11] Then the LORD said to Samuel, "See, I am about to do something in Israel that will make both ears of anyone who hears of it tingle. [12] On that day I will fulfill against Eli all that I have spoken concerning his house, from beginning to end. [13] For I have told him that I am about to punish his house forever, for the iniquity that he knew, because his sons were blaspheming God, and he did not restrain them. [14] Therefore I swear to the house of Eli that the iniquity of Eli's house shall not be expiated by sacrifice or offering forever."

[15] Samuel lay there until morning; then he opened the doors of the house of the LORD. Samuel was afraid to tell the vision to Eli. [16] But Eli called Samuel and said, "Samuel, my son." He said, "Here I am." [17] Eli said, "What was it that he told you? Do not hide it from me. May God do so to you and more also, if you hide anything from me of all that he told you." [18] So Samuel told him everything and hid nothing from him. Then he said, "It is the LORD; let him do what seems good to him."

[19] As Samuel grew up, the LORD was with him and let none of his words fall to the ground. [20] And all Israel from Dan to Beer-sheba knew that Samuel was a trustworthy prophet of the LORD.

Psalm 139:1-6, 13-18 (UM854)

[1] O LORD, you have searched me and known me.
[2] You know when I sit down and when I rise up;
    you discern my thoughts from far away.
[3] You search out my path and my lying down,
    and are acquainted with all my ways.
[4] Even before a word is on my tongue,
    O LORD, you know it completely.
[5] You hem me in, behind and before,
    and lay your hand upon me.
[6] Such knowledge is too wonderful for me;
    it is so high that I cannot attain it.
. . . .
[13] For it was you who formed my inward parts;
    you knit me together in my mother's womb.
[14] I praise you, for I am fearfully and wonderfully made.
    Wonderful are your works;
that I know very well.
[15]   My frame was not hidden from you,
when I was being made in secret,
    intricately woven in the depths of the earth.

[16] Your eyes beheld my unformed substance.
In your book were written
    all the days that were formed for me,
    when none of them as yet existed.
[17] How weighty to me are your thoughts, O God!
    How vast is the sum of them!
[18] I try to count them—they are more than the sand;
    I come to the end—I am still with you.

2 Corinthians 4:5-12

[5] For we do not proclaim ourselves; we proclaim Jesus Christ as Lord and ourselves as your slaves for Jesus' sake. [6] For it is the God who said, "Let light shine out of darkness," who has shone in our hearts to give the light of the knowledge of the glory of God in the face of Jesus Christ.

[7] But we have this treasure in clay jars, so that it may be made clear that this extraordinary power belongs to God and does not come from us. [8] We are afflicted in every way, but not crushed; perplexed, but not driven to despair; [9] persecuted, but not forsaken; struck down, but not destroyed; [10] always carrying in the body the death of Jesus, so that the life of Jesus may also be made visible in our bodies. [11] For while we live, we are always being given up to death for Jesus' sake, so that the life of Jesus may be made visible in our mortal flesh. [12] So death is at work in us, but life in you.

Mark 2:23—3:6

[23] One sabbath he was going through the grainfields; and as they made their way his disciples began to pluck heads of grain. [24] The Pharisees said to him, "Look, why are they doing what is not lawful on the sabbath?" [25] And he said to them, "Have you never read what David did when he and his companions were hungry and in need of food? [26] He entered the house of God, when Abiathar was high priest, and ate the bread of the Presence, which it is not lawful for any but the priests to eat, and he gave some to his companions." [27] Then he said to them, "The sabbath was made for humankind, and not humankind for the sabbath; [28] so the Son of Man is lord even of the sabbath."

3 Again he entered the synagogue, and a man was there who had a withered hand. [2] They watched him to see whether he would cure him on the sabbath, so that they might accuse him. [3] And he said to the man who had the withered hand, "Come forward." [4] Then he said to them, "Is it lawful to do good or to do harm on the sabbath, to save life or to kill?" But they were silent. [5] He looked around at them with anger; he was grieved at their hardness of heart and said to the man, "Stretch out your hand." He stretched it out, and his hand was restored. [6] The Pharisees went out and immediately conspired with the Herodians against him, how to destroy him.

Primary Hymns and Songs for the Day

454   "Open My Eyes, That I May See" (1 Sam, 2 Cor) (O)
       H-3   Chr-157; Org-108
451   "Be Thou My Vision" (1 Sam, 2 Cor)
       H-3   Hbl-15, 48; Chr-36; Org-153
       S-1   #319. Arr. for organ, voices in canon
497   "Send Me, Lord" (1 Sam)
       S-2   #173. Percussion Arr.
593   "Here I Am, Lord" (1 Sam)
       H-3   Chr-97; Org-54
2052   "The Lone, Wild Bird" (Pss)
261   "Lord of the Dance" (Mark)
       H-3   Chr-106; Org-81
660   "God Is Here" (2 Cor)
       H-3   Hbl-61; Chr-132; Org-2
       S-1   #4-5. Instr. and vocal Desc
3139   "We Cannot Measure How You Heal" (Mark)
       S-2   #33-37. Various treatments
463   "Lord, Speak to Me" (1 Sam) (C)
       H-3   Hbl-75; Chr-131; Desc-22; Org-18
       S-1   #52. Desc.

Additional Hymn Suggestions

400   "Come, Thou Fount of Every Blessing" (1 Sam)
419   "I Am Thine, O Lord" (1 Sam)
508   "Faith, While Trees Are Still in Blossom" (1 Sam)
582   "Whom Shall I Send?" (1 Sam)
584   "Lord, You Give the Great Commission" (1 Sam)
593   "Here I Am, Lord" (1 Sam)
581   "Lord, Whose Love Through Humble Service" (1 Sam, Mark)
2218   "You Are Mine" (1 Sam, 2 Cor)
139   "Praise to the Lord, the Almighty" (Pss) (O)
411   "Dear Lord, Lead Me Day by Day" (Pss)
474   "Precious Lord, Take My Hand" (Pss)
2046   "Womb of Life" (Pss)
2050   "Mothering God, You Gave Me Birth" (Pss)
2051   "I Was There to Hear Your Borning Cry" (Pss)
2117   "Spirit of God" (Pss)
2123   "Loving Spirit" (Pss)
2208   "Guide My Feet" (Pss)
2214   "Lead Me, Guide Me" (Pss)
3011   "All My Days" (Pss)
3019   "Bidden, Unbidden" (Pss)
430   "O Master, Let Me Walk with Thee" (Pss, Mark)
188   "Christ Is the World's Light" (2 Cor)
206   "I Want to Walk as a Child of the Light" (2 Cor)
356   "*Pues Si Vivimos*" ("When We Are Living") (2 Cor)
585   "This Little Light of Mine" (2 Cor)
679   "O Splendor of God's Glory Bright" (2 Cor)
2166   "Christ Beside Me" (2 Cor)
2204   "Light of the World" (2 Cor)
2218   "You Are Mine" (2 Cor)
2237   "As a Fire Is Meant for Burning" (2 Cor)
2172   "We Are Called" (2 Cor, Mark) (O)
3011   "All My Days" (2 Cor, Mark)
263   "When Jesus the Healer Passed Through Galilee" (Mark)
265   "O Christ, the Healer" (Mark)
425   "O Crucified Redeemer" (Mark)
427   "Where Cross the Crowded Ways of Life" (Mark)
441   "What Does the Lord Require" (Mark)
444   "O Young and Fearless Prophet" (Mark)
620   "One Bread, One Body" (Mark, Comm.)
629   "You Satisfy the Hungry Heart" (Mark, Comm.)
637   "*Una Espiga*" ("Sheaves of Summer") (Mark, Comm.)
2177   "Wounded World That Cries for Healing" (Mark)
2238   "In the Midst of New Dimensions" (Mark)
3120   "Amazing Abundance" (Mark)
3124   "How Shall I Come Before the Lord" (Mark)
3128   "Whatever You Do" (Mark)

Additional Contemporary Suggestions

S2139   "Oh, I Know the Lord's Laid His Hands on Me" (1 Sam, Pss)
M105   "Let My Words Be Few" (1 Sam)
M108   "Lead Me, Lord" (1 Sam)
M109   "He Knows My Name" (1 Sam, Pss)
M38   "In the Secret" ("I Want to Know You") (Pss)
M85   "The Potter's Hand" (Pss)
M101   "These Hands" (Pss)
S2032   "My Life Is in You, Lord" (2 Cor)
S2173   "Shine, Jesus, Shine" (2 Cor)
S2204   "Light of the World" (2 Cor)
S2235   "We Are Marching" ("*Siyahamba*") (2 Cor)
WS3038   "Mighty to Save" (2 Cor)
WS3105   "In Christ Alone" (2 Cor)
WS3108   "Tradin' My Sorrows" (2 Cor)
WS3163   "Walking in the Light of God" (2 Cor)
M249   "Marvelous Light" (2 Cor, Mark)
S2261   "Life-Giving Bread" (2 Cor, Mark, Comm.)
S2174   "What Does the Lord Require of You" (Mark)
WS3162   "Stand in Awe" (Mark)

Vocal Solos

"Be Thou My Vision" (1 Sam)
     V-6   p. 13
"Here I Am" (1 Sam)
     V-11   p. 19
"Shine, Jesus, Shine" (2 Cor)
     V-3(2)   p. 48

Anthems

"Lord, You Know Me Through and Through" (Pss)
Mozart, Arr. Hopson; MorningStar 50-9208
2-part mixed with keyboard

"Eternal Light, Shine in My Heart"
K. Lee Scott; MorningStar 50-8825
SATB with organ

Other Suggestions

Visuals:
     O   Listening, lamp, boy, old man, service to others, 3:4b, 5b, 9b
     P   Hand, pregnant woman, newborn child, baby examining fingers, hour glass
     E   Light/darkness, Christ, treasure chest, clay pots or urns (various sizes, some cracked), service to others
     G   wheat/bread, outstretched hands
Opening Prayer: BOW313 (1 Sam)
Call to Prayer: BOW196. "Call to Prayer" (Pss)
Prayer of Confession: BOW478 (1 Sam) or BOW480 (Pss)
Prayer: UM403. For True Life (1 Sam)
Prayer: BOW510. For Discernment (1 Sam)
Prayer: WSL51. "O Mysterious God" (1 Sam, Pss)
Words of Assurance: BOW476. "This is the message" (2 Cor)
Prayer: UM489 or BOW525 (1 Sam, 2 Cor)

1 Samuel 8:4-20 (11:14-15)

[4] Then all the elders of Israel gathered together and came to Samuel at Ramah, [5] and said to him, "You are old and your sons do not follow in your ways; appoint for us, then, a king to govern us, like other nations." [6] But the thing displeased Samuel when they said, "Give us a king to govern us." Samuel prayed to the LORD, [7] and the LORD said to Samuel, "Listen to the voice of the people in all that they say to you; for they have not rejected you, but they have rejected me from being king over them. [8] Just as they have done to me, from the day I brought them up out of Egypt to this day, forsaking me and serving other gods, so also they are doing to you. [9] Now then, listen to their voice; only— you shall solemnly warn them, and show them the ways of the king who shall reign over them."

[10] So Samuel reported all the words of the LORD to the people who were asking him for a king. [11] He said, "These will be the ways of the king who will reign over you: he will take your sons and appoint them to his chariots and to be his horsemen, and to run before his chariots; [12] and he will appoint for himself commanders of thousands and commanders of fifties, and some to plow his ground and to reap his harvest, and to make his implements of war and the equipment of his chariots. [13] He will take your daughters to be perfumers and cooks and bakers. [14] He will take the best of your fields and vineyards and olive orchards and give them to his courtiers. [15] He will take one-tenth of your grain and of your vineyards and give it to his officers and his courtiers. [16] He will take your male and female slaves, and the best of your cattle and donkeys, and put them to his work. [17] He will take one-tenth of your flocks, and you shall be his slaves. [18] And in that day you will cry out because of your king, whom you have chosen for yourselves; but the LORD will not answer you in that day."

[19] But the people refused to listen to the voice of Samuel; they said, "No! but we are determined to have a king over us, [20] so that we also may be like other nations, and that our king may govern us and go out before us and fight our battles." . . .

(11 [14] Samuel said to the people, "Come, let us go to Gilgal and there renew the kingship." [15] So all the people went to Gilgal, and there they made Saul king before the LORD in Gilgal. There they sacrificed offerings of well-being before the LORD, and there Saul and all the Israelites rejoiced greatly.)

Psalm 138 (UM853)

[1] I give you thanks, O LORD, with my whole heart;
    before the gods I sing your praise;
[2] I bow down toward your holy temple
      and give thanks to your name for your steadfast love and
            your faithfulness;
      for you have exalted your name and your word
      above everything.
[3] On the day I called, you answered me,
      you increased my strength of soul.
[4] All the kings of the earth shall praise you, O LORD,
      for they have heard the words of your mouth.
[5] They shall sing of the ways of the LORD,
      for great is the glory of the LORD.
[6] For though the LORD is high, he regards the lowly;
      but the haughty he perceives from far away.
[7] Though I walk in the midst of trouble,
      you preserve me against the wrath of my enemies;
you stretch out your hand,
      and your right hand delivers me.
[8] The LORD will fulfill his purpose for me;
      your steadfast love, O LORD, endures forever.
      Do not forsake the work of your hands.

2 Corinthians 4:13–5:1

[13] But just as we have the same spirit of faith that is in accordance with scripture—"I believed, and so I spoke"—we also believe, and so we speak, [14] because we know that the one who raised the Lord Jesus will raise us also with Jesus, and will bring us with you into his presence. [15] Yes, everything is for your sake, so that grace, as it extends to more and more people, may increase thanksgiving, to the glory of God.

[16] So we do not lose heart. Even though our outer nature is wasting away, our inner nature is being renewed day by day. [17] For this slight momentary affliction is preparing us for an eternal weight of glory beyond all measure, [18] because we look not at what can be seen but at what cannot be seen; for what can be seen is temporary, but what cannot be seen is eternal.

[5] For we know that if the earthly tent we live in is destroyed, we have a building from God, a house not made with hands, eternal in the heavens.

Mark 3:20-35

[20] And the crowd came together again, so that they could not even eat. [21] When his family heard it, they went out to restrain him, for people were saying, "He has gone out of his mind." [22] And the scribes who came down from Jerusalem said, "He has Beelzebul, and by the ruler of the demons he casts out demons." [23] And he called them to him, and spoke to them in parables, "How can Satan cast out Satan? [24] If a kingdom is divided against itself, that kingdom cannot stand. [25] And if a house is divided against itself, that house will not be able to stand. [26] And if Satan has risen up against himself and is divided, he cannot stand, but his end has come. [27] But no one can enter a strong man's house and plunder his property without first tying up the strong man; then indeed the house can be plundered.

[28] "Truly I tell you, people will be forgiven for their sins and whatever blasphemies they utter; [29] but whoever blasphemes against the Holy Spirit can never have forgiveness, but is guilty of an eternal sin"— [30] for they had said, "He has an unclean spirit."

[31] Then his mother and his brothers came; and standing outside, they sent to him and called him. [32] A crowd was sitting around him; and they said to him, "Your mother and your brothers and sisters are outside, asking for you." [33] And he replied, "Who are my mother and my brothers?" [34] And looking at those who sat around him, he said, "Here are my mother and my brothers! [35] Whoever does the will of God is my brother and sister and mother."

Primary Hymns and Songs for the Day

142   "If Thou But Suffer God to Guide Thee" (1 Sam, Pss, 1 Cor) (O)
     H-3   Chr-108; Desc-103; Org-179
533   "We Shall Overcome" (1 Cor)
2225   "Who Is My Mother, Who Is My Brother?" (Mark, Communion)
2223   "They'll Know We Are Christians" (Mark)
2234   "Lead On, O Cloud of Presence" (1 Sam, Mark) (C)
     H-3   Hbl-74; Chr-123; Desc-64; Org-71
     S-1   #9-197. Various treatments

Additional Hymn Suggestions

132   "All My Hope Is Firmly Grounded" (1 Sam)
435   "O God of Every Nation" (1 Sam)
443   "O God Who Shaped Creation" (1 Sam)
586   "Let My People Seek Their Freedom" (1 Sam)
345   "'Tis the Old Ship of Zion" (1 Sam, Pss, 1 Cor)
154   "All Hail the Power of Jesus' Name" (1 Sam, 1 Cor)
155   "All Hail the Power of Jesus' Name" (1 Sam, 1 Cor)
454   "Open My Eyes, That I May See" (1 Sam, 1 Cor)
505   "When Our Confidence Is Shaken" (1 Sam, 1 Cor)
506   "Wellspring of Wisdom" (1 Sam, 1 Cor)
356   *Pues Si Vivimos* ("When We Are Living") (1 Sam, 1 Cor, Mark)
84   "Thank You, Lord" (Pss)
2009   "O God Beyond All Praising" (Pss)
2061   "Praise Our God Above" ("Harvest Song") (Pss)
2205   "The Fragrance of Christ" (Pss)
332   "Spirit of Faith, Come Down" (1 Cor, Comm.)
333   "I'm Goin'a Sing When the Spirit Says Sing" (1 Cor)
479   "Jesus, Lover of My Soul" (1 Cor)
508   "Faith, While Trees Are Still in Blossom" (1 Cor)
511   "Am I a Soldier of the Cross" (1 Cor)
524   "Beams of Heaven as I Go" (1 Cor)
590   "Christ Loves the Church" (1 Cor)
517   "By Gracious Powers" (1 Cor)
534   "Be Still, My Soul" (1 Cor)
610   "We Know That Christ Is Raised" (1 Cor)
623   "Here, O My Lord, I See Thee" (1 Cor, Comm.)
2196   "We Walk by Faith and Not by Sight" (1 Cor)
2206   "Without Seeing You" (1 Cor)
363   "And Can It Be that I Should Gain" (1 Cor, Mark)
368   "My Hope Is Built" (1 Cor, Mark)
548   "In Christ There Is No East or West" (1 Cor, Mark)
180   "O Jesus, My King" ("*Jesús Es Mi Rey Soberano*") (Mark)
261   "Lord of the Dance" (Mark)
267   "O Love, How Deep" (Mark)
444   "O Young and Fearless Prophet" (Mark)
445   "Happy the Home When God Is There" (Mark)
447   "Our Parent, by Whose Name" (Mark)
576   "Rise Up, O Men of God" (Mark)
2177   "Wounded World That Cries for Healing" (Mark)
2236   "Gather Us In" (Mark)
3072   "Cast Out, O Christ" (Mark)

Additional Contemporary Suggestions

S2190   "Bring Forth the Kingdom" (1 Sam, 1 Cor)
S2188   "The Family Prayer Song" ("As for Me and My House") (1 Sam, Mark)
S2016   "Glorify Thy Name" (Pss)
S2036   "Give Thanks" (Pss)
S2070   "He Is Exalted" (Pss)
S2195   "In the Lord I'll Be Ever Thankful" (Pss)
SP18   "I Exalt You" (Pss)
SP45   "Be Exalted, O God" ("I Will Give Thanks") (Pss)
SP65   "We Bow Down" (Pss)
M4   "Let It Rise" (Pss)
WS3023   "Forever" (Pss)
WS3027   "Hallelujah" ("Your Love Is Amazing") (Pss)
WS3014   "You Are Good" (Pss)
WS3040   "You Are My All in All" (Pss)
M189   "Your Love, Oh Lord" (Pss)
M257   "Came to My Rescue" (Pss)
M73   "My Redeemer Lives" (1 Cor)
WS3008   "Open the Eyes of My Heart" (1 Cor)
S2162   "Grace Alone" (1 Cor, Mark)
S2151   "I'm So Glad Jesus Lifted Me" (Mark)
WS3013   "Sing the Praise of God Our Maker" (Mark)

Vocal Solos

"That Someday Is Now" (Pss, 1 Cor)
   V-8   p. 259
"And Can It Be that I Should Gain" (1 Cor, Mark)
   V-1   p. 29

Anthems

"We Shall Overcome" (2 Cor)
Arr. Tom Trenney; Augsburg 9781506414010
SATB with djembe

"Lord, for Thy Tender Mercy's Sake" (Mark)
Richard Farrant; Pavanne HL 08301649
SATB a cappella

Other Suggestions

Visuals:
   O   Crown, purple, Samuel, symbols of political power
   P   crown, rejoicing, victory
   E   Bible, new growth coming out of decay, heavenly home
   G   Crowns, kingdoms/house divided, chains, strength, family

Call to Worship: S2225, stanza 1. "Who Is My Mother, Who Is My Brother?" (Mark, Comm.)
Prayer: UM429. "For Our Country" (1 Sam)
Prayer: UM495. "The Sufficiency of God" (1 Sam)
See The Abingdon Worship Annual 2018 *for more ideas.*

1 Samuel 15:34–16:13

[34] Then Samuel went to Ramah; and Saul went up to his house in Gibeah of Saul. [35] Samuel did not see Saul again until the day of his death, but Samuel grieved over Saul. And the LORD was sorry that he had made Saul king over Israel.

16 The LORD said to Samuel, "How long will you grieve over Saul? I have rejected him from being king over Israel. Fill your horn with oil and set out; I will send you to Jesse the Bethlehemite, for I have provided for myself a king among his sons." [2] Samuel said, "How can I go? If Saul hears of it, he will kill me." And the LORD said, "Take a heifer with you, and say, 'I have come to sacrifice to the LORD.' [3] Invite Jesse to the sacrifice, and I will show you what you shall do; and you shall anoint for me the one whom I name to you." [4] Samuel did what the LORD commanded, and came to Bethlehem. The elders of the city came to meet him trembling, and said, "Do you come peaceably?" [5] He said, "Peaceably; I have come to sacrifice to the LORD; sanctify yourselves and come with me to the sacrifice." And he sanctified Jesse and his sons and invited them to the sacrifice.

[6] When they came, he looked on Eliab and thought, "Surely the LORD's anointed is now before the LORD." [7] But the LORD said to Samuel, "Do not look on his appearance or on the height of his stature, because I have rejected him; for the LORD does not see as mortals see; they look on the outward appearance, but the LORD looks on the heart." [8] Then Jesse called Abinadab, and made him pass before Samuel. He said, "Neither has the LORD chosen this one." [9] Then Jesse made Shammah pass by. And he said, "Neither has the LORD chosen this one." [10] Jesse made seven of his sons pass before Samuel, and Samuel said to Jesse, "The LORD has not chosen any of these." [11] Samuel said to Jesse, "Are all your sons here?" And he said, "There remains yet the youngest, but he is keeping the sheep." And Samuel said to Jesse, "Send and bring him; for we will not sit down until he comes here." [12] He sent and brought him in. Now he was ruddy, and had beautiful eyes, and was handsome. The LORD said, "Rise and anoint him; for this is the one." [13] Then Samuel took the horn of oil, and anointed him in the presence of his brothers; and the spirit of the LORD came mightily upon David from that day forward. Samuel then set out and went to Ramah.

Psalm 20

[1] The LORD answer you in the day of trouble!
    The name of the God of Jacob protect you!
[2] May he send you help from the sanctuary,
    and give you support from Zion.
[3] May he remember all your offerings,
    and regard with favor your burnt sacrifices. *[Selah]*
[4] May he grant you your heart's desire,
    and fulfill all your plans.
[5] May we shout for joy over your victory,
    and in the name of our God set up our banners.
May the LORD fulfill all your petitions.
[6] Now I know that the LORD will help his anointed;
    he will answer him from his holy heaven
    with mighty victories by his right hand.
[7] Some take pride in chariots, and some in horses,
    but our pride is in the name of the LORD our God.
[8] They will collapse and fall,
    but we shall rise and stand upright.
[9] Give victory to the king, O LORD;
    answer us when we call.

2 Corinthians 5:6-10 (11-13), 14-17

[6] So we are always confident; even though we know that while we are at home in the body we are away from the Lord—[7] for we walk by faith, not by sight. [8] Yes, we do have confidence, and we would rather be away from the body and at home with the Lord. [9] So whether we are at home or away, we make it our aim to please him. [10] For all of us must appear before the judgment seat of Christ, so that each may receive recompense for what has been done in the body, whether good or evil.

([11] Therefore, knowing the fear of the Lord, we try to persuade others; but we ourselves are well known to God, and I hope that we are also well known to your consciences. [12] We are not commending ourselves to you again, but giving you an opportunity to boast about us, so that you may be able to answer those who boast in outward appearance and not in the heart. [13] For if we are beside ourselves, it is for God; if we are in our right mind, it is for you.) [14] For the love of Christ urges us on, because we are convinced that one has died for all; therefore all have died. [15] And he died for all, so that those who live might live no longer for themselves, but for him who died and was raised for them.

[16] From now on, therefore, we regard no one from a human point of view; even though we once knew Christ from a human point of view, we know him no longer in that way. [17] So if anyone is in Christ, there is a new creation: everything old has passed away; see, everything has become new!

Mark 4:26-34

[26] He also said, "The kingdom of God is as if someone would scatter seed on the ground, [27] and would sleep and rise night and day, and the seed would sprout and grow, he does not know how. [28] The earth produces of itself, first the stalk, then the head, then the full grain in the head. [29] But when the grain is ripe, at once he goes in with his sickle, because the harvest has come."

[30] He also said, "With what can we compare the kingdom of God, or what parable will we use for it? [31] It is like a mustard seed, which, when sown upon the ground, is the smallest of all the seeds on earth; [32] yet when it is sown it grows up and becomes the greatest of all shrubs, and puts forth large branches, so that the birds of the air can make nests in its shade."

[33] With many such parables he spoke the word to them, as they were able to hear it; [34] he did not speak to them except in parables, but he explained everything in private to his disciples.

Primary Hymns and Songs for the Day

545 "The Church's One Foundation" (2 Cor) (O)
   H-3 Hbl-94; Chr-180; Desc-16; Org-9
   S-1 #25-26. Desc. and Harm.
383 "This Is a Day of New Beginnings" (2 Cor)
   H-3 Chr-196
2196 "We Walk by Faith" (2 Cor, Mark)
   H-3 Chr-21
356 *Pues Si Vivimos* ("When We Are Living") (2 Cor, Mark) (C)
   S-1 #320. Orff Instr. Arr.
   H-3 Chr-218; Org-155

Additional Hymn Suggestions

203 "Hail to the Lord's Anointed" (1 Sam)
454 "Open My Eyes, That I May See" (1 Sam)
497 "Send Me, Lord" (1 Sam)
593 "Here I Am, Lord" (1 Sam)
2123 "Loving Spirit" (1 Sam)
2238 "In the Midst of New Dimensions" (1 Sam)
2236 "Gather Us In" (1 Sam, Mark)
2279 "The Trees of the Field" (Pss)
160 "Rejoice, Ye Pure in Heart" (Pss)
161 "Rejoice, Ye Pure in Heart" (Pss)
292 "What Wondrous Love Is This" (2 Cor)
294 "Alas! and Did My Savior Bleed" (2 Cor)
359 "Alas! and Did My Savior Bleed" (2 Cor)
384 "Love Divine, All Loves Excelling" (2 Cor)
388 "O Come and Dwell in Me" (2 Cor)
421 "Make Me a Captive, Lord" (2 Cor)
508 "Faith, While Trees Are Still in Blossom" (2 Cor)
524 "Beams of Heaven as I Go" (2 Cor)
2046 "Womb of Life" (2 Cor)
2083 "My Song Is Love Unknown" (2 Cor)
2158 "Just a Closer Walk with Thee" (2 Cor)
2282 "I'll Fly Away" (2 Cor)
97 "For the Fruits of This Creation" (Mark)
118 "The Care the Eagle Gives Her Young" (Mark)
275 "The Kingdom of God" (Mark)
414 "Thou Hidden Love of God" (Mark)
565 "Father, We Thank You" (Mark)
583 *Sois la Semilla* ("You Are the Seed") (Mark)
694 "Come, Ye Thankful People, Come" (Mark)
707 "Hymn of Promise" (Mark)
2060 "God the Sculptor of the Mountains" (Mark)
2190 "Bring Forth the Kingdom" (Mark)
2211 "Faith Is Patience in the Night" (Mark)

Additional Contemporary Suggestions

UM393 "Spirit of the Living God" (1 Sam)
   S-1 #212 Vocal Desc.
S2164 "Sanctuary" (1 Sam)
M36 "Awesome in This Place" (1 Sam)
M49 "Refresh My Heart" (1 Sam, 2 Cor)
M262 "Desert Song" (Pss)
S2074 "Shout to the Lord" (Pss)
S2159 "Jesus, Draw Me Close" (2 Cor)
WS3102 "You Are My King" ("Amazing Love") (2 Cor)
SP158 "The Battle Belongs to the Lord" (2 Cor)
M67 "We Want to See Jesus Lifted High" (2 Cor)
M221 "Happy Day" (2 Cor)
M226 "Counting on God" (2 Cor)
M260 "I Will Rise" (2 Cor)
M266 "You Have Saved Us" (2 Cor)
M248 "One Way" (2 Cor, Mark)

M211 "I Will Not Forget You" (Mark)
M17 "This Kingdom" (Mark)
WS3186 "Days of Elijah" (Mark)
S2188 "The Family Prayer Song" (Father's Day)

Vocal Solos

"Brighter than the Sun" (2 Cor)
  V-5(1) p. 57
"Just a Closer Walk with Thee" (2 Cor)
  V-8 p. 323
"So Art Thou with Me" (Father's Day)
  V-9 p. 34

Anthems

"Sanctuary" (1 Sam)
Arr. Lloyd Larson; Hope C5805
SATB with piano

"Thanks Be to God" (Mark)
Allen Pote; Hope C-5881
SATB with keyboard, opt. oboe

Other Suggestions

Visuals:
  O Several vials of oil, anointing
  P Vials of oil, rejoicing, victory
  E Cross wrapped with white cloth, resurrection, reconciliation
  G Bag of seeds, several small plants, one larger plant, stalks of wheat

Call to Worship: S2124. "Come, O Holy Spirit, Come" (1 Sam)
Greeting: BOW450 (Ps 20) or BOW451 (Ps 72)
Opening Prayer: BOW459 (1 Sam) or BOW464 (Mark)
Prayer: BOW437, BOW441, BOW466 (Father's Day)
Prayer: BOW511. For God's Reign (1 Sam, Pss)
Prayer: BOW544. For Leaders (1 Sam)
Call to Prayer: UM388, stanza 1. "O Come and Dwell in Me" (2 Cor)
Affirmation of Faith: WSL78. "God loves us" (Mark)
Offering Prayer: WSL111. "Holy God, we give you" (2 Cor)
Prayer of Thanksgiving: BOW550 (2 Cor, Mark)
Blessing: BOW564 (1 Sam, 2 Cor)
Benediction: S2241. "The Spirit Sends Us Forth to Serve" (1 Sam)

1 Samuel 17:(1a, 4-11, 19-23), 32-49

(¹ªNow the Philistines gathered their armies for battle. . . . ⁴And there came out from the camp of the Philistines a champion named Goliath, of Gath, whose height was six cubits and a span. ⁵He had a helmet of bronze on his head, and he was armed with a coat of mail; the weight of the coat was five thousand shekels of bronze. ⁶He had greaves of bronze on his legs and a javelin of bronze slung between his shoulders. ⁷The shaft of his spear was like a weaver's beam, and his spear's head weighed six hundred shekels of iron; and his shield-bearer went before him. ⁸He stood and shouted to the ranks of Israel, "Why have you come out to draw up for battle? Am I not a Philistine, and are you not servants of Saul? Choose a man for yourselves, and let him come down to me. ⁹If he is able to fight with me and kill me, then we will be your servants; but if I prevail against him and kill him, then you shall be our servants and serve us." ¹⁰And the Philistine said, "Today I defy the ranks of Israel! Give me a man, that we may fight together." ¹¹When Saul and all Israel heard these words of the Philistine, they were dismayed and greatly afraid. . . .

¹⁹Now Saul, and they, and all the men of Israel, were in the valley of Elah, fighting with the Philistines. ²⁰David rose early in the morning, left the sheep with a keeper, took the provisions, and went as Jesse had commanded him. He came to the encampment as the army was going forth to the battle line, shouting the war cry. ²¹Israel and the Philistines drew up for battle, army against army. ²²David left the things in charge of the keeper of the baggage, ran to the ranks, and went and greeted his brothers. ²³As he talked with them, the champion, the Philistine of Gath, Goliath by name, came up out of the ranks of the Philistines, and spoke the same words as before. And David heard him. . . .)

³²David said to Saul, "Let no one's heart fail because of him; your servant will go and fight with this Philistine." ³³Saul said to David, "You are not able to go against this Philistine to fight with him; for you are just a boy, and he has been a warrior from his youth." ³⁴But David said to Saul, "Your servant used to keep sheep for his father; and whenever a lion or a bear came, and took a lamb from the flock, ³⁵I went after it and struck it down, rescuing the lamb from its mouth; and if it turned against me, I would catch it by the jaw, strike it down, and kill it. ³⁶Your servant has killed both lions and bears; and this uncircumcised Philistine shall be like one of them, since he has defied the armies of the living God." ³⁷David said, "The LORD, who saved me from the paw of the lion and from the paw of the bear, will save me from the hand of this Philistine." So Saul said to David, "Go, and may the LORD be with you!"

³⁸Saul clothed David with his armor; he put a bronze helmet on his head and clothed him with a coat of mail. ³⁹David strapped Saul's sword over the armor, and he tried in vain to walk, for he was not used to them. Then David said to Saul, "I cannot walk with these; for I am not used to them." So David removed them. ⁴⁰Then he took his staff in his hand, and chose five smooth stones from the wadi, and put them in his shepherd's bag, in the pouch; his sling was in his hand, and he drew near to the Philistine.

⁴¹The Philistine came on and drew near to David, with his shield-bearer in front of him. ⁴²When the Philistine looked and saw David, he disdained him, for he was only a youth, ruddy and handsome in appearance. ⁴³The Philistine said to David, "Am I a dog, that you come to me with sticks?" And the Philistine cursed David by his gods. ⁴⁴The Philistine said to David, "Come to me, and I will give your flesh to the birds of the air and to the wild animals of the field." ⁴⁵But David said to the Philistine, "You come to me with sword and spear and javelin; but I come to you in the name of the LORD of hosts, the God of the armies of Israel, whom you have defied. ⁴⁶This very day the LORD will deliver you into my hand, and I will strike you down and cut off your head; and I will give the dead bodies of the Philistine army this very day to the birds of the air and to the wild animals of the earth, so that all the earth may know that there is a God in Israel, ⁴⁷and that all this assembly may know that the LORD does not save by sword and spear; for the battle is the LORD's and he will give you into our hand."

⁴⁸When the Philistine drew nearer to meet David, David ran quickly toward the battle line to meet the Philistine. ⁴⁹David put his hand in his bag, took out a stone, slung it, and struck the Philistine on his forehead; the stone sank into his forehead, and he fell face down on the ground.

Psalm 9:9-20 [UM744]

⁹ The LORD is a stronghold for the oppressed,
   a stronghold in times of trouble.
¹⁰ And those who know your name put their trust in you,
   for you, O LORD, have not forsaken those who seek you.
¹¹ Sing praises to the LORD, who dwells in Zion.
   Declare his deeds among the peoples.
¹² For he who avenges blood is mindful of them;
   he does not forget the cry of the afflicted.
¹³ Be gracious to me, O LORD.
   See what I suffer from those who hate me;
   you are the one who lifts me up from the gates of death,
¹⁴ so that I may recount all your praises,
   and, in the gates of daughter Zion,
   rejoice in your deliverance.
¹⁵ The nations have sunk in the pit that they made;
   in the net that they hid has their own foot been caught.
¹⁶ The LORD has made himself known, he has executed judgment;
   the wicked are snared in the work of their own hands.
                                        Higgaion. [Selah]
¹⁷ The wicked shall depart to Sheol,
   all the nations that forget God.
¹⁸ For the needy shall not always be forgotten,
   nor the hope of the poor perish forever.
¹⁹ Rise up, O LORD! Do not let mortals prevail;
   let the nations be judged before you.
²⁰ Put them in fear, O LORD;
   let the nations know that they are only human. *[Selah]*

2 Corinthians 6:1-13

¹As we work together with him, we urge you also not to accept the grace of God in vain. ²For he says,

"At an acceptable time I have listened to you,
   and on a day of salvation I have helped you."

See, now is the acceptable time; see, now is the day of salvation! ³We are putting no obstacle in anyone's way, so that no fault may be found with our ministry, ⁴but as servants of God we have commended ourselves in every way: through great endurance, in afflictions, hardships, calamities, ⁵beatings, imprisonments, riots, labors, sleepless nights, hunger; ⁶by purity, knowledge, patience, kindness, holiness of spirit, genuine love, ⁷truthful speech, and the power of God; with the weapons of righteousness for the right hand and for the left; ⁸in honor and dishonor, in ill repute and good repute. We are treated as impostors, and yet are true; ⁹as unknown, and yet are well known; as dying, and see—we are alive; as punished, and yet not killed; ¹⁰as sorrowful, yet always rejoicing; as poor, yet making many rich; as having nothing, and yet possessing everything.

¹¹We have spoken frankly to you Corinthians; our heart is wide open to you. ¹²There is no restriction in our affections, but only in yours. ¹³In return—I speak as to children—open wide your hearts also.

Mark 4:35-41

³⁵On that day, when evening had come, he said to them, "Let us go across to the other side." ³⁶And leaving the crowd behind, they took him with them in the boat, just as he was. Other boats were with him. ³⁷A great windstorm arose, and the waves beat into the boat, so that the boat was already being swamped. ³⁸But he was in the stern, asleep on the cushion; and they woke him up and said to him, "Teacher, do you not care that we are perishing?" ³⁹He woke up and rebuked the wind, and said to the sea, "Peace! Be still!" Then the wind ceased, and there was a dead calm. ⁴⁰He said to them, "Why are you afraid? Have you still no faith?" ⁴¹And they were filled with great awe and said to one another, "Who then is this, that even the wind and the sea obey him?"

Primary Hymns and Songs for the Day

519   "Lift Every Voice and Sing" (1 Sam, 2 Cor) (O)
       H-3   Chr-128

377   "It Is Well with My Soul" (2 Cor, Mark)
       H-3   Chr-113

2191   "Eternal Father, Strong to Save" (Mark)
       H-3   Chr-63; Desc-74; Org-89

512   "Stand By Me" (Mark) (C)
       H-3   Chr-177

Additional Hymn Suggestions

473   "Lead Me, Lord" (1 Sam)
513   "Soldiers of Christ, Arise" (1 Sam)
523   "*Saranam, Saranam*" ("Refuge") (1 Sam)
3100   "Jesus Paid It All" (1 Sam)
517   "By Gracious Powers" (1 Sam, Pss)
522   "Leave It There" (1 Sam, Pss)
533   "We Shall Overcome" (1 Sam, Pss)
110   "A Mighty Fortress Is Our God" (1 Sam, Pss, Mark)
577   "God of Grace and God of Glory" (1 Sam, Pss, Mark) (C)
2053   "If It Had Not Been for the Lord" (1 Sam, Pss)
2218   "You Are Mine" (1 Sam, Mark)
107   "*La Palabra Del Señor Es Recta*" ("Righteous and Just Is the Word of Our Lord") (Pss)
2001   "We Sing to You, O God" (Pss)
2030   "The First Song of Isaiah" (Pss)
2216   "When We Are Called to Sing Your Praise" (Pss)
450   "Creator of the Earth and Skies" (2 Cor)
510   "Come, Ye Disconsolate" (2 Cor)
511   "Am I Soldier of the Cross" (2 Cor)
514   "Stand Up, Stand Up for Jesus" (2 Cor)
730   "O Day of God, Draw Nigh" (2 Cor)
2255   "In the Singing" (2 Cor, Comm.)
2211   "Faith Is Patience in the Night" (2 Cor, Mark)
122   "God of the Sparrow, God of the Whale" (Mark)
129   "Give to the Winds Thy Fears" (Mark)
341   "I Sought the Lord" (Mark)
368   "My Hope Is Built" (Mark)
476   "Lonely the Boat" (Mark)
509   "Jesus, Savior, Pilot Me" (Mark)
525   "We'll Understand It Better By and By" (Mark)
529   "How Firm a Foundation" (Mark) (O)
530   "Are Ye Able" (Mark)
532   "Jesus, Priceless Treasure" (Mark)
534   "Be Still, My Soul" (Mark)
479   "Jesus, Lover of My Soul" (Mark)
2142   "Blessed Quietness" (Mark)
2146   "His Eye Is on the Sparrow" (Mark)
2212   "My Life Flows On" ("How Can I Keep from Singing") (Mark)
3101   "Love Lifted Me" (Mark)
3144   "When the Waves Are Crashing" (Mark)

Additional Contemporary Suggestions

S2139   "Oh, I Know the Lord's Laid His Hands on Me" (1 Sam)
M244   "Jesus Paid It All" (1 Sam)
S2054   "Nothing Can Trouble" (1 Sam, Pss)
S2144   "Someone Asked the Question" (Pss)
M237   "My Savior Lives" (Pss)
M245   "No Sweeter Name" (Pss)
SP2   "Ah, Lord God" (1 Sam, Pss)
S2021   "What a Mighty God" (1 Sam, Pss)
       WS3016

SP4   "Great and Mighty Is He" (1 Sam, Pss)
S2040   "Awesome God" (1 Sam, Mark)
SP158   "The Battle Belongs to the Lord" (1 Sam, 2 Cor)
M67   "We Want to See Jesus Lifted High" (2 Cor)
M226   "Counting on God" (2 Cor)
M227   "I Will Boast" (2 Cor)
UM507   "Through It All" (2 Cor)
S2057   "Be Still and Know That I Am God" (Mark)
S2064   "O Lord, You're Beautiful" (Mark)
S2213   "Healer of Our Every Ill" (Mark)
WS3032   "Across the Lands" (Mark)
WS3105   "In Christ Alone" (Mark)
M177   "How Can I Keep from Singing" (Mark)
M258   "You Never Let Go" (Mark)

Vocal Solos

"What God Hath Promised" (2 Cor)
     V-8   p. 297
"Jesus, Lover of My Soul" (Mark)
     V-1   p. 37
"It Is Well with My Soul" (Mark)
     V-5(2)   p. 35
"His Eye Is on the Sparrow" (Mark)
     V-8   p. 166

Anthems

"The House of David" (1 Sam)
Z. Randall Stroope; MorningStar 50-2571
SATB with organ and optional bracc and percussion

"How Can I Keep from Singing" (Mark)
Mark Hayes; Lorenz 10/4659L
SATB with piano

Other Suggestions

Visuals:

    O   Armor, sword/spear, slingshot, stones, bag
    P   Globe, scales of justice, rejoicing
    E   Clock set for worship hour, all ages enduring hardship, poor smiling
    G   Boat, storm at sea, fear, peace, calm, sleeping, Jesus in command

Call to Worship: UM473. "Lead Me, Lord" (1 Sam)
Act of Congregational Centering: BOW472 (Mark)
Greeting: BOW327 (1 Sam, Mark)
Opening Prayer: BOW464 (Mark) or BOW466 (2 Cor)
Prayer of Confession & Assurance: BOW478 (1 Sam, Mark)
Prayer: BOW337, BOW506, or BOW522 (2 Cor)
Prayer: BOW513 or BOW524 (1 Sam, Mark)
Prayer: BOW542. For Those in Military Service (1 Sam)
Scripture Response: UM534, stanza 2. "Be Still, My Soul" (Mark)
Dismissal: BOW559 (1 Sam, 2 Cor)

2 Samuel 1:1, 17-27

¹After the death of Saul, when David had returned from defeating the Amalekites, David remained two days in Ziklag. . . .

¹⁷David intoned this lamentation over Saul and his son Jonathan. ¹⁸ (He ordered that The Song of the Bow be taught to the people of Judah; it is written in the Book of Jashar.) He said:
¹⁹Your glory, O Israel, lies slain upon your high places!
    How the mighty have fallen!
²⁰Tell it not in Gath,
    proclaim it not in the streets of Ashkelon;
or the daughters of the Philistines will rejoice,
    the daughters of the uncircumcised will exult.
²¹You mountains of Gilboa,
    let there be no dew or rain upon you,
    nor bounteous fields!
For there the shield of the mighty was defiled,
    the shield of Saul, anointed with oil no more.
²²From the blood of the slain,
    from the fat of the mighty,
the bow of Jonathan did not turn back,
    nor the sword of Saul return empty.
²³Saul and Jonathan, beloved and lovely!
    In life and in death they were not divided;
they were swifter than eagles,
    they were stronger than lions.
²⁴O daughters of Israel, weep over Saul,
    who clothed you with crimson, in luxury,
    who put ornaments of gold on your apparel.
²⁵How the mighty have fallen
    in the midst of the battle!
Jonathan lies slain upon your high places.
²⁶   I am distressed for you, my brother Jonathan;
greatly beloved were you to me;
    your love to me was wonderful,
    passing the love of women.
²⁷How the mighty have fallen,
    and the weapons of war perished!

Psalm 130 (UM848)

¹Out of the depths I cry to you, O LORD.
²   Lord, hear my voice!
Let your ears be attentive
    to the voice of my supplications!
³If you, O LORD, should mark iniquities,
    Lord, who could stand?
⁴But there is forgiveness with you,
    so that you may be revered.
⁵I wait for the LORD, my soul waits,
    and in his word I hope;
⁶my soul waits for the Lord
    more than those who watch for the morning,
    more than those who watch for the morning.
⁷O Israel, hope in the LORD!
    For with the LORD there is steadfast love,
    and with him is great power to redeem.
⁸It is he who will redeem Israel
    from all its iniquities.

2 Corinthians 8:7-15

⁷Now as you excel in everything—in faith, in speech, in knowledge, in utmost eagerness, and in our love for you—so we want you to excel also in this generous undertaking.

⁸I do not say this as a command, but I am testing the genuineness of your love against the earnestness of others. ⁹For you know the generous act of our Lord Jesus Christ, that though he was rich, yet for your sakes he became poor, so that by his poverty you might become rich. ¹⁰And in this matter I am giving my advice: it is appropriate for you who began last year not only to do something but even to desire to do something—¹¹now finish doing it, so that your eagerness may be matched by completing it according to your means. ¹²For if the eagerness is there, the gift is acceptable according to what one has—not according to what one does not have. ¹³I do not mean that there should be relief for others and pressure on you, but it is a question of a fair balance between ¹⁴your present abundance and their need, so that their abundance may be for your need, in order that there may be a fair balance. ¹⁵As it is written,
    "The one who had much did not have too much,
    and the one who had little did not have too little."

Mark 5:21-43

²¹When Jesus had crossed again in the boat to the other side, a great crowd gathered around him; and he was by the sea. ²²Then one of the leaders of the synagogue named Jairus came and, when he saw him, fell at his feet ²³and begged him repeatedly, "My little daughter is at the point of death. Come and lay your hands on her, so that she may be made well, and live." ²⁴So he went with him.

And a large crowd followed him and pressed in on him. ²⁵Now there was a woman who had been suffering from hemorrhages for twelve years. ²⁶She had endured much under many physicians, and had spent all that she had; and she was no better, but rather grew worse. ²⁷She had heard about Jesus, and came up behind him in the crowd and touched his cloak, ²⁸for she said, "If I but touch his clothes, I will be made well." ²⁹Immediately her hemorrhage stopped; and she felt in her body that she was healed of her disease. ³⁰Immediately aware that power had gone forth from him, Jesus turned about in the crowd and said, "Who touched my clothes?" ³¹And his disciples said to him, "You see the crowd pressing in on you; how can you say, 'Who touched me?'" ³²He looked all around to see who had done it. ³³But the woman, knowing what had happened to her, came in fear and trembling, fell down before him, and told him the whole truth. ³⁴He said to her, "Daughter, your faith has made you well; go in peace, and be healed of your disease."

³⁵While he was still speaking, some people came from the leader's house to say, "Your daughter is dead. Why trouble the teacher any further?" ³⁶But overhearing what they said, Jesus said to the leader of the synagogue, "Do not fear, only believe." ³⁷He allowed no one to follow him except Peter, James, and John, the brother of James. ³⁸When they came to the house of the leader of the synagogue, he saw a commotion, people weeping and wailing loudly. ³⁹When he had entered, he said to them, "Why do you make a commotion and weep? The child is not dead but sleeping." ⁴⁰And they laughed at him. Then he put them all outside, and took the child's father and mother and those who were with him, and went in where the child was. ⁴¹He took her by the hand and said to her, "Talitha cum," which means, "Little girl, get up!" ⁴²And immediately the girl got up and began to walk about (she was twelve years of age). At this they were overcome with amazement. ⁴³He strictly ordered them that no one should know this, and told them to give her something to eat.

Primary Hymns and Songs for the Day

117   "O God, Our Help in Ages Past" (2 Sam) (O)
     H-3   Hbl-87; Chr-143; Desc-93; Org-132
     S-1   #293-296. Various treatments
474   "Precious Lord, Take My Hand" (2 Sam, Pss, Mark)
427   "Where Cross the Crowded Ways of Life" (2 Cor, Mark)
     H-3   Chr-178, 180; Org-44
     S-1   #141-3 Various treatments
434   "*Cuando El Pobre*" ("When the Poor Ones") (2 Cor, Mark)
534   "Be Still, My Soul" (2 Sam, Pss, Mark)
     H-3   Chr-36
2153   "I'm Gonna Live So God Can Use Me" (2 Cor) (C)

Additional Hymn Suggestions

708   "Rejoice in God's Saints" (2 Sam) (O)
709   "Come, Let Us Join Our Friends Above" (2 Sam)
510   "Come, Ye Disconsolate" (2 Sam, Pss, Mark)
515   "Out of the Depths I Cry to You" (2 Sam, Pss, Mark)
518   "O Thou, in Whose Presence" (2 Sam, Pss)
700   "Abide with Me" (2 Sam, Pss)
2110   "Why Has God Forsaken Me?" (2 Sam, Pss)
2136   "Out of the Depths" (2 Sam, Pss)
2216   "When We Are Called to Sing Your Praise" (2 Sam, Pss)
2213   "Healer of Our Every Ill" (2 Sam, Pss, Mark)
3131   "Hear My Prayer, O God" (2 Sam, Pss, Mark)
458   "Dear Lord, for All in Pain" (2 Sam, Pss, Mark)
3131   "Hear My Prayer, O God" (Pss)
3142   "I Love the Lord" (Pss)
250   "Once in Royal David's City" (2 Cor)
372   "How Can We Sinners Know" (2 Cor)
554   "All Praise to Our Redeeming Lord" (2 Cor)
2236   "Gather Us In" (2 Cor, Comm.)
3143   "Jesus, You Are the New Day" (2 Cor, Mark)
262   "Heal Me, Hands of Jesus" (2 Cor, Mark)
263   "When Jesus the Healer Passed Through Galilee" (Mark)
265   "O Christ, the Healer" (Mark)
266   "Heal Us, Emmanuel, Hear Our Prayer" (Mark)
274   "Woman in the Night" (Mark)
337   "Only Trust Him" (Mark)
340   "Come, Ye Sinners, Poor and Needy" (Mark)
341   "I Sought the Lord" (Mark)
351   "Pass Me Not, O Gentle Savior" (Mark)
357   "Just As I Am, Without One Plea" (Mark, Comm.)
367   "He Touched Me" (Mark)
370   "Victory in Jesus" (Mark)
632   "Draw Us in the Spirit's Tether" (Mark, Comm.)
2104   "An Outcast among Outcasts" (Mark)
2266   "Here Is Bread, Here Is Wine" (Mark, Comm.)
3101   "Love Lifted Me" (Mark)
437   "This Is My Song" (Independence Day)

Additional Contemporary Suggestions

S2215   "Cares Chorus" (2 Sam, Pss)
WS3049   "Wait for the Lord" (Pss)
WS3099   "Falling on My Knees" (Pss)
WS3141   "Holy Darkness" (Pss)
S2244   "People Need the Lord" (Pss, Mark)
S2036   "Give Thanks" (2 Cor)
S2163   "He Who Began a Good Work in You" (2 Cor)
S2176   "Make Me a Servant" (2 Cor)
S2195   "In the Lord I'll Be Ever Thankful" (2 Cor)

WS3177   "Here I Am to Worship" (2 Cor)
M98   "Take This Life" (2 Cor)
M101   "These Hands" (2 Cor)
S2064   "Oh Lord, You're Beautiful" (Mark)
S2086   "Open Our Eyes, Lord" (Mark)
UM123   "El-Shaddai" (Mark)
     S-2   #54 Verses for Soloist
UM328   "Surely the Presence of the Lord" (Mark)
     S-2   #200 Stanzas for soloist
UM347   "Spirit Song" (Mark)
UM349   "Turn Your Eyes upon Jesus" (Mark)
UM394   "Something Beautiful" (Mark)
S2040   "Awesome God" (Mark)
S2139   "Oh, I Know the Lord's Laid His Hands on Me" (Mark)
S2151   "I'm So Glad Jesus Lifted Me" (Mark)
S2152   "Change My Heart, O God" (Mark)
M177   "How Can I Keep from Singing" (Mark)
M258   "You Never Let Go" (Mark)

Vocal Solos

"Like a Child" (2 Sam, Pss)
     V-8   p. 356
"Out of the Depths I Cry to Thee" (Pss)
     V-9   p. 16

Anthems

"Out of the Depths" (Pss)
Richard Frost; MorningStar 50-3209
SATB with piano and violin

"There Is an Everlasting Kindness" (Mark)
Arr. Lloyd Larson; Hope C5803
SATB with piano and optional C-Instrument

Other Suggestions

Grief can be addressed today, related to 2 Sam. Additional resources include: UM652, BOW548, BOW183, WSL209, and WSL213. Stewardship can be emphasized, using 2 Cor.
Visuals:
   O   Bow/sword, mourning, dead soldiers
   P   Darkness, prayer, patient waiting, early dawn, Ps 130:5, 6a
   E   Kindness, Jesus, poverty/wealth, full offering plate
   G   Boat, child dead/woman reaching, child well/woman rejoicing, Jesus healing
Introit: WS3177, M116. "Here I Am to Worship" (2 Cor)
Greeting: BOW327 (2 Sam, Pss) or 455 (Mark)
Opening Prayer: BOW464 (Mark)
Prayer of Confession: BOW487 or BOW491 (Pss, Mark)
Canticle: UM516. "Canticle of Redemption" (Pss) See S-1, p. 386.
Prayer: UM461. For Those Who Mourn (2 Sam)
Prayer: UM446. Serving the Poor (2 Cor)
Prayer: BOW500. For Blessing, Mercy, and Courage (Mark)
Prayers: BOW545-546. For Those Who Suffer (2 Sam, Mark)
Prayers for Healing: BOW627-BOW629, WSL209 (Mark)
Prayer: WSL203. "God of all nations" (Independence Day)
Prayers: BOW442, BOW515, BOW516 or BOW526 (Independence Day)
Prayer Response: S2200 "O Lord, Hear My Prayer" (Pss)
Benediction: UM665. "Go Now in Peace" (Mark)

2 Samuel 5:1-5, 9-10

[1]Then all the tribes of Israel came to David at Hebron, and said, "Look, we are your bone and flesh. [2]For some time, while Saul was king over us, it was you who led out Israel and brought it in. The LORD said to you: It is you who shall be shepherd of my people Israel, you who shall be ruler over Israel." [3]So all the elders of Israel came to the king at Hebron; and King David made a covenant with them at Hebron before the LORD, and they anointed David king over Israel. [4]David was thirty years old when he began to reign, and he reigned forty years. [5]At Hebron he reigned over Judah seven years and six months; and at Jerusalem he reigned over all Israel and Judah thirty-three years. . . .

[9]David occupied the stronghold, and named it the city of David. David built the city all around from the Millo inward. [10]And David became greater and greater, for the LORD, the God of hosts, was with him.

Psalm 48 (UM782)

[1]Great is the LORD and greatly to be praised
in the city of our God.
His holy mountain, [2]beautiful in elevation,
is the joy of all the earth,
Mount Zion, in the far north,
the city of the great King.
[3]Within its citadels God
has shown himself a sure defense.
[4]Then the kings assembled,
they came on together.
[5]As soon as they saw it, they were astounded;
they were in panic, they took to flight;
[6]trembling took hold of them there,
pains as of a woman in labor,
[7]as when an east wind shatters
the ships of Tarshish.
[8]As we have heard, so have we seen
in the city of the LORD of hosts,
in the city of our God,
which God establishes forever. *[Selah]*
[9]We ponder your steadfast love, O God,
in the midst of your temple.
[10]Your name, O God, like your praise,
reaches to the ends of the earth.
Your right hand is filled with victory.
[11]   Let Mount Zion be glad,
let the towns of Judah rejoice
because of your judgments.
[12]Walk about Zion, go all around it,
count its towers,
[13]consider well its ramparts;
go through its citadels,
that you may tell the next generation
[14]   that this is God,
our God forever and ever.
He will be our guide forever.

2 Corinthians 12:2-10

[2]I know a person in Christ who fourteen years ago was caught up to the third heaven—whether in the body or out of the body I do not know; God knows. [3]And I know that such a person—whether in the body or out of the body I do not know; God knows—[4]was caught up into Paradise and heard things that are not to be told, that no mortal is permitted to repeat. [5]On behalf of such a one I will boast, but on my own behalf I will not boast, except of my weaknesses. [6]But if I wish to boast, I will not be a fool, for I will be speaking the truth. But I refrain from it, so that no one may think better of me than what is seen in me or heard from me, [7]even considering the exceptional character of the revelations. Therefore, to keep me from being too elated, a thorn was given me in the flesh, a messenger of Satan to torment me, to keep me from being too elated. [8]Three times I appealed to the Lord about this, that it would leave me, [9]but he said to me, "My grace is sufficient for you, for power is made perfect in weakness." So, I will boast all the more gladly of my weaknesses, so that the power of Christ may dwell in me. [10]Therefore I am content with weaknesses, insults, hardships, persecutions, and calamities for the sake of Christ; for whenever I am weak, then I am strong.

Mark 6:1-13

[1]He left that place and came to his hometown, and his disciples followed him. [2]On the sabbath he began to teach in the synagogue, and many who heard him were astounded. They said, "Where did this man get all this? What is this wisdom that has been given to him? What deeds of power are being done by his hands! [3]Is not this the carpenter, the son of Mary and brother of James and Joses and Judas and Simon, and are not his sisters here with us?" And they took offense at him. [4]Then Jesus said to them, "Prophets are not without honor, except in their hometown, and among their own kin, and in their own house." [5]And he could do no deed of power there, except that he laid his hands on a few sick people and cured them. [6]And he was amazed at their unbelief.

Then he went about among the villages teaching. [7]He called the twelve and began to send them out two by two, and gave them authority over the unclean spirits. [8]He ordered them to take nothing for their journey except a staff; no bread, no bag, no money in their belts; [9]but to wear sandals and not to put on two tunics. [10]He said to them, "Wherever you enter a house, stay there until you leave the place. [11]If any place will not welcome you and they refuse to hear you, as you leave, shake off the dust that is on your feet as a testimony against them." [12]So they went out and proclaimed that all should repent. [13]They cast out many demons, and anointed with oil many who were sick and cured them.

Primary Hymns and Songs for the Day

400	"Come, Thou Fount of Every Blessing" (2 Cor) (O)	
	H-3	Chr-57; Desc-79; Org-96
	S-1	#244. Desc.
2037	"I Sing Praises to Your Name" (Pss)	
2130	"The Summons" (Mark)	
584	"Lord, You Give the Great Commission" (Mark)	
	H-3	Hbl-61; Chr-132; Org-2
	S-1	#4-5. Instr. and Vocal Desc.
568	"Christ for the World We Sing" (Mark) (C)	
	H-3	Hbl-49, 53; Chr-56; Desc-57; Org-63
	S-1	#185-186. Desc. and Harm.

Additional Hymn Suggestions

206	"I Want to Walk as a Child of the Light" (2 Sam)
473	"Lead Me, Lord" (2 Sam)
3096	"Gentle Shepherd" (2 Sam)
518	"O Thou, in Whose Presence" (2 Sam, 2 Cor)
732	"Come, We That Love the Lord" (2 Sam, Pss)
733	"Marching to Zion" (2 Sam, Pss)
77	"How Great Thou Art" (Pss)
139	"Praise to the Lord, the Almighty" (Pss)
726	"O Holy City, Seen of John" (Pss)
727	"O What Their Joy and Their Glory Must Be" (Pss)
731	"Glorious Things of Thee Are Spoken" (Pss)
88	"Maker, in Whom We Live" (Pss, 2 Cor)
2208	"Guide My Feet" (Pss, 2 Cor, Mark)
340	"Come, Ye Sinners, Poor and Needy" (2 Cor)
365	"Grace Greater than Our Sin" (2 Cor)
378, 4091	"Amazing Grace" (2 Cor)
386	"Come, O Thou Traveler Unknown" (2 Cor)
480	"O Love That Wilt Not Let Me Go" (2 Cor)
505	"When Our Confidence Is Shaken" (2 Cor)
507	"Through It All" (2 Cor)
581	"Lord, Whose Love Through Humble Service" (2 Cor, Mark)
582	"Whom Shall I Send?" (2 Cor, Mark)
2149	"Living for Jesus" (2 Cor, Mark)
257	"We Meet You, O Christ" (Mark)
263	"When Jesus the Healer Passed Through Galilee" (Mark)
358	"Dear Lord and Father of Mankind" (Mark) (Alternate Text "Parent of Us All")
497	"Send Me, Lord" (Mark)
567	"Heralds of Christ" (Mark) (O)
569	"We've a Story to Tell to the Nations" (Mark) (C)
573	"O Zion, Haste" (Mark)
582	"Whom Shall I Send?" (Mark)
589	"The Church of Christ in Every Age" (Mark)
649	"How Shall They Hear the Word of God" (Mark)
664	"Sent Forth by God's Blessing" (Mark) (C)
2197	"Lord of All Hopefulness" (Mark)
2239	"Go Ye, Go Ye into the World" (Mark) (C)
2243	"We All Are One in Mission" (Mark)
2260	"Let Us Be Bread" (Mark, Comm.)
2241	"The Spirit Sends Us Forth to Serve" (Mark) (C)

Additional Contemporary Suggestions

M103	"How Great Are You, Lord" (Pss)
SP58	"Great Is the Lord Almighty!" (Pss)
SP40	"God Will Make a Way" (Pss)
S2022	"Great Is the Lord" (Pss)
M126	"Famous One" (Pss)
M234	"Awesome Is the Lord Most High" (Pss)
M237	"My Savior Lives" (Pss, 2 Cor)

M243	"Beautiful Savior" (Pss, 2 Cor))
S2036	"Give Thanks" (2 Cor)
S2162	"Grace Alone" (2 Cor)
S2055	"You Are My Hiding Place" (2 Cor)
WS3104	"Amazing Grace" ("My Chains Are Gone") (2 Cor)
WS3040	"You Are My All in All" (2 Cor)
M26	"The Power of Your Love" (2 Cor)
M92	"All Things Are Possible" (2 Cor)
WS3042	"Shout to the North" (2 Cor)
M164	"Good to Me" (2 Cor)
S2208	"Guide My Feet" (Mark, 2 Cor)
WS3004	"Step by Step" (Mark)
M55	"Jehovah Reigns" (Mark)
M122	"Every Move I Make" (Mark)
S2040	"Awesome God" (Mark)
S2184	"Sent Out in Jesus' Name" (Mark)
S2186	"Song of Hope" (Mark)
SP143	"Carry the Light" (Mark) (C)
WS3180	"As We Part for the Towns And Cities"

Vocal Solos

"O Thou That Tellest Good Tidings to Zion" (2 Sam, Pss)
"Rejoice Greatly, O Daughter of Zion" (2 Sam, Pss)
 V-2
"What God Hath Promised" (2 Cor)
 V-8   p. 297
"God Will Make a Way" (with "He Leadeth Me") (Pss, Mark)
 V-3   p. 9
"Gospel Train" (Mark)
 V-7   p. 74

Anthems

"Come, Thou Fount of Every Blessing" (2 Cor)
Arr. Victor Johnson; Choristers Guild CGA1279
SATB with piano

"Amazing Grace" ("My Chains Are Gone") (2 Cor)
Arr. Joel Raney; Hope 5644 (SATB) or 5807 (SAB)
SATB or SAB with piano

Other Suggestions

Visuals:
O	Shepherd, crown, oil
P	People at worship, fear, globe, right hand
E	Clay vessels of varying sizes/conditions, handicap sign
G	Teams of two, staff, sandals, tunic, oil

Greeting: BOW452 (Pss)
Prayer: BOW502. For the Church (Mark)
Response to Scripture: UM206, refrain. "I Want to Walk as a Child of the Light" (2 Sam)
Response: UM77, stanza 1. "How Great Thou Art" (Pss)
Prayer of Thanksgiving: BOW550 (2 Cor)
Closing Prayer: WSL163. "From where we are" (Mark)
Benediction: WS3183. "As We Go" (Pss, Mark)

2 Samuel 6:1-5, 12b-19

[1]David again gathered all the chosen men of Israel, thirty thousand. [2]David and all the people with him set out and went from Baale-judah, to bring up from there the ark of God, which is called by the name of the LORD of hosts who is enthroned on the cherubim. [3]They carried the ark of God on a new cart, and brought it out of the house of Abinadab, which was on the hill. Uzzah and Ahio, the sons of Abinadab, were driving the new cart [4]with the ark of God; and Ahio went in front of the ark. [5]David and all the house of Israel were dancing before the LORD with all their might, with songs and lyres and harps and tambourines and castanets and cymbals. . . .

[12b]So David went and brought up the ark of God from the house of Obed-edom to the city of David with rejoicing; [13]and when those who bore the ark of the LORD had gone six paces, he sacrificed an ox and a fatling. [14]David danced before the LORD with all his might; David was girded with a linen ephod. [15]So David and all the house of Israel brought up the ark of the LORD with shouting, and with the sound of the trumpet.

[16]As the ark of the LORD came into the city of David, Michal daughter of Saul looked out of the window, and saw King David leaping and dancing before the LORD; and she despised him in her heart.

[17]They brought in the ark of the LORD, and set it in its place, inside the tent that David had pitched for it; and David offered burnt offerings and offerings of well-being before the LORD. [18]When David had finished offering the burnt offerings and the offerings of well-being, he blessed the people in the name of the LORD of hosts, [19]and distributed food among all the people, the whole multitude of Israel, both men and women, to each a cake of bread, a portion of meat, and a cake of raisins. Then all the people went back to their homes.

Psalm 24 (UM755)

[1]The earth is the LORD's and all that is in it,
  the world, and those who live in it;
[2]for he has founded it on the seas,
  and established it on the rivers.
[3]Who shall ascend the hill of the LORD?
  And who shall stand in his holy place?
[4]Those who have clean hands and pure hearts,
  who do not lift up their souls to what is false,
  and do not swear deceitfully.
[5]They will receive blessing from the LORD,
  and vindication from the God of their salvation.
[6]Such is the company of those who seek him,
  who seek the face of the God of Jacob. [Selah]
[7]Lift up your heads, O gates!
  and be lifted up, O ancient doors!
  that the King of glory may come in.
[8]Who is the King of glory?
  The LORD, strong and mighty,
  the LORD, mighty in battle.
[9]Lift up your heads, O gates!
  and be lifted up, O ancient doors!
  that the King of glory may come in.
[10]Who is this King of glory?
  The LORD of hosts,
  he is the King of glory. [Selah]

Ephesians 1:3-14

[3]Blessed be the God and Father of our Lord Jesus Christ, who has blessed us in Christ with every spiritual blessing in the heavenly places, [4]just as he chose us in Christ before the foundation of the world to be holy and blameless before him in love. [5]He destined us for adoption as his children through Jesus Christ, according to the good pleasure of his will, [6]to the praise of his glorious grace that he freely bestowed on us in the Beloved. [7]In him we have redemption through his blood, the forgiveness of our trespasses, according to the riches of his grace [8]that he lavished on us. With all wisdom and insight [9]he has made known to us the mystery of his will, according to his good pleasure that he set forth in Christ, [10]as a plan for the fullness of time, to gather up all things in him, things in heaven and things on earth. [11]In Christ we have also obtained an inheritance, having been destined according to the purpose of him who accomplishes all things according to his counsel and will, [12]so that we, who were the first to set our hope on Christ, might live for the praise of his glory. [13]In him you also, when you had heard the word of truth, the gospel of your salvation, and had believed in him, were marked with the seal of the promised Holy Spirit; [14]this is the pledge of our inheritance toward redemption as God's own people, to the praise of his glory.

Mark 6:14-29

[14]King Herod heard of it, for Jesus' name had become known. Some were saying, "John the baptizer has been raised from the dead; and for this reason these powers are at work in him." [15]But others said, "It is Elijah." And others said, "It is a prophet, like one of the prophets of old." [16]But when Herod heard of it, he said, "John, whom I beheaded, has been raised."

[17]For Herod himself had sent men who arrested John, bound him, and put him in prison on account of Herodias, his brother Philip's wife, because Herod had married her. [18]For John had been telling Herod, "It is not lawful for you to have your brother's wife." [19]And Herodias had a grudge against him, and wanted to kill him. But she could not, [20]for Herod feared John, knowing that he was a righteous and holy man, and he protected him. When he heard him, he was greatly perplexed; and yet he liked to listen to him. [21]But an opportunity came when Herod on his birthday gave a banquet for his courtiers and officers and for the leaders of Galilee. [22]When his daughter Herodias came in and danced, she pleased Herod and his guests; and the king said to the girl, "Ask me for whatever you wish, and I will give it." [23]And he solemnly swore to her, "Whatever you ask me, I will give you, even half of my kingdom." [24]She went out and said to her mother, "What should I ask for?" She replied, "The head of John the baptizer." [25]Immediately she rushed back to the king and requested, "I want you to give me at once the head of John the Baptist on a platter." [26]The king was deeply grieved; yet out of regard for his oaths and for the guests, he did not want to refuse her. [27]Immediately the king sent a soldier of the guard with orders to bring John's head. He went and beheaded him in the prison, [28]brought his head on a platter, and gave it to the girl. Then the girl gave it to her mother. [29]When his disciples heard about it, they came and took his body, and laid it in a tomb.

Primary Hymns and Songs for the Day

213	"Lift Up Your Heads, Ye Mighty Gates" (Pss) (O)
	H-3 Hbl-50; Chr-129; Desc-101; Org-167
	S-1 #334-5. Desc. and Harm.
2091	"The King of Glory Comes" (2 Sam, Pss) (O)
99	"My Tribute" ("To God Be the Glory") (Eph)
	V-8 p.5 Vocal Solo
	S-2 #130. Stanza for soloist
377	"It Is Well with My Soul" (Eph) (C)
	H-3 Chr-113

Additional Hymn Suggestions

2020	"Praise the Lord with the Sound of Trumpet" (2 Sam)
68	"When in Our Music God Is Glorified" (2 Sam)
87	"What Gift Can We Bring" (2 Sam, Pss)
93	Let All the World in Every Corner Sing" (2 Sam, Pss)
96	"Praise the Lord Who Reigns Above" (2 Sam, Pss)
101	"From All That Dwell Below the Skies" (2 Sam, Pss)
149	*Cantemos al Señor"* ("Let's Sing unto the Lord") (2 Sam, Pss)
3018	"Creation Sings" (2 Sam, Pss)
312	"Hail the Day That Sees Him Rise" (Pss)
2044	"My Gratitude Now Accept, O God (Pss)
3082	"Who Is He" (Pss)
121	"There's a Wideness in God's Mercy" (Eph)
141	"Children of the Heavenly Father" (Eph)
182	"Word of God, Come Down on Earth" (Eph)
194	"Morning Glory, Starlit Sky" (Eph)
325	"Hail, Thou Once Despised Jesus" (Eph)
362	"Nothing but the Blood" (Eph)
369	"Blessed Assurance" (Eph)
370	"Victory in Jesus" (Eph)
378, 4091	"Amazing Grace" (Eph)
365	"Grace Greater than Our Sin" (Eph)
355	"Depth of Mercy" (Eph)
3097	"Depth of Mercy" (Eph)
2236	"Gather Us In" (Eph, Comm.)
2248	"Baptized in Water" (Eph, Baptism)
2276	"Glory to God in the Highest" (Eph)
2155	"Blest Are They" (Eph, Mark)
108	"God Hath Spoken by the Prophets" (Mark)
511	"Am I a Soldier of the Cross" (Mark)
525	"We'll Understand It Better By and By" (Mark)
529	"How Firm a Foundation" (Mark)
530	"Are Ye Able" (Mark)
534	"Be Still, My Soul" (Mark)
708	"Rejoice in God's Saints" (Mark)
711	"For All the Saints" (Mark)
2089	"Wild and Lone the Prophet's Voice" (Mark)
2283	"For All the Saints" (Mark)

Additional Contemporary Suggestions

S2028	"Clap Your Hands" (2 Sam)
UM123	"El Shaddai" (2 Sam)
M63	"I Could Sing of Your Love Forever" (2 Sam)
M140	"We Will Dance" (2 Sam)
M152	"Be Glorified" (2 Sam)
M36	"Awesome in This Place" (2 Sam, Pss)
S2272	"Holy Ground" (2 Sam, Pss)
WS3188	"Hosanna" (Pss)
M70	"No Higher Calling" (Pss)
M83	"Just Let Me Say" (Pss)
S2039	"Holy, Holy" (Eph)
S2088	"Lord, I Lift Your Name on High" (Eph)
S2162	"Grace Alone" (Eph)

S2163	"He Who Began a Good Work in You" (Eph)
WS3027	"Hallelujah" ("Your Love Is Amazing") (Eph)
WS3187	"We Fall Down" (Eph)
WS3102	"You Are My King" ("Amazing Love") (Eph)
WS3104	"Amazing Grace" ("My Chains Are Gone") (Eph)
WS3119	"Take, O Take Me as I Am" (Eph)
M7	"I Believe in Jesus" (Mark)
S2213	"Healer of Our Every Ill" (Mark)
UM507	"Through It All" (Mark)
UM527	"Do, Lord, Remember Me" (Mark)
UM533	"We Shall Overcome" (Mark)

Vocal Solos

"I Will Sing of Thy Great Mercies" (2 Sam, Eph)
    V-4   p. 43
"My Cup Overflows" (Pss)
    V-8   p. 302
"Lift Up Your Heads" (Pss)
    V-10   p. 38
"And Can It Be that I Should Gain" (Eph)
    V-1   p. 29
"Amazing Grace" (Eph)
    V-8   p. 56

Anthems

"In Christ an Inheritance Is Ours" (Eph)
Michael D. Costello; MorningStar 60-6010
SATB with flute, oboe, and organ, opt. cello

"It Is Well with My Soul" (Eph)
Arr. René Clausen; MorningStar 50-5211
SATB divisi with organ

Other Suggestions

This would be a good day to recognize musicians or dedicate a new instrument. See BOW604, BOW606 and WSL185 for suggestions.
Visuals:

O	Ark of Covenant, man dancing (video "David")
P	Earth/sea/river, bowl/water/towel, hand with heart, gates
E	Adoption papers, Christus Rex, last will and testament, rejoicing
G	Feasting, dancing, dinner platter

Call to Worship: BOW199 (2 Sam)
Greeting: BOW450 (2 Sam)
Prayer of Confession: BOW494 (Pss)
Prayer of Confession: WSL43. "We often act" (Eph)
Psalter: UM212. Psalm 24
Prayer: WSL48. "Oh Lord, our God" (Pss)
Prayer: UM69 (2 Sam, Eph) or 713 (Mark)
Scripture Response: UM261, refrain. "Lord of the Dance" (2 Sam)
Scripture Response: UM712, stanza 1. "I Sing a Song of the Saints of God" (Mark)
Prayer of Thanksgiving: BOW557 (Pss)
Dismissal: BOW559 (2 Sam, Mark)
Benediction: M87. "Let the Peace of God Reign" (Eph)

2 Samuel 7:1-14a

¹Now when the king was settled in his house, and the LORD had given him rest from all his enemies around him, ²the king said to the prophet Nathan, "See now, I am living in a house of cedar, but the ark of God stays in a tent." ³Nathan said to the king, "Go, do all that you have in mind; for the LORD is with you."

⁴But that same night the word of the LORD came to Nathan:⁵ Go and tell my servant David: Thus says the LORD: Are you the one to build me a house to live in? ⁶I have not lived in a house since the day I brought up the people of Israel from Egypt to this day, but I have been moving about in a tent and a tabernacle. ⁷Wherever I have moved about among all the people of Israel, did I ever speak a word with any of the tribal leaders of Israel, whom I commanded to shepherd my people Israel, saying, "Why have you not built me a house of cedar?" ⁸Now therefore thus you shall say to my servant David: Thus says the LORD of hosts: I took you from the pasture, from following the sheep to be prince over my people Israel; ⁹and I have been with you wherever you went, and have cut off all your enemies from before you; and I will make for you a great name, like the name of the great ones of the earth. ¹⁰And I will appoint a place for my people Israel and will plant them, so that they may live in their own place, and be disturbed no more; and evildoers shall afflict them no more, as formerly, ¹¹from the time that I appointed judges over my people Israel; and I will give you rest from all your enemies. Moreover the LORD declares to you that the LORD will make you a house. ¹²When your days are fulfilled and you lie down with your ancestors, I will raise up your offspring after you, who shall come forth from your body, and I will establish his kingdom. ¹³He shall build a house for my name, and I will establish the throne of his kingdom forever. ¹⁴ᵃI will be a father to him, and he shall be a son to me.

Psalm 89:20-37 (UM807)

²⁰"I have found my servant David;
   with my holy oil I have anointed him;
²¹ my hand shall always remain with him;
   my arm also shall strengthen him.
²² The enemy shall not outwit him,
   the wicked shall not humble him.
²³ I will crush his foes before him
   and strike down those who hate him.
²⁴ My faithfulness and steadfast love shall be with him;
   and in my name his horn shall be exalted.
²⁵ I will set his hand on the sea
   and his right hand on the rivers.
²⁶ He shall cry to me, 'You are my Father,
   my God, and the Rock of my salvation!'
²⁷ I will make him the firstborn,
   the highest of the kings of the earth.
²⁸ Forever I will keep my steadfast love for him,
   and my covenant with him will stand firm.
²⁹ I will establish his line forever,
   and his throne as long as the heavens endure.
³⁰ If his children forsake my law
   and do not walk according to my ordinances,
³¹ if they violate my statutes
   and do not keep my commandments,
³² then I will punish their transgression with the rod
   and their iniquity with scourges;
³³ but I will not remove from him my steadfast love,
   or be false to my faithfulness.
³⁴ I will not violate my covenant,
   or alter the word that went forth from my lips.

³⁵ Once and for all I have sworn by my holiness;
   I will not lie to David.
³⁶ His line shall continue forever,
   and his throne endure before me like the sun.
³⁷ It shall be established forever like the moon,
   an enduring witness in the skies." [Selah]

Ephesians 2:11-22

¹¹So then, remember that at one time you Gentiles by birth, called "the uncircumcision" by those who are called "the circumcision"—a physical circumcision made in the flesh by human hands—¹²remember that you were at that time without Christ, being aliens from the commonwealth of Israel, and strangers to the covenants of promise, having no hope and without God in the world. ¹³But now in Christ Jesus you who once were far off have been brought near by the blood of Christ. ¹⁴For he is our peace; in his flesh he has made both groups into one and has broken down the dividing wall, that is, the hostility between us. ¹⁵He has abolished the law with its commandments and ordinances, that he might create in himself one new humanity in place of the two, thus making peace, ¹⁶and might reconcile both groups to God in one body through the cross, thus putting to death that hostility through it. ¹⁷So he came and proclaimed peace to you who were far off and peace to those who were near; ¹⁸for through him both of us have access in one Spirit to the Father. ¹⁹So then you are no longer strangers and aliens, but you are citizens with the saints and also members of the household of God, ²⁰built upon the foundation of the apostles and prophets, with Christ Jesus himself as the cornerstone. ²¹In him the whole structure is joined together and grows into a holy temple in the Lord; ²²in whom you also are built together spiritually into a dwelling place for God.

Mark 6:30-34, 53-56

³⁰The apostles gathered around Jesus, and told him all that they had done and taught. ³¹He said to them, "Come away to a deserted place all by yourselves and rest a while." For many were coming and going, and they had no leisure even to eat. ³²And they went away in the boat to a deserted place by themselves. ³³Now many saw them going and recognized them, and they hurried there on foot from all the towns and arrived ahead of them. ³⁴As he went ashore, he saw a great crowd; and he had compassion for them, because they were like sheep without a shepherd; and he began to teach them many things. . . .

⁵³When they had crossed over, they came to land at Gennesaret and moored the boat. ⁵⁴When they got out of the boat, people at once recognized him, ⁵⁵and rushed about that whole region and began to bring the sick on mats to wherever they heard he was. ⁵⁶And wherever he went, into villages or cities or farms, they laid the sick in the marketplaces, and begged him that they might touch even the fringe of his cloak; and all who touched it were healed.

Primary Hymns and Songs for the Day

116	"The God of Abraham Praise" (2 Sam) (O)
	H-3　　Hbl-62, 95; Chr-59; Org-77
	S-1　　#211. Harm.
540	"I Love Thy Kingdom, Lord" (2 Sam, Eph)
	H-3　　Hbl-16; Chr-106; Desc-97; Org-147
	S-1　　#311. Desc. and Harm.
546	"The Church's One Foundation" (2 Sam, Eph)
	H-3　　Hbl-94; Chr-180; Desc-16; Org-9
	S-1　　#25-26. Desc. and Harm.
358	"Dear Lord and Father of Mankind" (Mark)
	H-3　　Hbl-56; Chr-61; Org-124
	S-2　　#151. Intro.
	#152. Violin Desc.
559	"Christ Is Made the Sure Foundation" (Eph) (C)
	H-3　　Chr-49; Desc-103; Org-180
	S-1　　#346. Desc.

Additional Hymn Suggestions

123	"El-Shaddai" (2 Sam)
	S-2　　#54 Verses for Vocal Solo
580	"Lead On, O King Eternal" (2 Sam) (O)
463	"Lord, Speak to Me" (2 Sam, Pss)
115	"How Like a Gentle Spirit" (2 Sam, Eph)
541	"See How Great a Flame Aspires" (2 Sam, Eph)
WS3041	"Praise Him" (Pss, Eph)
529	"How Firm a Foundation" (Pss, Eph)
188	"Christ Is the World's Light" (Eph)
377	"It Is Well with My Soul" (Eph)
550	"Christ, from Whom All Blessings Flow" (Eph)
552	"Here, O Lord, Your Servants Gather" (Eph)
2135	"When Cain Killed Abel" (Eph)
2158	"Just a Closer Walk with Thee" (Eph)
2175	"Together We Serve" (Eph)
2185	"For One Great Peace" (Eph)
2218	"You Are Mine" (Eph)
2220	"We Are God's People" (Eph)
2228	"Sacred the Body" (Eph)
3125	"Peace for the Children" (Eph)
3127	"I Have a Dream" (Eph)
3147	"Built on a Rock" (Eph)
3156	"One Is the Body" (Eph, Comm.)
2128	"Come and Find the Quiet Center" (Eph, Mark)
178	"Hope of the World" (Eph, Mark)
187	"Rise, Shine, You People" (Mark)
261	"Lord of the Dance" (Mark)
263	"When Jesus the Healer Passed Through Galilee" (Mark)
266	"Heal Us, Emmanuel, Hear Our Prayer" (Mark)
277	"Tell Me the Stories of Jesus" (Mark)
381	"Savior, Like a Shepherd Lead Us" (Mark)
427	"Where Cross the Crowded Ways of Life" (Mark)
472	"Near to the Heart of God" (Mark)
492	"Prayer Is the Soul's Sincere Desire" (Mark)
494	*Kum Ba Yah* ("Come by Here") Mark)
2202	"Come Away with Me" (Mark)
3043	"You, Lord, are Both Lamb and Shepherd" (Mark)

Additional Contemporary Suggestions

S2139	"Oh, I Know the Lord's Laid His Hands on Me" (2 Sam)
UM143	"On Eagle's Wings" (2 Sam, Pss)
	S-2　　#143. Stanzas for soloist
S2002	"I Will Call Upon the Lord" (Pss)
S2066	"Praise the Name of Jesus" (Pss)

WS3023	"Forever" (Pss)
WS3027	"Hallelujah" ("Your Love Is Amazing") (Pss)
WS3034	"God of Wonders" (Pss)
M28	"Who Can Satisfy My Soul Like You?" (Pss)
M93	"Rock of Ages" (Pss)
S2043	"Alleluia" (Eph)
S2156	"Give Peace" ("*Da Pacem Cordium*") (Eph)
S2159	"Jesus, Draw Me Close" (Eph)
S2164	"Sanctuary" (Eph)
S2224	"Make Us One" (Eph)
S2226	"Bind Us Together" (Eph)
WS3105	"In Christ Alone" ("My Hope Is Found") (Eph)
SP177	"Cornerstone" (Eph)
M9	"Firm Foundation" (Eph)
S2058	"Shepherd Me, O God" (Mark)
S2064	"Oh Lord, You're Beautiful" (Mark)
S2244	"People Need the Lord" (Mark)
S2266	"Here Is Bread, Here Is Wine" (Mark, Comm.)
WS3032	"Across the Lands" (Mark)
WS3093	"Fill My Cup, Lord" (Mark, Comm.)
WS3135	"In God Alone" (Mark)
M104	"There Is None Like You" (Mark)
M260	"I Will Rise"

Vocal Solos

"How Firm a Foundation" (Eph)
　　V-6　　p. 31
"Just a Closer Walk with Thee" (Eph)
　　V-8　　p. 323
　　V-5(2)　　p. 31
"Serenity" (Mark)
　　UM499

Anthems

"Cornerstone" (Eph)
Arr. Heather Sorenson; Hal Leonard 125214
SATB with piano

"Loving Shepherd of Thy Sheep" (Mark)
John Rutter; Hinshaw HMC1192
SATB a cappella

Other Suggestions

Visuals:
　　O　　Cedar, churches under construction
　　P　　Rock, star of David, oil, genealogical chart, father/son
　　E　　Walls crumbling, family, Christian unity, cornerstone
　　G　　Resting, boat, sheep, healing, cloak with fringe
Introit: UM164. "Come, My Way, My Truth, My Life" (Mark)
Introit: S2057. "Be Still and Know That I Am God" (Eph)
Greeting: BOW307, BOW455, or BOW456 (Eph, Mark)
Call to Worship or Communion: WSL65. "Jesus said" (Mark)
Opening Prayer: BOW460 (Mark)
Prayer of Confession: BOW492 or BOW493 (Eph)
Litany: BOW495. For the Church and the World (Eph, Mark)
Prayer: BOW503 or BOW506. For the Church (Eph)
Prayer: BOW546. For Those Who Suffer (Mark)
Scripture Response: UM541, stanza 1. "See How Great a Flame Aspires" (2 Sam, Eph)
Prayer of Thanksgiving: BOW551 (Mark)
Response: UM93, stanza 1. "Let All the World" (2 Sam)
Dismissal: BOW559 (Eph)
Benediction: S2171. "Make Me a Channel of Your Peace" (Eph)

2 Samuel 11:1-15

¹In the spring of the year, the time when kings go out to battle, David sent Joab with his officers and all Israel with him; they ravaged the Ammonites, and besieged Rabbah. But David remained at Jerusalem.

²It happened, late one afternoon, when David rose from his couch and was walking about on the roof of the king's house, that he saw from the roof a woman bathing; the woman was very beautiful. ³David sent someone to inquire about the woman. It was reported, "This is Bathsheba daughter of Eliam, the wife of Uriah the Hittite." ⁴So David sent messengers to get her, and she came to him, and he lay with her. (Now she was purifying herself after her period.) Then she returned to her house. ⁵The woman conceived; and she sent and told David, "I am pregnant."

⁶So David sent word to Joab, "Send me Uriah the Hittite." And Joab sent Uriah to David. ⁷When Uriah came to him, David asked how Joab and the people fared, and how the war was going. ⁸Then David said to Uriah, "Go down to your house, and wash your feet." Uriah went out of the king's house, and there followed him a present from the king. ⁹But Uriah slept at the entrance of the king's house with all the servants of his lord, and did not go down to his house.¹⁰When they told David, "Uriah did not go down to his house," David said to Uriah, "You have just come from a journey. Why did you not go down to your house?" ¹¹Uriah said to David, "The ark and Israel and Judah remain in booths; and my lord Joab and the servants of my lord are camping in the open field; shall I then go to my house, to eat and to drink, and to lie with my wife? As you live, and as your soul lives, I will not do such a thing." ¹²Then David said to Uriah, "Remain here today also, and tomorrow I will send you back." So Uriah remained in Jerusalem that day. On the next day, ¹³David invited him to eat and drink in his presence and made him drunk; and in the evening he went out to lie on his couch with the servants of his lord, but he did not go down to his house.

¹⁴In the morning David wrote a letter to Joab, and sent it by the hand of Uriah. ¹⁵In the letter he wrote, "Set Uriah in the forefront of the hardest fighting, and then draw back from him, so that he may be struck down and die."

Psalm 14 (UM746)

¹Fools say in their hearts, "There is no God."
　　They are corrupt, they do abominable deeds;
　　there is no one who does good.
²The LORD looks down from heaven on humankind
　　to see if there are any who are wise,
　　who seek after God.
³They have all gone astray, they are all alike perverse;
　　there is no one who does good,
　　no, not one.
⁴Have they no knowledge, all the evildoers
　　who eat up my people as they eat bread,
　　and do not call upon the LORD?
⁵There they shall be in great terror,
　　for God is with the company of the righteous.
⁶You would confound the plans of the poor,
　　but the LORD is their refuge.
⁷O that deliverance for Israel would come from Zion!
　　When the LORD restores the fortunes of his people,
　　Jacob will rejoice; Israel will be glad.

Ephesians 3:14-21

¹⁴For this reason I bow my knees before the Father, ¹⁵from whom every family in heaven and on earth takes its name. ¹⁶I pray that, according to the riches of his glory, he may grant that you may be strengthened in your inner being with power through his Spirit, ¹⁷and that Christ may dwell in your hearts through faith, as you are being rooted and grounded in love. ¹⁸I pray that you may have the power to comprehend, with all the saints, what is the breadth and length and height and depth, ¹⁹and to know the love of Christ that surpasses knowledge, so that you may be filled with all the fullness of God.

²⁰Now to him who by the power at work within us is able to accomplish abundantly far more than all we can ask or imagine, ²¹to him be glory in the church and in Christ Jesus to all generations, forever and ever. Amen.

John 6:1-21

¹After this Jesus went to the other side of the Sea of Galilee, also called the Sea of Tiberias. ²A large crowd kept following him, because they saw the signs that he was doing for the sick. ³Jesus went up the mountain and sat down there with his disciples. ⁴Now the Passover, the festival of the Jews, was near. ⁵When he looked up and saw a large crowd coming toward him, Jesus said to Philip, "Where are we to buy bread for these people to eat?" ⁶He said this to test him, for he himself knew what he was going to do. ⁷Philip answered him, "Six months' wages would not buy enough bread for each of them to get a little." ⁸One of his disciples, Andrew, Simon Peter's brother, said to him, ⁹"There is a boy here who has five barley loaves and two fish. But what are they among so many people?" ¹⁰Jesus said, "Make the people sit down." Now there was a great deal of grass in the place; so they sat down, about five thousand in all. ¹¹Then Jesus took the loaves, and when he had given thanks, he distributed them to those who were seated; so also the fish, as much as they wanted. ¹²When they were satisfied, he told his disciples, "Gather up the fragments left over, so that nothing may be lost." ¹³So they gathered them up, and from the fragments of the five barley loaves, left by those who had eaten, they filled twelve baskets. ¹⁴When the people saw the sign that he had done, they began to say, "This is indeed the prophet who is to come into the world."

¹⁵When Jesus realized that they were about to come and take him by force to make him king, he withdrew again to the mountain by himself.

¹⁶When evening came, his disciples went down to the sea, ¹⁷got into a boat, and started across the sea to Capernaum. It was now dark, and Jesus had not yet come to them. ¹⁸The sea became rough because a strong wind was blowing. ¹⁹When they had rowed about three or four miles, they saw Jesus walking on the sea and coming near the boat, and they were terrified. ²⁰But he said to them, "It is I; do not be afraid." ²¹Then they wanted to take him into the boat, and immediately the boat reached the land toward which they were going.

Primary Hymns and Songs for the Day

102	"Now Thank We All Our God" (John) (O)	
	H-3	Hbl-78; Chr-140; Desc-81; Org-98
	S-1	#252-254. Various treatments
111	"How Can We Name a Love" (Eph)	
	H-3	Hbl-99; Chr-102, 197; Org-159
	S-1	#326. Transposition in D major
175	"Jesus, the Very Thought of Thee" (Eph)	
	H-3	Hbl-52; Chr-90; Desc-92; Org-131
	S-1	#291-292. Desc. and Harm.
191	"Jesus Loves Me" (Eph, John)	
	H-3	Chr-117
599	"Break Thou the Bread of Life" (John, Comm.) (C)	
	H-3	Chr-44; Org-15

Additional Hymn Suggestions

425	"O Crucified Redeemer" (2 Sam)
439	"We Utter Our Cry" (2 Sam)
441	"What Does the Lord Require" (2 Sam)
3124	"How Shall I Come Before the Lord" (2 Sam)
2048	"God Weeps" (2 Sam, Pss)
3098	"Dust and Ashes" (2 Sam, Pss)
120	"Your Love, O God" (2 Sam, Eph)
358	"Dear Lord and Father of Mankind" (2 Sam, John) (Alternate Text: "Parent of Us All")
2027	"Now Praise the Hidden God of Love" (Pss, Eph)
98	"To God Be the Glory" (Eph)
267	"O Love, How Deep" (Eph)
356	*"Pues Si Vivimos"* ("When We Are Living") (Eph)
372	"How Can We Sinners Know" (Eph)
388	"O Come and Dwell in Me" (Eph)
414	"Thou Hidden Love of God" (Eph)
539	"O Spirit of the Living God" (Eph)
551	"Awake, O Sleeper" (Eph)
627	"O the Depth of Love Divine" (Eph)
3039	"Jesus, the Saving Name" (Eph)
3122	"Christ Has Broken Down the Wall" (Eph)
3150	"Father, We Have Heard You Calling" (Eph)
129	"Give to the Winds Thy Fears" (John)
350	"Come, All of You" (John)
368	"My Hope Is Built" (John)
427	"Where Cross the Crowded Ways of Life" (John)
444	"O Young and Fearless Prophet" (John)
476	"Lonely the Boat" (John)
479	"Jesus, Lover of My Soul" (John)
507	"Through It All" (John)
509	"Jesus, Savior, Pilot Me" (John)
510	"Come, Ye Disconsolate" (John)
512	"Stand By Me" (John)
525	"We'll Understand It Better By and By" (John)
529	"How Firm a Foundation" (John)
532	"Jesus, Priceless Treasure" (John)
534	"Be Still, My Soul" (John)
599	"Break Thou the Bread of Life" (John, Comm.)
612	"Deck Thyself, My Soul, with Gladness" (John, Comm.)
617	"I Come with Joy" (John, Comm.)
629	"You Satisfy the Hungry Heart" (John, Comm.)
631	"O Food to Pilgrims Given" (John, Comm.)
2142	"Blessed Quietness" (John)
2202	"Come Away with Me" (John)
2218	"You Are Mine" (John)
2236	"Gather Us In" (John, Comm.)
2261	"Life-Giving Bread" (John, Comm.)
3093	"Fill My Cup, Lord" (John, Comm.) UM641 (refrain only)

Additional Contemporary Suggestions

S2174	"What Does the Lord Require of You" (1 Sam)
S2053	"If It Had Not Been for the Lord" (Pss)
S2131	"Humble Thyself in the Sight of the Lord" (Pss)
UM347	"Spirit Song" (Eph)
S2073	"Celebrate Love" (Eph)
S2141	"There's a Song" (Eph)
S2143	"O Lord, Your Tenderness" (Eph)
S2150	"Lord, Be Glorified" (Eph)
WS3140	"Give Me Jesus" (Eph)
M13	"Be Glorified" (Eph)
M25	"No Greater Love" (Eph)
M37	"He Is Able" (Eph)
M63	"I Could Sing of Your Love Forever" (Eph)
M152	"Be Glorified" (Eph)
M273	"Amazed" (Eph)
M278	"Jesus Died My Soul to Save" (Eph)
SP50	"Think about His Love" (Eph)
WS3032	"Across the Lands" (John)
WS3105	"In Christ Alone" (John)
S2072	"Amen, Amen" (John)
UM628	"Eat This Bread" (John, Comm.)

Vocal Solos

"Wondrous Love" (Eph)	
V-6	p. 47
"May the Mind of Christ" (Eph)	
V-8	p. 114
"Give Me Jesus" (Eph)	
V-3(1)	p. 53
V-8	p. 256

Anthems

"Christ Has Broken Down the Wall" (Eph)
Mark Miller; Choristers Guild CGA1224
SATB with piano

"O Love, How Deep" (Eph)
Everett Titcomb; Alfred GCMR02226
SATB with organ

Other Suggestions

Visuals:

O	Bath towel, sword
P	Broken bread, fear, rescue, rejoicing
E	Kneeling in prayer, globe, flags of nations, missions, love
G	Dried fish, 5 loaves, 12 baskets, boat, storm, Jesus walking

Call to Worship: S2118. "Holy Spirit, Come to Us" (Pss)
Greeting: BOW449 (2 Sam)
Opening Prayer: BOW460 (2 Sam, Pss, Eph)
Call to Prayer: S2207. "Lord, Listen to Your Children"
Prayer of Confession and Assurance: BOW478 (2 Sam, John)
Prayer: BOW510 (2 Sam, Eph)
Prayer: WSL55, BOW431, UM446 (John, Comm.)
Prayer: BOW522 or BOW525 (Pss)
Response: BOW193. "Prayer for Wisdom" (Pss)
Scripture Response: UM441, stanza 2. "What Does the Lord Require?" (2 Sam)
Scripture Response: UM292, stanza 2. "What Wondrous Love Is This" (Eph)
Offering Prayer: WSL134. "Loving Father" (John)
Blessing: BOW529. A Prayer of Saint Patrick (Eph)

2 Samuel 11:26–12:13a

[26] When the wife of Uriah heard that her husband was dead, she made lamentation for him. [27] When the mourning was over, David sent and brought her to his house, and she became his wife, and bore him a son.

But the thing that David had done displeased the LORD, 12 and the LORD sent Nathan to David. He came to him, and said to him, "There were two men in a certain city, the one rich and the other poor. [2] The rich man had very many flocks and herds; [3] but the poor man had nothing but one little ewe lamb, which he had bought. He brought it up, and it grew up with him and with his children; it used to eat of his meager fare, and drink from his cup, and lie in his bosom, and it was like a daughter to him. [4] Now there came a traveler to the rich man, and he was loath to take one of his own flock or herd to prepare for the wayfarer who had come to him, but he took the poor man's lamb, and prepared that for the guest who had come to him." [5] Then David's anger was greatly kindled against the man. He said to Nathan, "As the LORD lives, the man who has done this deserves to die; [6] he shall restore the lamb fourfold, because he did this thing, and because he had no pity."

[7] Nathan said to David, "You are the man! Thus says the LORD, the God of Israel: I anointed you king over Israel, and I rescued you from the hand of Saul; [8] I gave you your master's house, and your master's wives into your bosom, and gave you the house of Israel and of Judah; and if that had been too little, I would have added as much more. [9] Why have you despised the word of the LORD, to do what is evil in his sight? You have struck down Uriah the Hittite with the sword, and have taken his wife to be your wife, and have killed him with the sword of the Ammonites. [10] Now therefore the sword shall never depart from your house, for you have despised me, and have taken the wife of Uriah the Hittite to be your wife. [11] Thus says the LORD: I will raise up trouble against you from within your own house; and I will take your wives before your eyes, and give them to your neighbor, and he shall lie with your wives in the sight of this very sun. [12] For you did it secretly; but I will do this thing before all Israel, and before the sun." [13a] David said to Nathan, "I have sinned against the LORD."

Psalm 51:1-12 (UM785)

[1] Have mercy on me, O God,
    according to your steadfast love;
according to your abundant mercy
    blot out my transgressions.
[2] Wash me thoroughly from my iniquity,
    and cleanse me from my sin.
[3] For I know my transgressions,
    and my sin is ever before me.
[4] Against you, you alone, have I sinned,
    and done what is evil in your sight,
so that you are justified in your sentence
    and blameless when you pass judgment.
[5] Indeed, I was born guilty,
    a sinner when my mother conceived me.
[6] You desire truth in the inward being;
    therefore teach me wisdom in my secret heart.
[7] Purge me with hyssop, and I shall be clean;
    wash me, and I shall be whiter than snow.
[8] Let me hear joy and gladness;
    let the bones that you have crushed rejoice.
[9] Hide your face from my sins,
    and blot out all my iniquities.
[10] Create in me a clean heart, O God,
    and put a new and right spirit within me.
[11] Do not cast me away from your presence,
    and do not take your holy spirit from me.
[12] Restore to me the joy of your salvation,
    and sustain in me a willing spirit.

Ephesians 4:1-16

[1] I therefore, the prisoner in the Lord, beg you to lead a life worthy of the calling to which you have been called, [2] with all humility and gentleness, with patience, bearing with one another in love, [3] making every effort to maintain the unity of the Spirit in the bond of peace. [4] There is one body and one Spirit, just as you were called to the one hope of your calling, [5] one Lord, one faith, one baptism, [6] one God and Father of all, who is above all and through all and in all.

[7] But each of us was given grace according to the measure of Christ's gift. [8] Therefore it is said,
    "When he ascended on high he made captivity itself a captive;
    he gave gifts to his people."
[9] (When it says, "He ascended," what does it mean but that he had also descended into the lower parts of the earth? [10] He who descended is the same one who ascended far above all the heavens, so that he might fill all things.) [11] The gifts he gave were that some would be apostles, some prophets, some evangelists, some pastors and teachers, [12] to equip the saints for the work of ministry, for building up the body of Christ, [13] until all of us come to the unity of the faith and of the knowledge of the Son of God, to maturity, to the measure of the full stature of Christ. [14] We must no longer be children, tossed to and fro and blown about by every wind of doctrine, by people's trickery, by their craftiness in deceitful scheming. [15] But speaking the truth in love, we must grow up in every way into him who is the head, into Christ, [16] from whom the whole body, joined and knit together by every ligament with which it is equipped, as each part is working properly, promotes the body's growth in building itself up in love.

John 6:24-35

[24] So when the crowd saw that neither Jesus nor his disciples were there, they themselves got into the boats and went to Capernaum looking for Jesus.

[25] When they found him on the other side of the sea, they said to him, "Rabbi, when did you come here?" [26] Jesus answered them, "Very truly, I tell you, you are looking for me, not because you saw signs, but because you ate your fill of the loaves. [27] Do not work for the food that perishes, but for the food that endures for eternal life, which the Son of Man will give you. For it is on him that God the Father has set his seal." [28] Then they said to him, "What must we do to perform the works of God?" [29] Jesus answered them, "This is the work of God, that you believe in him whom he has sent." [30] So they said to him, "What sign are you going to give us then, so that we may see it and believe you? What work are you performing? [31] Our ancestors ate the manna in the wilderness; as it is written, 'He gave them bread from heaven to eat.'" [32] Then Jesus said to them, "Very truly, I tell you, it was not Moses who gave you the bread from heaven, but it is my Father who gives you the true bread from heaven. [33] For the bread of God is that which comes down from heaven and gives life to the world." [34] They said to him, Sir, give us this bread always.

[35] Jesus said to them, "I am the bread of life. Whoever comes to me will never be hungry, and whoever believes in me will never be thirsty."

Primary Hymns and Songs for the Day
546	"The Church's One Foundation" (Eph) (O)
	H-3 Hbl-94; Chr-180; Desc-16; Org-9
	S-1 #25-26. Desc. and Harm.
355	"Depth of Mercy" (2 Sam, Pss)
	H-3 Chr-63, 100
	S-1 #53. Desc.
3097	"Depth of Mercy" (2 Sam, Pss, Eph)
628	"Eat This Bread" (John, Comm.)
629	"You Satisfy the Hungry Heart" (John, Comm.)
	S-1 #144. Four-part setting of refrain
3093	"Fill My Cup, Lord" (John, Comm.) (C)
	UM641 (refrain only)

Additional Hymn Suggestions
358	"Dear Lord and Father of Mankind" (2 Sam)
	(Alternate Text: "Parent of Us All")
421	"Make Me a Captive, Lord" (2 Sam) (O)
439	"We Utter Our Cry" (2 Sam)
441	"What Does the Lord Require" (2 Sam)
3124	"How Shall I Come Before the Lord" (2 Sam)
3098	"Dust and Ashes" (2 Sam, Pss)
357	"Just as I Am, Without One Plea" (2 Sam, Pss)
417	"O For a Heart to Praise My God" (Pss)
3140	"Give Me Jesus" (Pss, Eph)
108	"God Hath Spoken by the Prophets" (Eph)
410	"I Want a Principle Within" (Eph)
505	"When Our Confidence Is Shaken" (Eph)
547	"O Church of God, United" (Eph)
551	"Awake, O Sleeper" (Eph)
554	"All Praise to Our Redeeming Lord" (Eph)
555	"Forward Through the Ages" (Eph)
604	"Praise and Thanksgiving Be to God" (Eph, Baptism)
620	"One Bread, One Body" (Eph, Comm.)
649	"How Shall They Hear the Word of God" (Eph)
709	"Come, Let Us Join Our Friends Above" (Eph)
712	"I Sing a Song of the Saints of God" (Eph)
3109	"Living Spirit, Holy Fire" (Eph)
3150	"Father, We Have Heard You Calling" (Eph)
3155	"The Lord of Life, a Vine Is He" (Eph)
3156	"One Is the Body" (Eph, Comm.)
2175	"Together We Serve" (Eph)
2220	"We Are God's People" (Eph)
2229	"We Are One in Christ Jesus" (Eph)
2240	"One God and Father of Us All" (Eph)
2269	"Come, Share the Lord" (Eph, Comm.)
2261	"Life-Giving Bread" (Eph, John, Comm.)
2260	"Let Us Be Bread" (Eph, John, Comm.)
2221	"In Unity We Lift Our Song" (Eph, John)
3169	"You Feed Us, Gentle Savior" (Eph, John, Comm.)
127	"Guide Me, O Thou Great Jehovah" (John)
350	"Come, All of You" (John)
565	"Father, We Thank You" (John)
624	"Bread of the World" (John, Comm.)
631	"O Food to Pilgrims Given" (John, Comm.)
2126	"All Who Hunger" (John, Comm.)
2236	"Gather Us In" (John, Comm.)
3170	"What Feast of Love" (John, Comm.)
3173	"Table of Plenty" (John, Comm.)

Additional Contemporary Suggestions
S2174	"What Does the Lord Require of You" (2 Sam)
S2152	"Change My Heart, O God" (2 Sam, Pss)
S2133	"Give Me a Clean Heart" (2 Sam, Pss)
S2157	"Come and Fill Our Hearts" (Pss)
WS3103	"Purify My Heart" (Pss)
WS3188	"Hosanna" (Pss)
M50	"Refiner's Fire" (Pss)
M26	"The Power of Your Love" (Pss)
M35	"White as Snow" (Pss)
M153	"Give Us Clean Hands" (Pss)
M224	"Because of Your Love" (Pss)
M251	"Grace Like Rain" (Pss, Eph)
M77	"Above All" (Eph)
WS3023	"Forever" (Eph)
S2162	"Grace Alone" (Eph)
S2222	"The Servant Song" (Eph)
S2223	"They'll Know We Are Christians" (Eph)
S2224	"Make Us One" (Eph)
2227	"We Are the Body of Christ" (Eph)
S2226	"Bind Us Together" (Eph)
S2026b	"Halle, Halle, Halleluja" (John)
S2071	"Jesus, Name above All Names" (John)
S2132	"You Who Are Thirsty" (John, Comm.)
S2264	"Come to the Table" (John, Comm.)
WS3167	"Feed Us, Lord" (John, Comm.)
M32	"Holy and Anointed One" (John)
WS3093	"Fill My Cup, Lord" (John, Comm.)
	UM641 (refrain only)
WS3099	"Hungry" ("Falling on My Knees") (John)
M159	"All Who Are Thirsty" (John)
M160	"Enough" (John)

Vocal Solos
"A Contrite Heart" (Pss)
  V-4   p. 10
"Turn My Heart to You" (Pss)
  V-5(2)   p. 14
"One Bread, One Body" (Eph, John, Comm.)
  V-3(2)   p. 40
"Life Indeed" (John, Comm.)
  V-8   p. 271

Anthems
"*Kyrie Eleison*" (2 Sam, Pss)
Schubert/ed. Pfautsch; Hope LP-3711
SATB with keyboard

"Bread of the World" (John)
Mark Burrows/Arr. McDonald; Lorenz 10/4224L
SATB with piano

Other Suggestions
Visuals:
O	Lamb, sword
P	Water, hyssop, snow, rejoicing, heart, baptism
E	Unity, no. 1, baptism, gifts, building, Christ, ministry, binding
G	Boat, seal, bread, feeding, pitcher of water, flowing water

Greeting and Opening Prayer: BOW454 and 461 (2 Sam, Pss)
Prayer of Confession: BOW486 (Pss, Eph)
Response: UM483, UM484 or S2275. "*Kyrie*" (Pss)
Response: UM482 or S2277. "Lord, Have Mercy" (Pss)
Prayer: UM353, UM366, UM456, or UM535 (2 Sam, Pss)
Prayer: UM713. All Saints (Eph)
Prayer: WSL55, BOW431, or BOW399 Week 2 (John)
Prayers: BOW505 and BOW506. For the Church (Eph)
Prayer of Thanksgiving: BOW554 (Eph, John)
Blessing: BOW564 (John)

2 Samuel 18:5-9, 15, 31-33

[5] The king ordered Joab and Abishai and Ittai, saying, "Deal gently for my sake with the young man Absalom." And all the people heard when the king gave orders to all the commanders concerning Absalom.

[6] So the army went out into the field against Israel; and the battle was fought in the forest of Ephraim. [7] The men of Israel were defeated there by the servants of David, and the slaughter there was great on that day, twenty thousand men. [8] The battle spread over the face of all the country; and the forest claimed more victims that day than the sword.

[9] Absalom happened to meet the servants of David. Absalom was riding on his mule, and the mule went under the thick branches of a great oak. His head caught fast in the oak, and he was left hanging between heaven and earth, while the mule that was under him went on. . . .

[15] And ten young men, Joab's armor-bearers, surrounded Absalom and struck him, and killed him. . . .

[31] Then the Cushite came; and the Cushite said, "Good tidings for my lord the king! For the LORD has vindicated you this day, delivering you from the power of all who rose up against you." [32] The king said to the Cushite, "Is it well with the young man Absalom?" The Cushite answered, "May the enemies of my lord the king, and all who rise up to do you harm, be like that young man." [33] The king was deeply moved, and went up to the chamber over the gate, and wept; and as he went, he said, "O my son Absalom, my son, my son Absalom! Would I had died instead of you, O Absalom, my son, my son!"

Psalm 130 (UM848)

[1] Out of the depths I cry to you, O LORD.
[2]   Lord, hear my voice!
Let your ears be attentive
    to the voice of my supplications!
[3] If you, O LORD, should mark iniquities,
    Lord, who could stand?
[4] But there is forgiveness with you,
    so that you may be revered.
[5] I wait for the LORD, my soul waits,
    and in his word I hope;
[6] my soul waits for the Lord
    more than those who watch for the morning,
    more than those who watch for the morning.
[7] O Israel, hope in the LORD!
    For with the LORD there is steadfast love,
    and with him is great power to redeem.
[8] It is he who will redeem Israel
    from all its iniquities.

Ephesians 4:25–5:2

[25] So then, putting away falsehood, let all of us speak the truth to our neighbors, for we are members of one another. [26] Be angry but do not sin; do not let the sun go down on your anger, [27] and do not make room for the devil. [28] Thieves must give up stealing; rather let them labor and work honestly with their own hands, so as to have something to share with the needy. [29] Let no evil talk come out of your mouths, but only what is useful for building up, as there is need, so that your words may give grace to those who hear. [30] And do not grieve the Holy Spirit of God, with which you were marked with a seal for the day of redemption. [31] Put away from you all bitterness and wrath and anger and wrangling and slander, together with all malice, [32] and be kind to one another, tenderhearted, forgiving one another, as God in Christ has forgiven you.

[5] Therefore be imitators of God, as beloved children, [2] and live in love, as Christ loved us and gave himself up for us, a fragrant offering and sacrifice to God.

John 6:35, 41-51

[35] Jesus said to them, "I am the bread of life. Whoever comes to me will never be hungry, and whoever believes in me will never be thirsty. . . .

[41] Then the Jews began to complain about him because he said, "I am the bread that came down from heaven." [42] They were saying, "Is not this Jesus, the son of Joseph, whose father and mother we know? How can he now say, 'I have come down from heaven'?" [43] Jesus answered them, "Do not complain among yourselves. [44] No one can come to me unless drawn by the Father who sent me; and I will raise that person up on the last day. [45] It is written in the prophets, 'And they shall all be taught by God.' Everyone who has heard and learned from the Father comes to me. [46] Not that anyone has seen the Father except the one who is from God; he has seen the Father. [47] Very truly, I tell you, whoever believes has eternal life. [48] I am the bread of life. [49] Your ancestors ate the manna in the wilderness, and they died. [50] This is the bread that comes down from heaven, so that one may eat of it and not die. [51] I am the living bread that came down from heaven. Whoever eats of this bread will live forever; and the bread that I will give for the life of the world is my flesh."

Primary Hymns and Songs for the Day

178	"Hope of the World" (Eph, John) (O)
	H-3 Chr-100
	S-1 #343. Desc.
	S-2 #189. Intro.
136	"The Lord's My Shepherd, I'll Not Want" (2 Sam)
	H-3 Chr-75, 188
2261	"Life-Giving Bread" (John, Comm.)
474	"Precious Lord, Take My Hand" (2 Sam, Pss) (C)
	H-3 Chr-164; Org-116

Additional Hymn Suggestions

443	"O God Who Shaped Creation" (2 Sam) (O)
458	"Dear Lord, for All in Pain" (2 Sam, Pss)
515	"Out of the Depths I Cry to You" (2 Sam, Pss)
534	"Be Still, My Soul" (2 Sam, Pss)
700	"Abide with Me" (2 Sam, Pss)
2110	"Why Has God Forsaken Me?" (2 Sam, Pss)
2136	"Out of the Depths" (2 Sam, Pss)
355	"Depth of Mercy" (2 Sam, Pss)
3097	"Depth of Mercy" (2 Sam, Pss)
510	"Come, Ye Disconsolate" (2 Sam, John)
3131	"Hear My Prayer, O God" (Pss)
3141	"Holy Darkness" (Pss)
399	"Take My Life, and Let It Be" (Eph)
430	"O Master, Let Me Walk with Thee" (Eph)
431	"Let There Be Peace on Earth" (Eph)
608	"This Is the Spirit's Entry Now" (Eph)
2082	"Woke Up This Morning" (Eph)
2167	"More Like You" (Eph)
2205	"The Fragrance of Christ" (Eph)
2213	"Healer of Our Every Ill" (Eph)
350	"Come, All of You" (John)
127	"Guide Me, O Thou Great Jehovah" (John)
612	"Deck Thyself, My Soul, with Gladness" (John, Comm.)
616	"Come, Sinners, to the Gospel Feast" (John, Comm.)
624	"Bread of the World" (John, Comm.)
627	"O the Depth of Love Divine" (John, Comm.)
629	"You Satisfy the Hungry Heart" (John, Comm.)
630	"Become to Us the Living Bread" (John, Comm.)
631	"O Food to Pilgrims Given" (John)
633	"The Bread of Life for All Is Broken" (John, Comm.)
2060	"God the Sculptor of the Mountains" (John)
2062	"The Lily of the Valley" (John)
2126	"All Who Hunger" (John, Comm.)
2132	"You Who Are Thirsty" (John)
2236	"Gather Us In" (John)
3168	"Come to the Table of Grace" (John, Comm.)
3169	"You Feed Us, Gentle Savior" (John, Comm.)
3170	"What Feast of Love" (John, Comm.)
3173	"Table of Plenty" (John, Comm.)
672	"God Be with You Till We Meet Again" (2 Sam, John) (C)
673	"God Be with You Till We Meet Again" (2 Sam, John) (C)

Additional Contemporary Suggestions

WS3142	"I Love the Lord" (Pss)
WS3099	"Hungry" ("Falling on My Knees") (Pss, John)
S2039	"Holy, Holy" (Eph)
S2073	"Celebrate Love" (Eph)
S2108	"O How He Loves You and Me!" (Eph)
S2145	"I've Got Peace Like a River" (Eph)
S2161	"To Know You More" (Eph)

WS3103	"Purify My Heart" (Eph)
WS3151	"The Jesus in Me" (Eph)
M38	"In the Secret" ("I Want to Know You") (Eph)
S2026b	"Halle, Halle, Halleluja" (John)
S2038	"Father, I Adore You" (John)
S2071	"Jesus, Name above All Names" (John)
S2204	"Light of the World" (John)
S2264	"Come to the Table" (John, Comm.)
UM628	"Eat This Bread" (John, Comm.)
UM640	"Take Our Bread" (John, Comm.)
WS3093	"Fill My Cup, Lord" (John, Comm.)
	UM641 (refrain only)
WS3167	"Feed Us, Lord" (John, Comm.)
M32	"Holy and Anointed One" (John)
M159	"All Who Are Thirsty" (John)
M160	"Enough" (John)
M264	"Song of Hope" ("Heaven Come Down") (John)

Vocal Solos

"Out of the Depths I Cry to Thee" (Pss)
    V-9   p. 16
"Like a Child" (Pss, Eph)
    V-8   p. 356
"Christ Living Within You" (Eph)
    V-8   p. 177
"Maybe the Rain"
    V-5(2)   p. 27

Anthems

"Grieve Not the Holy Spirit of God" (Eph)
T. Tertius Noble; H.W. Gray / Alfred 00-GCMR00409
SATB and tenor solo with organ

"Gather Us In" (John)
Haugen/Arr. Hayes; Alfred 42503
SATB with piano

Other Suggestions

Visuals:
O	Tree limb, man weeping
P	Waiting for dawn, forgiveness, praying hands, weeping
E	Setting sun, children, sacrificial offering, portrait of Christ
G	Bread, love feast, communion, anointing with oil, baptism

Greeting: BOW453 (2 Sam, John)
Opening Prayer: BOW469 (John)
Canticle: UM516. "Canticle of Redemption" (Pss)
Prayer: UM461. For Those Who Mourn (2 Sam)
Prayer: UM481. The Prayer of Saint Francis (Eph)
Prayer: BOW514. "For the Mind of Christ" (Eph)
Call to Communion: BOW431 by Andy Langford (John)
Communion Prayer: BOW431 by Dunlap-Berg (John)
Benediction: S2161. "To Know You More" (Eph)

1 Kings 2:10-12; 3:3-14

[10] Then David slept with his ancestors, and was buried in the city of David. [11] The time that David reigned over Israel was forty years; he reigned seven years in Hebron, and thirty-three years in Jerusalem. [12] So Solomon sat on the throne of his father David; and his kingdom was firmly established. . . .

3 [3] Solomon loved the LORD, walking in the statutes of his father David; only, he sacrificed and offered incense at the high places. [4] The king went to Gibeon to sacrifice there, for that was the principal high place; Solomon used to offer a thousand burnt offerings on that altar. [5] At Gibeon the LORD appeared to Solomon in a dream by night; and God said, "Ask what I should give you." [6] And Solomon said, "You have shown great and steadfast love to your servant my father David, because he walked before you in faithfulness, in righteousness, and in uprightness of heart toward you; and you have kept for him this great and steadfast love, and have given him a son to sit on his throne today. [7] And now, O LORD my God, you have made your servant king in place of my father David, although I am only a little child; I do not know how to go out or come in. [8] And your servant is in the midst of the people whom you have chosen, a great people, so numerous they cannot be numbered or counted. [9] Give your servant therefore an understanding mind to govern your people, able to discern between good and evil; for who can govern this your great people?"

[10] It pleased the Lord that Solomon had asked this. [11] God said to him, "Because you have asked this, and have not asked for yourself long life or riches, or for the life of your enemies, but have asked for yourself understanding to discern what is right, [12] I now do according to your word. Indeed I give you a wise and discerning mind; no one like you has been before you and no one like you shall arise after you. [13] I give you also what you have not asked, both riches and honor all your life; no other king shall compare with you. [14] If you will walk in my ways, keeping my statutes and my commandments, as your father David walked, then I will lengthen your life."

Psalm 111 (UM832)

[1] Praise the LORD!
I will give thanks to the LORD with my whole heart,
    in the company of the upright, in the congregation.
[2] Great are the works of the LORD,
    studied by all who delight in them.
[3] Full of honor and majesty is his work,
    and his righteousness endures forever.
[4] He has gained renown by his wonderful deeds;
    the LORD is gracious and merciful.
[5] He provides food for those who fear him;
    he is ever mindful of his covenant.
[6] He has shown his people the power of his works,
    in giving them the heritage of the nations.
[7] The works of his hands are faithful and just;
    all his precepts are trustworthy.
[8] They are established forever and ever,
    to be performed with faithfulness and uprightness.
[9] He sent redemption to his people;
    he has commanded his covenant forever.
    Holy and awesome is his name.
[10] The fear of the LORD is the beginning of wisdom;
    all those who practice it have a good understanding.
    His praise endures forever.

Ephesians 5:15-20

[15] Be careful then how you live, not as unwise people but as wise, [16] making the most of the time, because the days are evil. [17] So do not be foolish, but understand what the will of the Lord is. [18] Do not get drunk with wine, for that is debauchery; but be filled with the Spirit, [19] as you sing psalms and hymns and spiritual songs among yourselves, singing and making melody to the Lord in your hearts, [20] giving thanks to God the Father at all times and for everything in the name of our Lord Jesus Christ.

John 6:51-58

[51] "I am the living bread that came down from heaven. Whoever eats of this bread will live forever; and the bread that I will give for the life of the world is my flesh."

[52] The Jews then disputed among themselves, saying, "How can this man give us his flesh to eat?" [53] So Jesus said to them, "Very truly, I tell you, unless you eat the flesh of the Son of Man and drink his blood, you have no life in you. [54] Those who eat my flesh and drink my blood have eternal life, and I will raise them up on the last day; [55] for my flesh is true food and my blood is true drink. [56] Those who eat my flesh and drink my blood abide in me, and I in them. [57] Just as the living Father sent me, and I live because of the Father, so whoever eats me will live because of me. [58] This is the bread that came down from heaven, not like that which your ancestors ate, and they died. But the one who eats this bread will live forever."

Primary Hymns and Songs for the Day
60	"I'll Praise My Maker While I've Breath" (Pss, Eph) (O)
	H-3　Chr-109; Org-105
	S-2　#141. Harm.
500	"Spirit of God, Descend upon My Heart" (Eph)
	H-3　Chr-175; Desc-77; Org-94
	S-2　#125-128. Various treatments
2254	"In Remembrance of Me" (John, Comm.)
624	"Bread of the World" (John, Comm.) (C)

Additional Hymn Suggestions
407	"Close to Thee" (1 Kgs)
410	"I Want a Principle Within" (1 Kgs)
411	"Dear Lord, Lead Me Day by Day" (1 Kgs)
441	"What Does the Lord Require" (1 Kgs)
451	"Be Thou My Vision" (1 Kgs)
3124	"How Shall I Come Before the Lord" (1 Kgs)
140, 4011	"Great Is Thy Faithfulness" (1 Kgs, Pss)
430	"O Master, Let Me Walk with Thee" (1 Kgs, Pss)
73	"O Worship the King" (Pss, Eph) (O)
2004	"Praise the Source of Faith and Learning" (Pss, Eph)
2121	"O Holy Spirit, Root of Life" (Pss, Eph)
2195	"In the Lord I'll Be Ever Thankful" (Pss, Eph)
2216	"When We Are Called to Sing Your Praise" (Eph)
2255	"In the Singing" (Eph, Comm.)
68	"When in Our Music God Is Glorified" (Eph)
395	"Take Time to Be Holy" (Eph)
537	"Filled with the Spirit's Power" (Eph)
539	"O Spirit of the Living God" (Eph)
164	"Come, My Way, My Truth, My Life" (John)
339	"Come, Sinners, to the Gospel Feast" (John)
616	"Come, Sinners, to the Gospel Feast" (John, Comm.)
630	"Become to Us the Living Bread" (John)
631	"O Food to Pilgrims Given" (John, Comm.)
2060	"God the Sculptor of the Mountains" (John)
2062	"The Lily of the Valley" (John)
2263	"Broken for Me" (John, Comm.)

Additional Contemporary Suggestions
S2174	"What Does the Lord Require of You" (1 Kgs)
WS3004	"Step by Step" (1 Kgs)
M72	"Jesus, Lover of My Soul" ("It's All about You") (1 Kgs)
M104	"There Is None Like You" (1 Kgs)
UM84	"Thank You, Lord" (Pss)
S2040	"Awesome God" (Pss)
S2022	"Great Is the Lord" (Pss)
SP2	"Ah, Lord God" (Pss)
SP58	"Great Is the Lord Almighty!" (Pss)
SP102	"Great Are You, Lord" (Pss)
M103	"How Great Are You, Lord" (Pss)
M126	"Famous One" (Pss)
M224	"Because of Your Love" (Pss)
S2036	"Give Thanks" (Eph)
S2144	"Someone Asked the Question" (Eph)
S2173	"Shine, Jesus, Shine" (Eph)
S2038	"Father, I Adore You" (John)
S2266	"Here Is Bread, Here Is Wine" (John, Comm.)
WS3099	"Hungry" ("Falling on My Knees") (John)
M32	"Holy and Anointed One" (John)
M159	"All Who Are Thirsty" (John, Comm.)
M160	"Enough" (John)
M253	"Jesus Messiah" (John, Comm.)
M264	"Song of Hope" ("Heaven Come Down") (John)

Vocal Solos
"Be Thou My Vision" (1 Kgs)
　V-6　p. 13
"Now Thank We All Our God" (Pss)
　V-6　p. 8
"Thanks to God" (Pss)
　V-8　p. 296
"Author of Life Divine" (Eph, John)
　V-1　p. 39

Anthems
"O for a Closer Walk" (1 Kgs)
Arr. Joey Hoelscher; Alfred 00-44577
SATB with piano, opt. Instr.

"The Bread That I Will Give" (John)
James Biery; GIA Publications G-5935
SATB a cappella

Other Suggestions
Visuals:
O	Crown, scepter, royal robe, people exhibiting wisdom
P	Images of creation, feasting, heart, humble praise
E	Singing, musical instruments, hymnal, worship/revelry
G	Communion broken bread, chalice, crucifix

Call to Worship: S2265. "Time Now to Gather" (John, Comm.)
Greeting: BOW451 (1 Kgs, Pss)
Opening Prayer: BOW468 (1 Kgs)
Canticle: UM112. "Canticle of Wisdom" (1 Kgs) See S-1, p. 377.
Prayer of Confession: UM586 or BOW487 (1 Kgs, Eph)
Intercessory Prayer: UM429. For Our Country (1 Kgs)
Prayer: BOW399 Week 2 or BOW431 (John)
Prayer: BOW510, BOW525, or BOW530 (1 Kgs, Pss, Eph)
Response: WSL47 or BOW193 (1 Kgs, Pss)
Offering Prayer: WSL109. "O great and holy God" (Eph)
Prayer of Thanksgiving: BOW555 (1 Kgs, Eph)
Response: UM84. "Thank You, Lord" (Pss)
Blessing: BOW564 (1 Kgs, Pss, John)

1 Kings 8: (1, 6, 10-11), 22-30, 41-43

(¹Then Solomon assembled the elders of Israel and all the heads of the tribes, the leaders of the ancestral houses of the Israelites, before King Solomon in Jerusalem, to bring up the ark of the covenant of the LORD out of the city of David, which is Zion. . . . ⁶Then the priests brought the ark of the covenant of the LORD to its place, in the inner sanctuary of the house, in the most holy place, underneath the wings of the cherubim. . . . ¹⁰And when the priests came out of the holy place, a cloud filled the house of the LORD, ¹¹so that the priests could not stand to minister because of the cloud; for the glory of the LORD filled the house of the LORD. . . .)

²²Then Solomon stood before the altar of the LORD in the presence of all the assembly of Israel, and spread out his hands to heaven. ²³He said, "O LORD, God of Israel, there is no God like you in heaven above or on earth beneath, keeping covenant and steadfast love for your servants who walk before you with all their heart, ²⁴the covenant that you kept for your servant my father David as you declared to him; you promised with your mouth and have this day fulfilled with your hand. ²⁵Therefore, O LORD, God of Israel, keep for your servant my father David that which you promised him, saying, 'There shall never fail you a successor before me to sit on the throne of Israel, if only your children look to their way, to walk before me as you have walked before me.' ²⁶Therefore, O God of Israel, let your word be confirmed, which you promised to your servant my father David.

²⁷"But will God indeed dwell on the earth? Even heaven and the highest heaven cannot contain you, much less this house that I have built! ²⁸Regard your servant's prayer and his plea, O LORD my God, heeding the cry and the prayer that your servant prays to you today; ²⁹that your eyes may be open night and day toward this house, the place of which you said, 'My name shall be there,' that you may heed the prayer that your servant prays toward this place. ³⁰Hear the plea of your servant and of your people Israel when they pray toward this place; O hear in heaven your dwelling place; heed and forgive. . . .

⁴¹"Likewise when a foreigner, who is not of your people Israel, comes from a distant land because of your name ⁴²—for they shall hear of your great name, your mighty hand, and your outstretched arm—when a foreigner comes and prays toward this house, ⁴³then hear in heaven your dwelling place, and do according to all that the foreigner calls to you, so that all the peoples of the earth may know your name and fear you, as do your people Israel, and so that they may know that your name has been invoked on this house that I have built.

Psalm 84 (UM804)

¹How lovely is your dwelling place,
  O LORD of hosts!
²My soul longs, indeed it faints
  for the courts of the LORD;
my heart and my flesh sing for joy
  to the living God.
³Even the sparrow finds a home,
  and the swallow a nest for herself,
  where she may lay her young,
at your altars, O LORD of hosts,
  my King and my God.
⁴Happy are those who live in your house,
  ever singing your praise. *[Selah]*
⁵Happy are those whose strength is in you,
  in whose heart are the highways to Zion.
⁶As they go through the valley of Baca
  they make it a place of springs;
  the early rain also covers it with pools.

⁷They go from strength to strength;
  the God of gods will be seen in Zion.
⁸O LORD God of hosts, hear my prayer;
  give ear, O God of Jacob! *[Selah]*
⁹Behold our shield, O God;
  look on the face of your anointed.
¹⁰For a day in your courts is better
  than a thousand elsewhere.
I would rather be a doorkeeper in the house of my God
  than live in the tents of wickedness.
¹¹For the LORD God is a sun and shield;
  he bestows favor and honor.
No good thing does the LORD withhold
  from those who walk uprightly.
¹²O LORD of hosts,
  happy is everyone who trusts in you.

Ephesians 6:10-20

¹⁰Finally, be strong in the Lord and in the strength of his power. ¹¹Put on the whole armor of God, so that you may be able to stand against the wiles of the devil. ¹²For our struggle is not against enemies of blood and flesh, but against the rulers, against the authorities, against the cosmic powers of this present darkness, against the spiritual forces of evil in the heavenly places. ¹³Therefore take up the whole armor of God, so that you may be able to withstand on that evil day, and having done everything, to stand firm. ¹⁴Stand therefore, and fasten the belt of truth around your waist, and put on the breastplate of righteousness. ¹⁵As shoes for your feet put on whatever will make you ready to proclaim the gospel of peace. ¹⁶With all of these, take the shield of faith, with which you will be able to quench all the flaming arrows of the evil one. ¹⁷Take the helmet of salvation, and the sword of the Spirit, which is the word of God.

¹⁸Pray in the Spirit at all times in every prayer and supplication. To that end keep alert and always persevere in supplication for all the saints. ¹⁹Pray also for me, so that when I speak, a message may be given to me to make known with boldness the mystery of the gospel, ²⁰for which I am an ambassador in chains. Pray that I may declare it boldly, as I must speak.

John 6:56-69

⁵⁶"Those who eat my flesh and drink my blood abide in me, and I in them. ⁵⁷Just as the living Father sent me, and I live because of the Father, so whoever eats me will live because of me. ⁵⁸This is the bread that came down from heaven, not like that which your ancestors ate, and they died. But the one who eats this bread will live forever." ⁵⁹He said these things while he was teaching in the synagogue at Capernaum.

⁶⁰When many of his disciples heard it, they said, "This teaching is difficult; who can accept it?" ⁶¹But Jesus, being aware that his disciples were complaining about it, said to them, "Does this offend you? ⁶²Then what if you were to see the Son of Man ascending to where he was before? ⁶³It is the spirit that gives life; the flesh is useless. The words that I have spoken to you are spirit and life. ⁶⁴But among you there are some who do not believe." For Jesus knew from the first who were the ones that did not believe, and who was the one that would betray him. ⁶⁵And he said, "For this reason I have told you that no one can come to me unless it is granted by the Father."

⁶⁶Because of this many of his disciples turned back and no longer went about with him. ⁶⁷So Jesus asked the twelve, "Do you also wish to go away?" ⁶⁸Simon Peter answered him, "Lord, to whom can we go? You have the words of eternal life. ⁶⁹We have come to believe and know that you are the Holy One of God."

Primary Hymns and Songs for the Day

514	"Stand Up, Stand Up for Jesus" (Eph) (O)	
	H-3	Chr-177; Org-177
	S-2	#192-194. Various treatments
2042	"How Lovely, Lord, How Lovely" (Pss)	
	H-3	Hbl-70; Chr-174; Desc-76; Org-90
600	"Wonderful Words of Life" (John)	
	H-3	Chr-221; Org-186
513	"Soldiers of Christ, Arise" (Eph) (C)	
	H-3	Hbl-55; Chr-60; Desc-30; Org-27
	S-1	#86-88. Various treatments
178	"Hope of the World" (Eph, John) (C)	
	H-3	Chr-100
	S-1	#343. Desc.
	S-2	#189. Intro.

Additional Hymn Suggestions

88	"Maker, in Whom We Live" (1 Kgs) (O)
93	"Let All the World in Every Corner Sing" (1 Kgs)
103	"Immortal, Invisible, God Only Wise" (1 Kgs)
119	"O God in Heaven" (1 Kgs)
3009	"Praise God for This Holy Ground" (1 Kgs)
2142	"Blessed Quietness" (Pss)
2206	"Without Seeing You" (Pss)
352	"Standing in the Need of Prayer" (Eph)
374	"Standing on the Promises" (Eph)
435	"O God of Every Nation" (Eph)
530	"Are Ye Able" (Eph)
575	"Onward, Christian Soldiers" (Eph)
580	"Lead On, O King Eternal" (Eph)
670	"Go Forth for God" (Eph) (C)
2202	"Come Away with Me" (Eph)
358	"Dear Lord and Father of Mankind" (Eph, John) (Alternate Text: "Parent of Us All")
369	"Blessed Assurance" (John)
462	"'Tis so Sweet to Trust in Jesus" (John)
596	"Blessed Jesus, at Thy Word" (John)
598	"O Word of God Incarnate" (John)
630	"Become to Us the Living Bread" (John, Comm.)
2254	"In Remembrance of Me" (John, Comm.)
2263	"Broken for Me" (John, Comm.)
2265	"Time Now to Gather" (John, Comm.)

Additional Contemporary Suggestions

S2272	"Holy Ground" (1 Kgs)
WS3036	"There's No One in This World Like Jesus" ("*Hakuna wakaita sa Jesu*") (1 Kgs)
SP2	"Ah, Lord God" (1 Kgs)
M36	"Awesome in This Place" (1 Kgs)
M93	"Rock of Ages" (1 Kgs.)
M128	"You Are God Alone" (1 Kgs)
S2080	"All I Need Is You" (Pss)
S2025	"As the Deer" (Pss)
M28	"Who Can Satisfy My Soul Like You?" (Pss)
M60	"Better Is One Day" (Pss)
M110	"Love You So Much" (Pss)
WS3112	"Breathe" (Pss, John)
WS3040	"You Are My All in All" (Pss, Eph)
WS3042	"Shout to the North" (Eph)
S2055	"You Are My Hiding Place" (Eph)
SP158	"The Battle Belongs to the Lord" (Eph)
M67	"We Want to See Jesus Lifted High" (Eph)
M92	"All Things Are Possible" (Eph)
M164	"Good to Me" (Eph)
S2038	"Father, I Adore You" (John)

S2266	"Here Is Bread, Here Is Wine" (John, Comm.)
UM628	"Eat This Bread" (John, Comm.)
WS3099	"Hungry" ("Falling on My Knees") (John)
M7	"I Believe in Jesus" (John)
M32	"Holy and Anointed One" (John)
M72	"Jesus, Lover of My Soul" (John)
M159	"All Who Are Thirsty" (John)
M160	"Enough" (John)

Vocal Solos

"Lord, Listen to Your Children" (1 Kgs, Eph)
    V-8   p. 168
"Ivory Palaces" (Pss)
    V-8   p. 136

Anthems

"Great Is Thy Faithfulness" (1 Kgs)
Arr. Joseph M. Martin; Hope C-5657
SATB with piano

"Psalm 84: *Cantique de Jean Racine*" (Pss)
Faure/Hopson; Carl Fisher CM8042
SATB with keyboard

Other Suggestions

Visuals:

O	Praying hands, temple (church), hand, outstretched arm
P	Churches, sparrows and nest, rain, water pooling, door
E	Armor, praying hands, people in prayer
G	Bread/wine/communion, line drawn, question mark, Christ

Call to Worship: S2273, BOW187. "Jesus, We Are Here" (Eph)
Opening Prayer: BOW467 (John)
Prayer of Confession: BOW486 (1 Kgs, Eph)
Sung Prayers: S2201. "Prayers of the People" (Pss, Eph)
Prayer: UM423. Finding Rest in God (Pss)
Prayer: BOW399 Week 2 or BOW431 (John)
Prayer: BOW504, BOW521, or BOW528 (Eph)
Prayer: BOW516. For the Nation (1 Kgs, Eph)
Response: S2193. "Lord, Listen to Your Children Praying" (Pss, Eph)
Scripture Response: UM600, stanza 1. "Wonderful Words of Life" (John)
Prayer: WSL81. "Creator God, how lovely" (Pss, Comm.)
Prayer of Thanksgiving: BOW553 (Eph, John)
Response: S2262. "Let Us Offer to the Father" (Pss, Eph)
Blessing: BOW564 (Eph, John)
Benediction: S2281. "May You Run and Not Be Weary" (Eph)

SCRIPTURE INDEX

WORSHIP PLANNING SHEET 1

Date: _____ Color:_____

Preacher: _____

Liturgist: _____

Selected Scripture: _____

Selected Hymns   No.   Placement

_____

_____

_____

_____

Psalter #_____

Keyboard Selections

Title   Composer   Placement

_____

_____

_____

Anthems

Title   Choir   Composer   Placement

_____

_____

Vocal Solos

Title   Singer   Composer   Placement

_____

_____

Other Ideas:

Acolytes: _____

Head Usher: _____

Altar Guild Contact: _____

Other Participants: _____

_____

WORSHIP PLANNING SHEET 2

Date: _____ Sunday: _____ Color: _____

Preacher: _____

Liturgist: _____

Opening Voluntary   Composer

_____

_____

Hymn   Tune Name   No.

_____

Opening Prayer: _____

Prayer for Illumination: _____

First Lesson: _____

Psalter: _____

Second Lesson: _____

Gospel Lesson: _____

Hymn   Tune Name   No.

_____

Response to the Word: _____

Prayers of the People: _____

Offertory   Composer

_____

Communion Setting: _____

Communion Hymns   Tune Name   No.

_____

_____

Closing Hymn   Tune Name   No.

_____

Benediction: _____

Closing Voluntary   Composer

_____

CONTEMPORARY WORSHIP PLANNING SHEET

Because of the diversity in orders of worship, you will want to adjust this planning sheet to meet the needs of your worship planning team. A common order used would consist of three to four opening praise choruses and lively hymns, a time of informal prayers of the congregation along with songs of prayer, reading of the primary scripture for the day, a drama or video to illustrate the day's theme, a message from the preacher, a testimony on the theme for the day (if a drama or video was not presented earlier), followed by closing songs appropriate to the mood of the service and the message. Any offering would usually be taken early in the service, and Holy Communion would normally take place following the message. Special music (solos, duets, instrumental music) can be used wherever it best expresses the theme of the service.

Date: _____ Sunday: _____

Thematic Emphasis or Topic: _____

Color: _____ Visual Focus: _____

Opening Songs:

_____

_____

Prayer Songs:

_____

Scripture Selection(s):

_____

Drama or Video:

_____

Message Title:

_____

Testimony: _____

Special Music:

_____

Closing Songs:

_____

Preacher: _____ Music Leader: _____

Worship Facilitator: _____ Prayer Leader: _____

NOTES

2017–2018 Lectionary Calendar

Lectionary verses and worship suggestions in this edition of *The UM Planner*
relate to the unshaded dates in the calendar below.
Lectionary Year A: September 3, 2017–November 26, 2017
Lectionary Year B: December 3, 2017–August 26, 2018

2017

| JANUARY 2017 |||||||
S	M	T	W	T	F	S
1	2	3	4	5	6	7
8	9	10	11	12	13	14
15	16	17	18	19	20	21
22	23	24	25	26	27	28
29	30	31				

| FEBRUARY 2017 |||||||
S	M	T	W	T	F	S
			1	2	3	4
5	6	7	8	9	10	11
12	13	14	15	16	17	18
19	20	21	22	23	24	25
26	27	28				

| MARCH 2017 |||||||
S	M	T	W	T	F	S
			1	2	3	4
5	6	7	8	9	10	11
12	13	14	15	16	17	18
19	20	21	22	23	24	25
26	27	28	29	30	31	

| APRIL 2017 |||||||
S	M	T	W	T	F	S
						1
2	3	4	5	6	7	8
9	10	11	12	13	14	15
16	17	18	19	20	21	22
23	24	25	26	27	28	29
30						

| MAY 2017 |||||||
S	M	T	W	T	F	S
	1	2	3	4	5	6
7	8	9	10	11	12	13
14	15	16	17	18	19	20
21	22	23	24	25	26	27
28	29	30	31			

| JUNE 2017 |||||||
S	M	T	W	T	F	S
				1	2	3
4	5	6	7	8	9	10
11	12	13	14	15	16	17
18	19	20	21	22	23	24
25	26	27	28	29	30	

| JULY 2017 |||||||
S	M	T	W	T	F	S
						1
2	3	4	5	6	7	8
9	10	11	12	13	14	15
16	17	18	19	20	21	22
23	24	25	26	27	28	29
30	31					

| AUGUST 2017 |||||||
S	M	T	W	T	F	S
		1	2	3	4	5
6	7	8	9	10	11	12
13	14	15	16	17	18	19
20	21	22	23	24	25	26
27	28	29	30	31		

| SEPTEMBER 2017 |||||||
S	M	T	W	T	F	S
					1	2
3	4	5	6	7	8	9
10	11	12	13	14	15	16
17	18	19	20	21	22	23
24	25	26	27	28	29	30

| OCTOBER 2017 |||||||
S	M	T	W	T	F	S
1	2	3	4	5	6	7
8	9	10	11	12	13	14
15	16	17	18	19	20	21
22	23	24	25	26	27	28
29	30	31				

| NOVEMBER 2017 |||||||
S	M	T	W	T	F	S
			1	2	3	4
5	6	7	8	9	10	11
12	13	14	15	16	17	18
19	20	21	22	23	24	25
26	27	28	29	30		

| DECEMBER 2017 |||||||
S	M	T	W	T	F	S
					1	2
3	4	5	6	7	8	9
10	11	12	13	14	15	16
17	18	19	20	21	22	23
24	25	26	27	28	29	30
31						

2018

| JANUARY 2018 |||||||
S	M	T	W	T	F	S
	1	2	3	4	5	6
7	8	9	10	11	12	13
14	15	16	17	18	19	20
21	22	23	24	25	26	27
28	29	30	31			

| FEBRUARY 2018 |||||||
S	M	T	W	T	F	S
				1	2	3
4	5	6	7	8	9	10
11	12	13	14	15	16	17
18	19	20	21	22	23	24
25	26	27	28			

| MARCH 2018 |||||||
S	M	T	W	T	F	S
				1	2	3
4	5	6	7	8	9	10
11	12	13	14	15	16	17
18	19	20	21	22	23	24
25	26	27	28	29	30	31

| APRIL 2018 |||||||
S	M	T	W	T	F	S
1	2	3	4	5	6	7
8	9	10	11	12	13	14
15	16	17	18	19	20	21
22	23	24	25	26	27	28
29	30					

| MAY 2018 |||||||
S	M	T	W	T	F	S
		1	2	3	4	5
6	7	8	9	10	11	12
13	14	15	16	17	18	19
20	21	22	23	24	25	26
27	28	29	30	31		

| JUNE 2018 |||||||
S	M	T	W	T	F	S
					1	2
3	4	5	6	7	8	9
10	11	12	13	14	15	16
17	18	19	20	21	22	23
24	25	26	27	28	29	30

| JULY 2018 |||||||
S	M	T	W	T	F	S
1	2	3	4	5	6	7
8	9	10	11	12	13	14
15	16	17	18	19	20	21
22	23	24	25	26	27	28
29	30	31				

| AUGUST 2018 |||||||
S	M	T	W	T	F	S
			1	2	3	4
5	6	7	8	9	10	11
12	13	14	15	16	17	18
19	20	21	22	23	24	25
26	27	28	29	30	31	

| SEPTEMBER 2018 |||||||
S	M	T	W	T	F	S
						1
2	3	4	5	6	7	8
9	10	11	12	13	14	15
16	17	18	19	20	21	22
23	24	25	26	27	28	29
30						

| OCTOBER 2018 |||||||
S	M	T	W	T	F	S
	1	2	3	4	5	6
7	8	9	10	11	12	13
14	15	16	17	18	19	20
21	22	23	24	25	26	27
28	29	30	31			

| NOVEMBER 2018 |||||||
S	M	T	W	T	F	S
				1	2	3
4	5	6	7	8	9	10
11	12	13	14	15	16	17
18	19	20	21	22	23	24
25	26	27	28	29	30	

| DECEMBER 2018 |||||||
S	M	T	W	T	F	S
						1
2	3	4	5	6	7	8
9	10	11	12	13	14	15
16	17	18	19	20	21	22
23	24	25	26	27	28	29
30	31					